New Perspectives on Negative Campaigning

Why Attack Politics Matters

Edited by Alessandro Nai and
Annemarie S. Walter

ecpr PRESS

First published by the ECPR Press in 2015

This paperback edition published by the ECPR Press in 2016

Cover: © Bup #163634792 ShutterStock

The ECPR Press is the publishing imprint of the European Consortium for Political Research (ECPR), a scholarly association, which supports and encourages the training, research and cross-national co-operation of political scientists in institutions throughout Europe and beyond.

ECPR Press
Harbour House
Hythe Quay
Colchester
CO2 8JF
United Kingdom

Typeset by Lapiz Digital Services

Printed and bound by Lightning Source

British Library Cataloguing in Publication Data

A catalogue record for this book is available from the British Library

HARDBACK ISBN: 978-1-785-521-28-7
PAPERBACK ISBN: 978-1-785-522-36-9
PDF ISBN: 978-1-785-521-93-5
EPUB ISBN: 978-1-785-521-94-2
KINDLE ISBN: 978-1-785-521-95-9

www.ecpr.eu/ecprpress

ECPR Press Series Editors:
Peter Kennealy (European University Institute)
Peter Mair (Leiden University)
... academic editorial board ...
and supported by ...

... published by ECPR Press include in Pardue ... author Series

The European Parliament as a ... and Administrative ... ...
9781907...

... Change, Catharsis ... and Political ... ...

... and ...

... and Why ... Coalitions ... after the Lisbon ...
9781...

... the ... Social Movement in Time of Crisis
9781...

... on the Pardue ... resource supply ... for information about new ...
... publications.

This one is for Clem
– AN

For my Father
– ASW

Contents

PART THREE: THE EFFECTS OF NEGATIVE CAMPAIGNING

Abbreviations

ADQ	Action Démocratique du Québec
AIM	Affective Intelligence Model
AKP	Adalet ve Kalkınma Partisi
AL	Alternative List
ANAP	Anavatan Partisi
AP	Adalet Partisi
AQ	Buss and Perry Aggression Questionnaire
AUTNES	Austrian National Election Study
BDP	Bürgerlich-Demokratische Partei Schweiz
BFI	Big Five Inventory
BP	Birlik Partisi
BZÖ	Bündnis Zukunft Österreich
CAQ	Coalition Avenir Québec
CDA	Christen Democratisch Appèl
CDU	Christlich Demokratische Union Deutschlands
CHES	Chapel Hill Expert Survey
CHP	Cumhuriyet Halk Partisi
CMAG	Campaign Media Analysis Group
CMD	Center for Media and Democracy
CMP	Comparative Manifesto Project
CSU	Christlich-Soziale Union in Bayern
CVP	Christlichdemokratische Volkspartei der Schweiz
D66	Democraten 66
DIC	Deviance Information Criterion
DMA	Designated Market Areas
DP	Demokrat Parti
DPTE	Dynamic Process Tracing Environment
ELM	Elaboration-Likelihood Model
EVP	Evangelische Volkspartei der Schweiz
FAPERJ	Fundação de Amparo à Pesquisa do Estado do Rio de Janeiro
FDP	Freisinnig-Demokratische Partei
FP	Fazilet Partisi

FPÖ	Freiheitliche Partei Österreichs
GAL/TAN	Green/alternative/libertarian vs. traditional/authoritarian/nationalist
GLES	German Longitudinal Election Study
GLP	Green Liberal Party
GP	Green Party
GRP	Gross Rating Points
HADEP	Halkın Demokrasi Partisi
HGPE	Horário Gratuito de Propaganda Eleitoral
ICCL	Irish Council for Civil Liberties
IDEA	International Institute for Democracy and Electoral Assistance
IPAS	Impulsive/Premeditated Aggression Scale
MCMC	Markov Chain Monte Carlo
MHP	Milliyetçi Hareket Partisi
MNP	Milli Nizam Partisi
MSP	Milli Selamet Partisi
NEO-PI-R	NEO-Personality Inventory Revised
NHS	National Health Service
NSC	National Security Council
OCEAN	Openness, Conscientiousness, Extraversion, Agreeableness, Neuroticism
OI	Oireachtas Inquiries
OLS	Ordinary Least Squares
ON	Option Nationale
ORF	Österreichischer Rundfunk
OTS	Originaltext-Service
ÖVP	Österreichische Volkspartei
PCA	Principal Component Analysis
PDT	Partido Democrático Trabalhista
PEB	Party Election Broadcasts
PEI	Perceptions of Electoral Integrity survey
PLQ	Parti Libéral du Québec
PQ	Parti Québecois
PR	Proportional Representation
PSDB	Partido da Social Democracia Brasileira
PSOL	Partido Socialismo e Liberdade
PT	Partido dos Trabalhadores
PV	Partido Verde

PvdA	Partij van de Arbeid
PVQ	Parti Vert du Québec
QS	Québec Solidaire
RDD	Random-Digit Dial
RP	Refah Partisi
RQ	Research Question
RTR	Real-Time Response
SBC	Swiss Broadcasting Corporation
SMD	Single-Member District
SP	Saadet Partisi
SP	Socialist Party
SPD	Sozialdemokratische Partei Deutschlands
SPÖ	Sozialdemokratische Partei Österreichs
SVP	Schweizerische Volkspartei
TİP	Türkiye İşçi Partisi
TIPI	Ten Item Personality Inventory/Measure
TRT	Turkish Radio and Television
VMS	Video Monitoring Service
VVD	Volkspartij voor Vrijheid en Democratie

List of Figures and Tables

Figures

Tables

Contributors

BARBARA ALLEN is Ada M. Harrison Distinguished Teaching Professor of the Social Sciences, Professor and former chair of the Department of Political Science, Carleton and former Director of Women's Studies at Carleton College, Northfield, MN (United States) as well as Senior Research Fellow of the Vincent and Elinor Ostrom Workshop in Political Theory and Policy Analysis at Indiana University (United States). She has received fellowships for various projects including her book, *Tocqueville, Covenant, and the Democratic Revolution*, from the Bush Foundation, the National Endowment for the Humanities and the Earhart Foundation. She has published a number of articles on election campaign news coverage and political advertising and was awarded the American Political Science Association Rowman and Littlefield Innovations in Teaching Award in 2005. She has received fellowships for various projects from the Bush Foundation and the National Endowment for the Humanities and the Earhart Foundation. In addition to studies of political communication, she has conducted community-based participatory research on topics of concern to Deaf Americans. Most recently she directed the award-winning feature length documentary, *Signing On: Stories of Deaf Breast Cancer Survivors, their Families and Community*.

WILLIAM L. BENOIT is a Professor of Communication Studies at Ohio University (United States). He developed the Functional Theory of Political Campaign Communication. He has published articles and books on political TV spots and debates from election campaigns in the United States and other countries. His most recent books, published in 2014, are *A Functional Analysis of Presidential Television Advertisements* (2nd edition, Lexington Books) and *Political Election Debates: Informing Voters About Policy and Character* (Lexington Books).

LAURENT BERNHARD is a postdoctoral researcher at the University of Zurich (Switzerland). His PhD thesis focused on the campaign strategies adopted by political actors in the context of direct-democratic campaigns. Together with Marco Steenbergen (University of Zurich), he currently leads a project that deals with populism in Western Europe in the framework of the research programme NCCR Democracy.

ANDRÉ BLAIS is professor in the department of political science at the Université de Montréal (Canada). He is the leader of the Making Electoral Democray Work Project and the chair of the Planning Committee of the Comparative Study of Electoral Systems (CSES). He is a fellow of the Royal Society of Canada, and a research fellow with the Centre for the Study of Democratic Citizenship (CSDC), the Centre interuniversitaire de recherche en économie quantitative (CIREQ), and the Center for Interuniversity Research Analysis on Organizations (CIRANO). He is past president of the Canadian Political Science Association. His research interests are elections, electoral systems, turnout, public opinion, and methodology.

MARIAN BOHL is a PhD candidate at University of Zurich (Switzerland). After undergraduate studies at the University of Mannheim and Johns Hopkins University, he joined the 'Making Electoral Democracy Work' project at University of Zurich. His research interests are election campaigning as well as regional and national electoral behaviour.

DAMIEN BOL is a postdoctoral fellow at the Canadian Research Chair in Electoral Studies of the University of Montreal (Canada). He receives his PhD from the University of Louvain in 2013. His research fields are comparative politics and political methodology. He is particularly interested in comparative political institutions and political behaviour. His work appears in the *European Journal of Political Research*, *West European Politics*, *Party Politics*, and *Political Research Quarterly* (among other journals).

FELIPE BORBA is a professor in the department of political science at the Federal University of The State of Rio de Janeiro and a postdoctoral researcher at State University of Rio de Janeiro (Brazil). His research interests are Brazilian politics, electoral behaviour, political communication, public opinion, and electoral campaign. Felipe Borba is also a political consultant and works for different candidates and parties in Brazil.

WOUTER DE NOOY is Associate Professor in the Department of Communication Science at the University of Amsterdam (The Netherlands) and a member of the Amsterdam School of Communication Research ASCoR. His research interests include political communication and social network analysis.

MARTIN DOLEZAL is a post-doctoral researcher for the Austrian National Election Study (AUTNES) and Assistant Professor (Universitätsassistent) at the Department of Government, University of Vienna (Austria). Dolezal has published on various aspects of party competition, electoral behaviour, and 'unconventional' modes of political participation. He is, amongst others, co-author of *West European Politics in the Age of Globalization* (2008) and *Political Conflict in Western Europe* (2012).

LAURENZ ENNSER-JEDENASTIK is a post-doctoral researcher at the University of Vienna's Department of Government (Austria) with a research interest in political parties, coalition politics, patronage, and politicisation in the public sector. He is the author of a number of publications, including articles in the *European Journal of Political Research*, *West European Politics*, *Party Politics*, *Political Studies*, and *Governance*.

FRANÇOIS GÉLINEAU holds the Research Chair in Democracy and Parliamentary Institutions at Université Laval (Canada). He is Associate Professor of Political Science. His research and teaching interests include the study of elections and electoral behaviour in a comparative perspective. His work has been published in some of the best journals of the discipline, such as the *British Journal of Political Science*, *Political Research Quarterly*, *Electoral Studies*, the *Journal of Elections, Public Opinion and Parties*, and *Publius*.

VALENTINA HOLECZ is completing her Master Degree in Political Science at the University of Geneva (Switzerland). She joined the SNFS research project 'Offensive Discourse in Political Arenas' in 2014. Her present research interests are questions about political behaviour, feminist theory and the use of torture in democracy.

JAN KLEINNIJENHUIS is professor of Communication Science at the VU University Amsterdam (Vrije Universiteit Amsterdam) (The Netherlands). He received his PhD in 1990 at the Political Science Department of VU University Amsterdam. His research interests include the selection and content of political and economic news, and the effects of news on citizens and stakeholders.

RICHARD R. LAU is Distinguished Professor of Political Science and Director of the Center for the Experimental Study of Politics and Psychology at Rutgers University (United States). His research focuses on information processing, political advertising, and voter decision-making. Recent books include *Negative Campaigning: An Analysis of U.S. Senate Elections* (with Gerry Pomper, Rowman Littlefield, 2004) and *How Voters Decide: Information Processing During Election Campaigns* (with David Redlawsk, Cambridge, 2006).

JÜRGEN MAIER is Professor of Political Communication at the University of Koblenz-Landau (Germany). His research focuses on media coverage of politics and its effects, political attitudes, electoral behaviour, and on quantitative methods. Within these fields he is specialised on televised debates, political scandals, experimental designs, and real-time response measurement.

MARIO MARCHESINI is a graduate student at University of Geneva (Switzerland). After undergraduate studies in International Relations at University of Geneva he started a Master of Arts in Political Science in the same university. He joined the research project 'Offensive Discourse in Political Arenas: Forms, Causes, and Effects of Negativism in Politics' in 2014.

WOLFGANG C. MÜLLER is Professor of Democratic Governance at the University of Vienna (Austria). Previous appointments included Chair and Director of the Mannheim Centre for European Social Research (MZES) at the University of Mannheim. Currently he is Speaker and Principal Investigator of the

Austrian National Election Study (AUTNES). Since 2013 he is co-editor of *West European Politics*. His research interests include government coalitions, political parties, and political institutions.

ALESSANDRO NAI is Project Manager and Research Associate at the Electoral Integrity Project (University of Sydney). He served until recently as lecturer in empirical methods at the Department of Political Science and International Relations at the University of Geneva (Switzerland). His work deals with citizens' behaviour in referenda and elections, political psychology, and campaigning effects. He is currently co-directing a three-year SNSF research project (2012–15) on negative campaigning in Switzerland, with a special focus on its causes and effects. He has been a visiting fellow at the Rutgers University, United States (2008–09) and at the University of Sydney, Australia (2014). His most recent work has been published in the *Journal of Political Marketing, European Journal of Political Research, Electoral Studies, Social Science Quarterly* and the *Swiss Political Science Review*.

ADRIEN PETITPAS is an undergraduate student at the University of Geneva (Switzerland). He joined the SNFS research project 'Offensive Discourse in Political Arenas' in 2014 and he is currently working on a meta-analysis on the individual effects of negative campaigning. His present research interests are the role of affect and cognitive mechanisms on political attitudes.

DAVID P. REDLAWSK is Professor of Political Science at Rutgers University in New Brunswick, NJ (United States). His most recent book is *The Positive Case for Negative Campaigning*, with Kyle Mattes (University of Chicago Press). He is also the author (with Caroline Tolbert and Todd Donovan) of *Why Iowa? How Caucuses and Sequential Elections Improve the Presidential Nominating Process* (University of Chicago Press). His book with Richard Lau, *How Voters Decide: Information Processing in an Election Campaign*, (Cambridge University Press) won the 2007 Alexander George Award for best Book in Political Psychology from the International Society of Political Psychology.

THERESA REIDY is a Lecturer in the Department of Government at University College Cork (Ireland), where she teaches Irish politics, political economy and public finance. Her research interests lie in the areas of public finance and electoral behaviour in Ireland. She is co-convener of the PSAI specialist group Voters, Parties and Elections and co-editor of *Irish Political Studies*.

TRAVIS N. RIDOUT is Thomas S. Foley Distinguished Professor of Government and Public Policy and Associate Professor in the School of Politics, Philosophy and Public Affairs at Washington State University (United States). He is also co-director of the Wesleyan Media Project and serves as chair of the Political Communication section of the American Political Science Association. Ridout received his Ph.D. in political science from the University of Wisconsin-Madison in 2003, and his research on political campaigns and political advertising has appeared in the *American Journal of Political Science, British Journal of Political Science, Journal of Politics, Political Communication, Political Behavior, Political Psychology, Annual Review of Political Science*, and in several book chapters. Ridout's most recent book, *The Persuasive Power of Campaign Advertising*, was published in 2011 with Temple University Press.

BEN SANOGO-WILLERS studied economics and political science at Leuphana University Lunebourg (Germany). He is currently finishing his Master studies in political science at the University of Geneva.

DANIEL STEVENS is an Associate Professor in the Department of Politics and International Relations at the University of Exeter (United Kingdom). He works primarily on questions surrounding political communication and political behaviour in the United States and the United Kindgom. He has published on these topics in the *American Journal of Political Science, Journal of Politics, British Journal of Political Science, Political Research Quarterly*, and *Public Opinion Quarterly* among others.

JANE SUITER is a political scientist in the School of Communications at Dublin City University (Ireland). Her research is in political communications and in deliberative and participative democracy. She was deputy research director of the Irish Constitutional Convention and is a member of the ECPR standing group on Democratic Innovations and co-convener of the PSAI specialist group Voters, Parties and Elections.

EMRE TOROS is an Associate Professor of Political Science at Atilim Unversity, Ankara (Turkey). He has carried out his academic studies in several universities including Bilkent University (Turkey), Malmö University (Sweden) and Stanford University (United States). His research interest is mainly on political methodology, electoral studies and Turkish politics and his articles appeared in journals like *International Journal of Forecasting, Social Indicators Research, Turkish Studies* and *Asia-Europe Journal*.

ANNEMARIE S. WALTER is a Marie Curie Fellow in the School of Politics and International Relations at the University of Nottingham (United Kingdom). She received her PhD in 2012 at the University of Amsterdam (The Netherlands). She was previously affiliated as Assistant Professor to the Communication Science Department at the VU University of Amsterdam (The Netherlands). She currently works on a three year Marie Curie/ NRF research project (2014–17) entitled 'CSNCC': Comparative Study of Negative Campaigning and its Consequences. She published numerous articles in international peer-reviewed journals such as *Comparative Political Studies, Political Studies, Party Politics, Acta Politica* and the *Harvard International Journal of Press/Politics*.

Preface and Acknowledgements

Have you ever witnessed, in a political debate, television advertisement, public rally or any other form of political discussion, speakers 'going dirty' on their opponent? We would be more than surprised if you had not. 'Dirty' discourse – i.e. 'negative campaigning', as politicians, journalists and other observers frequently name it – is a common feature of modern politics. Attacks targeting a rivalling candidate on his past performance (*'Mitt Romney's economic plan: It didn't work then, it won't work now'*, pro-Obama advertisement for the US 2012 presidential election), his policy propositions (*'Are the President's kids more important than yours? ... Protection for [his] kids, and gun free zones for ours'*, NRA advertisement for the US 2012 presidential election), his traits (*'In which direction will John Kerry lead?'*, pro-Bush advertisement for the 2004 US presidential election) or attacks just smearing mud on to him (*'Would Romney have killed Bin Laden?'*, pro-Obama advertisement for the US 2012 presidential election) make up a significant part of today's campaigns during elections, referenda and beyond.

Negative campaigning is an interesting phenomenon, which can be found varying in levels and shapes in virtually every country. Negative campaigning is not only disliked by political pundits, journalists and the public but might, according to some, also have harmful effects on the public such as increased cynicism and decreased trust for the political elite. Others suggest however positive effects, such as increased attention and mobilisation. From an academic perspective, negative campaigning is at the crossroad of political actors' strategies and voters' responses to political discourse (attitudes and behaviour). From a non-academic perspective, negative campaigning exemplifies the idea of politics as dirty business conducted by self-involved cowboys with no respect, no morale and no sense of civic duty. If you have never heard someone pushing this argument, just walk into the nearest pub and talk about politics and politicians with the first person you bump into. However, what is negative campaigning and can it be measured? What causes negative campaigning? And what are its effects? This book sheds some light on these questions.

This book originates from the workshop 'Going Dirty: Negative Campaigning in Elections and Referenda and its Effects on Citizens' Attitudes and Behaviour', held at the 2013 ECPR Joint Session Workshops (Mainz, Germany, 11–16 March 2013). The workshop attracted about twenty scholars from Europe, North America and beyond. Some chapters in this volume were presented during the workshop and some are new (e.g. Chapters Two, Six, Eight, Thirteen, Fourteen, Fifteen, Sixteen and Seventeen).

First and foremost, our gratitude goes to the authors that contributed to this book. To those who were present at the Mainz workshop we are grateful for their participation in this project and their commitment since the very first day. To those who wrote the additional chapters, we thank you for 'joining the ship' and helping this book to navigate to your hands. We also would like to thank the scholars that attended the workshop but did not write a chapter for this book for their excellent comments and insights. This book is unique in the sense that it is the first edited volume that brings together work from scholars studying negative campaigning in the United States and scholars examining negative campaigning in other parts of the world. We hope this is the beginning of more fruitful international collaborations with as ultimate goal to come to a general theory on negative campaigning.

We are very grateful to ECPR Press for believing in this book ever since the workshop in Mainz. We would like to acknowledge especially former editor Peter Triantafillou, Alexandra Segerberg, Laura Pugh and Kate Hawkins, who helped us throughout the process and were more than willing to answer our questions.

This book is written for several different readerships. First of all, it is written for scholars working on negative campaigning or more generally on political campaign dynamics. Second, this book is written for both undergraduate as well as graduate students interested in or attending a course on electoral behaviour, competition among political elites, political marketing and election campaigning. Finally, this book is written for the general public as negative campaigning is a phenomenon debated in the public domain. Negative campaigning, especially when elections loom, frequently features in the headlines in newspapers and magazines. For example, on its 20 January 2012 edition, *New York Magazine* featured on the cover a trio of battered candidates (Newt Gingrich, Barak Obama and Mitt Romney – the latter even missing a tooth) with the caption '*The bloodiest campaign ever (you ain't seen nothing yet)*'. In its 14 April 2012 edition, *The Economist* went even further, portraying the two leading candidates Romney and Obama playing a lethal version of baseball, the first holding a grenade while the latter a nail-spiked bat, ready to swing ('*The hardball campaign*'). Maybe newspapers and magazines pay so much attention to negative campaigning because discussing 'dirty politics' simply increases readers' attention, the same way as depicting normal and happy people makes the tabloid sales drop. However, our guess is that there is a substantial interest in negative campaigning and dirty politics also beyond academia.

This book is a must read for anyone who wishes to take an informed stance in this public debate. Whatever your background, dear reader, thank you for getting through these initial lines and we hope that what follows might satisfy your curiosity.

Alessandro Nai and Annemarie S. Walter
June 2015

Chapter One

The War of Words: The Art of Negative Campaigning

Alessandro Nai and Annemarie S. Walter

In probably one of the most notorious and beloved radio broadcasts, aired in October 1938, actor and soon-to-be filmmaker Orson Welles portrayed an on-going alien invasion via a series of mock news bulletins. The described attack on earth reportedly provoked panic in those who listened and, later, widespread outrage in the media once the deception was uncovered. Beyond the guilty amusement of the anecdote, Welles' scam perfectly illustrates how news media can arouse attention, anxiety, and outrage.

The attacks that this volume will deal with are – fortunately – not as deadly as those described in Welles' mock invasion. They do, however, arouse attention and anxiety, and they certainly stimulate public outrage. As with Welles' examples, they also receive substantial media coverage. The attacks we deal with here make up a considerable share of today's political campaigns and debates.

In contemporary political history, examples of negative campaign messages abound,[1] from the disturbing 'Daisy' advertisement of Lyndon Johnson attacking his Republican opponent Barry Goldwater in the 1964 United States (US) presidential election campaign, to the famed 'Willie Horton – Dukakis on crime' advertisement that tries to disqualify democratic candidate Michael Dukakis in the 1988 US presidential election campaign, or the more recent NRA advertisement criticising Barack Obama for his support for public schools as 'gun free zones' in the 2012 US presidential election campaign. Outside the US notorious examples of political attacks can also be found, from Valéry Giscard d'Estaing's catchy 'you don't have monopoly on hearts, Mr. Mitterrand' in the 1974 French presidential election campaign, to the quite distressing 'demon eyes' poster with the text 'New Labour, New Danger' portraying hostility towards Tony Blair in the 1997 United Kingdom (UK) general election campaign.

Attacks constitute an important part of campaign messages. To illustrate, Freedman and Goldstein (1999: 1194) found that about half of the advertisements aired during the 1997 Virginia Gubernatorial race were negative; Lau and Pomper

---

1. *See* Mark (2006) for an excellent historical introduction on the use (and misuse) of negative campaigning. We also encourage curious readers to access John Geer's 'Attack Ad Hall of Fame'. Available at http://www.press.uchicago.edu/Misc/Chicago/284996.html (last accessed 22 September 2014).

(2004: 29) showed that the share of negative statements of the Republican and Democratic candidates for US Senate elections was on average about 35 per cent between 1992 and 2002; Geer (2006: 37) reports that on average 30 per cent of the advertisements aired in US presidential campaigns were negative; Walter (2014b: 29) claims that the average level of negative appeals in party election broadcasts aired in parliamentary election campaigns in the Netherlands, Britain and Germany between 1980 and 2006 was 30 per cent; and Nai (2013: 55) reports that about 8 per cent of the advertisements were negative in Swiss direct-democratic campaigns between 1999 and 2005. Negative campaigning is thus a universal phenomenon.

Negative messages are not only a key component of today's political campaigns and debates, but also of its coverage. Nowadays, it is far from rare that media coverage of political races focuses on the extent that candidates attack each other, the increasingly aggressive nature of these races and its detrimental effects on voters (see Brooks 2006; Geer 2012; Ridout and Smith 2008). Voters exposed to negative campaign messages would not only potentially lower their evaluation of the attacker's target, but also lose trust in politicians, the political system and are eventually less likely to participate in the electoral process (Ansolabehere and Iyengar 1995; Lemert et al. 1999). If there lies any truth in these claims there is a good reason to be worried, as elections are cornerstone to any functioning democracy. Public opinion on negative campaigning is quite clear: voters are not fond of negative campaign messages and dislike trait attacks even more so than issue attacks (see e.g. Fridkin and Kenney 2011a; Johnson-Cartee and Copeland 1989).[2] In addition, a substantial part of the electorate thinks that modern campaigns are 'too negative'.[3] In this sense, concerns raised by politicians, journalists and voters make the use and effects of negative campaigning an important topic in the public debate.

However, the debate about negative campaigning not only takes place in the public domain, as academic attention for negative campaigning has grown considerably over the years. This becomes apparent when conducting a quick and simple bibliometric check.[4] Figures 1.1 and 1.2 show that the number of academic articles referring to negative campaigning has dramatically increased; for the first decade of the twenty-first century, about one out of 100 articles on politics referred somehow to negative campaigning, and one out of 2,000 articles on politics had references to negative campaigning in its title. To compare, one out of 1,500 articles on politics published between 2000 and 2010 referred to the term 'issue ownership' in its title. See also Fridkin and Kenney (2014).

---

2. But see Mattes and Redlawsk (2015).

3. For instance, the PEW January 2012 report states that about 50% of Americans described the early stages of the 2012 US presidential election campaign as 'too negative', and 55% described them even as 'dull'. Online. Available at http://www.people-press.org/2012/01/18/campaign-2012-too-negative-too-long-dull (last accessed 22 September 2014).

4. Scores in Figure 1.1 and 1.2 are based on Google Scholar search results. The number of articles referring to negativity has been found by using the search following string: 'negative campaign' or 'negative advertising' or 'attack advertising'. The number of articles on politics has been obtained by using the following search string: politic or politics or political or policy.

Figure 1.1: Number of articles referring to negative campaigning by 100 articles on politics

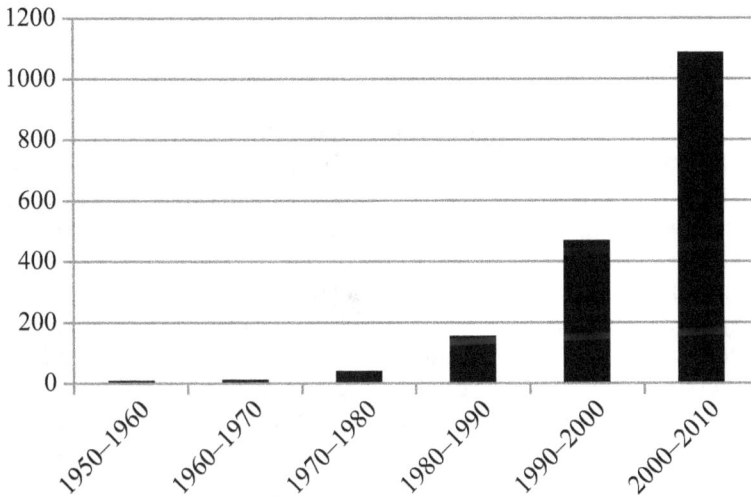

Figure 1.2: Number of articles referring to negative campaigning in its title by 100 articles on politics

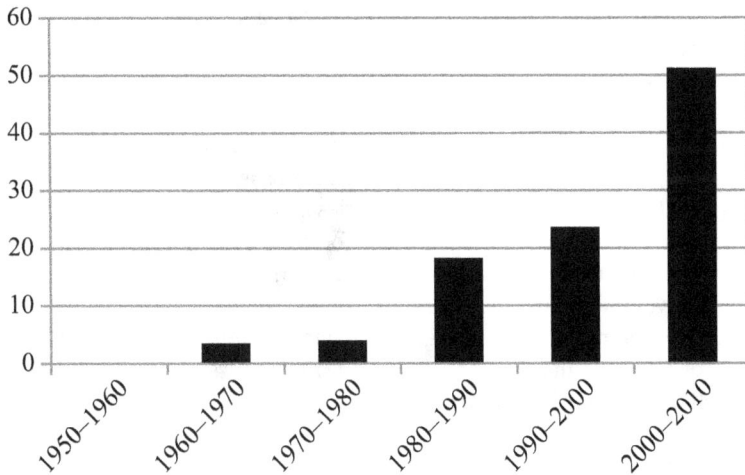

Since the seminal work of Ansolabehere and Iyengar (1995) that marks the beginning of negative campaigning as a new field, a considerable amount of research has been conducted. Was negative campaigning mainly associated with harmful effects on voters' attitudes, behaviour and the political system (e.g. Ansolabehere and Iyengar 1995; Ansolabehere *et al.* 1994; Ansolabehere *et al.* 1999; Lemert *et al.* 1999)? Nowadays a non-negligible part of academia points to its potentially beneficial effects (*see* e.g. Finkel and Geer 1998; Freedman and Goldstein 1999; Martin 2004; Geer 2006). Next to research on effects, scholars have been actively trying to map the occurrence and features of negative campaigning, increasingly also outside the US (*see* e.g. Geer 2006; Benoit 1999; West 2005; Van Heerde-Hudson 2011; Walter 2014b). These studies show that negative campaigning is a universal phenomenon (Fridkin and Kenney 2014). In addition, researchers have been puzzled by the question: what makes political actors decide to 'go negative'? Do they attack their opponent out of strategic considerations or is the use of negative tactics rooted in their personality or ideology? They have found various explanatory factors for negative campaigning, but have not solved this puzzle yet (e.g. Skaperdas and Grofman 1995; Theilman and Wilhite 1998; Haynes and Rhine 1998). Finally, some scholars (Jamieson, Waldman and Sherr 2000; Freedman and Goldstein 1999; Sigelman and Kugler 2003; Fridkin and Kenney 2008) took it upon themselves to reflect on the concept of negative campaigning itself, and more specifically about what does it entail and whether and how it can be measured. Is what is negative not in the eye of the beholder?

The work on negative campaigning looks predominantly at the US case. This is likely to come from the hegemonic position of the US in the discipline of political science[5] and the prominent role that election campaigns play in the US political arena. The length and the large amount of money spent in the US presidential election campaign exceeds campaign practices in all other countries, as far as we know. The prominent role of election campaigns in US politics make the study of election campaigns in the US a field of study in itself, unlike in many other countries. In addition, negative campaigning is commonly associated with US political culture; according to Scher (1997: 27) negativity is endemic in the US culture, 'as American as apple pie'. Assuming that the study of negative campaigning is limited to the context of US elections is, however, wrong. Negative campaigning has been studied in other countries than the US and outside the context of presidential and parliamentary elections, for instance in direct-democratic votes (e.g. Nai 2013, 2014; Nai and Sciarini 2015; Bernhard in this volume; Bol and Bohl in this volume), Buddhist Brāhmaṇical law texts (Freiberger 2009) and in elections for supranational on non-governmental organisations, such as the 2012 election for Chair of the African Union (AU) Commission (Maru 2012) or the 2011 election for the FIFA presidency.[6]

---

5. The hegemonic position of the US in the field can be referred from indicators such as, e.g. number of published articles, schools' and departments' rankings, and journal citation reports.

6. *See* for example http://www.thenational.ae/sport/football/pro-league-chief-fifa-election-race-may-yet-have-a-twist (last accessed 21 October 2014).

Table 1.1: Studies referring to negative campaigning beyond the US case by country

Country	References
Afghanistan	Sharan and Heathershaw (2011)
Algeria	Bouandel (2004)
Argentina	D'Adamo and Garcia-Beaudoux (2004)
Australia	Benoit and Henson (2007); Benoit *et al.* (2013a); Dickenson (2014); Miskin and Grant (2004); Salmond (2011); Stewart (2006); Wilson and Turnbull (2001)
Austria	Dolezal *et al.* (Chapter Ten in this volume); Hobolt *et al.* (2008); Hofer (2007; 2008); Lengauer (2012); Plasser *et al.* (1995); Plasser *et al.* (2003); Plasser and Ulram (2007)
Azerbaijan	Nikolayenko (2012)
Belarus	Nikolayenko (2012)
Belgium	Dassonneville (2010); Hobolt *et al.* (2008); Hooghe and Vissers (2008)
Bolivia	Freidenberg (2007)
Botswana	Maundeni (2005)
Brazil	Boas (2005); Borba (2012); Borba (Chapter Eleven in this volume); Da Silveira and De Mello (2011); Desposato (2007)
Bulgaria	Cholova (2013)
Cambodia	Sullivan (2005)
Canada	Attallah and Burton (2001); Belley (2003); Benoit and Henson (2007); Benoit *et al.* (2013b); Gélineau and Blais (Chapter Four in this volume); Marland (2003); Salmond (2011)
Chile	Boas (2009)
China and Taiwan	Chang (2000); Li (2008); Rawnsley (1997); Shih (2001); Sullivan (2008); Sullivan and Sapir (2012a, 2012b); Wen *et al.* (2004)
Colombia	Ocampo Salgado (2012); Restrepo Echavarría (2012)
Costa Rica	Fernández (1994); Urcuyo (2010)
Cote d'Ivoire	Cook (2011)

Table 1.1 (*continued*)

Country	References
Croatia	Haramija and Poropat Darrer (2014)
Cyprus	Hobolt *et al*. (2008)
Czech Republic and Czechoslovakia	Hobolt *et al*. (2008); Williams (2003)
Denmark	Elmelund-Præstekær (2008, 2009, 2010, 2011); Elmelund-Præstekær and Svensson (2014); Håkansson (2006); Hansen and Pedersen (2008); Hobolt *et al*. (2008)
Dominican Republic	Hartlyn (1990)
Ecuador	Constante Fiscal (2012); Freidenberg (2007)
Egypt	Khalifa (2013)
El Salvador	Azpuru (2010); Barnes (1998)
Estonia	Hobolt *et al*. (2008); Tigasson (2009)
Fiji	Fraenkel (2000); Lal (1988)
Finland	Carlson and Djupsund (2001); Carlson and Strandberg (2008); Hobolt *et al*. (2008); Strandberg (2007)
France	Choi and Benoit (2009); Dolez and Laurent (2007); Hobolt *et al*. (2008); Holtz-Bacha *et al*. (1994); Kaid and Holtz-Bacha (1995); Yanoshevsky (2009); Yoon *et al*. (2005)
Georgia	Nikolayenko (2012)
Germany	De Nooy and Maier (Chapter Seventeen in this volume); Håkansson (2006); Hobolt *et al*. (2008); Holtz-Bacha (2001); Kaid and Holtz-Bacha (1995); Maier (Chapter Eight in this volume); Reinemann and Maurer (2005); Salmond (2011); Schweitzer (2010, 2011); Walter *et al*. (2014)
Ghana	Hinson and Tweneboah-Koduah (2010); Rauschenbach and Carey (2013); Tietaah (2013)
Greece	Benoit (2007); Hobolt *et al*. (2008); Lappas *et al*. (2008); Samaras and Papathanassopoulos (2006); Yannas and Lappas (2005)
Guam	Shuster (2004)
Honduras	Kennedy *et al*. (1993)
Hungary	Hobolt *et al*. (2008)

Table 1.1 (*continued*)

Country	References
India	Gupta (2000); Kumar and Pathak (2012)
Indonesia and Bali	Altmeyer (2014); Aspinall *et al.* (2011); Rhoads (2012)
Iran	Alinejad (2009); Kasmani (2013)
Iraq	Al-Rawi and Gunter (2013)
Ireland	Brandenburg (2005); Hobolt *et al.* (2008); Reidy and Suiter (Chapter Eighteen in this volume)
Israel	Benoit and Shaefer (2006); Doron and On (1983); Kaid and Holtz-Bacha (1995)
Italy	Ceron and D'Adda (2013); Curini (2011); Curini and Martelli (2010); Hobolt *et al.* (2008); Kaid and Holtz-Bacha (1995); Salmond (2011)
Jamaica	Heron (2008)
Japan	Curini (2011); Park (1997); Salmond (2011)
Kazakhstan	Kennedy (2006); Timur (2006)
Kenya	Horowitz (2012); Kagwanja (2009)
Kuwait	Alqaseer (2013)
Latvia	Hobolt *et al.* (2008)
Lebanon	Salloukh (2006)
Lesotho	Southall (1994); Venter (2003)
Luxembourg	Hobolt *et al.* (2008)
Malawi	Matchaya (2010)
Malaysia	Case (2001); Hai and Ming (2006)
Mexico	Beltran (2007); Freidenberg (2007); Hughes and Guerrero (2009); Moreno (2004); Portillo (2012); Valverde Loya (2006)
Moldova	Way (2003)
Mongolia	Finch (2002)
Morocco	Willis (2004)
Namibia	Glover (2000)

Table 1.1 (*continued*)

Country	References
New Zealand	Lees-Marshment (2009); Salmond (2011); Stewart (2006); Ridout and Walter (2013); Ridout and Walter (Chapter Sixteen in this volume)
Nicaragua	Barnes (1998); Freidenberg (2007); Pastor (1990)
Nigeria	Edegoh *et al.* (2013); Olatunji and Adekunle Akinjogbin (2011); Olujide *et al.* (2011); Opeibi (2005); Taiwo (2013)
Northern Ireland	Benoit and Benoit-Bryan (2014)
Norway	Håkansson (2006); Midtbø (2011); Salmond (2011)
Panama	Freidenberg (2010)
Peru	Boas (2005); Freidenberg (2007); McClintock (2006); Schmidt (2000)
Philippines	Karan *et al.* (2009); Perron (2009)
Poland	Hobolt *et al.* (2008); Szczerbiak (2001)
Portugal	De Almeida and Freire (2005); Hobolt *et al.* (2008)
Republic of Macedonia	Emruli *et al.* (2011)
Romania	Momoc (2012)
Russia	Denisov (1996); Hutcheson (2001); Sigelman and Shiraev (2002)
Rwanda	Pitts (2011)
Scotland	Benoit and Benoit-Bryan (2014)
Serbia	Nikolayenko (2012)
Sierra Leone	Harris (2003)
Slovakia	Hobolt *et al.* (2008); Hrbková and Zagrapan (2014)
Slovenia	Deželan and Maksuti (2012); Hobolt *et al.* (2008)
Solomon Islands	Premdas and Steeves (1981)
Somaliland and Somalia	Kibble and Walls (2012)
South Africa	Fourie (2011); Fourie and du Plessis (2011); Kersting (2009); Lodge (2001)

Table 1.1 (*continued*)

Country	References
South Korea	Choi and Benoit (2009); Kim and Cho (2004); Kwon and Lee (2004); Morris (1998); Schafferer (2006)
Spain	Di Bonito (2014); García-Beaudoux and D'Adamo (2007); Hobolt *et al.* (2008); Salmond (2011)
Sweden	Åsard (1989); Håkansson (2006); Hobolt *et al.* (2008); Salmond (2011)
Switzerland	Bernhard (Chapter Nine in this volume); Bol and Bohl (Chapter Seven in this volume); Hänggli (2010); Lanz and Nai (2015); Marquis (2006); Nai (2013, 2014a, 2014b); Nai and Sciarini (2015)
Tanzania	Reuster-Jahn (2008)
Thailand	Murray (1996)
The Netherlands	De Nooy and Kleinnijenhuis (Chapter Five in this volume); Hobolt *et al.* (2008); Salmond (2011); Walter (2009, 2014a); Walter and van der Brug (2013); Walter *et al.* (2014); Walter and Vliegenthart (2010)
Turkey	Polat (2009); Toros (Chapter Twelve in this volume); Toros (2015)
Ukraine	Benoit and Klyukovski (2006); Dyczok (2005); Nikolayenko (2012)
United Kingdom	Benoit and Benoit-Bryan (2013, 2014); Benoit *et al.* (2013a); Dean (2005); Dickenson (2014); Hobolt *et al.* (2008); Kaid and Holtz-Bacha (1995); Ridout and Walter (Chapter Sixteen in this volume); Salmond (2011); Sanders and Norris (2005); Savigny (2005); Scammell and Langer (2006); Turner (2001); Van Heerde-Hudson (2011); Walter *et al.* (2014)
Uruguay	Cardona (unpublished)
Venezuela	Cyr (2013); Gallucci (2005); Molina and Pérez Baralt (1999)
Wales	Benoit and Benoit-Bryan (2014)
Yemen	Al-Yemeni (2003)
Zambia	Ihonvbere (1995); Venter (2003)
Zanzibar	Bakari and Makulilo (2012)
Zimbabwe	Kangira (2006); Makamani (2011); Venter (2003)

Note: We do not claim that the literature overview presented in Table 1.1 is exhaustive.

Table 1.1 provides an overview of research mentioning negative campaigning beyond the US case. The overview is most likely biased towards Western countries, as we are limited by our language abilities when listing studies written in a language other than English. It has to be noted that some studies listed do not provide empirical analyses, but are just descriptive case studies of specific elections or periods (e.g. Dolez and Laurent 2007; Hutcheson 2001; Kersting 2009; Taiwo 2013; Williams 2003). Furthermore, some studies listed do not have negative campaigning as their main focus, but touch upon its occurrence in a more general discussion of a specific case. Especially in emerging democracies such as, e.g. Cambodia, Kenya, Lesotho, Namibia or Sierra Leone, the use of mud-slinging and attacks during election campaigns is discussed within a more general framework of electoral malpractices, corruption, violence and the quest for electoral integrity (e.g. Glover 2000; Harris 2003; Kagwanja 2009; Southall 1994; Sullivan 2005). Table 1.1 illustrates that although many studies outside the US case do refer to negative campaigning, research in countries outside Western democracies is less abundant, more recent, and primarily descriptive.

Regardless, the numerous and wide array of articles published, the field of negative campaigning is still in its infancy (Fridkin and Kenney 2012). One of its limitations is its predominant focus on the US and lack of comparative work (Fridkin and Kenney 2014; Walter 2012), which is a prerequisite to come to a general theory on negative campaigning and to be able to take contextual variables into account that are likely to affect the use and effectiveness of negative campaigning. However, before this endeavour of truly comparative work can be undertaken a great deal of path-clearing needs to be done. Scholars are likely to face various challenges, such as the extent to which the concepts, indicators and methods developed in the US can be used to study negative campaigning in other geographical contexts or in general whether the concepts, indicators and methods used to study attack behaviour in the present also capture attack behaviour in election campaigns of the past.

This edited volume brings together work of American and non-American scholars for the first time, examining negative campaigning and its effects in various (geographical) contexts. With this volume we aim not only to increase awareness among these two groups of scholars of each other's work and foster international collaboration, but identify and take away the hurdles for large cross-national and temporal studies in the future which could bring us closer to a general theory on negative campaigning.

Existing literature examines negative campaigning along the three core questions that dominate the field, namely what is negative campaigning and how can we measure it? What are the causes of 'going negative'? What are the effects of negative campaigning? These are the three questions that guide this volume and they will be further introduced in the next part of this chapter.

What is negative campaigning and how can we measure it?

How to define and measure the concept of negative campaigning is an essential but difficult task that scholars face. In the literature definitions of negative campaigning abound (*see* Table 1.2 for some examples), they differ in which aspects they

Table 1.2: Examples of definitions of negative campaigning

Concept	Definition	Reference
Attack advertisements	'Ads [that] "create negative images" of political opponents by stressing negative attributes concerning their positions, character, or record'	Pfau and Louden (1994: 325)
Attack advertising	'Candidates criticize, discredit, or belittle their opponents rather than promoting their own ideas and programs'	Ansolabehere *et al.* (1994: 829)
Attack function of campaign messages	'Criticisms of the opponent, [versus] acclaims (positive statements about the candidate) ... and defenses (refutations of attacks)'	Benoit (2015, *see* Chapter Two in this volume)
Incivility	'Attacks that go beyond facts and differences, and move instead towards name-calling, contempt, and derision of the opposition'	Brooks and Geer (2007: 1)
Negative advertisements	'Spots that focused entirely on the opponent were considered negative, those focusing on the sponsoring candidate were positive, and those doing both were contrasting'	Martin (2004: 551)
Negative appeal	'Concentrate on the perceived weaknesses of their opponent's policy proposals, prior policy failures, and/or personal peccadilloes'	Lau and Rovner (2009: 286)
Negative campaigning	'Talking about the opponent criticizing his or her programs, accomplishments, qualifications, and so on. Positive campaigning is just the opposite: talking about one's own accomplishments, qualifications, programs, etc.'	Lau and Pomper (2001: 805–806)
Negative message	'Candidates choose to focus on ... their opponents' failures'	Brooks and Geer (2007: 2)
Negativism in political campaigns	'A speech act or communication that contains one or more attacks that are personally, voluntarily and directly addressed toward political opponents'	Nai (2013: 46)
Negativity in campaigns	'Campaigns stressing their opponent's shortcomings than their own strengths'	Lau (1982: 373)
Offensive campaign	'Campaign aimed at targeting political opponents ... in an attempt to become voters' preferred party by diminishing positive feelings for opposing candidates or parties'	Walter *et al.* (2014b: 551)
Opponent-oriented advertisements	'Negative or "attack" ads that emphasize negative aspects of the opponent's candidacy'	Kahn (1993: 487)

Table 1.2 (*continued*)

Concept	Definition	Reference
Uncivil advertisement	'Explicit use of harsh, shrill, or pejorative adjectives describing candidates, their policies, or their personal traits'	Fridkin and Kenney (2011a: 311–312)
'Wedge' politics	Campaign tactics that involve 'targeting unpopular or stigmatized social issues or groups as a way of defining "mainstream politics" and linking politics opponents to their support of these issues or groups, [aiming at] undermining the support base of key politics opponents'	Wilson and Turnbull (2001: 385)

Note: The overview of definitions presented in Table 1.2 is not exhaustive.

emphasise, but are similar in their core principle: negative campaigning refers to the act of attacking the opponent on his programme, values, record or character instead of advocating his own programme, values, record or character (e.g. Benoit 1999; Geer 2006; Lau and Pomper 2004). This is called the directional dimension of the concept of negative campaigning. The way that most researchers define negative campaigning nowadays excludes an evaluative dimension, the notion that negative discourse is bad, unfair, dishonest and illegitimate in contrast to positive discourse that is good, fair, honest and legitimate (e.g. Mayer 1996; Jamieson 1992). These are considered to be empirical issues rather than matters of definition or judgement. However, this evaluative dimension is commonly used to describe negative campaigning by journalists, politicians, campaign managers and the public. To illustrate, a study among political consultants (Swint 1998) shows that the majority considers a campaign message to be negative only if it contains information that is untruthful, deceptive or irrelevant to the campaign. It does not matter to them whether it is an attack on the issues or traits of the candidate. To voters it does, they regard trait attacks as more unfair than issue attacks (Kahn and Kenney 1999a). The exclusion of these aspects from the definition of negative campaigning employed by scholars is why journalists, politicians, political consultants, voters and scholars often fail to understand each other when discussing negative campaigning. In addition, it helps to understand that what academics define as negative campaigning is not necessarily perceived as such by the public. This is, according to some scholars (*see* Sigelman and Kugler 2003), one of the reasons that research on negative campaigning effects is so inconclusive. However, the choice to exclude the evaluative dimension when defining negative campaigning is also most likely to be motivated by measurement issues. Defining negative campaigning solely on the basis of its directional dimension avoids subjective judgement, i.e., negative campaigning being in the eye of the beholder (Brooks 1997). Scholars do not only agree to the directional dimension of negative campaigning, they also concur on its function: negative campaigning is a means to diminish the positive feelings voters might have towards a political opponent (Lau *et al.* 2007).

As well as the decision of how to define negative campaigning, scholars also have to choose how to measure the phenomenon. These two decisions are not independent, as the chosen definition affects the measurement of negative campaigning. Scholars strive to guarantee the validity and reliability of their measurements. Negative campaigning can be gauged in various ways; two frequent methods used are systematic content analysis and survey analysis among voters. Each of these two methods requires researchers to make difficult decisions and face shortcomings.

As negative rhetoric is a component of political discourse, researchers measuring the use of negative messages by political actors most often conduct systematic content analysis of qualitative data. Those data are retrieved from a wide range of communication channels, such as party manifestos (e.g. Curini 2011; Elmelund-Præstekær 2010), press releases (e.g. Norris *et al.* 1999; Haynes *et al.* 2002; Rußmann, 2012), newspaper advertisements (e.g. Nai 2013, 2014a; Nai and Sciarini 2015), television spots (Benoit 2007; Martin 2004; Walter 2014a), campaign posters (e.g. Vliegenthart 2012), political debates (e.g. Glantz *et al.* 2013; Benoit 2007; Walter and Vliegenthart 2010), letters in newspapers (Elmelund-Præstekær 2010), websites (e.g. Hooghe and Vissers 2008; Schweitzer 2010; Druckman *et al.* 2010), newspaper reports on campaigns (Ansolabehere *et al.* 1994; Lau and Pomper 2004; Wicks and Souley 2003) and social media (Carlson and Strandberg 2008; Salmond 2011). The choice of campaign source is of importance as studies have shown that the level and content of negative messages differs across campaign means (Walter and Vliegenthart 2010; Elmelund-Præstekær 2010). Ideally, researchers should examine more than one campaign mean. Coding messages from only one particular campaign mean might lead to over or underestimation of the level of negative campaigning and its content. Due to incomplete documentation of campaign material or money constraints, not always the population of campaign materials is examined, but a sample is drawn. The difference between samples is a source for inconsistent findings across studies.

Next, scholars have to decide which content analysis method they will use to analyse these campaign sources. Most content analysis methods are only developed to examine the occurrence and content of negative campaigning in text and not in visuals (an exception is the Videostyle Method of Kaid and Johnston 2001). Scholars generally neglect images as it is difficult to attain an acceptable level of reliability, as images resonate differently with different people. Nevertheless, scholars thereby ignore an important part of the campaign message, especially since visual messages are stronger than textual messages and they do not always support one another. For instance, the text in an advertisement can be positive, but the image of the candidate shown negative. Consequently, this can lead to a bias in the data collection.

The content analysis methods used for measuring negative campaigning differ furthermore in the unit of analysis. The main divide is between methods that take the campaign mean as the unit of analysis and methods that use a subunit as the unit of analysis. Especially studies examining negative campaigning on the basis of televised advertisements are inclined to take the advertisement as the unit of analysis (*see* e.g. Goldstein and Freedman 2002). As a result, the measure of negative campaigning is less precise, as one only gauges the predominant campaign mode. Methods that make use of a subunit, i.e. the claim, appeal, argument, idea unit (*see* for instance Geer 2006; Benoit 1999; Jamieson, Waldmann and Sherr 2000) are not only more precise, they are more easily applied across campaign means. Allen and Stevens (*see* Chapter Three) provide an overview of the five most prominent coding schemes used to measure the tone of campaign messages. They show that the selection of coding scheme affects especially the results of studies examining the effects of negativity.

Manual content analysis, prominently used in the field of negative campaigning, has in general two disadvantages. First of all, content analysis is a particularly expensive and time-consuming method. Huge amounts of materials have to be gathered, usually through lengthy archive work. Once the materials have been collected and in the case of visual and sound material also transcribed, researchers still need to do the rather tedious work of coding its content. The raw material needs to be dissected into units of analysis, such as 'quasi-sentences' (e.g. Lowe *et al*. 2011) and then the content of these units needs to be coded in accordance with pre-existing coding schemes to yield a quantitative assessment of the text, for instance the share of attack messages. The second drawback of this method is the risk of measurement error. Measurement error can have various sources, such as vague coding schemes, inconsistent coding over time and subjective interpretation of the coder. For example, a coder asked to retrieve the use of 'populist appeals' in party manifestos can be unconsciously tempted to find more occurrences from a party he dislikes. Data reliability is usually ensured by extensive training and the use of multiple coders. The latter allows for calculation of inter-coder agreement measures such as Krippendorff's alpha (Hayes and Krippendorff 2007). However, time and money constraints often limit the number of coders.

An alternative to manual content analysis is automated content analysis, which relies on classifying and scaling algorithms that translate texts into numbers. A wide range of automated content analysis methods and techniques exists. The most common and 'intuitive' methods make use of pre-existing or automatically generated dictionaries. Dictionaries use the rate at which key words appear in a text to classify documents into categories or to measure the extent to which documents belong to particular categories (Grimmer and Stewart 2013: 8). These methods enable the coding of a vast amount of textual data and automatically summarise its content. Automated content analysis methods are gaining momentum in political science. Examples of the use of automated content analysis are studies measuring sentiment in political texts (Young and Soroka 2012; van Atteveld *et al*. 2008), political opinions in blogs (Hopkins and King 2010), senate agenda setting in press releases (Grimmer 2010), and leaders' foreign policy orientations (Dille and Young 2000). The quality of results generated by automated content analysis is dependent on human performance such as defining relevant and sound dictionaries, supervising automated tasks and validating the results produced. Two of the four basic principles of automated text analysis, as discussed by Grimmer and Stewart (2013) are that 'quantitative methods augment humans, do not replace them' (2013: 4), and the need to 'validate, validate, validate' (2013: 5). However, if carefully executed, automated content analysis methods can facilitate coding tasks and reduce its time and costs. The use of automated content analysis has not yet penetrated the field of negative campaigning.

Next to content analysis, scholars make use of voter surveys to gauge negative campaigning (e.g. Pattie *et al.* 2011; Sigelman and Kugler 2003; Sides, Lipsitz, Grossmann 2010; Ridout and Franz 2008; Brooks 1997). These scholars argue that the 'reality' does not matter, but that it is about how voters perceive the campaign, in particular if we wish to understand the effects of negative campaigning. They argue that there is considerable disagreement between voters' perceptions of negative campaigning and negative campaigning as measured by scholars (Sigelman and Kugler 2003; Ridout and Franz 2008). This disagreement is claimed to be a source of inconclusive findings in the scholarly debate on the effects of negative campaigning (Sigelman and Kugler 2003). Ridout and Franz (2008) found that voters perceptual measures of negative campaigning only correlated within a range of 0.4 to 0.6 with various measures of negative campaigning based on content analysis.

Gauging voters' perceptions of negative campaigning through survey analysis is a useful method to measure its effects, as content analysis measures fall short of capturing the way campaigns are seen by voters whose decision-making we are trying to explain (Sigelman and Kugler 2003). In addition, using voters' campaign perceptions might be cost efficient as they can possibly be integrated in the (panel) survey that also gauges voters' responses to the campaign, instead of combining content analysis measures with survey data. When one matches survey data with content analysis data, one has to make sure that the voters in the survey were actually exposed to the content during the campaign and this is most often difficult to ascertain. Measuring negative campaigning on the basis of voters' survey analysis also has its limitations, as campaign perceptions vary widely from voter to voter and are subject to biases of various types, such as party identification and memory (Sigelman and Kugler 2003; Brooks 1997). Voters often perceive their own candidate's campaign as less negative and there is the risk that their evaluation only reflects the most recent considerations in their minds, such as the last campaign means seen (Brooks 1997; Sigelman and Kugler 2003). In addition, this method also prevents doing historical mapping of negative campaigning.

In the first section of this book an alternative to these two methods is presented by Gélineau and Blais (Chapter Four); they attempt to measure the tone of political campaigns through expert judgements: a method whereby a selected pool of experts provides an informed evaluation of the tone of the campaign. With the exception of Ansolabehere *et al.* (1994) that make use of expert judgements to validate their data yielded with content analysis, expert judgements have not been used to measure negative campaigning. However, political consultants in the US have been used for thought experiments on the question when one makes use of negative campaigning (*see* Theilmann and Wilhite, 1998; Swint 1998). The use of expert evaluations is not new as such and its use is not confined to the field of political communication. Expert judgements have been used for instance to measure party positions, *see* the Chapel Hill Expert Survey (CHES; Hooghe *et al.* 2010; Bakker *et al.* 2015) and the quality of elections worldwide, *see* the Perceptions of Electoral Integrity dataset (PEI; Norris *et al.* 2013). The use of expert judgements to measure negative campaigning has some advantages, namely it avoids the need for gathering and coding large amounts of campaign materials as the experts evaluate the overall campaign. Usually, researchers measuring negative campaigning through content analysis rely on a specific campaign mean with the assumption that the campaign mean can serve as proxy for all communication in the campaign. However, as argued previously, the level and features of negative campaigning differ across campaign means (Walter and Vliegenthart 2010; Elmelund-Præstekær 2010). The potential low costs and not having to rely on a particular campaign mean make expert evaluations suitable for comparative research. To what extent expert judgements resemble aggregate voter perceptions of negative campaigning is however unknown. Future research should test the usefulness of expert judgements in the field of negative campaigning. However, we expect that alternative methods to content analysis and voters' campaign perceptions will become more prominent in the study of negative campaigning. The first part of this book contains contributions to this conceptual and measurement debate.

Functional theory

One of the prominent theories and methods in the field that defines and measures negative campaigning is Benoit's Functional Theory (Benoit 1999; Benoit *et al.* 2003b; Benoit 2007). Functional Theory argues that political campaign discourse possesses one encompassing goal, namely winning the election by convincing enough citizens to cast their voters for one candidate.[7] Therefore candidates and parties wish to appear preferable to voters, consequently political candidates and parties will produce messages intended to make them appear better than their opponents. Political rhetors have but three options available for convincing voters that they are the better choice: they can acclaim (engage in self-praise of one's positive accomplishments or qualities), they can attack (criticise other candidates' failures or negative qualities) and they can defend (refute attacks). These three utterances can occur on two topics, namely policy and character (Benoit 1999; Benoit *et al.* 2003b). Benoit's Functional Theory measures negative campaigning through systematic content analysis. The unit of analysis used to measure negative campaigning is a theme, the part of the text that addressed a coherent idea. Because these utterances are enthymematic, themes vary in length from a phrase

---

7.   The notion that political campaign discourse has one encompassing goal is contested by European scholars (Strøm and Müller 1999; Elmelund-Præstekær 2008; 2010; Walter 2012; Walter *et al.* 2014; Hansen and Pedersen 2008) that argue that in multiparty systems winning not necessarily brings parties office or policy influence in contrast to two-party systems, such as the US.

to several sentences. Themes are then classified as claims, attacks or defences. Other utterances are not analysed. Benoit's Functional Theory is explained in more detail in Chapter Two. The strength of a functional approach to campaign discourse is that it can be used to measure negative campaign rhetoric across all kinds of campaign means, not only televised advertisements.

As Benoit's Functional Theory has been used in several (single) country studies that examine the content of campaign advertisements and debates (e.g. Benoit and Shaefer 2006; Benoit *et al.* 2013a) we are able to make an indirect country comparison of the use of negative campaigning (*see* Table 1.3). Table 1.3 is an adapted version of the results presented in Benoit's book (2007) *Communication in Political Campaigns.* We are able to compare the use of attack behaviour in sixteen different countries, while keeping constant both the definition of negative campaigning, as well as the method of measurement.[8] However, other variables such as the sample size and the kind of campaign materials coded still differ. As 'true' comparative work is rare (notable exceptions are Walter 2012; Walter, Van der Brug and Van Praag 2014; Salmond 2011; Kaid and Holtz-Bacha 2006; Kaid and Holtz-Bacha 1995) the overview presented in Table 1.3 is valuable as it provides an unique picture of the use of negative campaigning across countries. Negative campaigning is not an American phenomenon as it can be found in all countries studied. The findings show that acclaims are used more often than attacks when communicating with voters, with the exception of France, Scotland and the Ukraine. In addition, the overview shows that there is considerable variation across countries in the use of negative campaigning and that negative campaigning is more frequently used in debates than television advertisements. The level of negative campaigning ranges between 7 per cent in the 1995 Polish parliamentary election campaign and 43 per cent in the US presidential election campaigns when measured on the basis of televised advertisements. When we gauge the use of negative campaigning on the basis of televised election debates, the level ranges between 23 per cent in the 2009 German parliamentary election and 49 per cent for Scotland in the 2010 UK parliamentary campaign. These results show that there is room for 'true' comparative work not only mapping this phenomenon, but also explaining its differences in level and characteristics across geographical contexts.

In this volume Benoit's theory serves as a baseline for defining and measuring negative campaigning.[9] Some contributors make use of Benoit's theory, others do not; the latter will reflect on how their approach to negative campaigning differs from Benoit's.

---

8. Wen *et al.* (2004) and Lee and Benoit (2004) deviate from the other studies studying negative campaigning in television advertisements. Although they make use of Functional Theory they use a different coding unit, they used the entire spot as coding unit.

9. By choosing Benoit's Functional Theory of Campaign Discourse as a baseline in the book, the editors of the book do not claim that this theory should be preferred over others when examining negative campaigning. We have chosen to work with one of the most prominent theories as a baseline with the goal to make the book more coherent and clear for its readers, as the contributors will make use of Functional Theory or define how their approach to negative campaigning is different.

Table 1.3: Overview functions of political communication for selected countries and elections

Country	Election(s)	Channel	Attacks(%)	Acclaims(%)	Defences(%)	Ref.
Australia	2007	Debate	43	49	9	d
Britain	1992, 1997	Television spots	31	69	–	a
Britain	2010	Debate	36	60	4	f
Canada	2006	Debate	25	69	5	d
France	1988	Television spots	25	75	–	a
France	1988–95	Debate	33	61	6	a
France	2007	Debate	33	53	14	e
France	2012	Debate	41	40	20	e
Germany	1992	Television spots	32	68	–	a
Germany	2009	Debate	23	61	15	h
Greece	1996	Television spots	29	71	–	a
Israel	1992	Television spots	42	58	–	a
Israel	1984–99	Debate	38	50	12	a
Italy	1992	Television spots	15	85	–	a

Table 1.3 (*continued*)

Country	Election(s)	Channel	Attacks(%)	Acclaims(%)	Defences(%)	Ref.
Northern Ireland (UK)	2010	Debate	29	52	19	c
Poland	1995	Television spots	7	93	–	a
Russia	1996	Television spots	28	72	–	a
Scotland (UK)	2010	Debate	49	40	12	c
South Korea	1963–92	Television spots*	33	67	–	a
South Korea	2002	Television spots	27	72	1	a
South Korea	1997–2002	Debate	35	55	10	a
Taiwan	1996	Television spots*	19	81	–	a
Taiwan	2000	Television spots	35	63	3	a
Taiwan	2004	Debate	46	49	5	a
Turkey	1995	Television spots	11	89	–	a
Ukraine	2004	Debate	48	43	9	a
US - Non-presidential	1974–2008	Television spots	30	70	–	b
US - Presidential general	1952–2012	Television spots	43	57	–	b

Table 1.3 (*continued*)

Country	Election(s)	Channel	Attacks(%)	Acclaims(%)	Defences(%)	Ref.
US - Presidential primary	1952–2012	Television spots	**29**	71	–	b
US - Presidential primary	2012	Debate	**30**	67	3	g
Wales (UK)	2010	Debate	**39**	56	5	c

Note: Table adapted from Benoit (2007: 173–174); additional references were added in the last column.

* Sample includes newspapers advertisements.

[a] Benoit (2007) (some results are drawn from additional work by Benoit himself and other scholars : 173–174; Tables 6.16 and 6.18).

[b] Benoit (Chapter Two in this volume).

[c] Benoit and Benoit-Bryan (2014).

[d] Benoit (2013a).

[e] Choi and Benoit (2013).

[f] Benoit and Benoit-Bryan (2014).

[g] Glantz *et al.* (2013).

[h] De Nooy and Maier (Chapter Seventeen in this volume); the authors also include a fourth category ('self-criticism') that we excluded from the percentages shown here.

What are the causes and effects of negative campaigning?

Next to this conceptual and measurement debate scholars struggle to answer two questions: (1) what are the causes of negative campaigning; and (2) what are the effects of negative campaigning? Numerous studies (e.g. Geer 2006; Benoit 1999; Buell and Sigelman 2008; West 2005; Jamieson *et al.* 2000; Kaid and Johnston 1991; Walter 2014b; Salmond 2011; Kaid and Holtz-Bacha 2006; Kaid and Holtz-Bacha 1995) mapping negative campaigning point out the considerable variation in its level, not only across geographical contexts as shown in Table 1.3, but also within. The level of negative campaigning fluctuates between elections and within these elections between the competing candidates or parties. Several scholars (e.g. Theilmann and Wilhite 1998; Davis and Ferrantino 1996; Haynes and Rhine 1998; Kahn and Kenney 2004) have devoted their work to trying to explain this variation. What is it that makes a candidate or party decide to go negative? What are the characteristics of the attacker, target and context that affect the use of negative campaigning? *See* Table 1.4 for examples of variables that are found to affect the use of negative campaigning.

According to some scholars (e.g. Benoit 1999; Geer 2006; Abbe *et al.* 2001; Fowler and Ridout 2010) the level of negative campaigning does not just fluctuate over time, but is on the rise. Geer (2006) reports that on average there has been a 2.7 percentage point increase in negativity across each of the twelve US presidential campaigns that took place between 1960 and 2004. West (2005) finds that in 1952, 25 per cent of the advertisements were negative in contrast to the 58 per cent in 2004. These scholars argue that the nature of election campaigns is changing; they are becoming increasingly aggressive filled with frequent and harsh attacks. To the scholars, journalists, politicians and voters that believe negative campaigning to be a harmful phenomenon this is a concerning development. Therefore, research on the causes of negative campaigning, the factors that stimulate the use of these campaign tactics becomes even more meaningful. US scholars in particular suggest an increase in negative campaigning (*see* Chapter Six). The question then arises whether the American political system has certain characteristics that stimulate attack behaviour. Several single country studies already suggest that not all explanatory factors for the use of negative campaigning in the US matter or work the same in countries with a different political system (e.g. Hansen and Pedersen 2008; Elmelund-Præstekær 2010; Walter 2014b). Comparative work would not be an unnecessary luxury to examine the influence of the geographical and election context in which negative campaigning takes place. The puzzle on the causes of negative campaigning is discussed in more detail in Chapter Six. All of the chapters in the second section of this book are also devoted to this question.

Last but not least, what are the effects of negative campaigning? This question is core to the most prominent debate in the field of negative campaigning. An incredible wealth of work published in the last half-century has shown that political campaigns matter (e.g. Farrell and Schmitt-Beck 2002). Campaigns have the power to generate attention, put issues on the political agenda, shape and reframe ideas, persuade inattentive minds, mobilise citizens and ultimately, with a little luck, put

Table 1.4: Examples of causes of negative campaigning

Causes	References
Attack behaviour of the opponent	Lau and Pomper (2001b, 2004); Damore (2002); Krebs and Holian (2007); Haynes and Rhine (1998); Geer (2006); De Nooy and Kleinnijenhuis (Chapter Five in this volume)
Campaign budget	Lau and Pomper (2001); Johnson-Cartee and Copeland (1991)
Campaign professionalisation	Geer (2012); Walter (2014b); Abbe *et al.* (2001)
Coalition potential	Elmelund-Præstekær (2008; 2010); Walter and Van der Brug (2013); Walter *et al.* (2014); Hansen and Pedersen (2008)
Competitiveness of the campaign	Swint (1998); Damore (2002); Hale, Fox and Farmer (1996); Kahn and Kenney (1999b); Theilmann and Wilhite (1998); Freedman and Goldstein (2002); Franz *et al.* (2008); Nai and Sciarini (2015)
Direct legislation instrument	Nai and Sciarini (2015)
Electoral volatility	Mair (2004)
Gender candidate	Fridkin Kahn (1993); Benze and Declercq (1985); Lau and Pomper (2004); Kahn and Kenney (2004); Walter (2013); Maier (Chapter Eight in this volume)
Issue ownership	Damore (2002); Elmelund-Præstekær (2011)
Mediatisation	Geer (2012); Walter (2014b); Haynes and Rhine (1998); Peterson and Djupe (2005); Ridout and Smith (2008)
Office holder	Lau and Pomper (2004); Druckman *et al.* (2010); Benoit (2007); Hansen and Pedersen (2008); Elmelund-Præstekær (2010); Walter and Van der Brug (2013); Schweitzer (2010)
Party/candidate affiliation	Theilmann and Whilhite (1998); Lau and Pomper (2001b); Druckman *et al.* (2010); Sigelman and Buell Jr. (2003); Elmelund-Præstekær (2010); Nai and Sciarini (2015)
Party system	Ridout and Walter (2013); Walter, Van der Brug and Van Praag (2014); Walter (2014b); Hansen and Pedersen (2008); Plasser and Plasser (2002); Elmelund-Præstekær (2010)
Polarisation	Geer (2006); Elmelund-Præstekær and Svensson (2014)

Table 1.4 (*continued*)

Causes	References
Prospect of electoral failure	Damore (2002); Harrington and Hess (1996); Nai and Sciarini (2015); Skaperdas and Grofman (1995); Walter *et al.* (2014); Hale *et al.* (1996)
Race candidate	Krebs and Holian (2007)
Timing of advertising	Borba (Chapter Eleven in this volume); Damore (2002); Elmelund-Præstekær 2011); Haynes *et al.* (2006); Nai and Sciarini (2015); Peterson and Djupe (2005); Ridout and Holland (2010); Damore (2002); Haynes and Rhine (1998); Freedman and Goldstein (2002)
Type of race	Peterson and Djupe (2005); Kahn and Kenney (1999b), Lau and Pomper (2001b); Damore (2002); Druckman *et al.* (2010)

Note: The overview of causes presented in Table 1.4 is not exhaustive.

contestants ahead in the race. However, does it also matter whether one runs a positive or negative campaign? To say that the tone of the campaign matters is probably not that of a risky statement, nevertheless the answer to the question – *in which way the tone of the campaign matters*? – is less straightforward to answer.

In a nutshell, the existing literature is at the same time abundant, as well as incongruent as to what effects negative campaigning yield. To give a few examples, negative campaign messages have been found to be perceived as less informative than positive campaign messages (Pinkleton *et al.* 2002), to enhance voters' levels of 'issue information' (Ansolabehere *et al.* 1994), to be beneficial for the attacker (Kaid 1997; Fridkin and Kenney 2004; Arceneaux and Nickerson 2005; Coulter 2008), to harm the attacker (Basil *et al.* 1991; Hitchon and Chang 1995; Lau and Pomper 2002), to demobilise voters and depress turnout (Ansolabehere and Iyengar 1995; Ansolabehere *et al.* 1994; Wattenberg and Brians 1999; Lemert *et al.* 1999; Lawton and Freedman 2001), to enhance turnout (Finkel and Geer 1998; Freedman and Goldstein 1999; Kahn and Kenney 2004; Niven 2006; Jackson and Carsey 2007), to increase issue ambivalence (Nai 2014a), to decrease political trust (Pinkleton *et al.* 2002; Brader 2005), to increase political interest (Pinkleton and Garramone 1992; Bartels 2000; Brader 2005), to reduce the likelihood that voters cast a vote in line with his or her preferences (Lanz and Nai 2015) and to shrink perceived political efficacy (Ansolabehere and Iyengar 1995; Finkel and Geer 1998; Craig and Kane 2000; Brader 2005. *See* also Table 1.5). These examples show that negative campaigning first of all can affect a wide range of phenomena, from voters' unconscious psychological predisposition (attention, learning, knowledge) to voters' attitudes (partisanship, trust, political efficacy) and behaviour (turnout, support for a candidate).

Table 1.5: Examples of effects of negative campaigning

Effects	References
Affect for attacker or sponsor	Arceneaux and Nickerson (2005); Hitchon and Chang (1995); Kahn and Kenney (2004); Pinkleton (1997)
Affect for target	Arceneaux and Nickerson (2005); Fridkin and Kenney (2004); Kahn and Kenney (2004); Pinkleton (1997)
Ambivalence	Lanz and Nai (2015); Nai (2014a)
Anxiety	Martin (2004)
Approval of Congress	Globetti and Heterington (2000)
Belief in citizen's duty to work	Pinkleton *et al.* (2002)
Correct voting	Lau and Redlawsk (Chapter Fifteen in this volume); Nai (2015)
Cynicism	Cappella and Jamieson (1997); Valentino *et al.* (2001); Yoon *et al.* (2005)
Election outcomes (real)	Lau and Pomper (2004)
Election outcomes (predicted)	Mattes *et al.* (2010)
Faith in elections	Geer (2006)
Implicit/explicit evaluation of candidates	Carraro *et al.* (2010); Carraro and Castelli (2010)
Information search	Lau and Redlawsk (Chapter Fifteen in this volume)
Interest in campaign	Brader (2005); Brader and Corrigan (2006)
Interest in politics	Brooks and Geer (2007); Kahn and Kenney (1999)
Knowledge of candidates' positions	Craig *et al.* (2005); Niven (2006); Stevens (2009)
Media use	Nai (2014c); Pinkleton *et al.* (1998)
Memory for or recall of advertisement	Brader (2005); Brians and Wattenberg (1996); Hitchon and Chang (1995)
Opinion formation and change	James and Hensel (1991); Nai (2014b, 2014c)
Perceived usefulness of candidates' information	Sides *et al.* (2003); Pinkleton *et al.* (2002)
Political efficacy	Brader (2005); Craig and Kane (2000); Freedman and Goldstein (1999); Wattenberg and Brians (1999); Jackson *et al.* (2005); Pinkleton *et al.* (2002); Thorson *et al.* (2000)

Table 1.5 (*continued*)

Effects	References
Public mood	Rahn and Hirshorn (1999); Thorson *et al.* (2000)
Trust in government	Brader (2005); Brooks and Geer (2007); Craig and Kane (2000); Geer (2006); Lau and Pomper (2004); Pinkleton *et al.* (2002)
Turnout (actual)	Ansolabehere *et al.* (1999); Finkel and Geer (1998); Lau and Pomper (2004)
Turnout (intended)	Ansolabehere and Iyengar (1995); Brader (2005); Brader and Corrigan (2006); Garramone *et al.* (1990); Min (2004)
Turnout (reported)	Jackson and Carsey (2007); Kahn and Kenney (2004); Lemert *et al.* (1999); Nai (2013)
Vote intention or choice	Brader (2005); Kaid (1997); Lemert *et al.* (1999); Min (2004); Rahn and Hirshorn (1999)

Note: The overview of effects presented in Table 1.5 is not exhaustive.

Second, they show that scholars expect either negative effects of negative campaigning or positive effects. According to the first group (e.g. Ansolabehere and Iyengar 1995; Ansolabehere *et al.* 1994; Wattenberg and Brians 1999; Lemert *et al.* 1999; Lawton and Freedman 2001) voters perceive attacks as vile, which deepens the gap between voters and the political elite, which in turn can depress political trust, involvement and participation. The latter group of scholars (e.g. Finkel and Geer 1998; Pinkleton and Garramone 1992; Bartels 2000; Brader 2005) argues that negative campaigning arouses attention, which increases the salience of issues and that again can stimulate political involvement and participation. Empirical evidence has been found that supports both expectations, which are based on distinct paradigms. If demobilisation arguments 'rely on a reading of the cultural tastes of the mass public, ... the mobilization arguments rely on a reading of the psychology of negative information' (Martin 2004: 547). This puzzle becomes even more complicated, as recent research suggests that identical negative messages have different effects depending on the sponsor (e.g. Nai 2013), the type of negative messages (e.g. Brooks and Geer 2007; Kahn and Kenney 1999a; Fridkin and Kenney 2011a; Min 2004) and the time of exposure (Krupnikov 2014). More research is needed to bring clarity in this complex debate. The debate on negative campaigning is like the other parts of the field dominated by studies examining the US. Although we do not expect that voters across geographical contexts differ substantially, it is possible that the political system affects the effectivenes of negative campaigning (Fridkin and Kenney 2012), therefore research in non-US settings is more than welcome. The last section of this volume is devoted to the question: what are the effects of negative campaigning?

Book outline

This book consists of three sections, each containing contributions assessing one of the following questions: What is negative campaigning and how can we measure it? What causes negative campaigning? What are its effects?

The first part deals with the definition and measurement of negative campaigning. In Chapter Two, Bill Benoit introduces in detail his Functional Theory of Political Campaign Discourse. Functional Theory is one of the most prominent theories in the field of negative campaigning. Functional Theory is used as a theoretical benchmark throughout this volume.

In Chapter Three, Barbara Allen and Daniel Stevens discuss the issue of measuring negative campaigning using systematic content analysis. Existing research varies significantly on the way negative campaigning is identified and categorised. The authors present results of an original study in which negative advertisements of the 2008 US presidential election were coded according to five different coding schemes. The goal of the study was to examine whether these coding schemes yield different results on the level of negative campaigning and its effects. Their results show, first of all, that the five different coding methods correlate strongly when it comes to the level of negative campaigning. However, their study also highlights that relatively minor differences in coding negative campaigning can result in significantly different findings when these measurements are used to estimate the *effects* of negative campaigning on turnout. Therefore, Allen and Stevens conclude their study with the warning that researchers need to be careful about the methodological choices that they make.

In Chapter Four, François Gélineau and André Blais explore the merits and limits of expert judgements to measure the tone of electoral campaigns. They start from the premise that compared to the traditional coding of party manifestos and advertisements, expert judgements constitute a quicker, cheaper, and more indirect method. The authors compare results from systematic content analysis of television advertisements for the 2012 Quebec general election with expert judgements obtained through the administration of a short Internet questionnaire. Their findings show that both instruments generate consistent results when ranking the level of negative campaigning by the main political parties, with the exception of one party. Gélineau and Blais also find a fairly consistent pattern concerning the targets of each party's attacks on the basis of expert judgements as well as content analysis of the video advertisements. The authors conclude that expert judgements are a promising avenue for measuring negative campaigning.

In Chapter Five, Wouter de Nooy and Jan Kleinnijenhuis propose to improve measuring negative campaigning with the concept of consonance, using dynamic network models, and measuring negative campaigning (attacks) as well as its counterpart (support) at the level of statements in the context of multi-party systems. They use the 2006 Dutch parliamentary election campaign as a case study and test a model that predicts the choice between support or attack on the basis of the pattern of *preceding* statements of all parties. Contrary to the mainly static statistical models usually used to predict negative campaigning in the case of a two-party or majoritarian system, their approach is based on repeated measurements of attack behaviour during the campaign. Their results show that consonance predictors help to explain political actors' choice between support and attack behaviour. De Nooy and Kleinnijenhuis conclude that consonance adds to our understanding of negative campaigning in coalition-governed party systems, and that it is worthwhile to analyse negative campaigning as a campaign dynamic, that is as a series of time-ordered decisions of parties and candidates instead of measuring negative campaigning as a characteristic of the overall campaign.

The second part of this volume deals with the causes of negative campaigning, i.e., the reasons for political actors to 'go dirty' on their opponents. First, in Chapter Six Annemarie Walter and Alessandro Nai present an overview on the causes of negative campaigning. They argue that negative campaigning is merely a strategic choice that political actors make and they continue to list the various attacker, target and contextual characteristics that affect their decision to go negative. In addition, they discuss the claim that negative campaigning is on the rise and the various general developments that would be causing this increase. Finally, they reflect on the state of this part of the field and point to various avenues for further research.

In Chapter Seven, Damien Bol and Marian Bohl argue that, as for single-member districts democracies, in PR democracies also the impact of the electoral competition on the decision of parties and candidates to go negative matters. The authors offer a test of the classic American-based theories of negative campaigning in four electoral campaigns in Switzerland, where the influence of pre-electoral agreements on the composition of the executive is rather limited, respectively the 2011 Zurich federal and cantonal campaigns, and the 2011 Lucerne federal and cantonal campaigns. Bol and Bohl find patterns that are in line with the electoral explanation of negative campaigning.

In Chapter Eight, Jürgen Maier analyses attack behaviour of male and female candidates in the context of German televised election debates. He examines content analysis data of all televised American-style election debates aired in Germany in the run-ups to national or state elections between 1997 and 2013. Maier finds no significant difference between male and female candidates in their attack behaviour; female candidates act as tough as male candidates. However, the author points to the existence of an interaction between gender and debate experience with respect to the share of issue-based attacks. Female candidates do not create more fact-based discussions and one can expect more criticism on policy from experienced female candidates. Furthermore, as the participation of female candidates in political debates increases, women tend to focus more on issues than men. However, if female candidates are debate novices they make issue-based attacks as often as inexperienced male candidates.

In Chapter Nine, Laurent Bernhard studies the use of negative campaigning in the context of Swiss direct-democratic campaigns, which are characterised by three major features: (1) a narrow scope and mainly issue oriented; (2) competition between two opposing campaigns; (3) a large number of participating organisations stemming from different backgrounds. Bernhard takes into account various elements of negative campaigning and proposes an encompassing message typology, which draws the distinction between the general campaign tone (i.e. positive or negative) and three forms of appeals – arguments, emotions, and heuristics. Through data obtained in interviews with campaign managers, he shows among others that opponents of ballot propositions (i.e. the defenders of the status quo) outclass their rivals in terms of negative campaigning. This basic pattern holds true both for the general direction, as well as for each of the three components of the message classification used.

In Chapter Ten, Martin Dolezal, Laurenz Ennser-Jedenastik and Wolfgang Müller examine which factors affect the use of negative campaigning by political parties in the Austrian multiparty system. In addition, the authors present a new method for measuring negative campaigning based on relational content analysis of party press releases, which allows for exploring the dynamics of this strategy over the course of a campaign as information on behaviour of the parties is gathered daily. They find that opposition parties and populist right wing parties are statistically as likely to resort to negative campaigning as other parties. They highlight that parties in government are more likely to be targeted than those in opposition. In addition, they find that large parties are attacked more frequently than small parties and that sharing government office decreases attack behaviour between parties with exception of grand coalitions.

In Chapter Eleven, Felipe Borba discusses presidential candidates' advertisement strategies in Brazilian elections. In Brazil candidates face a complex structure of incentives when deciding on the frequency, place and time that they will broadcast their political advertisements. Candidates vying for political posts must adapt their strategies to the imposed scheduling system that determines beforehand according to a lot, the day and time slots that they are allowed to broadcast advertisements. The author presents the results of the 2006 and 2010 presidential campaigns, comprising both the first and second round of voting. The analysis builds upon a dataset that contains content analysis data of all presidential advertisements aired in these two elections linked to detailed broadcasting information, such as number of times aired and exact date and time broadcasted. Borba shows that candidates for federal executive branch posts follow a specific pattern when they decide to attack an opponent. More specifically, his results suggest that despite the risk of punishment as a result of the 'right of rebuttal' rule, candidates do not shy away from attacking their opponents. The results of this study indicate that candidates rather attack in night-time slots than during the day. In addition, he finds that presidential candidates' advertisement strategies differ on the basis of their standing in the polls and between election rounds.

In Chapter Twelve, Emre Toros assesses the usefulness of the theory on negative campaigning for the Turkish case, both within and among different levels of government (national and local). Although it has been interrupted by three military coups, the Turkish Republic has been a multiparty democracy since the mid-1940s and the party and electoral system has brought alternations in government. On the basis of data gathered by manifest and latent content analysis of news articles, Toros finds that the dominant tone of election campaigns in

Turkey is negative, that the level of negative campaigning increases in periods of single party government and that the tone does not differ between general and local elections.

In Chapter Thirteen, Alessandro Nai, Valentina Holecz, Mario Marchesini, Adrien Petitpas and Ben Sanogo-Willers present a preliminary analysis on how personality traits may affect the use of negative campaigning. The authors use data gathered in experimental debate simulations with undergraduates, where personality traits were measured through the standard battery of questions of the Big-Five Inventory (BFI). The results show that attack behaviour differs across personality traits. Attacks are more likely among individuals scoring high on extraversion and low on agreeableness. Furthermore, the higher the level of neuroticism, the more the individual attacks. The traits of conscientiousness and openness to experience seem not to be related to attack behaviour.

The third part of this volume deals with how negative campaigning affects politics. In their overview in Chapter Fourteen, the first chapter of the third part, Alessandro Nai and Annemarie Walter argue that it matters whether candidates or parties make use of negative campaigning and discuss the various effects that negative campaigning can have on voters' attitudes and behaviour. First of all, they discuss the effects of negative campaigning on the psychological foundations of electoral behaviour, such as opinion formation, information processes and issue knowledge gain. Second, they reflect on the effects of negative campaigning on electoral attitudes, such as affect for the candidate or party and vote intention. Third, they discuss how negative campaigning affects general political attitudes, such as political interest, political efficacy and political trust. Implicitly this chapter reflects also on the question whether negative campaigning hurts our democracy? Finally, they mention the shortcomings of studies in this part of the field and suggest several avenues for further research.

In Chapter Fifteen, Rick Lau and David Redlawsk explore whether and how negative advertisements affect voters' information processing and decision strategies. The authors report results obtained using a unique dynamic information processing technique that allowed them to observe voter decision-making while the decisions were being made. Participants were randomly exposed to mock (although realistic) candidates' advertisements from Democrat and Republican candidates containing generic attacks on their opponents, attacks specifically targeting the opponent's healthcare policy and positive statements about the candidate's own healthcare policy. Lau and Redlawsk find that it is more effective for Democrats to attack Republicans than for Republicans to attack Democrats. On the topic of information processing, they find that negative advertisements were slightly easier to remember than positive ones. Overall, subjects searched more for information when both candidates ran a positive campaign or both candidates ran a negative campaign. Furthermore, negative advertisements seem to inspire about twice as much advertisement-specific search (i.e. for the policies or themes addressed in the advertisements) than positive advertisements. Finally, they show that the tone of candidates' advertising strategies is related to correct voting, but not in any straightforward manner.

In Chapter Sixteen, Travis Ridout and Annemarie Walter examine to what extent the news media cover political advertising and how they cover that advertising – two factors that can amplify or mitigate the effects of negative advertising. Comparing print media coverage of televised political advertising in New Zealand, the UK and the US, the authors find that the volume of coverage varies considerably across countries, but not so much within the media system. Remarkably, Ridout and Walter find not much variation across countries in the extent to which advertising is *described* as negative, even if there was a great divergence in the tone of the advertisements that journalists decided to emphasise. Their findings suggest that, given the large variation in media amplification of negative advertising, the potential effects of negative campaigning on voters are larger in some countries than others, respectively the US, where the volume of advertising is overwhelming at times. In sum, the idea that the media privilege negativity in their coverage is not generally backed by their findings. Although there are considerable mentions of negativity in news coverage, the amount of discussion they receive is generally on par with their proportion of all advertising.

In Chapter Seventeen, Wouter de Nooy and Jürgen Maier investigate the influence of negative candidate statements on viewers of the 2009 German televised election debate using Real-Time Response (RTR) data. The authors refine the analysis of RTR data by comparing the effect of attacks to acclaims and defences, by simultaneously considering characteristics of the speaker and characteristics of the viewers and by analysing the interplay between statement and viewer characteristics in great detail. Surprisingly, De Nooy and Maier find that the source of the statement has the most general and strongest effect on candidate evaluation; viewers tend to evaluate the candidate who is speaking more positively regardless of the kind of statement or the viewer's party identification. The authors also find that conservative viewers are more inclined to improve their evaluation of candidate Angela Merkel while she is speaking than left-wing viewers. In addition left-wing viewers evaluated candidate Frank-Walter Steinmeier more favourable regardless of whether he attacked or was targeted by his opponent. This partisan bias could not be found for evaluations of Merkel among conservative viewers. Their results also suggest indirectly that there are probably additional characteristics of viewers and statements that help to explain candidate evaluations, for example the non-verbal characteristics that accompany the candidates' statements.

In Chapter Eighteen, Theresa Reidy and Jane Suiter examine negative campaigning at two referendums in Ireland. Using pre-referendum opinion poll data and a post referendum survey, Reidy and Suiter explore whether negative campaigning is a feature of referendums, the extent to which it is used by both 'yes' and 'no' campaigners and which type of voter is most likely to be influenced by these negative campaign messages. They find that negative campaign messages, part of both referenda campaigns, provide voters with arguments for a 'yes' vote as well as a 'no' vote. They show that campaign messages resonate differently among groups of voters across the two referenda. Knowledge is a significant voter characteristic in the regression models of both referenda. At both referenda, older voters were more likely to recall positive arguments and higher social classes and farmers were more likely to recall positive messages. However, at the Fiscal Treaty referendum, older voters were also most likely to recall negative arguments from the 'no' side.

In Chapter Nineteen, Annemarie Walter and Alessandro Nai wrap up the edited volume and reflect on the goal set out in this introduction and the various contributions of the book. They conclude that the various unique contributions in this book point out the need for comparative research in the field of negative campaigning, the challenges that comparative research would involve and propose several solutions to these challenges. With its theoretical and methodological contributions, numerous studies in non-US settings and some comparative work this volume helps clear the path for the comparative endeavour necessary to come to this general theory on negative campaigning.

PART ONE

DEFINING AND MEASURING NEGATIVE
CAMPAIGNING

Chapter Two

Functional Theory: Negative Campaigning in Political Television Spots

William Benoit

In the second American presidential debate of 1992, President George H. W. Bush said 'We hear all the negatives. When you're president you expect this. Everybody's running against the incumbent.' Governor Clinton responded with 'This is not mud slinging. This is fact slinging' (15th October 1992). This exchange from this debate illustrates a concern held by many about attacks in political campaigns: mud-slinging is an unsavoury campaign practice. This chapter focuses on negative advertising in political television spots.

This chapter is founded on the Functional Theory of Political Campaign Discourse (e.g. Benoit 2007). Communication generally, and political campaign communication in particular, is an interaction between people. Functional Theory focuses primarily on mediated communication (e.g. television spots, debates, webpages) and it privileges politicians or message senders and the messages they create and disseminate. Of course, we must never forget that the audience is a vital component of communication – after all, citizens cast the votes that decide elections – and some scholarships focus on receivers, investigating how voters construe and react to messages (*see* e.g. Popkin 2004; Lodge and Taber 2013). Television spots are a particularly important message form for several reasons: Politicians and political parties rely heavily on advertisements, millions of voters are exposed to advertisements, which can have significant effects on voters, they can reach voters who are less interested in politics and therefore less likely to obtain information from such sources as political debates or campaign news. This chapter focuses on political advertising.

The first political television spot in history was run by William Benton in 1950 in his campaign for the US Senate seat from Connecticut (Wisconsin Public Television 2001). Since 1952, American presidential campaigns have used this message form in both primary and general campaign phases (*see* e.g. Benoit 1999, 2014a), and the practice of campaigning via the airwaves has spread to other offices (*see* e.g. Brazeal and Benoit 2006) and also other countries (*see* e.g. Kaid and Holtz-Bacha 1995).

Huge amounts of money are expended on political television advertising. The Center for Responsive Politics (2012) reported, for example, that over two billion dollars was spent on the American presidential campaign by Obama, Romney, the Democratic National Committee, the Republican National Committee, and outside groups. More money, of course, was spent on races for other offices, such as governor, the US Senate and House, mayor, and for elective offices in other countries. Candidates and political parties have good reason to rely on television spots: Meta-analysis confirms that exposure to these messages can increase issue knowledge, affect perceptions of the candidates' character, change attitudes toward candidates, alter candidate preference, have an agenda-setting effect, and influence vote likelihood (Benoit *et al.* 2007). It is important to realise that a given advertisement does not affect everyone, or affect all voters in the same way – but advertisements clearly have substantial effects on viewers.

Ansolabehere and Iyengar (1995) report that attack advertisements increase issue knowledge, are particularly persuasive for Republicans and Independents, and cause disillusionment, distrust of the political system, and decreased turnout (particularly for Democrats) at the election polls. However, subsequent research has raised serious questions about the claim that negative advertisements depress voter turnout (*see* e.g. Finkel and Geer 1998; Kahn and Kenney 1999a; Wattenberg and Brians 1999).

Allen and Burrell's (2002) meta-analysis contrasts positive and negative political advertising. They found comparatively small differences between these kinds of advertisements on attitude toward position, the target of the attack, and vote intention, and a larger backlash effect against the sponsor in negative advertisements. This finding suggests that negative advertising probably damages the sponsor of the advertisement more than the target of the attack. Lau *et al.* (2007) report another meta-analysis of the effects of negative versus positive political television spots. Negative spots tend to be more memorable and impart more issue knowledge than positive spots but they do not affect vote choice more than positive advertisements. Negative advertisements tend to reduce political efficacy and trust in government but are not related to lower rates of voter turn-out. Thus, overall the data do not indicate that negative advertisements are more effective or powerful than positive advertisements; both advertisements are capable of influencing voters. Nor is there good evidence that negative advertising generally demobilises voters.

Some studies investigate the circumstances under which political advertising is likely to attack (*see* e.g. Damore 2002; Elmelund-Præstekær 2010; Sullivan and Sapir 2012a, Chapter Six in this volume). Several potential factors that influence the nature of political television spots have been identified (Benoit 2014a) including incumbency (challengers tend to attack more), standing in public opinion polls (those behind usually attack more than leaders), being attacked (attacks against a candidate tends to encourage counter attacks from the targets), competitiveness of race (attacking is positively related to competitiveness), and sponsor of advertisements (advertisements from political parties are usually more negative than advertisements from candidates).

Lau and Pomper observed that 'negative campaigning has a bad reputation' (2004: 25). Broder (2002), a journalist rather than an academic, wrote that 'the advertisements people are seeing are relentlessly negative: loaded words and nasty implications about the opposition candidates, often never a hint as to why a voter should support the person paying for the TV spot.' In line with these sentiments, people have a tendency to dismiss negative advertisements as either trivial or evil if not both. Of course, there is no question that some messages deserve to be condemned but all political campaign messages generally, and all political advertisements specifically, are not the same. Is it reasonable to argue, as Governor Clinton did in the debate quoted earlier, that some attacks should not be considered to be mud-slinging? This chapter explores the nature of televised political advertisements.

It is vital that scholars understand the context of the political campaigns they study. Countries have varied media systems and different laws governing political advertising, such as limiting the time period during which political advertising can be used (Kaid and Holtz-Bacha 2006). In the United Kingdom (UK), for example, political candidates are prohibited from running television spots. Political parties are allowed to air Party Election Broadcasts but 'the maximum length of [PEBs] has declined progressively, from 30 minutes in 1955 to four minutes 40 seconds' (Scammell and Langer 2006: 76). We must not assume that the constraints operating in one country necessarily operate in another.

Dimensions of political advertising

It is useful to conceptualise political advertising as having three key dimensions: veracity, function, and topic. Each of these concepts will be discussed in turn in this section.

One potential reason to condemn attacks in political campaigns is the fact that candidates can make false or misleading statements in advertisements. There is no question that lies and deception are used in advertising and must be excoriated when they occur. However, it is simply not the case that all negative advertising lacks veracity. For example, Fact Check scrutinised political spots in the 2012 Florida presidential primary campaign, concluding that 'many of the attacks are accurate' (2012a). So attacks in political campaigns are not necessarily false. On the other hand, false or misleading statements can occur in positive advertising. A pro-Gingrich super-PAC, Winning Our Future, ran a spot called 'Renew Prosperity' in the run-up to the South Carolina Republican Primary of 2012. Fact Check (2012a) explained that this advertisement falsely claims that Newt Gingrich 'slashed' spending in his four years as House Speaker. Federal spending went up 18 per cent from 1995 to 2000, the time frame mentioned in the ad. In addition, the advertisement credits Gingrich for 'record-breaking surpluses.' There were surpluses for four straight years – from fiscal years 1998 through 2002 – but Gingrich already had left Congress in January 1999. The largest of those surpluses came in fiscal year 2000, when Gingrich was already out of office.

Geer argues correctly that people tend to incorrectly assume that positive advertisements are true whereas negative advertisements are false: 'We tend to evaluate the content of attack advertisements and assume positive advertising is reasonable and accurate. Perhaps this inconsistency helps explain why Bob Squire once said, "most lies in politics are told in positive advertisements"' (2006: 3). So although it is clearly wrong to use lies and deceit in political advertising, these qualities are not inherent qualities of political attacks. We must deplore false or misleading statements whether positive or negative; however, it is a mistake to assume that all negative advertising should be condemned for this reason.

The Functional Theory of Political Campaign Discourse (Benoit 2007) posits that political campaign messages have three functions: acclaims (positive statements about the candidate), attacks (criticisms of the opponent), and defences (refutations of attacks). Defences are most common in debates where they comprise about 5 per cent to 10 per cent of utterances; refutations of attacks typically account for only about 1 per cent of the statements in television spots (Benoit 2007). Accordingly, this chapter on political advertising focuses on the first two functions; acclaims and attacks. Acclaims are self-praise, offered by the candidate (and by surrogate supporters), whereas attacks are criticisms levelled at an opposing candidate. Political advertising from candidates in general is largely positive, although they do contain a substantial amount of attacks; advertisements aired by groups and political parties tend to rely more heavily than candidates on attacks (Benoit 2007). Candidates prefer to have surrogates attack more often than they do; they presumably hope that any voters who feel a backlash against attacks will blame the surrogate more than the candidate (although of course some voters might blame both, thinking they are in cahoots). Furthermore, if we think that campaigns are negative, that belief may stem in large part from news coverage of political campaigns: News coverage of political campaigns is consistently more negative than the candidates themselves. This relationship has been confirmed in American general election presidential campaigns (Benoit *et al.* 2005); American presidential primary campaigns (Benoit *et al.* 2010b); American Senate, gubernatorial, and mayoral campaigns (Benoit *et al.* 2013b); and in campaigns for prime minister in Australia, Canada, and the UK (Benoit *et al.* 2013a).

Geer argues that negativity can be good for democracy; one reason is that 'attacks are more likely to be supported by evidence than self-promotional claims' (p. 65; *see* also Henson and Benoit 2010). Functional Theory (Benoit 2007) considers a citizen's vote choice as an informal variant of cost-benefit analysis. Vote choice is not considered an instance of formal cost-benefit analysis because voters do not assign quantitative values to pros (acclaims) or cons (attacks) – nor do voters engage in mathematical operations (i.e. adding or averaging) of the information they possess. Still, positive ideas about a candidate (if persuasive to a voter) can help make that candidate appear more desirable; negative ideas about an opponent (if accepted by a voter) can make the opponent appear less desirable. The key point here is that we need (accurate) positive and negative information about candidates to make an informed vote choice. Attacks therefore play a crucial role in helping voters decide which candidate is preferable by identifying possible drawbacks or weaknesses of a candidate. If attacks could somehow be magically prohibited, campaign advertising might sound something like this:

Candidate 1: 'I will promote economic growth.'

Candidate 2: 'I will jump-start the economy.'

Candidate 1: 'I am a candidate you can trust.'

Candidate 2: 'I am worthy of your trust.'

Candidate 1: 'I will stem the tide of illegal immigration.'

Candidate 2: 'I can fix the problem of illegal immigrants.'

Candidate 1: 'I care about people.'

Candidate 2: 'People know I care about them.'

Hearing only positive statements tells voters nothing about the possible disadvantages of candidates, which hamstrings decision-making. The best way for voters to make a choice between candidates is to know both the pros and cons of competing candidates. So attacks, which can provide information about costs (when they are not false or misleading), are a vital part of political campaigns.

Political campaign messages can address two topics: policy, often referred to as 'issue,' and character, frequently called 'image' (Benoit 2007). Basically candidates can talk about what they do (policy) and who they are (character). Policy statements discuss governmental action (past or future) and problems amenable to governmental action. Character utterances concern the personalities or traits of candidates. The traditional terminology (issue, image) can be problematic because 'issue' has two meanings: policy and a disputed question. When character is questioned in a campaign, this means that image (character) is an issue (a disputable question). Furthermore, image can mean perception, which could suggest that voters have an image (perception) of the candidates' policy positions. Referring to the two possible topics of campaign discourse as policy and character avoids these potential problems. Research has established that news coverage of campaigns stresses character more, and policy less, than the candidates' messages (Benoit et al. 2013a; Benoit et al. 2013b; Benoit et al. 2010b; Benoit et al. 2005).

Both of these topics play important roles in vote choice. It is desirable to have a candidate who espouses the ends valued by a voter (policy) and a candidate who can be trusted (character) and has the ability to follow through on campaign promises. Furthermore, some crises arise during a presidency that could not have been anticipated or discussed during the campaign (the tragic events of 9/11 spring to mind as one such example). We must be able to trust our political leaders to make reasonable policy choices with regards to crises that arise during the candidate's term in office but on which he or she had no reason to take a position during the campaign. A political candidate (and indeed any human being) is, at base, a composite of what he or she has done or will do – policy – and who he or she is – character. Accordingly, political campaign messages address both policy and character.

Attacks versus acclaims on policy versus character

Functional Theory (Benoit 2007) argues that attacks and acclaims can occur on policy and character. Table 2.1 illustrates these four possibilities. A political campaign spot can (1) acclaim on policy, (2) acclaim on character, (3) attack on policy, and (4) attack on character. Of course, a given advertisement is not limited to a single option; many television spots use a combination of these approaches. For example, Benoit and Airne (2009) content analysed US Senate, House, and gubernatorial television spots from 2004, finding that 42 per cent of the advertisements in their sample contained both acclaims and attacks and 75 per cent of spots discussed both policy and character. This is an important reason for using the theme (idea, argument, claim) as the coding unit rather than the entire advertisement (some research classifies advertisements as either positive or negative, as either issue or image [acclaim or attack; policy or character]). The combination of function and topic can be a very important aspect of political campaign advertisements.

Johnson-Cartee and Copeland (1989) investigated voters' perceptions of the fairness of political campaign attacks. When asked to assess whether a variety of topics for attacks were fair, two clear groupings emerged in the data. Attacks on policy (e.g. stands on issues, political record, voting record) were considered fair by 83 per cent to 93 per cent of respondents. In sharp contrast, attacks on character (e.g. personal life, religion, family members) were thought to be fair by only 10 per cent to 21 per cent of voters. This suggests that attacks on character are more likely to be viewed unfavourably by voters than attacks on policy. I do not argue that attacks on character are wrong, that every voter despises character attacks, that such attacks are never appropriate, or that character attacks never help the candidate who uses them; however, messages which attack a candidate's character carry a clear risk that voters will view them as mud-slinging and unfair.

Table 2.1: Functions and topics of political campaign messages

	Policy	Character
Acclaim	My plan will create millions of jobs.	I care about people.
	Inflation dropped during my term in office.	You can trust me.
Attack	Under my opponent's administration the economy has stagnated.	You cannot trust my opponent.
	My opponent will raise taxes on the middle class.	My opponent does not understand ordinary people.

Nor is the possibility that voters will perceive character attacks as unfair the only reason to hesitate before levelling such charges. Pfau and Burgoon (1989) found that political campaign messages had larger effects on attitudes and vote intention when they attacked policy rather than character. Benoit (2004) examined the topics of attack and election outcome. The data came from seven American presidential message forms – primary television spots, primary debates, primary direct mail brochures, nomination acceptance addresses, general television spots, general debates, and general direct mail brochures – representing eighty-nine candidates and spanning fourteen campaigns (1948–2000). Election winners were more likely to attack on policy, and less likely to attack on character, than election losers. So, evidence suggests that attacks on policy (compared with attacks on character) have larger effects on voters, and other research finds that candidates who attack more on policy (and less on character) than opponents are more likely to win elections. Functional Theory does not argue that candidates should never attack their opponents' character, that such attacks will inevitably backfire, or that attacks on character will guarantee a lost election. But candidates should realise that attacks on policy may be more persuasive than attacks on character, and that candidates who attack too much on character risk alienating voters. We must also realise that cultural differences could come into play when political advertising in other countries besides the US are considered.

Content of political campaign advertisements

Research has established some contrasts between positive and negative television advertising. Geer (2006) reports that negative advertisements tend to discuss policy rather than character and attacks are more likely to include evidence than positive statements. Henson and Benoit (2010) analyse the use of evidence (statements for which a source is provided) in political advertisements using three samples: presidential primary advertisements, 1952–2008; presidential general advertisements, 1952–2004; and US Senate, US House, and gubernatorial spots from 2002. Only 8 per cent of themes were supported by an evidence source and evidence was very rare before the 1990s. Most of the statements in these advertisements were positive (70 per cent); however, when it was used, evidence was more likely to support attacks than acclaims.

Next I will discuss data from content analyses of political advertisements for several types of election campaigns: US presidential primary campaigns, US general election presidential elections, US Senate races, US House campaigns, US gubernatorial races, US local elections, and non-US political advertisements. The same data are not available for each of these types of campaigns (Benoit 2014a). Still, where possible I will answer these questions using these data: What is the distribution of functions (acclaims or attacks) in political advertising? What is the distribution of topics (policy or character) in political advertising? What is the distribution of attacks (policy or character) in political advertising? What is the distribution of functions between incumbents and challengers in political advertising? What is the distribution of functions of utterances on record in office (past deeds) for incumbents and challengers in political advertising? What are the functions of utterances on means (future plans) and ends (general goals) in political advertising?

The research summarised here compares the relative frequency of the two most common functions of political advertising, acclaims and attacks. The data establish that political television spots from candidates use more acclaims than attacks. *Chi-square goodness-of-fit* tests show that acclaims are significantly more common than attacks. These data are displayed in Table 2.2. I do not report the data from other countries separately, but every country in these data used more acclaims than attacks. Functional Theory explains that attacks have a potential drawback: Most voters say they dislike mud-slinging (e.g. Merritt 1984; Stewart 1975) so attacking too much could provoke a backlash from such voters. This potential backlash probably explains why candidates usually attack less often than surrogates (e.g. research on political advertising in the US has found that spots from candidates have fewer attacks than advertisements from political parties or groups; Benoit 2007). Hansen and Pedersen (2008) analysed political advertising in the 2005 Danish elections. Both newspaper advertisements and party election broadcasts had relatively few attacks (9 per cent in newspapers, 7 per cent in PEBs). Walter and Vliegenthart (2010) reported more acclaims than attacks in Dutch party election broadcasts.

The research summarised here found that overall, policy is discussed more frequently than character. This is the case in American presidential primary advertisements, American general presidential advertisements, and American non-presidential advertisements. Although I do not present the data from other countries separately here, I will note that of fourteen data sets, ten discussed policy more than character (the exceptions are Germany 1993, Turkey 1995, Greece 1996, and Taiwan 2000). Functional Theory (Benoit 2007) argues that in general presidents – and by extension, prime ministers and chancellors – are more about proposing/implementing policy than serving as role models. These data are reported in Table 2.3. Walter and

Table 2.2: Functions of political television spots

	Acclaims	Attacks	*Chi-square (df=1)*, p<0.0001
American presidential primary 1952–2012	**5,759 (71%)**	2,217 (29%)	650.96
American presidential general 1952–2012	**3,739 (57%)**	2,869 (43%)	114.54
American non-presidential 1974–2008	**15,708 (70%)**	6,733 (30%)	3,589.44
Non-US elections	**74%**	26%	–

Benoit (2014a). Defences excluded.

Table 2.3: Topics of political television spots

	Policy	Character	Chi-square (df=1), p<0.0001
American presidential primary	**4,337 (54%)**	3,639 (46%)	61.08
American presidential general	**4,057 (61%)**	2,551 (39%)	343.23
American non-presidential	**11,374 (54%)**	9,869 (46%)	106.62
Non-US elections	**61%**	39%	

Benoit (2014a).

Vliegenthart (2010) found more discussion of policy than character in Dutch party election broadcasts.

The summarised data here on topic of attack show that, when they attack, candidates criticise policy more often than they attack character. This difference is significant. The analysis presented above argues that attacks on character can be even more risky than attacks on policy. Table 2.4 displays these data.

Research in two of the three groups of advertisements – American presidential spots and American non-presidential spots – conformed to the prediction that incumbents acclaim more, and attack less, than challengers. In the data from non-US spots this prediction was not up-held. *See* Table 2.5 for these data. However, Hansen and Pedersen (2008) analysed newspaper advertisements and party election broadcasts in the 2005 Danish elections: Opposition parties attacked more frequently than the incumbent and supporting parties. Clearly more inquiry into incumbency status and political advertising is needed.

Virtually always the only candidate with a record in the office sought is the incumbent. The challenger usually has a record in other offices, but a record as president, or prime minister, or chancellor, is the best evidence of how one would do if elected to that office. This means that both incumbents and challengers discuss the incumbent's record more than they discuss the challenger's record (past deeds).

Table 2.4: Topics of attack in political television spots

	Policy	Character	Chi-square (df=1), p<0.0001
American presidential primary	**1,349 (61%)**	868 (39%)	104.36
American presidential general	**1,880 (66%)**	989 (34%)	276.71
American non-presidential	**2,498 (58%)**	1,783 (42%)	119.42
Non-US elections	**251 (60%)**	168 (40%)	16.04

Benoit (2014a).

Table 2.5: Functions of political television spots by incumbency

	Acclaims	Attacks	*Chi-square (df=1), p<0.0001*
American presidential general			
Incumbents	**1,933 (61%)**	1,222 (39%)	53.94,
Challengers	1,806 (52%)	**1,647 (48%)**	φ=0.09
American non-presidential			
Incumbents	**3,748 (78%)**	1,085 (22%)	304.49,
Challengers	2,461 (60%)	**1,607 (40%)**	φ=0.18
Non-US elections			
Incumbents	129 (57%)	97 (43%)	*n.s.*
Challengers	215 (70%)	92 (30%)	

Benoit (2014a). Defences excluded; Open-seat candidates excluded from non-presidential data.

Of course, when incumbents discuss their own past deeds, they acclaim; when challengers discuss the incumbent's past deeds, they attack. In all three sets of data, the incumbents acclaimed more, and attacked less, than the challengers when the candidates discussed their record in office. These data are displayed in Table 2.6.

Table 2.6: Functions of past deeds in political television spots by incumbency

	Acclaims	Attacks	*Chi-square (df=1), p<0.0001*
American presidential general			
Incumbents	**535 (55%)**	440 (45%)	274.6, φ=0.37
Challengers	212 (20%)	**867 (80%)**	
American non-presidential			
Incumbents	**1,272 (76%)**	400 (24%)	580.02, φ=0.46
Challengers	340 (30%)	**786 (70%)**	
Non-US elections			
Incumbents	**22 (73%)**	8 (27%)	21.87, φ=0.55
Challengers	8 (19%)	**35 (81%)**	

Benoit (2014a).

Now we turn to the question of the functions of one form of policy (general goals) and one form of character (ideals). Candidates used general goals and ideals significantly more often to acclaim than attack. Functional Theory (Benoit 2007) posits that many goals and ideals are easier to acclaim than attack (who could oppose goals such as more jobs or a secure country, or ideals such as justice?). These data can be found in Tables 2.7 and 2.8.

Conclusion

Political campaign messages are a vital component of the democratic process. Voters need to learn about the candidates (and parties) and their policy positions in order to effectively participate in the election; they need to hear what the leading candidates have to say. We must condemn false and misleading messages, but a lack of veracity can taint negative and positive messages alike. In order to assess the pros and cons of political candidates, voters must have access to both positive and negative messages. This means that attacks are a vital component of the democratic process. The fact that attacks are more likely than acclaims to be accompanied by evidence is noteworthy.

Table 2.7: Functions of general goals in political television spots

	Acclaims	**Attacks**	*Chi-square (df=1),* **p<0.0001**
American presidential primary	**1,802 (90%)**	198 (10%)	1,286.41
American presidential general	**1,048 (84%)**	198 (16%)	579.86
American non-presidential	**2,478 (89%)**	321 (11%)	1,658.82
Non-US elections	**44 (79%)**	12 (21%)	18.29

Benoit (2014a).

Table 2.8: Functions of ideals in political television spots

	Acclaims	**Attacks**	*Chi-square (df=1),* **p<0.0001**
American presidential primary	**663 (89%)**	81 (11%)	455.27
American presidential general	**348 (77%)**	102 (23%)	134.48
American non-presidential	**660 (86%)**	111 (14%)	390.92
Non-US elections	**52 (79%)**	14 (21%)	21.88

Benoit (2014a).

Both policy and character play key roles in assessing presidential candidates for it matters what we do and who we are. However, attacks on character open the candidates who make them to risks. Most voters (albeit not all of them) consider attacks on policy to be fair and attacks on character to be unfair. Attacks on policy are more persuasive than attacks on character – and candidates who attack more on policy, and less on character, are more likely to win elections than their opponents. Mud-slinging does not have a universally accepted definition, but the most common definition of this concept is attacks on character – and messages that do so open candidates to risks. This does not mean that a political candidate should never attack an opponent's character, but it does mean doing so is risky and so character attacks probably should be done in moderation.

Content analysis of political television advertising establishes that overall acclaims are more common than attacks. Candidate television spots stress policy more than character in the US (except for House advertisements, which are evenly split between these two topics); more studies on political advertising in other countries find that policy is more common than character but there are several exceptions noted above. Particularly in research on US elections (but also from Europe) shows that incumbents acclaim more, and attack less, than challengers in political advertising. This relationship is especially strong when the candidates are discussing record in office (past deeds). Political commercials tend to use fewer attacks (and more acclaims) when discussing general goals and ideals. Results similar to these have been found with televised election debates (Benoit 2014b).

Political advertising is an important element of contemporary political campaigns. It is important to consider the three dimensions of these campaign messages: veracity, function, and policy. Given the ubiquity and importance of this message form we need to learn more about political advertising around the world. Much of the research in this area focuses on American advertising, although research on political advertising in other countries is an important component of the literature. Still, future research should address this imbalance.

Chapter Three

What is Negative about Negative Advertisements?

Barbara Allen and Daniel Stevens

Research on 'negativity' must first define the meaning of the term. Common definitions in political science and political communication, as reflected in this volume, include Lau and Pomper's (2000: 2) description of, 'talking about the opponent – his or her programmes, accomplishments, qualifications, associates, and so on – with the focus, usually, on the defects of these attributes,' Geer's (2006: 29) of a negative appeal as, 'any criticism or reason to vote against the opposition,' and Benoit's of 'attacks' as criticisms of the opponent (*see* Chapter Two in this volume). Although, each of these definitions pertains to research on American political advertising, they are – and have been – easily applied to other communication mediums such as debates or newspaper coverage (Ridout and Franz 2008), and to advertising and media in other countries such as Denmark (Elmelund-Præstekær 2010), the Netherlands (Walter and Vliegenthart 2010), Taiwan (Sullivan and Sapir 2012a), and the United Kingdom (UK) (Sanders and Norris 2005; van Heerde-Hudson 2011). They indicate widespread agreement on what we mean by negativity.[1]

Operationalising negativity is more complex, however. Whereas there is broad consensus on what negativity is, there is variation in the way negativity is identified and categorised. Some of this variation pertains to what is analysed: using the example of advertising that will be the focus of this chapter, some research examines a sample of advertisements – 'prominent' advertisements for example (West 2005) – while other studies look at all the advertisements in an election; some research looks at advertisements made (Diamond and Bates 1992), others at advertisements aired (Goldstein and Freedman 2002). But additional variation stems from how exactly to code the 'tone' of an advertisement. For example, researchers have dealt differently with advertisements that combine positive and negative messages, some regarding advertisements with *any* negative content as 'negative,' while others view messages that combine negative and positive as 'comparative' or 'contrast.' Some research has recognised the distinction between negative and contrast advertisements but ultimately combined them on the grounds

---

1. Academic researchers now appear to agree that definitions of negativity should not include an evaluative dimension, i.e. that 'negativity' is also bad or undesirable, or that positivity is good or uplifting. These are considered to be empirical issues rather than matters of definition or judgement.

that they are 'functionally equivalent' (Goldstein and Freedman 2002), while other research argues that they are very different (Jamieson 2000). In addition, for some the unit of analysis is the advertisement (e.g. Goldstein and Freedman 2002), while others code discrete appeals (Geer 2006) or 'idea units' (Jamieson 2000), within an advertisement, and make further distinctions between issues and traits. Studying the tone of a newspaper article or a debate raises similar quandaries: does the researcher focus on sentences, paragraphs, the tone of an entire article in a newspaper or an entire answer in a debate?

It is this variation – in the operationalisation of tone – that is the subject of this chapter. Other studies have examined variation in tone *across* different media to see whether they provide different impressions of the negativity of a campaign, e.g. local news versus advertising (Franz and Ridout 2008). But this leaves a more fundamental question unanswered: does variation in the operationalisation of negativity *within* a medium lead us to different conclusions? We present the first study, to our knowledge, that takes the same universe of messages – political advertisements in the 2008 campaign – and pits different coding schemes against each other *using the same coders* (other comparisons have used secondary data) to see whether they provide different pictures of campaign negativity and its effects. The short answer is that while different coding schemes by and large converge on the same findings our study indicates that researchers need to be careful about the potential consequences of different choices.

Measuring 'negativity' in advertising

How has research conceived of and measured negativity in political advertising? The answer to these questions may matter for two reasons. First, the perception of trends in the use of negativity may depend on whether a single disparaging statement about one's opponent is seen as making an entire advertisement negative or whether the majority of the advertisement must be in this vein for it to be negative. Second, definitions of negativity make psychological assumptions about the individual voter, either explicit or implicit, that could be consequential for our understanding of the impact of tone.

To illustrate, we will start with trends in presidential elections and the United States (US). For West (2005), an advertisement is negative if it contains *any* pejorative statement about the opponent. By this measure the vast majority of prominent advertisements made in the 1988 presidential election, 83 per cent, or about five in every six, were negative. While the year 1968 was very negative, it was followed by a steep decline in 1972 and 1976. The 1980s witnessed an upward trend, with 1984 and 1988 the most negative of all, but in the 1990s there was some decline (59 per cent). In earlier work, Jamieson calls an advertisement negative if the *majority* of the advertisement consists of such information. By her reckoning (1992: 270) presidential campaigns from 1952 to 1976 were very similar in terms of negativity, 1980 was notably negative, and 1984 and 1988 were closer to previous campaigns, though marginally more negative. But in her later analysis, Jamieson (2000) divides the discourse contained in political spots into 'advocacy,' which promotes the sponsor's position, 'attack,' which focuses on criticism of the opponent, and 'contrast,' in which the two positions are compared. By this measure, 1952 becomes the most attack-oriented campaign. While there has been something of an upward trend since 1976, no recent election has been as negative. In an ostensibly similar measure to Jamieson's 1992 standard, Kaid and Johnston (1991) code by the positive or negative '*focus*' of the advertisement – sponsor or opponent. According to their analysis of presidential elections from 1960 to 1988, 1964 was the most negative campaign of all, and the trend has been slightly upward since 1968, without again reaching the level of 1964. They classify 37 per cent of advertisements in 1988 as negative compared to West's 83 per cent. Kaid and Johnston's (2001) later study, which includes 1992 and 1996, shows these two races to be the most negative campaigns of all. Finally, moving away from the advertisement or spot as the unit of analysis, Finkel and Geer (1998) and Geer (2006) break advertisements down into 'appeals.' For example, an advertisement might include appeals related to a candidate's record on inflation or defence, or be about moral values. They then code individual appeals as negative or positive, calculate the average proportion of negative and positive appeals from the candidates, and take the difference as the 'advertising tone' for that election. By this measure the 1964 election was also notably negative, and since 1976 there has been a steady decline in tone. The elections of 1984, 1988, 1992, and 1996 were all more negative in advertising tone than 1964.

In his work on negativity, Geer (2006) also compares many of these measures to his – West's, Jamieson's and Kaid and Johnston's – but adds Benoit's (1999). While Geer recognises the kinds of differences in the amounts of negativity *within* elections that these different coding schemes throw up, he points out that the trends in negativity they all show are similar and that the correlations between measures are mostly at 0.8 or above. Nevertheless, if one is interested in the effects of negativity within an election, as many analysts are, by West's reckoning prospective voters were barraged with negative advertising in 1988, at least in the 'prominent advertisements.' Yet according to Kaid and Johnston only one in three advertisements were negative that year. Jamieson finds no trend in the number of negative advertisements between 1952 and 1988 (1992, Appendix I Chart 4–3), whereas Geer indicates a steady decline in tone since 1976.

While they are illustrative of the potential consequences of duelling definitions of tone, in these examples it is not just the operationalisation of negativity that varies but also the advertisements that are coded from eras in which information about advertisements made versus advertisements aired is harder to obtain. We therefore do not know how much of the variation is due to different advertisements coded and how much is due to different ways of coding negativity. In the last few election cycles in the US, however, researchers have had access to Campaign Media Analysis Group (CMAG) data, which provide details of all the presidential advertisements that were made and aired to the vast majority of the US population.[2] Electronic resources also make negativity in other media, such as transcripts of debates, newspaper content, even direct mail, much easier to obtain than in the past. The availability of such data reduces any problems related to coding of different samples of materials and means that most of the variation in researchers' findings about levels of negativity – if they were coding the same universe of messages – would stem from different operationalisations of negativity.

By our reading, five methods of coding the tone of advertising messages have emerged over the last fifteen years in political science and political communication, two of which – the Geer and Jamieson methods – appear in Geer's (2006) comparison:[3]

Goldstein and Freedman method

Goldstein (1997) and later Goldstein and Freedman (2000; 2002) pioneered the use of CMAG data. They combined these data on advertisements made and aired with the Wisconsin Advertising Project's method of coding the tone of advertisements (which has remained unchanged now that the research has moved to the Wesleyan Media Project). Coders are asked: 'In your judgment, is the primary purpose of the advertisement to promote a specific candidate, to attack a candidate or to contrast the candidates?' Possible responses are 'attack,' (negative), 'promote' (positive), and 'contrast.' Thus the unit of analysis in this method is the advertisement and advertisement tone has three categories.

Freedman and Goldstein method

In another paper, Freedman and Goldstein (1999) describe a slightly different method, using a five-point scale. The variation is in how they deal with contrast advertisements (*see* their Appendix A). Advertisements with positive *and* negative appeals were split into three further categories of 'balanced' (given a '3' on the scale), 'predominantly negative, with a token mention of the sponsoring candidate' (a '4'), and, by implication – the third category is not explicitly mentioned in the article – more positive than negative ('2'). For the purposes of analysis, however, they took the average score given by multiple coders on their five-point scale, rounded to the nearest integer. They categorised only the middle category ('3') as a contrast advertisement, with a '1' or '2' on the five-point scale being a positive advertisement and a '4' or '5' a negative advertisement. Thus, the unit of analysis in this method is the advertisement and advertisement tone has five categories that are then collapsed into three.

---

2. Jamieson (2000) had access to television station logs, providing her with information on when and where advertisements aired.

3. Benoit's functional analysis of advertisements, described in Chapter Two, has a longer pedigree. More importantly, it also correlates almost perfectly with Geer's measure (Geer 2006: 37). Thus, our findings with regard to Geer's method can be extrapolated to Benoit's.

Kahn and Kenney method

Kahn and Kenney (1999a: 879–880) describe their approach to categorising tone as follows: 'we estimated the amount of negative information in each advertisement, including criticism of the opponent (i.e. negative information about issues or personality characteristics). We placed each commercial into one of three categories: no negative message (score=0), a minor emphasis on negativity (score=1), and a major emphasis on negative (score=2).'

Kahn and Kenney's method deals differently again with advertisements that mix positive and negative appeals: if the emphasis on negativity is 'minor' it is placed in the second category but if it is 'major' the advertisement is placed in the same category as advertisements that are purely negative. The unit of analysis in this method is the advertisement and advertisement tone has three categories.

Jamieson method

Jamieson (2000) breaks advertisements down into 'idea units' that pertain to issues or candidates' traits. She then codes the purpose of these idea units as 'attack' or 'advocacy.' Advertisements are given an 'attack score' based on the total number of words in the idea units categorised as attack as a proportion of the total number of words in the advertisement. Idea units that are about values or that are tag lines such as, 'Concerned about Barack Obama's naive foreign policy? You should be.' are excluded from the denominator. In Jamieson's (2000: 113) analysis, advertisements that contain more than 90 per cent attack words are attack advertisements, 30 per cent to 70 per cent attack words are contrast, and advertisements that are less than 30 per cent attack words are positive. The 71 per cent to 90 per cent range remains ambiguous in Jamieson's study – perhaps she found no advertisements with scores in this range. Thus, for Jamieson the unit of analysis is ultimately the advertisement and advertisement tone has three categories, but those categories are the result of the aggregation of idea units.[4]

Geer method

Geer's (2006) approach is similar to Jamieson's in that he divides advertisements into distinct 'appeals' that are directed at issues, traits or values that are positive or negative in tone. But Geer differs from Jamieson by not aggregating up from separate appeals to categorising the tone of the entire advertisement. He argues that there is so much variation within the category of contrast advertisements that

---

4.   In her analysis of the impact of advertisements, Jamieson calculates an 'attack weight' for each advertisement, based on multiplying the attack score by the length of the advertisement in seconds and a measure of exposure or reach within each television market in the US calculated from Gross Ratings Points (GRPs). For our purposes, however, it is her operationalisation of tone that is important.

aggregation could mislead us about the overall tone of an ad campaign: 'These data underscore the advantage of a more precise measure for assessing the overall content of political advertising' (2006: 35). Thus, in the Geer method the unit of analysis is the appeal and issue, trait or value appeals are either positive or negative in tone.[5]

Not only are there subtle variations in these methods regarding what negativity is but also, our second point, in terms of how their protagonists think negativity in political advertising is likely to affect individuals. On the one hand, if the vast majority of an advertisement must be negative to be classified as a negative advertisement, as in Jamieson's scheme, the claim is that only when the scales tip very firmly toward negativity is an individual affected by 'negativity.' Advertisements that are predominantly negative in content are apparently experienced differently. Kahn and Kenney's most extreme category of advertisements that have a 'major emphasis' on negativity appears to make a similar assumption. Certainly, from Jamieson's method, the implication is that advertisements in which there is a mixture of positive and negative content, even if the negative messages outweigh the positive messages two to one, are not judged as harshly. This suggests that positive information is given more weight than negative information in that a little positive content dilutes a lot of negative content – 'Pundits and scholars who collapse all attack advertisements into the catchall category 'negative campaigning' are treating the complex world of political advertisements in a simplistic manner that is not shared by the citizenry at large' (Jamieson 2000: 79). Indeed, Jamieson's analysis of the 1996 presidential election indicates that contrast advertisements had a positive effect on turnout and negative or attack advertisements had a smaller negative effect. Geer's measure, on the other hand, gives negative and positive information equal weight, which implies that this is also what individuals do. Geer is also explicit in the quote above that treating advertisements as the unit of analysis rather than appeals could lead to misleading conclusions about the negativity of campaigns and thus, by implication, to the effects of negativity on individuals.

Studies of negativity in campaigns outside the US, such as some of those in this volume, face the same dilemmas about how to code the negativity of other media such as posters, press releases, or debate statements. For example, is a predominantly negative statement about an opponent in a debate that also includes some comparison categorically different from a statement that does not make such a comparison? The answers to such questions matter to our understanding of negativity. We ask two questions in this chapter: 1) Do differences in the operationalisation of the coding of negativity lead to different conclusions about the negativity of a campaign? 2) Do variations in the operationalisation of the coding of negativity lead to different conclusions about the relationship between the negativity of a campaign and dependent variables such as turnout?

---

5. Value appeals are similar to Benoit's (Chapter Two in this volume) category of messages about 'goals and ideals.'

Data

We trained a team of undergraduates to watch and code all of the presidential advertisements from the 2008 campaign in the US, along with advertisements for the US Senate and US congressional races in Minnesota. Our universe of advertisements included advertisements aired on behalf of the candidates and covered the networks and cable television as well as radio. These were provided to us by Video Monitoring Service (VMS[6]), a US company that offers media intelligence to its clients. Thus, all the advertisements we analyse here were aired in these races – we are not mixing 'advertisements aired' and 'advertisements made.' In total, we analysed the tone of 531 unique advertisements[7] that aired more than 700,000 times in 2008. Our team coded the negativity of all 531 advertisements using each of the five methods – Goldstein and Freedman, Freedman and Goldstein, Kahn and Kenney, Jamieson, and Geer – described above.[8] Coders were blind to the purpose of this study.[9]

As we outlined above, previous research that has focused on similar questions to ours has either compared negativity across different media with different coders (e.g. Franz and Ridout 2008) or has compared the coding of negativity for the same medium, advertising, but with different samples of advertisements and different coders (Geer 2006). This does not allow us to separate variation that is due to different media and coders from variation that derives from different methods of operationalising negativity. By keeping the medium constant and using the same coders our study allows us to isolate variation due to the operationalisation of negativity, which we have argued is a more fundamental question than variation by medium: before we compare negativity across different media we should be sure that researchers are not drawing very different conclusions about negativity and its effects because of different conceptions of negativity *within* the same medium.

Analysis

Figure 3.1 presents our first look at the levels of negativity in advertisements in 2008 according to the five measures. The unit of analysis is the advertisement,

---

6. http://www.vmsinfo.com/

7. The term 'unique' refers to the fact that some advertisements are essentially identical but may mention a different state, depending on where they air, or the text may be the same but in Spanish rather than English. Like Geer (2006), when we examine the tone of the advertisements made in the campaign, we do not include such advertisements more than once but count them as the same advertisement in order to avoid biasing our results. However, when we look at the campaign in terms of advertisements aired later in the chapter, we include unique and 'duplicate' advertisements from the presidential race – 654 in total.

8. An additional trained coder examined a subsample of forty-five of the advertisements and coded tone independently. Krippendorff's Alphas for intercoder reliability were above 0.8 for the Jamieson, Geer, Goldstein and Freedman, and Freedman and Goldstein measures, and 0.78 for the Kahn and Kenney method. These levels of agreement are more than sufficient for our purposes.

9. Indeed, the main purpose of the study was to assess the truth of the claims made in political advertising; coders had no motivation to try to make different coding methods 'agree' because they were unaware of how the data on tone would be used.

Figure 3.1: The tone of advertisements in the US in 2008 according to five different methods of coding negativity (no.=531)

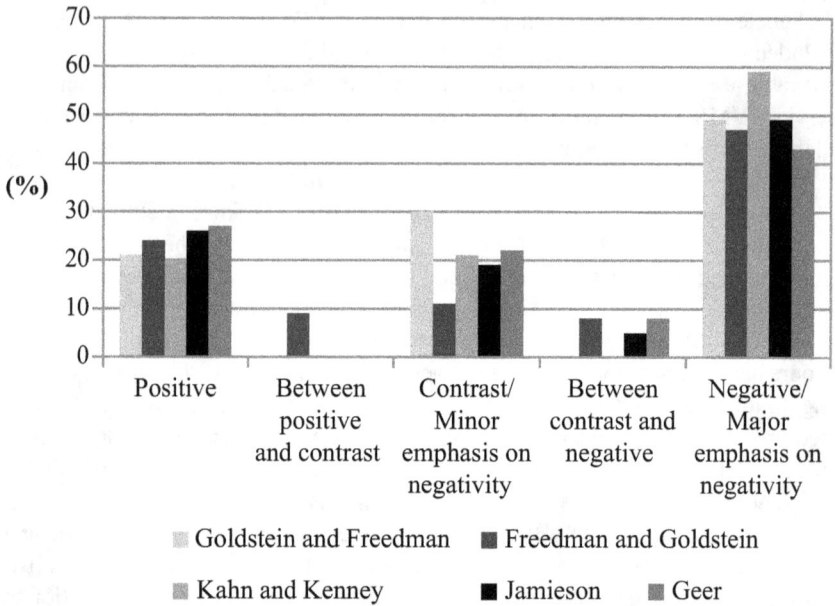

Notes: Goldstein and Freedman = Goldstein and Freedman's three-category measure; Freedman and Goldstein = Freedman and Goldstein's five-category measure; Kahn and Kenney = Kahn and Kenney's three-category measure; Jamieson = Jamieson's 'attack score' approach, where advertisements with 0 per cent – 29 per cent attack words are positive or advocacy, 30 per cent – 70 per cent are contrast, 71 per cent – 90 per cent are between contrast and attack, and 91 per cent plus are negative. Geer = Geer's proportion of negative appeals in each advertisement, categorised using the same system as Jamieson's. Where there are no bars for a category it is because the category is excluded from an author's coding scheme.

which requires some additional explanation. First, we noted above that Jamieson's method leaves ambiguous classification of advertisements with 71 per cent to 90 per cent attack words; we put these advertisements into a fourth, 'Between contrast and negative' category in Figure 1, equivalent to Freedman and Goldstein's 'predominantly negative with token mention of the sponsor' category. Second, although Geer's unit of analysis is the appeal, for the purposes of Figure 3.1 we classified advertisements into four categories from Geer's method – positive, contrast, between contrast and negative, and negative – using the same thresholds as for Jamieson's method, e.g. 90+ per cent negativity constitutes a negative advertisement – but based on the proportion of negative appeals in the advertisement rather than the proportion of attack words. Third, for the Freedman and Goldstein method we present the full five categories in

Figure 3.1 for informational purposes, although we reiterate that they ultimately collapses these five categories into three.

Figure 3.1 shows that there is a great deal of overlap between the different methods. They converge, for example, on indicating that between 20 per cent and 27 per cent of the advertisements in 2008 were positive. There is more discrepancy at the other extreme, negative advertisements or advertisements with a major emphasis on negativity, but that is largely because the Kahn and Kenney method places more advertisements in this category; all the other measures put the proportion of negative advertisements between 43 per cent and 49 per cent. Kahn and Kenney's method, on the other hand, identifies 59 per cent of advertisements as belonging in this category. It seems that their criteria, in which negative advertisements are divided according to minor or major emphasis on negativity, places more advertisements in the extreme category than others. Indeed, if we count the 'between contrast and negative advertisement' category, which three of the methods include but Kahn and Kenney do not, as 'negative' the range across the five methods narrows to between 49 per cent and 59 per cent negative, with all but Goldstein and Freedman's indicating that a majority of the advertisements belonged in this category.

Given these results, it is not surprising that there is also a high level of agreement about contrast advertisements. If we put Freedman and Goldstein's 'between positive and contrast advertisements' – 9 per cent of the total – into the contrast advertisement category, on the grounds that they are not purely positive advertisements – four of the five methods indicate the proportion of contrast advertisements to be between 19 per cent and 22 per cent. The outlier here is the Goldstein and Freedman method, in which 30 per cent of advertisements appear in the contrast category. The reason seems to be that their definition of a positive advertisement is somewhat tighter than, for example, Jamieson's, for whom only when more than 30 per cent of the words in an advertisement are negative does the advertisement move out of the 'positive' category.

In summary, Figure 3.1 indicates high levels of agreement across different methods, with discrepancies in proportions of advertisements placed in the categories of 'positive,' 'contrast' or 'negative' advertisements no greater than about 10 per cent and often much less. All methods indicate that roughly 50 per cent of the advertising in 2008 was negative, with the remaining 50 per cent of advertisements being split fairly evenly between positive and contrast advertising. To put these kinds of differences into perspective, in Geer's (2006) comparison of different methods of coding negativity for the 1960–96 elections, even if we exclude West there were discrepancies of more than 10 per cent between methods for the 1964, 1968, 1972, 1976, 1980, 1984 and 1996 elections. Thus, maximum differences of 10 per cent do not appear large.

Table 3.1 presents additional evidence based on the correlations between measures of levels of negativity using the different methods. In Table 3.1, rather than collapsing the Jamieson attack score and Geer's appeal measures into three categories we allow them to vary over their full range from zero to 100 for each advertisement, i.e. Jamieson's attack score and Geer's proportion of negative appeals

Table 3.1: Correlations between five different methods of measuring negativity (no.=531)

	Goldstein and Freedman	Freedman and Goldstein	Kahn and Kenney	Jamieson	Geer
Goldstein and Freedman	1				
Freedman and Goldstein	0.93	1			
Kahn and Kenney	0.89	0.93	1		
Jamieson	0.88	0.91	0.88	1	
Geer	0.87	0.91	0.88	0.92	1

for each advertisement. The correlations are universally high, with the *lowest* being the 0.87 correlation between the Goldstein and Freedman and Geer methods, which is still a very healthy correlation by any standard. Similarly, a factor analysis of the five methods shows only one very strong factor, with the factor loadings for all five methods greater than 0.9. We also examined different subsets of the data, such as just presidential advertisements, Republican versus Democrat advertisements, radio versus television advertisements, television advertisements that used more visual 'cuts' (to see whether more visual activity in an advertisement might open up greater disagreement between coders), and advertisements with more traits in them (perhaps the tone of issue oriented advertisements is easier to code). No matter how we sliced the data, the correlations between methods remained in excess of 0.8.

Thus, all of the evidence we have presented so far indicates that conclusions about the prevalence of negativity in a campaign would be only marginally affected by decisions like when the mixture of positive and negative appeals makes an ad 'negative' rather than 'contrast' and by the unit of analysis. This still does not quite answer the question of whether and why there might be disagreement about the tone of particular advertisements, however. We therefore examined the coding of specific advertisements among the 531. We would not expect to find instances in which one method describes an advertisement as positive and another as negative – and we do not. As Figure 1 suggested, where we see most instances of disagreement is with advertisements that mix negative and positive messages. For example, an advertisement from the Senate race in Minnesota received an attack score of twenty-one by the Jamieson method and about 13 per cent of the appeals were negative according to the Geer method, putting it in the advocacy or positive advertisement category, where it also belongs according to the Freedman and Goldstein method. Coding by the Kahn and Kenney method, however, places the same advertisement in their middle category of 'minor emphasis on negativity' and using the Goldstein and Freedman method made it a contrast advertisement according to our coders. In a few other instances, differences appear to arise between the methods that treat the advertisement as the unit of analysis and those that break them down into ideas or appeals. For example, when our coders broke down a National Rifle Association advertisement critical of Barack Obama on gun control into idea units for the Jamieson method, or into appeals for the Geer method, they gave it a Jamieson attack score of fifty, while the proportion of negative appeals by the Geer method was 62.5. This renders these advertisements contrast. But using the other three methods, where the unit of analysis is the advertisement, our coders put the same advertisement in the most negative category. The reason appears to be because the first half of the advertisement told a story about gun ownership, culminating in the line that, 'You might call it an heirloom, or just a wall hanger,' before going on to excoriate Obama for apparently calling 'it' an assault weapon. When the unit of analysis was the advertisement, coders did not see the first half of the advertisement as positive, but by the Jamieson and Geer methods it diluted the negativity of the ideas or appeals in the advertisement such as to put it in the contrast category.

Such differences are, however, both fairly limited and rare in our data. Nevertheless, so far we have only looked at the first of our two questions, differences in the coding of the negativity of advertisements made. Researchers are also usually interested in our second question, the effects of advertisements aired. It may be that when we look at negativity in this way small differences in the coding of individual advertisements become larger differences when we are trying to account for advertisements that often air thousands of times. Similarly, content analysis of negativity in debates or media coverage will code hundreds of cases, meaning that small but systematic differences in the coding of individual cases may become more consequential.

We examine this by looking at the relationship between negativity in advertisements aired in the presidential race and turnout in the 2008 presidential election according to the five methods. VMS provided us with data on how many times each presidential advertisement aired in 103 television markets in the US – the largest one hundred and three others – which cover more than 80 per cent of the population (the US is divided into 210 television markets, or 'Designated Market Area(s)' (DMA)). DMAs are smaller than states – Texas alone has seventeen – but they are larger than counties. We used census data on turnout by county and then aggregated up the counties in each DMA to obtain turnout in each DMA. It would be a mistake to simply use this turnout figure, however, because some areas will usually have higher turnout at elections than other areas, regardless of advertising; what we want to examine is the relationship between negativity and deviations from 'normal turnout' in a presidential election. Our dependent variable is therefore the per cent deviation from average turnout in the DMA over the five previous presidential elections (1988–2004).

For our estimates of negativity, knowing the tone of the advertisement according to each method and how often it aired allows us to calculate the five measures of the proportion of negative, contrast, and positive advertisements aired in each DMA. The Goldstein and Freedman method uses these exact categories. For the Freedman and Goldstein method, we categorised advertisements 'between positive and contrast' (*see* Figure 1) as positive and advertisements 'between contrast and negative' as contrast; for the Kahn and Kenney method, advertisements with no negativity were categorised as positive, advertisements with minor emphasis on negativity as contrast, and advertisements with major

Table 3.2: Estimated relationships between negativity and turnout according to five different methods (no.=103)

Negative advertisements

	Goldstein and Freedman	Freedman and Goldstein	Kahn and Kenney	Jamieson	Geer
Estimated relationship with turnout	0.15 (0.06)*	0.13 (0.06)*	−0.09 (0.07)	0.13 (0.06)*	0.16 (0.07)*

Contrast advertisements

	Goldstein and Freedman	Freedman and Goldstein	Kahn and Kenney	Jamieson	Geer
Estimated relationship with turnout	−0.24 (0.07)*	−0.19 (0.08)*	0.26 (0.12)*	−0.26 (0.08)*	−0.26 (0.08)*

Notes: *$p<0.05$ #$p<0.10$ (two-tailed test). Standard errors in parentheses. Models include controls for per cent black, per cent Hispanic, per cent in poverty, per cent in the labour force, and per cent with a higher education degree, according to census data, as well as the average age of adults, and the 'normal' Democrat and Republican votes in the DMA (average vote in presidential elections from 1988–2004).

emphasis on negativity as negative; with the Jamieson and Geer methods we also categorised advertisements 'between positive and contrast' as contrast. Thus for purposes of comparison we use the Geer method, in which the unit of analysis is the appeal, to categorise advertisements (employing the same criteria described in Figure 3.1).

Table 3.2 presents the results of separate regression models in which we first examined the relationship between the proportion of negative advertisements aired and turnout and then the relationship between the proportion of contrast advertisements aired and turnout according to each measure. The models control for the proportion of voting age adults in the DMA that are black, Hispanic, in poverty, in the labour force, and have a higher education degree, according to census data, as well as the average age of adults, and the 'normal' Democrat and Republican vote, also based on the previous five elections. We do not present those estimates here; our focus is solely on the estimated relationships between negativity and turnout.[10]

Four of the five methods provide very similar estimates of the effects of negativity, showing a statistically significant positive relationship between the proportion of negative advertisements and turnout in a DMA, ranging from 0.13 to 0.16, and a statistically significant negative relationship between the

---

10. The adjusted R^2 in the models is between 0.41 and 0.48.

proportion of contrast advertisements and turnout in a DMA, ranging from
−0.19 to −0.26. The outlier is Kahn and Kenney's measure, which indicates
no relationship between negative advertising and turnout and a positive
relationship between the proportion of contrast advertisements and turnout.
On closer inspection, this appears to be because, as Figure 3.1 showed, Kahn
and Kenney's method tends to put more advertisements with negative content
into their most extreme category. In the Philadelphia market, for example,
where all the other methods suggest that 34 per cent to 41 per cent of the
advertisements were negative, the Kahn and Kenney method indicates 51 per
cent. In the Charlotte market, while the other four measures indicate between
34 per cent and 44 per cent of the advertisements were negative the Kahn and
Kenney method suggests 56 per cent. Indeed, in more than 75 per cent of the
103 markets the Kahn and Kenney method indicates higher levels of negative
advertising than any other.

These differences can become particularly pronounced in markets where
there was relatively little advertising. Thus, we repeated the analysis of
Table 3.2 but divided the sample of DMAs into two − the fifty-two with the
fewest advertisements aired and the fifty-one with the most advertisements
aired − our reasoning being that if the different estimated relationships using
the Kahn and Kenney method are due to large discrepancies in markets where
few advertisements were aired, we should see similar estimated relationships
when we focus on the markets with the most airings. Table 3.3 presents the
results. Dividing the sample in this way limits sample size, as well as the
variance in dependent and independent variables, and we are thus less likely
to see statistically significant relationships, but our interest is also in the size
and signs of the estimated relationships. Table 3.3 confirms that the discrepancy
between the estimates using the Kahn and Kenney measure versus the other
measures is particularly pronounced in markets in which fewer advertisements
aired. The coefficients for the relationship between the proportion of negative
advertisements and turnout in these markets are between 0.00 and −0.03 for
the other four methods but it is −0.19 and statistically significant using the
Kahn and Kenney method. For markets with more airings there is also some
variation, with all the other methods indicating a negative relationship while
the coefficient using the Kahn and Kenney is 0.01; nevertheless, none of the
relationships is statistically significant, meaning we would not be led to different
conclusions by using any of the five methods in this case. The results for contrast
advertisements are similar in that all the measures other than Kahn and Kenney's
indicate a negative relationship with turnout in markets with fewer airings of
advertisements, with three of the four statistically significant at $p<0.10$ while the
relationship using the Kahn and Kenney method is positive. In addition, none
of the methods suggests a statistically significant relationship with turnout in
markets where more advertisements aired − all the coefficients are smaller than
their standard errors.

In sum, differences between the measures when we look at their relationships
with turnout are largely confined to the Kahn and Kenney method; all the others

Table 3.3: Estimated relationships between negativity and turnout controlling for the number of advertisements aired

Negative advertisements

	Goldstein and Freedman	Freedman and Goldstein	Kahn and Kenney	Jamieson	Geer
Estimated relationship with turnout in 52 markets with lowest number of airings	0.00 (0.09)	−0.03 (0.08)	−.019 (0.07)*	−0.02 (0.09)	−0.01 (0.10)
Estimated relationship with turnout in 51 markets with highest number of airings	−0.17 (0.20)	−0.21 (0.19)	0.01 (0.24)	−0.15 (0.20)	−0.06 (0.22)

Contrast advertisements

	Goldstein and Freedman	Freedman and Goldstein	Kahn and Kenney	Jamieson	Geer
Estimated relationship with turnout in 52 markets with lowest number of airings	−0.17 (0.08)#	−0.08 (0.10)	0.20 (0.15)	−0.17 (0.10)#	−0.17 (0.10)#
Estimated relationship with turnout in 51 markets with highest number of airings	0.09 (0.25)	0.24 (0.30)	−0.23 (0.31)	0.13 (0.29)	−0.12 (0.30)

Notes: *p<0.05 #p<0.10 (two-tailed test). Standard errors in parentheses. Models include controls for per cent black, per cent Hispanic, per cent in poverty, per cent in the labour force, and per cent with a higher education degree, according to census data, as well as the average age of adults, the 'normal' Democrat and Republican votes in the DMA (average vote in presidential elections from 1988–2004).

tell a similar story. The reason appears to be because the tendency for the Kahn and Kenney method to code more advertisements in the most negative category can be particularly exaggerated in markets where few advertisements aired. In markets with more advertisements, we see some variation in the sign of the relationships across the five methods, but none of these relationships approaches statistical significance, i.e. all five methods lead to the same substantive inferences about the relationship between negativity and turnout.

Discussion and conclusion

This chapter has provided a unique examination of different measures of negativity in a campaign. We asked two questions at the outset: Do differences in the operationalisation of the coding of negativity lead to different conclusions about the negativity of a campaign; and do variations in the operationalisation of the coding of negativity lead to different conclusions about the relationship between the negativity of a campaign and dependent variables such as turnout? Our results are reassuring on the first question and suggest the need for caution with respect to the second. On the one hand, while we pointed to the fact that the five different methods we examined – what we have termed the Goldstein and Freedman, Freedman and Goldstein, Kahn and Kenney, Jamieson, and Geer measures – make slightly different assumptions about how negativity affects individuals, they correlate very highly – at 0.87 and above – when our interest is in levels of negativity in a campaign. Thus, if researchers' focus is on the tone of a campaign, or when and whether a candidate or party 'goes negative,' our study suggests that variation in what constitutes a 'negative' versus a mixed or 'contrast' message, or variation in the unit of analysis makes little difference. On the other hand, when we turned to an examination of the *effects* of negativity – in our case to the relationships the five methods imply between advertisements aired and turnout – these relatively minor differences in the coding of negativity in individual advertisements can become much greater. We observed that while four methods provided similar answers about the relationship between negativity and turnout, the Kahn and Kenney method, which lead to more advertisements being coded in the most extreme negative category, suggested quite different relationships, particularly in markets where few advertisements aired.

Such differences in measures of negativity may be less consequential in countries like the UK where very few advertisements are aired compared to the US, but when the medium is negativity in newspapers or debates we may see similar patterns: small differences in the coding of the negativity of individual articles, for example, may become more substantial if the researcher then creates a measure that multiplies the negativity of hundreds of articles by likely exposure to them. What is the solution? We offer two possibilities in concluding this chapter. One is that researchers adopt more than one method by which to code negativity and check to see whether analysis using different measures converges on the same answers. It seems particularly important to be cognisant of different ways of categorising messages that mix positive and negative information. A second way forward is that researchers are simply more aware of the assumptions that lie behind their coding of negativity and, at a minimum, justify them, though it would be preferable to actually test for the robustness of different categories of tone by conducting experiments.

Chapter Four

Comparing Measures of Campaign Negativity: Expert Judgements, Manifestos, Debates, and Advertisements

François Gélineau and André Blais

The traditional way of measuring the tone of an electoral campaign is to content analyse the parties' and/or candidates' discourse. There are two methodological issues with this approach. The first concerns how to code party messages as positive, negative, or neutral. The second issue, which is the focus of this chapter, concerns the content to be analysed. The most commonly available source is party manifestos, which exist in the majority of countries. The problem is that party manifestos may not reflect the actual discourse employed by the parties or candidates, the actual discourse that voters are exposed to during the course of an election campaign. From that perspective televised debates and party advertisements seem more appropriate. Unfortunately, these sources are seldom universal or directly comparable across countries; many countries ban television advertisements and the format of television debates varies considerably over both time and space. The same applies to party websites, the purpose and format of which vary from one party to another.

Given all these problems, in this chapter we explore the merits and limits of expert judgements to ascertain the tone of electoral campaigns. We first place our research question in context with regards to the broader negative campaign literature. We then review the debate on the use of expert judgements in another domain, the analysis of party policy positions, where the pros and cons of expert judgements have been systematically discussed, and we explore the implications for the study of campaign negativity. We then present findings of experts' judgements about the negativity of the various parties' campaign in the 2012 election in the province of Quebec, and provide a preliminary evaluation of the value of asking experts to characterise the positivity/negativity of election campaigns.

Campaign negativity

Despite the fact that negative campaign communications have not increased significantly over the past few decades, at least in the American context (Lau and Rovner 2009), a growing literature has contributed to place this phenomenon at the centre of interest for scholars studying political campaigns and party strategy. An important part of this research has attempted to measure the effectiveness of negative political advertisements. All in all, the literature provides rather weak support for the claim that campaigns work in favour of the attacker (Lau *et al.* 2007) or that it produces a backlash effect on the attacker's support (Roese and Sande 1993).

Another segment of that literature has focused on the candidate/party motivation behind the decision to use negative attacks as a campaign strategy. Some have argued that the candidate's relative position in the campaign (frontrunner or not) is the key factor (Kern 1989, Jamieson and Campbell 1983, Skaperdas and Grofman 1995). Others have argued that the decision is primarily based on the candidate's own personal and ideological attributes (Harrington and Hess 1996; Kahn 1993; Kahn and Kenney 2000; Ansolabehere and Iyengar 1995; Procter *et al.* 1994). Yet others have claimed that campaign conditions determine whether negative campaigning will be used by candidates (Haynes and Rhine 1998).

All in all, this literature has faced the difficult task of measuring a phenomenon that is rather difficult to circumscribe. Some have even suggested that scholarly measurement of campaign negativity is often at variance with voters' perceptions, which are what matter in the end (Sigelman and Kugler 2003). Measurement of campaign negativity is thus at the core of our concerns.

Before directly addressing this question we will review the intense debate that has taken place about how to measure party positions in election campaigns, since many of the issues that we face when it comes to ascertaining the tone of party messages similarly arise when the goal is to identify party positions. We believe that a review of that debate provides a perspective that can be fruitfully applied to the measurement of campaign negativity.

The debate about party manifestos versus expert judgements to tap party positions

The analysis of party manifestos requires a significant cost and time investment. Expert judgements constitute a quicker, cheaper, and more indirect approach. After all, we are interested in what the parties tell voters, and the most logical way to proceed is to analyse the content of the messages. So, everything else being equal, and especially when cost is not a primary consideration, content analysis should be preferred.

Everything else is not equal, however. The fact is that doing an Internet survey to obtain expert judgements is a lot cheaper than content analysing party manifestos. We will elaborate on that in the next section, but perhaps as much emphasis should be given to the fact that an expert survey is much quicker to perform than a content analysis of party manifestos. This is a crucial consideration in research projects where the goal is to link party messages to voter choices, like Making Electoral Democracy Work (www.electoraldemocracy.com). There is often a delay of several years before the coded data from the Comparative Manifesto Project (CMP) are released. The CMP data are heavily used by researchers long after they have been collected, but the collection of content-based data can be a frustrating experience for projects dealing with a specific set of elections and a specific time horizon.

We should keep in mind that the analysis of party manifestos is itself a shortcut for researchers that are interested in the content of party messages conveyed to voters at the time of an election campaign. Ideally we would like to study a representative sample of these messages. In fact, party manifestos seem at first sight to be the least valid source of information, as very few voters read them or are even aware of their existence. The assumption has to be that party leaders and candidates know the manifestos and more or less repeat the messages contained in the manifestos when it comes to expressing positions on the issues of the day in their encounters with the media and voters. In other words, the party manifesto is also a proxy to identify the policy positions that are conveyed during a campaign.

This suggests a reason why party manifestos are more extensively examined than other types of party messages. It is easier and cheaper to retrieve and analyse the manifesto of a given party than to obtain and code all the speeches that a party leader delivers during the course of a campaign. Another reason is that manifestos exist (almost) everywhere while other forms of communication, such as television advertisements or debates, do not. Finally, the main objective of a party manifesto is to lay out what the party stands for. It is thus more useful for the study of party policy positions or ideology than for other matters (such as campaign tone).

A second question concerns the accuracy of measures based on manifestos and expert judgements. Ray (2007) notes that expert surveys explicitly assume a Downsian proximity space since experts are asked to locate each party from the extreme left to the extreme right, while the CMP reports the percentage of quasi sentences that are devoted to each of a set of themes, which are then classified as being on the left or right. This indicates the relative emphasis given to various issues, grounded in the saliency theory of party competition (Budge and Farlie, 1983). In this case, it is hard to argue that one measure is 'better' than the other, unless one is able to show that proximity theory is more or less valid than directional theory.

This highlights one contrast between the two approaches. Content analysis is usually performed by one or two coders, who code a great number of short messages contained in one individual document, while the expert survey invites many respondents to provide their general assessment of all the party messages. The great advantage of content analysis is that it is based on a specific assessment of a very specific message, according to a pre-established set of criteria. The main shortcoming is clearly that the analysis is limited to one particular document.

Those who rely on expert judgements have to concede that the individual measures that they obtain are more error prone. Each expert is asked to provide an evaluation of the general orientation of the party. That evaluation cannot be as precise as that of the coder who must make a similar decision regarding a quasi-sentence. The hope is that what is lost in precision in each response is compensated by the use of many experts; aggregating many responses should attenuate the random noise associated with each response. Furthermore, the experts base their judgements on their observation of a variety of sources, and not only a single document (the manifesto), and this should enhance the validity of the measure.

The last issue that we need to deal with is cross-temporal and cross-national variability. McDonald *et al.* (2007) report that expert surveys of left-right positions show much less variation, across both time and space, than CMP measures and they argue that as a consequence the latter are to be preferred.

McDonald *et al.* (2007) show that there is little dynamic variation in expert survey scores. As the authors point out, the survey approach is deemed to tap the longstanding core principles of a party and may thus miss some of the more specific changes in party positions. But the difference may also stem from the fact that the CMP is a saliency-based measure and that saliency is more variable than policy positions *per se*.

McDonald *et al.* (2007) also point out that party scores on the left-right scale are strongly associated with party family affiliations and yield little cross-national variation. The authors' interpretation is the following: 'The concept of left-right has no secure anchor. Experts are left to determine their own individual frame of reference. Each expert respondent may set his or her reference in accordance with, say, what it means to be centrist in the expert's own nation.' (McDonald *et al.* 2007: 74). The interpretation makes sense. The concern, however, holds only when it comes to characterising party positions on a broad scale whose meaning is far from clear and is prone to be interpreted differently across countries.

Much of the debate about the merits and limits of party manifestos versus expert judgements for the study of party positions hinges on views about the meaning of left and right, more specifically whether it makes sense or not to measure party positions on the basis of the relative emphasis given to various issues (as the CMP does) or to allow for different policy dimensions to be considered in different countries (as is the case with expert surveys).

It is more fruitful to think about the merits and limits of these two approaches with respect to the analysis of party positions on specific issues. The above discussion leads to the following observations:

1. Ideally, party positions should be tapped through the analysis of what the parties say, and from that perspective content analysis is to be preferred over expert surveys.
2. Ideally, all party messages should be considered and the focus on one particular document (party manifesto) is unfortunate. From that perspective, expert judgements, which are presumably based on the observation of many different sources, would seem to be preferable.
3. Coders' judgements are likely to be more accurate than experts' judgements to the extent that the former deal with specific statements contained in quasi-sentences while the latter are summary evaluations with less explicit rules about how to make these evaluations.
4. There are usually many more experts than coders, which should contribute to reducing measurement error.
5. Expert judgements are a lot cheaper than content analysis. One question, therefore, is whether the potential quality differential is worth the cost. Another question is whether expert judgements might produce better quality measures if we were to devote more resources to their development.

Prior research on campaign tone

Let us now consider what kind of approach has been used to study campaign tone. The first observation to be made is that to the best of our knowledge no previous study has resorted to expert surveys.[1] From that perspective the attempt in the MEDW project (www.electoraldemocracy.com) to ask experts to provide their assessment of the negativity of the various parties' campaigns is an innovation.

The second observation is that almost all studies focus on one single source in their content analysis and that the most frequent source is by far party advertisements. This is so because the great majority of studies have dealt with American elections, where television advertisements play a central role. The fact is that television advertisements play a less important role in many other settings; in fact they are banned in many European countries. Which sources to examine in a cross-national project is thus a huge challenge since communication between parties/candidates and voters is based on very different channels across countries. There is no dominant source that would be the equivalent of the party manifesto for the analysis of party positions. One reason is that the party position literature is solely interested in what the parties say about the issues of the day while the negative campaign literature would like to cover everything that the candidates and parties say in the course of a campaign.

It is useful to make at the outset one crucial distinction between direct and indirect sources of party messages. Direct sources concern messages that are conveyed by the political parties themselves, perhaps the most obvious example being party advertisements.[2] Indirect sources refer to media coverage of the campaign. In the latter case, researchers characterise the tone of a campaign by analysing television news or the print media; the approach consists in identifying what the media reports that party figures have said and coding all these statements, which can come from many different sources, as negative or not. The issue in this case is whether media coverage provides a good approximation of what the parties say during a campaign. The problem is that the media are likely to pay more attention to some messages than to others; the smaller parties are less likely to be covered, statements about the horserace will be highlighted, and negative news will get greater prominence. It can be argued, however, that most voters get most of their information from the media and that media coverage is a good proxy for the set of party messages that reach voters.

Let us focus on direct sources. What is most remarkable is that in all cases the analysis is based on one single source. As Lau and Rovner (2009: 286) note in their review of the literature, 'how one could actually get an overall negativism "score" for a campaign that included television ads... radio ads...

---

1. We have found one exception, an unpublished paper by Patterson and Shea (2001), cited in Lau *et al.* (2007), which relied on ratings of congressional elections by local newspaper editors.

2. We would also classify leaders' debates as direct, since leaders' messages are delivered directly to viewers (or listeners). The media sometime play an important role since journalists may feed questions or act as chairs or judges but they do not screen out what they deem to be less relevant.

newspaper advertisements, billboards, law signs, bumper stickers, and personal appearances ... is a question no one we know has ever tried to address.'[3]

Researchers typically analyse the document that they feel best represents the messages conveyed by the parties or candidates. In the US, the most frequent choice is television advertisements because they are under the full control of the parties; the parties/candidates devote a major fraction of their resources to these advertisements, and many voters are exposed to them, either directly or indirectly as they become part of the news coverage. A major problem, of course, is that there are no campaign television advertisements in many (perhaps most) countries and, as a consequence, television advertisements are not an option for cross-national projects. Cross-national studies of campaign negativity thus face a bigger challenge (compared to research on party positions) with respect to the documents to be examined. There is no equivalent to party manifestos.

Things are easier, however, on another front. As pointed out earlier, the debate about the respective merits and limits of party manifestos versus expert judgements is very much intertwined with the discussion of the meaning of the left-right scale. There is little ambiguity about what a negative message is: it is simply a message that refers in a negative fashion to one's opponents.[4]

What is most remarkable in the campaign negativity research is that a good number of studies rely on content analysis, but the content is not party messages *per se* but media coverage of party messages. The rationale for this approach is well explained by Lau and Pomper (2002):

> We rely on estimates of the campaign more broadly, we need a more comprehensive view. We rely on estimates of the nature of the campaign gathered from newspaper accounts of the election campaigns. These accounts include descriptions of political advertisements broadcast by the different candidates but they also include reports of a wide variety of other campaign activities. As such, our data are second-hand, relying on the judgements of political experts (i.e. political reporters)...'

In this sense the distinction between content analysis and expert judgements becomes somewhat blurred.

We also note that expert judgements are sometimes used to validate the findings of content analysis. This is the case in Ansolabehere *et al.* (1994). The non-experimental component of their study is based on a systematic content analysis of news coverage. The authors validated their classification of the thirty-fourth Senatorial elections 'by asking two major political consultants ... to rate each of

---

3. We should note, however, that Kahn and Kenney (1999a) use three different indicators of campaign negativity, one based on television advertisements, a second based on content analysis of press coverage, and a third resulting from interviews of campaign managers. The three indicators are examined separately.

4. Jamieson *et al.* (2000) have argued for a different typology (attack/contrast/advocate). We find the positive/negative typology (or continuum) simpler, once we allow for the possibility of a mixture of positive and negative messages.

the Senate campaigns on the same three-point scale. The consultants disagreed with our classification in only one instance ... and we deferred to their expertise' (p. 836). We find it interesting that, in the end, the authors put more confidence in the judgements of two experts than in their content analysis of 2,500 articles.

In short, the analysis of campaign tone relies either on a content analysis of television advertisements or of media coverage. Television advertisements can be used as the prominent source of party messages almost exclusively in the US and are therefore not very useful in a comparative perspective. Interestingly, we do not know of any comparative study based on other sources, such as leaders' debates. There have been quite a few analyses that have used media coverage of the campaign as an indirect source of information about the tone of the campaign. Such analyses lend themselves relatively easily to a comparative perspective though we have not come across any concrete example yet.

There are thus three methodological options when it comes to studying the tone of election campaigns. The first is the direct content analysis of party messages, the major question then being which source(s) to examine. The second is the indirect content analysis of media coverage, the major question being whether the media provide a good approximation of party messages. The third is the expert survey, the major question being how much trust we can have in these experts' overall assessments.

In this chapter, we compare expert judgements on the negative/positive character of the campaign to negativity scores obtained through the content analysis of television advertisements.

The Quebec 2012 general election

Historically, the Quebec party system has been relatively stable, dominated by two main political parties (Pelletier 2012; Montigny 2011). Since the late 1990s, the political landscape has changed slightly, with the arrival of a third party that managed to compete closely with the two historical parties in 2003 (with 18 per cent of the vote), 2007 (31 per cent), 2008 (16 per cent), and 2012 (27 per cent). In 2007, the party (*Action Démocratique du Québec*) even managed to form the official opposition by outvoting one of the two historical parties by a few points.

In 2012, six main political parties attracted over 99 per cent of the votes. These six political parties are also those that had produced a manifesto and presented candidates in a majority of the 125 electoral districts.

Since 1976, the *Parti Québécois* (PQ) and the *Parti Libéral du Québec* (PLQ) have formed the government in alternation. The PLQ is the only party that exists since 1867. The PQ was founded in the 1970s and the CAQ (formerly *Action Démocratique du Québec* (ADQ)) made its appearance on the political scenery in the mid-1990s.

At least since the 1970s, the Quebec political landscape has been dominated by a debate over the place of Quebec within the Canadian federation. While the PLQ has been a long-time defender of the federalist position, the PQ has been the front figure for the independence of the province. In the constitutional sphere, the PVQ tends to be more federalist, while QS and ON are clearly promoting Quebec's

Table 4.1: Result of the 2012 Quebec general election

Parti québécois (PQ)	31.95%
Parti libéral du Québec (PLQ)	31.20%
Coalition avenir Québec (CAQ)	27.05%
Québec solidaire (QS)	6.03%
Option nationale (ON)	1.89%
Parti vert du Québec (PVQ)	0.99%
	99.11%

independence. The CAQ (as was the case for the ADQ) has tried to avoid the constitutional issues to focus on public finance and economic development.

Using a left-right ideological scale, one would place the CAQ and the PLQ to the immediate-right of the middle point, and the PQ to the immediate-left. QS is further to the left while ON and the PVQ would place somewhere between QS and PQ. Figure 4.1 illustrates the positions of the Quebec political parties by using a two-dimensional grid in which the horizontal axis illustrates the left-right dimension, and the vertical axis, an approximation of the constitutional dimension.

Figure 4.1: The Quebec political landscape

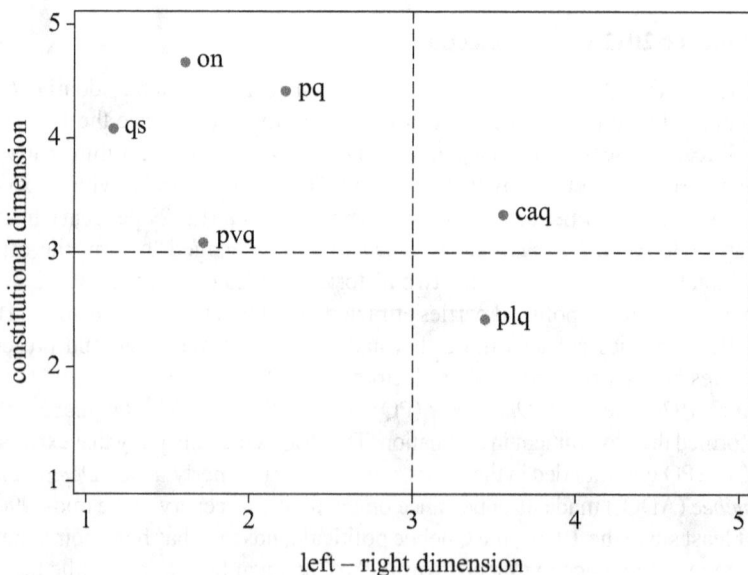

Source: www.votecompass.ca

Data analysis

The expert judgements were obtained through the administration of a short Internet questionnaire immediately after the 2012 Quebec general election. The questionnaire contained six questions measuring (1) the general tone of the campaign (negative/positive); (2) the target of each political party's attacks; (3) the main issue discussed by each party; (4) the clarity of their campaign; (5) the relative emphasis on the party leader; and (6) the main campaign method used by the parties. An invitation was sent to a total of seventy-nine experts. Thirty-three of them completed the questionnaire.

The content analysis of television advertisements was performed on a total of thirty-five advertisements. We coded an additional 111 video advertisements that were widely broadcast on the Web (mostly through YouTube), but not on television. In addition to providing a general measure of the tone of each party's campaign, the content analysis allows us to identify the target of the attacks of each political party.

For the content analysis, the advertisements were broken down into 826 quasi-sentences, using a coding scheme analogous to the one used by the Comparative Manifesto Project. Out of these quasi-sentences, we were able to identify a positive/negative tone (Benoit *et al.* 2003b; Benoit 2007) for 751 quasi-sentences: 132 from the advertisements that were broadcast on television and 619 for the others.

Figure 4.2: Positive/negative campaign by party

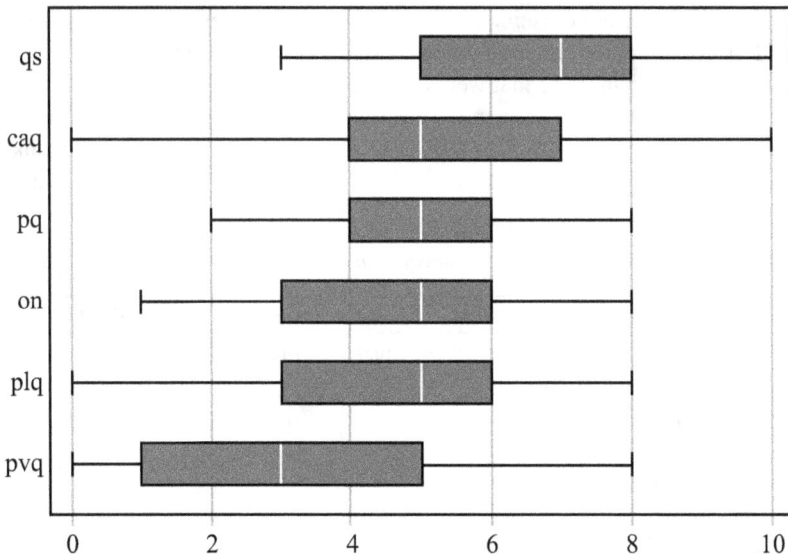

Expert survey

According to the experts, the tone of the 2012 Quebec election was located at the midpoint (4.85) of the zero to ten negative/positive scale. This value was obtained by simply averaging the 183 scores attributed to each party. Figure 4.2 breaks down these evaluations by political party. The mean score of each party ranks as follows (from most positive to most negative): QS (6.68), CAQ (5.16), PQ (4.94), ON (4.7), PLQ (4.39), and PVQ (3.10). While it is difficult to distinguish the tone of the four parties located in the middle, the PVQ and QS clearly stand out from the group.

The target of this negativity varied from one party to another. Table 4.2 illustrates how the experts perceived these targets. According to the experts, the PQ and PLQ mostly targeted each other, with 72 per cent of the PQ's attacks being directed at the PLQ and 69 per cent of the PLQ's attacks towards the PQ. For both parties, the second target was the CAQ, representing 28 per cent of their attacks. The CAQ's attacks were shared almost equally between the PQ (50 per cent) and the PLQ (47 per cent). ON followed a similar pattern, with 56 per cent of its attacks directed at the PLQ and 44 per cent at the PQ. The other two parties, QS and PVQ, mostly targeted the incumbent party, with 75 per cent and 94 per cent of their attacks directed at the PLQ.

Content analysis of televised advertisements

Out of the 751 quasi-sentences analysed, 202 (27 per cent) of them displayed a negative tone. Interestingly, with only 12 per cent of the quasi-sentences being negative, the advertisements that appeared on television were much less negative than those that were limited to the Internet, in which 30 per cent of the quasi-sentences had a negative tone. It appears that political parties did not broadcast their most negative advertisements on television. It is especially true of the CAQ and PLQ, for which the Internet advertisements contained over three times more negative content than those that were televised (*see* Table 4.3).

The overall ranking (from most positive to most negative) of the political parties is as follows: PQ, QS, CAQ, PLQ, ON, and PVQ. At first sight, the ranking that emerges of the content analysis is different from the one obtained with the

Table 4.2: Target of attacks (expert survey in per cent)

		PQ	PLQ	CAQ	QS	ON	PVQ
	PQ		69.0	50.0	14.3	44.0	5.9
	PLQ	71.9		46.7	75.0	56.0	94.1
Target	CAQ	28.2	27.6		10.7		
	QS						
	ON		3.5	3.3			
	PVQ						
	Total	100%	100%	100%	100%	100%	100%

Table 4.3: Campaign tone in video advertisements (per cent negative quasi-sentences)

	PQ	QS	CAQ	PLQ	ON	PVQ
Television	16.7	14.3	16.7	8.6	.	.
Internet	21.2	23.0	42.9	41.9	37.2	80.0
All	20.8	21.3	22.6	26.9	37.2	80.0

expert judgements. Yet, the Spearman rank order coefficient is 0.77, indicating a very consistent pattern.

Table 4.4 confirms the consistency of the two measures of campaign negativity. In both datasets the PVQ is ranked as the most negative. In four of the remaining five cases, the ranking only differs by one. The most important divergence is found with the PQ, which had more positive advertisements than what experts observed.

As for the target of these negative advertisements, Table 4.5 suggests that political parties mostly attacked the incumbent (PLQ). In every case with the exception of ON, the PLQ is the most frequent target of the negative advertisements. This is mostly consistent with the results of the expert survey. Yet, there are some nuances. The content analysis suggests that the PQ attacks were almost equally directed at the PLQ and the CAQ, while the expert survey indicated that the PQ target was mostly the PLQ. Similarly, the CAQ advertisements targeted mostly the PLQ, while the experts' perception was that it almost equally targeted the PLQ and the PQ.

Conclusion

This chapter has used responses to an expert survey along with the content analysis of video advertisements to measure the tone of the 2012 Quebec general election. Although the results of each instrument cannot be directly compared to one another to measure the absolute level of negativity of the campaign, we could assess the relative tone of each political party's campaign. We ranked the level of negativity of the main political parties and concluded that both instruments generate consistent results, with the exception of one party (PQ) for which experts gave a higher ranking (in terms of negativity) than what the advertisements seem to indicate. It is not clear why that is at this point. The answer may lie in other aspects of the campaign that are not captured by the advertisements. Our hypothesis is that the negative tone perceived by experts is related to the PQ leader's strategy in the televised debates and in some public speeches during the campaign.

Our analysis has also allowed us to identify the targets of each party's negative attacks, as perceived by the experts as well as through the content analysis of the video advertisements. Here too, we found a fairly consistent pattern. For most political actors, the party of the incumbent government was the main object of their attacks.

Table 4.4: Ranking of parties' campaigns (from most positive to most negative)

	Ranking		
	Experts	**Advertisements**	**Difference**
PLQ	5	4	−1
PQ	3	1	−2
CAQ	2	3	+1
QS	1	2	+1
ON	4	5	+1
PVQ	6	6	0

Table 4.5: Target of attacks (video advertisements in per cent)

		PQ	PLQ	CAQ	QS	ON	PVQ
Target	PQ		63.8	40.0	16.7	45.7	
	PLQ	51.5		60.0	83.3	28.6	100.0
	CAQ	48.5	36.2			2.9	
	QS					22.9	
	ON						
	PVQ						
	Total	100%	100%	100%	100%	100%	100%

We must stress that this was a first attempt to use expert judgements to ascertain the tone of a campaign and that we need to think about ways to improve how we survey expert judgements.

First, most obviously, we could/should provide a clear definition of what we mean by negativity to make sure that the experts are on the same page. Second, we need to think about how to improve the response rate among these experts. Thirdly, the survey could be conducted during the campaign rather than after, or even better, the experts could be surveyed let us say every week of the campaign and asked to ascertain the tone for each week. Fourth, the experts could be asked to rate the negativity of different types of messages (advertisements, leaders' speeches at party rallies, party websites). All possible improvements could of course increase the cost of these expert surveys. It remains to be determined whether, or under what circumstances, expert judgements provide better or lower quality data than other approaches, and also to ascertain the cost differential. Our claim is simply that expert surveys should be considered as a serious option, especially in the context of cross-national research.

What we need, then, are systematic comparisons of campaign negativity obtained through direct content analysis of party messages, indirect analysis through media coverage of the campaign, and expert judgements. This study provides a first step in that direction.

Chapter Five

Attack, Support, and Coalitions in a Multiparty System: Understanding Negative Campaigning in a Country with a Coalition Government

Wouter de Nooy and Jan Kleinnijenhuis[1]

The extensive body of work by Benoit, Geer, and other researchers has taught us a lot about the causes and consequences of negative campaigning in the US. As Benoit states in the Chapter Two of this volume, however, more work needs to be done to see whether the insights about attacks on electoral competitors generalise to other countries. This chapter addresses negative campaigning in a country with a coalition government. In multiparty proportional representation systems governed by coalitions, political parties and strategic voters in particular need to figure out the most probable coalition(s) during the election campaign. We posit that parties and voters deduce parties' coalition preferences from statements that parties make in the mass media, notably statements about other parties. Negative statements, that is, attacks on another party, suggest incompatibilities that are in the way of a viable coalition. But positive statements – expressions of support, which appear frequently in coalition government systems during campaigns – are equally important because they suggest agreement and cooperation. We conceive attacks and support as the two poles of a continuum. Note that expressions of support for another party are fundamentally different from positive campaigning as self-praise – one of the three functions specified in the Functional Theory of Political Campaign Discourse (Benoit 2007) – so we refer to support statements instead of positive campaigning to avoid confusion.

Parties may use intermediated attack and support statements strategically to suggest potential coalitions to the electorate. If support and attack statements cluster parties into blocs of mutually supporting parties that systematically attack parties in other blocs, voters will have the strong impression that blocs represent coalitions that are supported by parties, whereas coalitions combining parties from different blocs are unlikely to be successful. We expect this type of polarisation to occur because it is cognitively consonant and meeting the news value of consonance, even if the suggested coalitions are not desired by all parties involved or even unrealistic

---

1. We are grateful to Kristin Ramcke and Ada Sneekes who operationalised standing in the polls and coalition potential during their research internship in the Research Master program at the University of Amsterdam, Department of Communication Science.

according to the polls. There is group pressure to contribute to polarisation by aligning one's support and attacks to previous support and attack statements in the media. In our case study of the Dutch 2006 national election campaign, reported in the next section, media coverage of attacks and support among parties displayed two party blocs, which happened to match the two future coalitions that were preferred by most of the strategic voters. Note, however, that none of these coalitions was viable according to the polls whereas a coalition of the two major antagonists was the most probable majority coalition during the election campaign.

Support and attack being part of a group process, a dynamic network model is needed for analysing negative campaigning. We propose and test a model that predicts the choice between support and attack from the pattern of preceding statements among all parties. This is quite a different type of model than the mainly static models used to explain negative campaigning in two-party or majoritarian systems. It requires repeated measurements of negativity during the campaign, which we collect at the level of single statements reported in the media. Again, this is quite different from the assessment of overall negativity for entire election campaigns, which is a key measurement in many negative campaigning studies. In summary, we propose to extend theories of negative campaigning with the concept of consonance, using dynamic network models, and measuring negativity (attacks) as well as its counterpart (support) at the level of statements in the context of multi-party systems governed by coalitions.

Prospective coalitions and consonance

In a system with a coalition government, citizens vote for a party but they know they will be ruled by a coalition of parties. As a result, strategic voting may occur, that is, a citizen may vote for a party that is not her preferred party to avoid a detested coalition (McKelvey and Ordeshook 1972; Blais and Nadeau 1996; Cox and Shugart 1996; Duch et al. 2010). In the post-election wave of a panel survey conducted in the 2006 election campaign in the Netherlands (cf. Kleinnijenhuis et al. 2007a), for example, the preference for a specific government coalition was mentioned as the most important motive to vote for a specific party by no less than 11 per cent of the voters ($n=1,149$ valid responses). Strategic voters are assumed to be informed about the viability of coalitions, that is, the probability of having a majority of the votes (Laver and Schofield 1990). During the election campaign, polling results inform voters on the probability of a majority for particular coalitions.

We doubt that most voters take into account the probability of a majority for their preferred coalition. This doubt is supported by further results from the 2006 post-election survey as previously mentioned. Roughly three quarters of the CDA voters who mentioned a desired coalition as their primary reason to vote, answered in response to a follow-up question that they wanted a rightist CDA-VVD (Liberals) coalition. Strategic PvdA voters answered that they wanted a coalition of the PvdA with smaller leftist parties. These coalitions never achieved a majority in the polls during the campaign but interestingly they showed up as blocs in the support and attacks among parties reported in the media. Only one quarter of the strategic voters preferred a CDA–PvdA coalition featuring the two main antagonists during the campaign, which was the only coalition close to a majority.

We expect that voters pay attention especially to the intention or willingness of parties to enter coalitions, which must be read from statements that parties make in the media (e.g. Meffert and Gschwend 2011). Parties may explicitly state their preferred coalition partners before or during an election campaign but parties expecting to have a choice between different coalitions are unlikely to disclose their preferences because that would limit their room for manoeuvring during post-election coalition negotiations. As a consequence, voters must usually infer coalition preferences indirectly from the statements that parties make about each other in the media. We expect voters to pay special attention to support and attack statements.

The theory of cognitive dissonance (Festinger [1957] 1962) states that people try to avoid cognitive dissonance, that is, conflicting cognitions. Seeing one party attacking another party, one would believe that the two disagree. If two parties either both attack a third party, or both support a third party, then one expects that these two parties support each other. Consonance refers to the confirmation of such expectations by new or additional facts, and dissonance to their violation. A party under attack is expected to retaliate instead of praising the attacker. In this sense, reciprocity or tit-for-tat is consonant and so is simply repeating previous attacks or support (steadfastness): sticking to your strategy. Expectations pressure parties into consonant behaviour, that is, pressure them to respond with actions that are in line with expectations. This is particularly the case with statements reported by the media in contrast to paid advertisements because consonance is an important news value, that is, a reason for journalists to publish a piece of news (Galtung and Ruge 1965).

For consonance in affective interactions such as attacks and expressions of support, we turn to a precursor of cognitive dissonance, namely Fritz Heider's concept of balance (Heider 1946). Friends tend to support their friends' friends while they attack their friends' enemies (Cartwright and Harary 1956). It is straightforward to apply the latter theory, known as structural balance, to support and attack statements among political parties during an election campaign. If parties care about the impression that their actions are consonant, that is, in line with previous actions, they will tend to choose to attack if it increases structural balance more than support, while they will choose support in the opposite situation.

Balance concerns consonance in support and attack among three or more parties. We restrict ourselves to constellations of three parties: Ego (the focal party making a new statement on another party), Alter (the party that Ego makes a statement on), and Tertius (any other party). Ignoring the direction of previous support and attack statements, four situations can be distinguished:

1. Tertius is a common friend of Ego and Alter, that is, there is support between Ego and Tertius, as well as between Tertius and Alter. In this situation, balance predicts that Ego supports Alter according to the maxim: My friend's friend is my friend.
2. Tertius is a common enemy of Ego and Alter, that is, there are attacks between Ego and Tertius as well as between Tertius and Alter. In this

situation, balance also predicts that Ego supports Alter according to the maxim: My enemy's enemy is my friend.

3. Tertius is an ally to Ego but an adversary to Alter. Balance predicts that Ego attacks Alter to line up with Tertius: My friend's enemy is my enemy.
4. Tertius is an ally to Alter but an adversary to Ego. Balance again predicts that Ego attacks Alter: My enemy's friend is my enemy.

The four configurations are illustrated in Figure 5.1. A grey arc represents a new statement with the predicted value while black lines indicate statements made previously in the media. In Panels 1 and 2, support is predicted, which is indicated by the plus sign between parentheses as well as the solid grey arc. In Panels 3 and 4, attack is predicted as shown by both the minus sign between parentheses and the dashed grey arc. The direction of previous statements between Ego and Tertius or Alter and Tertius is not relevant, therefore, these statements are represented by undirected lines.

If the balance principle is applied systematically by all, the overall network structure has been proven to be polarised, that is, consisting of two blocs of actors with all support within blocs and all attacks among different blocs (Cartwright and Harary 1956). In the context of an election campaign, a bloc expresses cooperation between parties that makes the electorate expect it to be a fruitful coalition. A party pursuing a particular coalition may promote polarisation by strategically responding to support and attack among other parties. If successful, the polarised pattern of support and attack pressures other parties to act in accordance with the pattern, reinforcing the bloc and the image of a prospective coalition even if they would prefer not to. In our case study, we will present an example of this process.

Dynamic network model

We conceptualise negative campaigning as a choice between attacking and supporting another party in the media. The choice is supposed to depend on the pattern of previous support and attacks among all parties, so we need a model that takes into account both the temporal order of attack and support statements in the media and the network structure of preceding statements: a dynamic network model.

In our current approach, we take for granted the fact that a party makes a statement about another party at a particular moment. In other words, we do not try to predict when a party makes such a statement or which other party the statement is directed at (Walter 2014a). We acknowledge that these questions are not trivial but we leave them to be explored in further research, focusing now on the choice between attack and support. This focus allows us to considerably simplify the statistical model for dynamic networks proposed by De Nooy (2011) to a logistic regression model explaining the choice between attack and support for each relevant statement published in the media during an election campaign. The choice is predicted, among other things, from the network pattern of preceding attacks and support statements; the precise operationalisation of these network effects is

Figure 5.1: Four configurations of balance

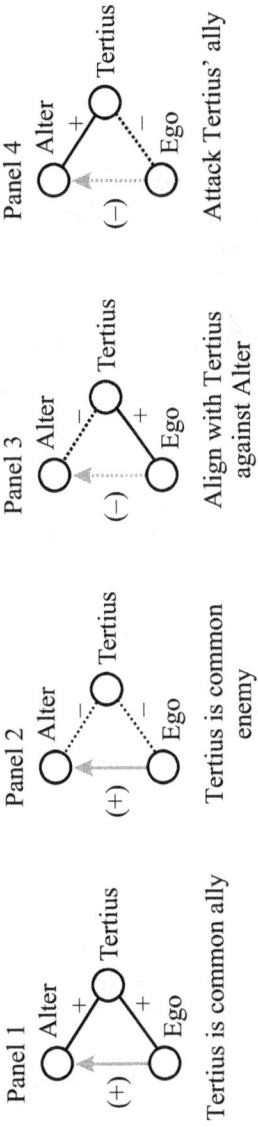

Panel 1

Alter   Tertius
+   +
(+)   Ego

Tertius is common ally

Panel 2

Alter   Tertius
−   −
(+)   Ego

Tertius is common enemy

Panel 3

Alter   Tertius
−   +
(−)   Ego

Align with Tertius against Alter

Panel 4

Alter   Tertius
+   −
(−)   Ego

Attack Tertius' ally

presented in the case study below. Suffice it to say now that the quality (attack versus support) of a statement is predicted at the time it appeared but that the same statement is part of the network pattern of preceding statements, hence a predictor, at later times. This is a characteristic of dynamic networks models: Interactions result from network structure but they also change network structure over time. This endogenous dynamic is in line with the concept of adaptive learning (Budge *et al.* 2010; Laver 2005) and with advocacy coalitions literature (Sabatier 1998; Weible *et al.* 2009).

Each party repeatedly appears both as the sender and as the target of a statement, so we must correct for dependencies among observations with a cross-nested multilevel model. In this model, we can incorporate characteristics of the sending party as well as the targeted party as additional predictors of attack or support, e.g. well-known predictors of going negative or being the object of negativity such as incumbency or being the frontrunner in the polls. Thus we can test whether the network effects hypothesised by consonance contribute to the explanation of attacks versus support over and above the effects of established predictors of negativity.

Measurement of negativity

The dynamic network model requires measurement of negativity for each moment during the campaign at which a party can respond to attack and support statements. In the case study reported below, newspapers and television news broadcasts appeared three times a day (morning, afternoon, evening), so we have to identify attacks and support statements for each part of each day. The basis for this is a content analysis of single statements reported in the media in accordance to the core sentence approach (Osgood *et al.* 1956; Helbling and Tresch 2011; van Cuilenburg *et al.* 1986; Kriesi *et al.* 2008). Note that this is in sharp contrast with the current practice of assessing the negativity of an entire campaign. To obtain such a detailed measurement, we used the iNET method for computer-assisted semantic network analysis (van Atteveldt 2008). The headlines and introductory paragraphs of newspaper stories and entire political items in television news bulletins were coded sentence-by-sentence by human coders. Each sentence was split into nuclear sentences linking one subject to one object with a predicate. The predicate indicates the valence of the sentence, which was coded on a scale ranging from '−1' (attack) to '+1' (support) with '0' indicating a neutral sentence. Attack refers to any negative sentence while any positive sentence is regarded as support.

An example of a supportive statement from our case, featuring the leader (Mark Rutte) of the large right-wing party (VVD) speaking about the leader (Balkenende) of the large centre-party (CDA) as well as the incumbent Prime Minister: 'Balkenende is a decent fellow. Reliable. Give him your wallet and you will receive an interest on it' (*Balkenende is een keurige vent. Betrouwbaar. Je geeft hem je portemonnee en je krijgt rente terug.*) *Trouw* newspaper, 11th November 2006.

This statement was coded as a positive statement by Rutte (VVD) on Balkenende (CDA). An example of an attack, which was coded as an attack by Verdonk (VVD) on Oosterhuis (SP, Socialist Party), which evidently reciprocated an earlier attack by Oosterhuis on Verdonk: 'Offended Verdonk does not want to debate with Oosterhuis (SP)' (*Beledigde Verdonk wil niet met Oosterhuis (SP) in debat*). *Trouw* newspaper, 14th November 2006.

Finally, all sentences with the same subject and object that appeared at the same time were combined with the average valence as the overall measure of support versus attack. The combined sentences best represent a party's statement about another party as it was portrayed in the media at that time.

Case study

In the remainder of this chapter, we apply the dynamic network model to a case study of the media coverage of the 2006 national election campaign in The Netherlands. In total, ten parties that gained seats in parliament after the 2006 elections were included in the analysis.

The data were gathered in a content analysis of the news coverage from 14th August to election day, which was 22nd November 2006 (Kleinnijenhuis *et al.* 2007a; Kleinnijenhuis *et al.* 2007b). The selected media included the five largest subscription-based national newspapers (*De Telegraaf, Algemeen Dagblad, de Volkskrant, NRC Handelsblad, nrc.next,* and *Trouw*), two free daily newspapers (*Spits* and *Metro*), and the prime time television news bulletins of the public channels (NOS) and a commercial channel (RTL4). The subscription-based national newspapers and television news programmes reach most Dutch citizens. The free daily newspapers are read mainly by commuters and youngsters who use public transport to go to schools and universities. Note that political advertising is rare in The Netherlands, so the news media constitute the major outlet for campaign messages.

Because the valence of support and attack statements concentrated heavily on the extremes, the values were dichotomised: positive is support (+1), negative is attack (0). Only thirty-one statements were exactly neutral; they were omitted from the analyses. Due to the inclusion of lagged values in the calculation of the consonance predictors (*see* next section), the statements issued in the first two weeks had to be excluded. A total of 705 statements remained for the analyses.

Operationalisation of consonance

Consonance was operationalised in several ways. The choice between attack and support of one party towards a specific other party can be explained with bilateral predictors, most notably with *steadfastness* and *reciprocity*, and with multilateral predictors, most notably with various indicators of *balance*. Bilateral predictors reproduce previously existing cleavages between pairs of parties, whereas multilateral predictors produce polarisation among all parties.

Steadfastness is simply the tendency to stick to your strategy and repeat previous attacks or support for another party. The steadfastness predictor was calculated as the preponderance of support statements over attack statements by the sending party on the targeted party in the preceding two weeks. A positive score indicates that a party more often supported than attacked the other party, while a negative score indicates the opposite. Steadfastness is expressed by a positive effect of this predictor: Previous support predicts new support, previous attacks predict a new attack.

Statements published longer ago are assumed to be less important, so a decay function was used with a half-life time of a week. While yesterday's support or attack counted for (almost) 100 per cent, a statement published a week ago counted only for 50 per cent, and a statement that was two weeks old counted for only 25 per cent. This approach is in line with the ideodynamic model proposed by David Fan (1996; Kleinnijenhuis and Fan 1999). It was also applied in the calculation of reciprocity and balance (*see* next section).

Reciprocity was calculated in the same way as steadfastness albeit that previous statements of the targeted party on the focal party (sender of the support/attack statement to be explained) were counted. A positive effect of this variable on the valence of the current statement indicates reciprocity: If the other party tended to support the focal party, the latter is more likely to support it in turn. The same principle applies to attacks.

Reciprocity turned out to be highly correlated with steadfastness ($R=0.86$), which is understandable because reciprocity creates conformity over time. If Party X attacks Party Y, Party Y reciprocates the attack, which is again reciprocated by Party X, then the last attack is indirectly a replication of the first attack, suggesting steadfastness while it originates from reciprocity. To correct for this spurious effect of steadfastness, a new steadfastness variable was created consisting of the residuals after regressing steadfastness on reciprocity (steadfastness_old = constant + b · reciprocity + steadfastness_new). The new steadfastness variable is by definition uncorrelated to reciprocity and its effect represents the minimum effect of steadfastness while the reciprocity effect shows the maximum effect that reciprocity may have had.

Balance was measured with indicators for each of the four configurations (*see* Figure 5.1). For each case, that is, for each sending-receiving pair of parties, the number of instances of each configuration was counted using the support and attack statements published in the media in the preceding two weeks. Again, a decay function with a half-life time of one week was used to weigh the counts. The common friend and common enemy counts should have a positive effect, that is, predict support rather than attack, if balance is at work, while the other two counts should have a negative effect, predicting attack rather than support.

Controls: Vote seeking

To test if consonance is really needed to explain negative campaigning, we included controls for other determinants of negativity that are common in the research literature. We categorise the controls by the three motives for party competition distinguished by Strøm (1990): vote seeking, policy seeking, and office seeking.

Vote seeking takes the polls as its point of departure. During the 2006 election campaign, three polling institutes regularly asked Dutch voters to name the party that they would vote for if elections would be on the current day: TNS Nipo, Maurice de Hond, and Synovate/Interview NSS. Polling results were collected from and compared across Internet sources.[2] Polls from different organisations that appeared on the same or consecutive days (usually Sundays and Mondays) were combined, using the average predicted number of seats that was linked to the date of the latest poll. Thus, seven measurements of poll standings were constructed, effective from 28th August, 26th September, 30th September, 30th October, 6th November, 13th November, and 21st November.

Winners/losers

Although the presumed beneficial effects of attacks for the attacker to the detriment of the attacked party (e.g. Harrington and Hess 1996) are not corroborated by all scientific evidence (Kleinnijenhuis *et al.* 2007b), many campaign leaders still seem to act upon the expectation that this effect will occur (Lau *et al.* 2007; Lau and Rovner 2009). The opponents most likely to be attacked are the 'candidates with status (be it a frontrunner position or the mantle of incumbency)' (Haynes and Rhine 1998: 709) so as to knock loose the floating voters that recently brought these opponents into winning positions. In a similar vein, winning in the polls may provoke attacks from other parties. It should be noted, however, that the parties with status or winning in the polls are also the parties that have most exposure in the media due to the news value of relevance (Galtung and Ruge 1965), so attacking them is also a strategy to obtain media attention (Hansen and Pedersen 2008; Geer 2009). Winning or losing in the polls was calculated as the difference in predicted seats between the last and the preceding poll.

Frontrunners

The literature on frontrunners suggests that attacks are launched especially by the runner-up in the polls (Damore 2002; Lau and Pomper 2001b; Skaperdas and Grofman 1995). Rising challengers may also provoke the frontrunner to attack (Skaperdas and Grofman 1995). The frontrunner and runner-up were identified as the parties with the largest and largest but one predicted number of seats in the latest combined poll. The Social-Democratic Party (PvdA) was the frontrunner and the Christian-Democratic Party (CDA) was the runner-up at the start of the campaign. The two parties changed roles near the end of October.

---

2. Online. Available http://www.nl.wikipedia.org/wiki/Tweede_Kamerverkiezingen_2006_-_peilingen/en.wikipedia.org/wiki/Dutch_general_election_2006, and http://www.marketingfacts.nl/berichten/20061123_maurice_de_hond_winnaar_tweede_kamerverkiezingen_2006 (accessed 19 June 2012).

Incumbents

Discrediting the opponent is also hypothesised to play a role in attacks by opposition parties on incumbent parties. To motivate a regime change, opposition parties must argue that the incumbent parties have done a bad job during their time in office (Trent and Friedenberg 2008; Lau and Pomper 2001b). Incumbent parties need to defend past policies, which implies that they are less likely to attack each other. In general, incumbents are hypothesised to be less involved in negative campaigning (Skaperdas and Grofman 1995), which was confirmed for news coverage in the Danish 2005 elections by Hansen and Pedersen (2008) and the presidential campaigns in Russia (Sigelman and Shiraev 2002), unless the race is highly competitive (Druckman *et al.* 2010). The CDA and the VVD were the two incumbent parties; the liberal party (D66), which left the executive coalition and caused its downfall, was not regarded as an incumbent in the analyses.

Controls: Policy seeking

(Static) left–right and Conservative–Progressive distances

If parties prefer coalitions in which they can optimally realise their policy goals, they should pursue a coalition with parties that are ideologically similar to themselves. As a consequence, they would be supportive of ideologically close parties and attack ideologically distant parties. Attacks are a valuable instrument for communicating policy differences or ideological differences with other parties in a multiparty system featuring more than a handful of parties (e.g. Ansolabehere and Iyengar 1995; Geer 2006). Similarly, support statements may be made in the media for signalling ideological similarities.

In Western democracies, the left–right dimension is the fundamental ideological ordering principle (e.g. Gallagher *et al.* 2005: 238–275). If attacks are meant to highlight ideological differences, they are expected between parties with distant positions on the left–right dimensions rather than parties that are close. In addition, parties vary also on a secondary ideological dimension in European democracies, *viz*, Conservative versus Progressive (GAL/TAN) (Marks *et al.* 2006). In the Netherlands this dimension dates back to the sixteenth century, but it still viable (Kleinnijenhuis and Pennings 2001). The ideological position of a party according to its pre-election programme was operationalised as a position on the left–right and Conservative–Progressive dimensions in the voting advice application Kieskompas, which was developed and operated at the Free University of Amsterdam (van Kersbergen and Krouwel 2008).[3] The scores of the parties on the left–right dimension in Kieskompas correlate highly with the scores in the Manifesto project (Volkens *et al.* 2012) for the eight parties classified in both sources (R=0.84). The Kieskompas scores were used because they also include the Conservative–Progressive dimension. These positions were used to calculate distances between each pair of parties.

---

3. Online. Available http://www.tweedekamer.kieskompas.nl/ (accessed 12 February 2013).

Dynamic left–right and Conservative–Progressive distances

Support and attacks, however, may also highlight agreement and disagreement on issues recently discussed in the media rather than fixed ideological positions. A dynamic measure of issue agreement was calculated from the reported statements by the selected parties and their representatives on all issues (5,279 statements on 377 different issues). The statements were collected in the same content analysis of election campaign coverage introduced above. Dynamic issue agreement between two parties was calculated as the number of issues that both parties supported or opposed minus the number of issues that one party supported while the other opposed it in the preceding two weeks. Prominent issues include taxes and government expenditures, social services, education, environment, and immigration and Islam. Again, a decay function was used with a half-life time of one week. Higher positive values of this predictor indicate stronger agreement on issues while more negative values indicate stronger disagreement. Because the issues debated in the preceding weeks and the stances expressed by political parties may change, the issue agreement score for a pair of parties is a dynamic (time-varying) predictor.

Controls: Office seeking

Finally, support and attack may be driven by office-seeking motives, that is, they may serve to maximise a party's opportunity to be included in the coalition negotiations and in the eventual executive coalition. To this end, parties should focus on majority coalitions and not let attacks spoil their relationship with the parties they need for a viable post-election majority coalition (Elmelund-Præstekær 2010). Laver and Schofield (1990) define a coalition as more viable if fewer parties participate and the ideological differences between participating parties are smaller. In this chapter, the focus is on ideological proximity on the main left–right ideological dimension.

Left–right diameter

Here we focus on ideological proximity on the left–right ideological dimension. For each pair of parties, the minimum number of parties and the ideological distance between the parties for a minimum winning coalition were determined. The predicted number of seats according to the latest polls was used to determine the number of seats of a coalition. Because the required minimum number of parties is usually three, only incidentally two and never more than four, the variation in number of parties is very limited and will be disregarded. The ideological diameter of a winning coalition was determined as the minimum of the largest difference in scores on the left–right dimension of all sets of up to four parties including the sender and receiver of the current support or attack statement. The higher this score, the larger the maximum ideological difference within a coalition with the other party, the lower the need to avoid attacking that party for office-seeking motives.

Large and close allies

In the case of Dutch election campaigns, three large parties – CDA, PvdA and VVD – traditionally play a pivotal role in executive coalitions. All parties, including the three large parties themselves, need at least one of the large parties for a majority coalition. As a consequence, parties may be expected to be friendly especially to the large party that is ideologically closest because this would be an unavoidable coalition partner. The predictor is a dummy indicating whether the receiving party is large (PvdA, CDA, or VVD) and closest to the sending party on at least one of the two ideological dimensions.

Results

The majority of statements (73 per cent) were attacks but a substantial number of statements expressed support (27 per cent). The balance variables were highly skewed, so they were transformed (logarithm) to obtain more normal distributions. Three models were tested (*see* Table 5.1). First, a variance components model was estimated including only random intercepts for the sending and receiving parties (Model 0); a baseline model to which the fit (DIC) of the other models can be compared. There is more variation among receiving parties (S^2=0.81) than among sending parties (S^2=0.15) regarding the odds of being supported rather than attacked. The differences among parties, however, are not significant, nor do they become significant in any of the other models, so we need not interpret the random intercepts in the models.

Model 1 includes the effects of vote seeking, policy seeking and office seeking explanations on the choice between supporting or attacking another party.

Vote seeking matters. Incumbency is the most important predictor in this dataset. Incumbents tend to attract relatively many attacks: The odds of receiving support over attack decrease by 84 per cent [b=−1.81, exp (−1.81)=0.16] for incumbents. Similarly, incumbents are more likely to attack; the odds of support decrease by 72 per cent, [b=−1.28, exp (−1.28)=0.28]. Controlling for these two tendencies, however, incumbents tend to be relatively supportive to each other because they are nearly five times as likely to support rather than attack each other [b=1.60, exp (1.60)=4.95]. In addition, winning in the polls increases the odds of receiving support over attack (b=0.11), indicating that parties tend to support rather than attack parties that are winning in the polls, most likely because parties realise that the best way to get the floating voters that recently came to vote for a winning party in the polls is to team up with that winning party – a bandwagon effect – or that they tend to attack rather than support parties that are losing in the polls, which may indicate wolf pack behaviour.

Policy and ideology seeking also matters. A larger distance on the left–right dimension decreases the odds of a supportive statement (b=−0.15), whereas more agreement on issues in the preceding two weeks increases the odds of exchanging support (b=0.02). Note that the last three predictors are not dichotomous, so the unstandardised parameters do not disclose relative effect size.

Table 5.1: Predicting support over attack, unstandardised results (MCMC estimation, 100,000 runs)

	Model 0		Model 1		Model 2	
Fixed part	**b**	**S.E.**	**b**	**S.E.**	**b**	**S.E.**
Constant/intercept	−0.59	0.335	0.09	0.416	−0.15	0.478
Vote seeking						
Winning/ losing (gm)			0.11**	0.041	0.14**	0.043
Sender is front-runner			−0.18	0.531	−0.09	0.523
Receiver is front-runner			0.03	0.343	−0.14	0.376
Sender is runner-up			0.42	0.564	0.33	0.551
Runner-up on front-runner			−0.61	0.637	0.02	0.683
Sender is front-runner * Winning/ losing (gm)			−0.05	0.064	−0.07	0.068
Receiver incumbent			−1.81***	0.423	−1.74***	0.491
Sender incumbent			−1.28*	0.552	−1.06	0.555
Sender and receiver incumbent			1.60**	0.555	1.21*	0.598
Policy seeking						
Left–right distance (gm)			−0.15*	0.062	−0.10	0.066
Conservative– Progressive distance (gm)			−0.08	0.062	−0.06	0.065
Dynamic issue agreement (gm)			0.02*	0.009	0.02	0.012
Office seeking						
Left–right diameter (gm)			0.20	0.109	0.08	0.123
Receiver is large and closest			−0.59	0.534	−0.85	0.569
Consonance						
Steadfastness					0.03	0.069

Table 5.1 (*continued*)

Fixed part	Model 0		Model 1		Model 2	
	b	S.E.	b	S.E.	b	S.E.
Reciprocity					0.18***	0.053
Tertius common friend					0.08	0.237
Tertius common enemy					0.35*	0.161
Align with Tertius against Alter					−0.19	0.190
Attack Tertius' ally					−0.15	0.201
Random part						
Level: Receiving party						
Intercept variance	0.81	0.620	0.08	0.158	0.12	0.255
Level: Sending party						
Intercept variance	0.15	0.273	0.23	0.421	0.22	0.460
Goodness of fit						
−2* loglikelihood						
DIC	783.44		726.69		721.35	
pD	12.53		19.59		25.83	
Units						
Receiving party	10		10		10	
Sending party	10		10		10	
Statements	705		705		705	

Note: (gm)=grand mean-centred. Wald χ^2 test: * $p<0.05$; ** $p<0.01$; *** $p<0.001$.
Bayesian MCMC estimation was used in MLwiN software (Browne 2004: 291).

Office seeking does not matter. Seemingly the parties did not care whether they supported enough other parties, and enough strong other parties, to enable a future majority coalition. The blocs of parties that supported each other according to the media simply did not qualify as majority coalitions.

Model 2 adds the consonance predictors. Controlling for them, the effects of the previously included predictors tend to decrease. As a result, policy seeking measured by ideological positions does not have a statistically significant effect on the choice between support and attack anymore. In addition, the effect of incumbency of the statement's sender is no longer significant. These effects are mainly replaced by a reciprocity effect: Support has higher odds of being reciprocated by support (b=0.18) and consequently attacks are likely to be followed by counterattacks. This effect is quite substantial because the predicted probability of a support statement rises from 22 per cent for a party at the average reciprocity score to 34 per cent for a party scoring one standard deviation above the average on the reciprocity predictor keeping all other predictors at their average or at their reference category. Parties partly act in accordance with a reciprocal tit-for-tat logic, as in the old days of segmentation and pillarisation.

The balance configurations have effects with the predicted signs – positive for Tertius as a common friend and Tertius as a common enemy, negative for aligning with Tertius against Alter and for attacking Tertius' ally – but Tertius as a common enemy is the only statistically significant effect. Again, the effect is substantial, raising the probability of support from 22 per cent for a party with average score to 33 per cent for a party scoring one standard deviation above the average. The presence of one or more common enemies seems to have triggered support among parties in this case study.

We visualised the marginal effects of the balance predictors to see their consequences in more detail (Figure 5.2). The marginal contribution of balance to the prediction of the odds of support over attack was calculated as the difference between the predicted logit of the full model (Model 2) and a model without the balance predictors. If the direction of the difference corresponds with the observed outcome, e.g. the marginal contribution is positive and a supportive statement was made, and the difference was substantial (at least half a standard deviation away from zero), the predictor was assumed to have contributed to a correct prediction. In the diagrams, solid arcs represent statements that correctly predicted support, dashed arcs represent predicted attacks, and arc width represents the square root of the number of statements that contributed to correct prediction of support or attack. The parties are located at their ideological positions and the two incumbent parties are represented by a square.

In the early stages of the campaign, balance mainly yielded support among the three large parties PvdA, CDA, and VVD (*see* Figure 5.2). Perhaps as a response to attacks from and on the smaller parties, the large parties tended to support each other. Note that there were quite some attacks between CDA and PvdA, especially in the second period (top right) during which the CDA campaigners attacked the PvdA on a daily basis, as a result of which the PvdA had to defend itself with counterattacks. This spiral of attacks and counterattacks was predicted by reciprocity, not balance and therefore they are not shown among the marginal effects of balance depicted in Figure 5.2. The marginal effects of balance suggest that the large parties ensured that their animosity did not align them into blocs with smaller parties even though the small left-wing parties – the SP and the GL – tried to lure the large left-wing party PvdA into a bloc by supporting it.

The relatively soft replies of the PvdA to the harsh attacks of the CDA and the small left-wing parties' display of affection for the PvdA did not go unnoticed. On 12th November the public television broadcaster NOS gave the floor to two senior

Figure 5.2: Marginal effects of balance over time

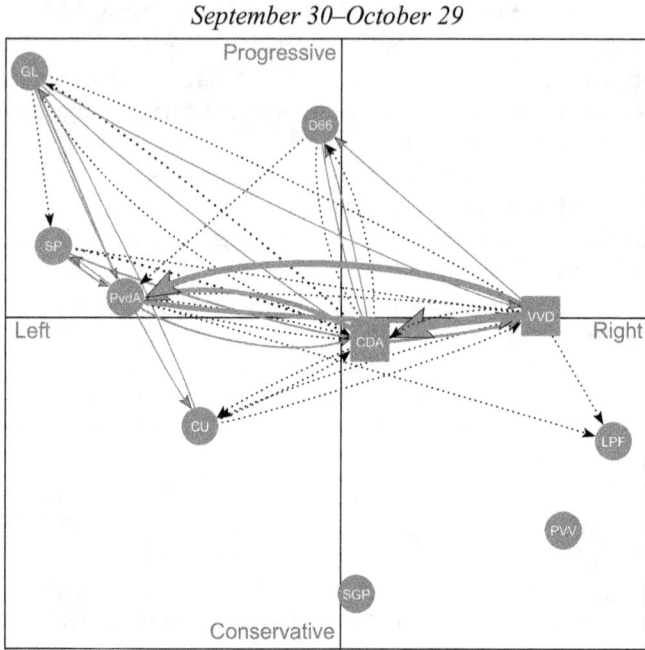

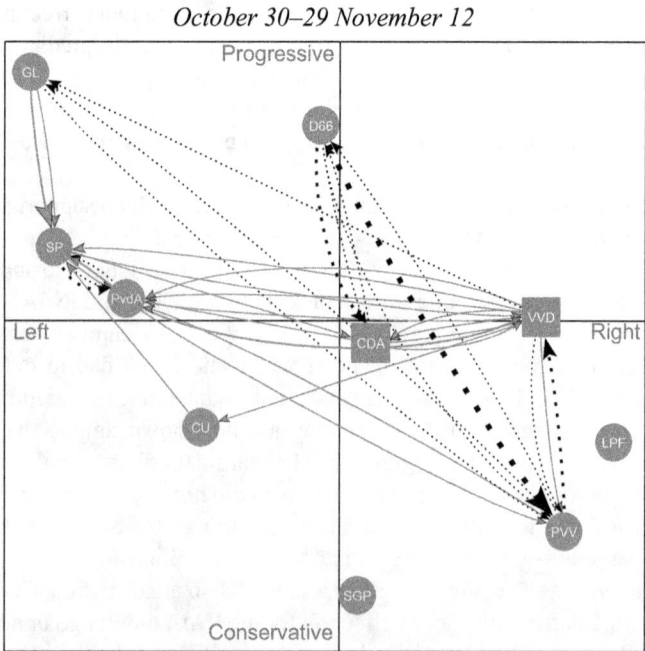

September 30–October 29

October 30–29 November 12

Key: solid arc=support, dashed arc=attack

November 13–20

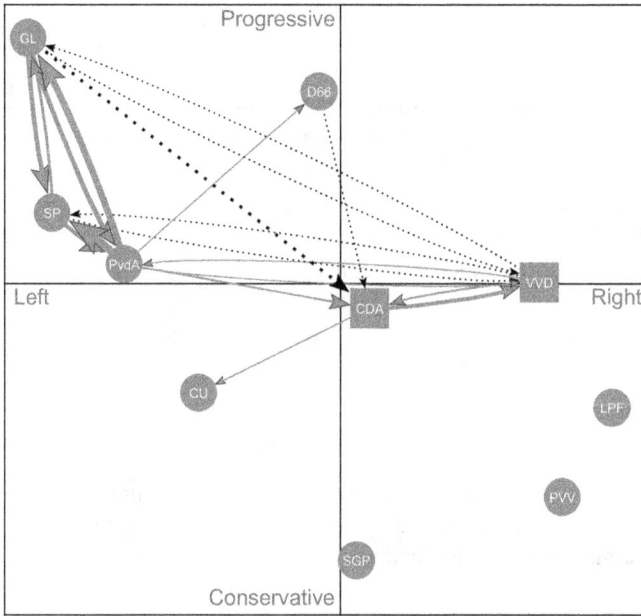

November 21–22

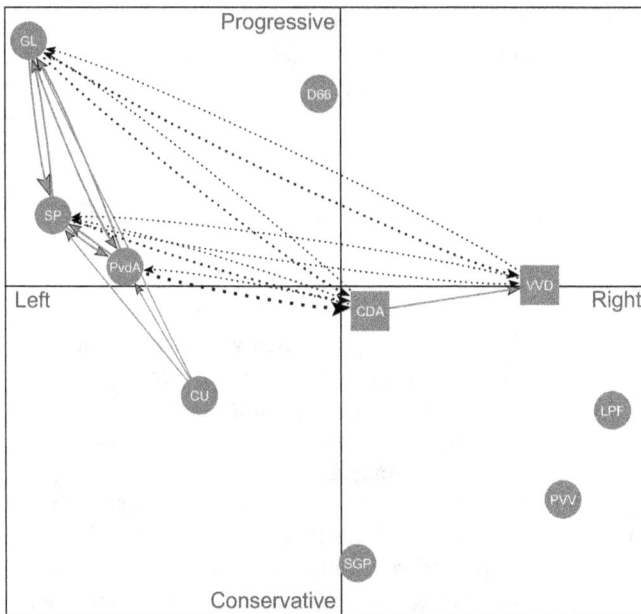

Key: solid arc=support, dashed arc=attack

PvdA senators who heavily criticised PvdA leader Bos for being soft against the CDA and for not showing an interest in the support from smaller left-wing parties. Although the polls predicted no majority at all for a left-wing coalition, and giving in would deter moderate voters to vote for the PvdA, the PvdA leader felt obliged to respond positively to the small left-wing parties. This resulted in a highly publicised media-event with the three left-wing party leaders expressing their agreement over a cup of tea (20 November). We conjecture that both the criticism ventured by the senators and the leader's action show the pressure to respond to attacks and support in a consonant way. After the meeting of the left-wing party leaders, balance established a clearly polarised situation with a left-wing faction and the two incumbent parties (CDA and VVD) (*see* Figure 5.2, [November 13–20]), which resulted in a completely balanced network in the last two days of the election campaign (*see* Figure 5.2, [November 21–22]).

Discussion

We set out to show that prospective coalitions are important to negative campaigning in systems governed by coalitions. In this type of system, assessing and suggesting parties' post-election coalition preferences is an important part of election campaigns, we argued, and both negative campaigning (attacks) and its counterpart (supporting other parties) are instrumental to these ends. Attacks and support statements express affective relations between parties, which have a tendency to form consonant patterns, displaying reciprocity and polarisation especially when they are broadcasted in the media.

We tested these ideas with a dynamic network model predicting the choice between support and attack among parties. Vote seeking motives related to incumbency and winning in the polls affected choice, as did policy-seeking motives linked to ideological distance. Office seeking motives did not explain why parties attacked each other. The future coalitions that were suggested by parties through their support for specific other parties were not majority coalitions according to the polls.

While controlling for the effects of vote seeking, policy seeking and office seeking, we showed that consonance predictors add to the explanation of support versus attack. The consonance hypothesis implies that campaigns will often result in polarisation between two blocs of parties, even when neither of these blocs will be capable of building a majority coalition with a limited number of parties after the elections. Additional survey data showed that three quarters of the voters whose main motive to vote for a specific party was to obtain a specific government coalition, actually wanted a government coalition of the blocs of parties that opposed each other during the campaign.

We may conclude that consonance adds to our understanding of negative campaigning in coalition-governed electoral systems although we should note that model fit (DIC) improved relatively little and that we have studied only one particular case. Cross-validation of the model on more cases is necessary to obtain more conclusive results but we claim that the present results indicate that consonance and supportive statements should not be ignored when researching negative campaigning in systems with coalition governments. Furthermore, the results suggest that it is worthwhile to analyse negativity as a campaign dynamic, that is, as a series of time-ordered decisions on the part of parties and candidates, instead of measuring negativity as a characteristic of an overall campaign.

Although we found that support and attack partly responded to previous support and attack among parties, and although public opinion data showed that voters took up the coalitions suggested by support and attack among parties in the media, we did not proof that this happened because parties meant to signal coalition preferences. Moreover, we have not investigated whether voters who interpret polarised factions as likely coalitions will become disappointed and cynical after the elections. We did not delve either in the presumably poor performance of government coalitions of parties that harshly attacked each other before the election campaign. This is an important venue for further research because it addresses consequences of support and attack strategies for democracy.

PART TWO

THE CAUSES OF NEGATIVE CAMPAIGNING

Chapter Six

Explaining the Use of Attack Behaviour in the Electoral Battlefield: A Literature Overview

Annemarie S. Walter and Alessandro Nai

Negative campaigning tactics, i.e. attacking the opponent on its issues or traits (Benoit 1999; Geer 2006) have received tremendous amounts of attention from scholars. However, scholarly research has focused largely on the question of what its effects are (*see* Lau *et al.* 2007). Notwithstanding the importance of this question, as some scholars (e.g. Ansolabehere and Iyengar 1995) suggest that negative campaigning might be harmful for democracy, i.e. negative campaigning would decrease turnout and increase levels of political cynicism towards politicians and the political system (*see* Chapter Fourteen), the equally interesting puzzle about why campaigns turn negative has received considerably less attention.

The scholars that do take on the challenge to explain the use of negative campaigning tend to study this phenomenon in the presidential, Senate and House races in the United States (US). As a result, the theory developed on the use of negative campaigning is somewhat limited in scope. However, in recent years (non-US) scholars have started to map and explain negative campaigning in other countries (*see* for instance Hansen and Pedersen 2008 and Elmelund-Præstekær 2010 on Denmark; Van Heerde-Hudson 2011 on the United Kingdom (UK); Ridout and Walter 2013 on New Zealand; Walter and Van der Brug 2013 on the Netherlands). Although still in its infancy the study of negative campaigning in non-US context has already provided us with some knowledge on the extent to which negative campaigning is present in other geographical settings and hints to whether the theory developed on the basis of the US case travels. Unfortunately, almost virtually no research has examined negative campaigning from a comparative perspective (a notable exception is Walter *et al.* 2014), thereby limiting our understanding whether systemic characteristics help to explain the presence of negative campaigning in political campaigns (Fridkin and Kenney 2012).

The work on negative campaigning can be divided in two camps, namely studies developing formal theoretical models focusing on the incentives of the political actor to attack (*see* e.g. Skaperdas and Grofman 1995) and studies that test prepositions on negative campaigning empirically with a range of statistical techniques (e.g. Lau and Pomper 2004). The empirical studies foremost make use of data collected using content analysis methods on paid publicity (advertisements, posters, leaflets, direct mail, party websites, press releases, twitter messages) and free publicity (newspaper articles, televised election debates). However, some work relies on expert interviews, survey or experimental data of campaign consultants when testing hypotheses on the use of negative campaigning (Swint 1998; Abbe *et al.* 2001; Theilmann and Wilhite 1998).

This chapter aims to give an overview of the literature explaining the use of negative campaigning. Which candidates/parties are likely to go negative and under which circumstances? This chapter proceeds as follows: we will first discuss the decision-making process preceding a (negative) campaign strategy and then the attacker's characteristics and the target's characteristics that make the use of negative campaigning more likely. We then reflect on the contextual (election and systemic) factors that are likely to affect the use of negative campaigning, including developments that are changing the overall context in which campaigns are waged nowadays. Finally, we talk about what still needs to be done and introduce the chapters included in this section of the book. By doing so this chapter not only aims to provide an overview of what has been done so far explaining negative campaigning, but also to pinpoint the 'grey areas' in existing literature and suggest avenues for future research.

Negativity as a strategic choice

First we will discuss negative campaigning – who does it and under what conditions? The literature examining these questions generally takes a rational choice perspective and argues that the decision to attack is a strategic one (Riker 1996; Lau and Pomper 2004). Political actors engage in a cost-benefit analysis before deciding whether to attack or not (Lau and Pomper 2004). It is posited that only once the expected benefits outweigh the costs, will negative campaigning be used in an electoral campaign. This decision to go negative is driven by the desire to attain a certain goal, namely to win the elections and negative campaigning can potentially increase a candidate's or party's vote share. Thus, a candidate or party resorts to negative campaigning in an attempt to become the voters' preferred choice by diminishing positive feelings for opposing candidates or parties (Lau *et al.* 2007; Budesheim *et al.* 1996). The opposite strategy of negative campaigning is positive campaigning, in which parties engage in acclamation or self-appraisal (Benoit 1999; Geer 2006). Positive campaigning is associated with strengthening a candidate's or party's base and mobilising adherents to cast their vote. Negative campaigning is considered to be a dangerous choice, as one runs the risk that the attacks will generate negative feelings toward the attacker instead of the target (Garramone 1984; Johnson-Cartee and Copeland 1991; Roese and Sande 1993). This risk is the so-called 'backlash' or 'boomerang' effect. Whether or not candidates or parties decide to attack depends on the expected balance between the losses their opponent will suffer from the attack and the risk they face from being perceived negatively.

Recent studies in non-US contexts where the party is the main actor in the political arena (Walter *et al.* 2014; Ridout and Walter 2013; Hansen and Pedersen 2008; Elmelund-Præstekær 2008, 2010) claim that the party system complicates this decision calculus. Parties in a multiparty system face a different cost-benefit analysis than parties in a two party system. The US literature argues that all candidates are vote seeking, a perspective that is insufficient when examining negative campaigning in a multiparty competition. Strøm and Müller (1999) assume parties to be rational actors whose behaviour is guided by three overarching political objectives: office, policy and votes. Within a two-party system, especially one with majority electoral districts, parties can concentrate on vote-seeking goals, as a majority of votes enables them to achieve office and to implement policy as a result. In contrast, parties operating within a multi-party system have to carefully balance their vote-, office- and policy-seeking objectives. In these systems, obtaining the most parliamentary seats does not automatically translate into government office or influence over policy. As a result, the costs of negative campaigning are higher in a multi-party system than in a two-party system, as parties not only need to worry about possible backlash effects, but also about potential post-election bargaining costs (Walter and Van der Brug 2013; Brants *et al.* 1982; Hansen and Pedersen 2008; Elmelund-Præstekær 2010). A campaign, which is fought too aggressively and too negatively, may damage parties' ability to govern together (for example *see* Sjöblom 1968; Brants *et al.* 1982; Kaid and Holtz-Bacha 2006). In addition, the rewards of negative campaigning in a multiparty system are less certain than in a two party system; as the number of parties increases it is less likely that the attacker will benefit from an attack (Elmelund-Præstekær 2008; 2010; Hansen and Pedersen 2008; Ridout and Walter 2013). Most models on vote choice rely at least implicitly on the concept of electoral utility and they assume that voters vote for the party from which they expect the highest utility (Van der Eijk *et al.* 2006). Voters have a choice set of preferred parties from which they choose at every election (Tillie 1995). As a result of negative campaigning, a voter's expected utility for voting for the attacked party may decline, but that may not result in an increase in the expected utility for the party doing the attacking (Tillie 1995). After the utility for the first preferred party is lowered, these voters are likely to vote for another party in their choice set. Especially in multiparty systems voters prefer or identify with more than one party, as it is likely that there are a number of fairly ideologically similar parties competing (Schmitt 2002; Tillie 1995; Van der Eijk and Niemöller 1983). Thus, parties in a multi-party system face a different cost-benefit structure and as a result have a more difficult task calculating the likelihood of success when going negative, than parties operating in a two-party system.

The decision calculus surrounding the choice whether to go negative in a political campaign is affected by various kinds of factors, respectively the political actors' traits, its opponents' traits and the characteristics of the context in which he operates (both race/election characteristics as well as systemic characteristics). Due to the dominance of single country studies examining negativity in the US context, where candidates are more important than parties, the literature has extensively examined candidate and race characteristics that affect negative campaigning, but not so much the influence of party and systemic characteristics. The more recent work on negative campaigning studying the phenomenon in other geographical contexts than the US has just scratched the surface. Characteristics of the attacker, characteristics of the target and contextual characteristics are insufficient to explain the 'rise' in negative campaigning, we therefore discuss more general developments that are argued to have altered the overall context in which (negative) campaigns are waged nowadays. In the rest of this chapter we will try to systematically discuss the type of factors that affect the candidate's or party's likelihood to go negative.

Characteristics of the attacker

The prime actor in American politics is the candidate, consequently the literature predominantly focuses on candidate' traits when attempting to explain the use of negative campaigning. Some of these characteristics can also be applied to settings where parties rather than candidates are the prime actors. First of all, there is a set of identity features that is argued to affect the likelihood of candidates using negative campaigning. The most prominent one is the gender of the candidate. A growing body of work focuses on topics relating to the differential use of negative campaigning by female and male candidates (e.g. Benze and Declercq 1985; Kahn and Kenney 2004; Lau and Pomper 2004) and the disparity in impact of negative campaigning for female and male candidates (and how this impact in turn affects male and female voters differently) (Brooks 2010; Chang and Hitchon 2004; Gordon et al. 2003; Fridkin et al. 2009; King and McConnell 2003). This body of work suggests that male and female candidates both campaign differently and experience different pay-offs. Female candidates who employ negative campaigning may find themselves acting at odds with public expectation of their behaviour, as societal stereotypes depict women as kind, helpful, sympathetic and passive in contrast to men who are depicted as independent, forceful and aggressive (Huddy and Terkildsen 1993; Fridkin and Kenney 2009; Kahn 1996). Negative campaigning might be seen as a campaign tactic more suitable for male candidates than female candidates, as negative campaigning is considered rather aggressive. Violating gender stereotypes can have negative electoral consequences, candidates might suffer a substantial backlash as voters tend to reject behaviour that conflicts with gender expectations (Trent and Friedenberg 2008; Kahn 1996). The work on gender and negative campaigning is inconclusive. Some studies support the idea that female candidates are hesitant to go negative due to societal gender stereotypes (Herrnson and Lucas 2006; Johnston and White 1994; Kahn and Kenney 2004), while other studies find no difference (Lau and Pomper 2001b; 2004) or even find that female candidates are more likely to go negative (Bystrom 2006; Evans et al. 2014). Walter (2013) found preliminary evidence that female party leaders were not more likely to go negative than male party leaders in Germany, the UK and the Netherlands, with exception of Conservative Party leader Margaret Thatcher. Thatcher was more prone than her male counterparts to engage in attack behaviour during parliamentary election campaigns. Maier (*see* Chapter Eight) examines attack behaviour in televised election debates aired in state and national election campaigns in Germany; he finds no evidence for different behaviour between male and female candidates, which is in line with the findings of Walter (2013). One could also argue that not the characteristics of the candidate himself matter, but those of his personnel that design and manage his election campaign. That is why Swint (1998) examines gender differences between male and female political consultants in their attitudes towards negative tactics and actual use. Overall, he finds only small differences in their perception of what constitutes negative campaigning. However, his survey data does suggest that female political consultants are in general less likely to go negative; in particular they are less likely than their male counterparts to attack an opponent on personal grounds.

Another candidate trait that is argued to affect the likelihood that the candidate runs a negative campaign is the candidate's race. Krebs and Holian (2007) suggest on the basis of the 2001 Los Angeles mayoral election that minority candidates are less likely to make use of attack behaviour than non-minority candidates. Candidates whose ethnic or racial status places them in a minority of the electorate must reach beyond their base of support to be able to win the elections, they often do so by waging a deracialised campaign, i.e. a campaign that de-emphasises racial issues and focuses on issues that transcend race. The core of a deracialised campaign is the aim to project a non-threatening image, which might be realised by avoiding confrontation and thus the use of negative campaigning (Krebs and Holian 2007).

Several US studies find that the party affiliation of the candidate matters (e.g. Theilmann and Whilhite 1998; Lau and Pomper 2001b; Druckman *et al.* 2010; Sigelman and Buell 2003). The work on this link between the candidate's party affiliation and tendency to attack is inconclusive and under-theorised. Some scholars (Theilmann and Wilhite 1998; Lau and Pomper 2001b; Grossmann 2009) argue that Republican candidates are more likely to attack than Democratic candidates, which they link to the findings that consultants who work for Republicans tend to be more open to attack strategies (Theilmann and Wilhite 1998; Francia and Herrnson 2007) and Democratic voters are less likely to approve of negative campaigning than Republican voters (e.g. Ansolabehere and Iyengar 1995). The notion that Republican consultants are more likely to go negative is not supported by all (Swint 1998). Others argue that Democratic candidates are more likely to attack (Druckman *et al.* 2009 and Sigelman and Buell 2003; Kaid 2004; Benoit 2007; Evans *et al.* 2014). No similar results are found in the European context (*see* for instance Elmelund-Præstekær 2010), with exception of Scammell and Langer (2006) who find that in the UK the Conservative Party is more likely to make use of negative campaigning than the Labour Party and the Liberal Democrats.

Second, a candidate's position in the campaign affects willingness to attack respectively challenger status and competitive standing. The main finding from several US studies (e.g. Lau and Pomper 2004; Druckman *et al.* 2009; Benoit 2007) is that the challenger status of a candidate matters as challengers are disadvantaged in the race compared to candidates that have an incumbency status. The latter can promote themselves, their work and their accomplishments on the basis of their official positions and duties. Incumbents are also more likely to receive media attention and as a result benefit from name recognition and established reputation (Swint 1998; Kaid and Holtz-Bacha 2006). As challengers do not often have a policy record which can serve as a strong basis for positive campaigning, they are in a position that they have to provide voters with reasons why they should vote for them (Benoit 1999; Kahn and Kenney 2004; Haynes and Rhine 1998; Harrington and Hess 1996; Theilmann and Wilhite 1998; Hale *et al.* 1996). However, they are also in a position that they do not have an office to loose and are therefore more prone to take a risk and wage a negative campaign. This finding also travels to other contexts such as parliamentary systems where parties are the prime actor and opposition parties are challenging the parties in government. Here it is also the case that opposition parties are disadvantaged and more willing to take a risk and go negative (both in two party systems as well as multiparty systems; e.g. Hansen and Pedersen 2008; Elmelund-Præstekær 2010; Walter and Van der Brug 2013; Schweitzer 2010). Walter *et al.* (2014) did not find such an effect in the UK, on the basis of attack behaviour in party election broadcasts between 1980 and 2006, but that is in accordance with the finding of Scammell and Langer (2006) that the Conservative Party as an incumbent party favours negative campaigning.

Another important factor is the competitive standing of the candidate, which most often is operationalised as his standing in the polls (Hale *et al.* 1996; Skaperdas and Grofman 1995; Kahn and Kenney 2004; Harrington and Hess 1996; Benoit 1999; Swint 1998; Nai and Sciarini 2015). The rationale is that candidates that are trailing behind in the polls or are losing are more willing to bear the risks of a backlash effect than candidates that are frontrunners or gaining in the polls (Damore 2002; Sigelman and Buell 2003; Hale *et al.* 1996; Skaperdas and Grofman 1995). Although the competitive standing of a political actor is likely to matter mixed results were found beyond the US case. In the UK parties that are losing in the polls tend to make more use of negative campaigning than parties that are gaining in the polls (Walter *et al.* 2014). The more recent work on multiparty systems has different findings. Elmelund-Præstekær (2008) shows that parties trailing behind are more likely to go negative, while Hansen and Pedersen (2008) and Elmelund-Præstekær (2010) only find partial support for Denmark. Walter *et al.* (2014) did not find such an effect for the Dutch and German multiparty systems. The inconclusive findings might be the result of the fact that operationalising a trailing or losing party is much more complicated in a multiparty system than in a two party system. For the concept of losing different points of reference can be chosen, namely, the position in the previous polls, the previous election results, or the position of a competing party (Kleinnijenhuis and Takens 2011).

Another indicator of competitive standing is the candidate's campaign budget size. Some studies (e.g. Lau and Pomper 2001b; Johnson-Cartee and Copeland 1991) argue that candidates with relatively fewer campaign sources than their opponents will be more likely to engage in negative campaigning (Lau and Pomper 2001b). These candidates need to win more votes with a smaller budget than their opponent and since negative campaigning is considered to be an efficient campaign tactic to win voters, they would be more willing to bare the risks and likely to attack. However, other studies (Damore 2002; Druckman *et al.* 2010; Swint 1998) find that candidates with a relatively large budget size in comparison to their opponents are more likely to engage in negative campaigning, as foremost they can afford to go negative, they have the resources to buy the advertisements and hire political consultants to do opponent research and develop advertisements.

Finally, a factor that affects the likelihood of going negative in a multiparty system is the party's coalition potential (e.g. Elmelund-Præstekær 2008; 2010; Walter and Van der Brug 2013; Walter *et al.* 2014; Hansen and Pedersen 2008). Parties in multiparty systems waging a negative campaign not only run the risks of backlash effect, but also the risk of alienating potential coalition partners. Consequently parties with low coalition potential have less too lose from negative campaigning, as their chances of being part of the government are slim to none from the beginning. Coalition potential is operationalised differently across various studies, such as the size of the party, years of government experience and the distance to the median party (*see* Walter and Van der Brug 2013; Elmelund-Præstekær 2010). In Germany and the Netherlands Walter *et al.* (2014) find that parties with less government experience are more likely to go negative. They do not find such an effect for government experience in the British two-party system where until recently coalition governments were absent. In addition, they find in Germany and the Netherlands that the further away parties are positioned from the median party, the more likely they are to make use of negative campaigning. In Britain they find the opposite, namely that the more close parties are positioned to the median party, the more likely they are to make use of negative campaigning. The study of Elmelund-Præstekær (2010) yielded similar results for the Danish case, parties that are positioned in the centre were less likely to go negative.

Characteristics of the target

The decision of whether to make use of negative campaigning is not only affected by characteristics of the attacker, but also by characteristics of the opponent, the potential target of the attack. Most studies modelling the decision to attack pay only limited attention to opponent's characteristics. However, characteristics of the opponent are modelled extensively in a separate strand of studies, which examines the question of whom to attack when going negative in a multi-candidate/party setting. Only a handful of studies have dealt with the decision-making processes of choosing a target when going negative (*see* Doron and On 1983; Elmelund-Præstekær 2008; Haynes and Rhine 1998; Ridout and Holland 2010; Sigelman and Shiraev 2002; Skaperdas and Grofman 1995; Walter 2014a; De Nooy and Kleinnijenhuis 2013; Sigelman and Buell 2008; *see* also Chapters Five and Ten in this book). This is the result of the dominance of studies examining negative campaigning in the US context. The decision of whom to attack only comes into play with intraparty competition in presidential nomination campaigns and in three candidate races in the US

(Walter 2014a). In the US independent and third party candidates have rarely any significant influence on the campaign (a notable exception being Ross Perot in the 1992 presidential race), as a result independent and third party candidates are in the game of negative campaigning often ignored by the major party candidates and thus seldom attacked (Benoit 1999). It follows that the choice of target in a two-party system is relatively clear-cut. Recent work (Walter 2014a; Elmelund-Præstekær 2008; *see* also Chapters Five and Ten in this book) has started to examine this question in the setting of multiparty systems, where the choice of whom to attack is much more complex. The choice of target is just as important as the decision to attack when attempting to understand the use of negative campaigning and one could argue that these decisions are intertwined and should be modelled separately. Thus, whether a candidate or party decides to attack is dependent on the characteristics of the opponent he faces.

First of all, the opponent's identity matters. Several studies have shown that male candidates are less likely to go negative if they face a female opponent than a male opponent. These male candidates refrain from attack behaviour as they fear an electoral backlash for 'beating up' a woman (Kahn and Kenney 2004; Benze and Declercq 1985). Societal norms generally hold that aggressive behaviour by men towards women is unacceptable. Thus, female candidates are less targeted than male candidates. Since the number of women running for office is still limited, we have no knowledge about situations in which female candidates have a female opponent.

Second, the position of the other candidate in the race matters, such as incumbency status (Sigelman and Shiraev 2002), competitive position (e.g. Gurian 1996; Haynes and Rhine 1998; Skaperdas and Grofman 1995) and ideological position (Gurian 1996; Doron and On 1983; *see* also Chapter Ten). Sigelman and Shiraev argue on the basis of the 1996 and 2002 Russian presidential campaign that challengers will primarily aim their attacks at the incumbent. This is in line with the arguments that challengers have to provide reasons to voters why they should be in office instead of the incumbent (Kahn and Kenney 2004; Hale *et al.* 1996). In addition, the incumbent is the winner of previous election and therefore also potentially the candidate most votes can be won from. Walter (2014a) and De Nooy and Kleinnijenhuis (*see* Chapter Five) also find that government parties are more frequently targeted than opposition parties in the Dutch multiparty system, as do Dolezal, Ennser-Jedenastik and Müller (*see* Chapter Ten) for the Austrian multiparty system.

Third, no candidate is expected to engage in negative campaigning against the weakest of his opponents – it is more advantageous to defeat a successful rival (Gurian 1996: 8). Negative campaigning will therefore almost always be directed against the so-called front-runner in the campaign, i.e. the largest candidate in the polls, and if the front-runner engages in negative campaigning it is against its strongest opponent (Skaperdas and Grofman 1995). This finding also seems to travel to the context of multiparty systems (Walter 2014a; Bol and Bohl, Chapter Seven; Dolezal *et al.*, Chapter Ten).

Furthermore, several scholars argue that not just the relative success of rivals matters, but also their ideological proximity (Haynes and Rhine 1998; Gurian 1996). Based on the Downsian notion of relative competition, candidates will try to eliminate the candidates close to their position, as they are competing for the same group of voters. Ridout and Holland argue the opposite, namely that candidates will refrain from attacking an opponent with the same ideological base in presidential nomination campaigns as they do not want to alienate potential voters that are needed in a later stage of the campaign, they find that Conservative candidates attack Liberal candidates instead of Moderate candidates. A party's position in the polls and its ideological proximity are not two mutually exclusive factors (Gurian 1996). Doron and On (1983) find in four Israeli parliamentary elections partial support for the notion that parties in a multiparty system will attack the largest party close to their position as that is where the most votes can be won. They also point out that parties in a multiparty system often compete in a multidimensional space, so the largest proximate party can be attacked on multiple dimensions. However, Walter (2014a) finds that the effect for ideological proximity is larger for small parties than large parties in the Dutch multiparty system.

In addition, in a multiparty system where parties not only take vote-seeking but also office-seeking considerations into account when deciding whether to attack, parties tend to refrain from attacking potential coalition partners (Elmelund-Præstekær 2008; Holtz-Bacha and Kaid 2006). Elmelund-Præstekær (2008) finds exemplary evidence for this in the 2008 Danish election campaign. Walter (2014a) finds mixed results for the Dutch case in the period 1980 to 2006 and suggests that a party's coalition potential is of minor importance in comparison to the other characteristics of the attacked party, or the relationship between the attacker and the attacked party. Dolezal *et al.* (*see* Chapter Ten) find for Austria that parties that share executive office, i.e. coalition partners are less likely to attack one another than other parties, with exception of parties that are part of a grand coalition. More work needs to be done in multiparty settings to test the relationship between attack behaviour and targeting potential coalition partners.

Finally, the behaviour of the opponent affects the likelihood of using negative campaigning as election campaigns are dynamic. When the opponent engages in negative campaigning, candidates themselves employ more negative campaigning (Lau and Pomper 2001b, 2004; Damore 2002; Krebs and Holian 2007; Haynes and Rhine 1998; Geer 2006). A similar effect is found in the Dutch multiparty system (*see* De Nooy and Kleinnijenhuis, Chapter Five). Political consultants also prepare for a negative campaign on both sides when they are involved in a campaign against a candidate with a history of negative attack behaviour (Swint 1998). This is likely to be the result of the conventional wisdom among campaign consultants that a candidate must respond to an attack with a counter attack (Haynes and Rhine 1998). This tit-for-tat effect, however, does not seem to apply across party lines in primaries; the negativity of one party's primary is not a good predictor of negativity in the other party's primary (Peterson and Djupe 2005).

Context characteristics

Candidates and parties do not compete in a vacuum, the electoral context affects the calculus candidates and political parties make with respect to negative campaigning (Damore 2002). Context characteristics are features such as the type of election, the competitiveness and openness of the race, the moment in the election campaign and political system characteristics. These context characteristics are often tightly intertwined with one another. As these context characteristics and their relation with negative campaigning have received less attention than the identity of the attacker and the target, we will only reflect on several context characteristics. Nevertheless, we are certain that there are more contextual features that affect the decision calculus of negative campaigning than mentioned in this section.

First of all, the type of race tends to affect candidates and parties likelihood to go negative. To illustrate, primary campaigns provide a fundamentally different element to the calculation that candidates make. Instead of weighing the benefits and risks in a single election, candidates need to forecast the impact this type of campaigning will have on their general election chances as well. The candidates want to win the primary, but they cannot alienate the supporters of their in-party opponent whose votes they need in order to win in the general election (Peterson and Djupe 2005). As a result, candidates might be more likely to make use of negative tactics towards the end of the election campaign as the number of candidates narrows (Haynes and Rhine 1998). Another example that the type of race matters, in open seat races the use of negative campaigning tends to be higher than in challenger and incumbency races (Kahn and Kenney 1999b, Lau and Pomper 2001b; Damore 2002; Druckman 2010). Often candidates for open seats behave as challengers because they lack the advantages afforded an incumbent (Kahn and Kenney 1999b).

Second, many scholars argue that candidates and parties are more willing to use negative campaigning while jeopardising a potential backlash effect when the race is competitive (e.g. Lau and Pomper 2004; Swint 1998; Damore 2002; Hale et al. 1996; Kahn and Kenney 1999b; Theilmann and Wilhite 1998; Elmelund-Præstekær 2008; Freedman and Goldstein 2002; Franz et al. 2008; Nai and Sciarini 2015). However, some scholars (Lau and Pomper 2001b; Lau and Pomper 2004; Herrnson and Lucas 2006) do not find a significant relationship between competitiveness and negativity or even the opposite. Francia and Herrnson (2007) find on the basis of a survey of candidates who ran in a variety of races from 1996 to 1998 in the US that candidates in non-competitive races were most likely to endorse negative campaign tactics. According to Mair (1997) two factors are needed for electoral competition, namely the availability of an electoral market and rewards associated with electoral gains. Walter et al. (2014) did not find significant results in Germany, the UK and the Netherlands when testing the first prerequisite of whether the likelihood of going negative increases when the size of the electoral market grows, operationalised as the number of voters that are undecided between two or more parties. However, extensive evidence exists for the second prerequisite, when the rewards increase so does the use of negative campaigning. Haynes and

Rhine (1998) show that negative campaigning increases prior to delegate rich contests (such as New Hampshire, Super Tuesday, New York) and important events (Haynes and Rhine 1998). In particular, the electoral rewards are high in close races when both candidates have a chance of winning. US-based research shows that in these close races, the overall negativity from both candidates increases as they are more willing to use negative campaigning while jeopardising a potential backlash effect (e.g. Buell and Sigelman 2008; Damore 2002; Druckman *et al.* 2009; Kahn and Kenney 2004; Lau and Pomper 2004; Theilmann and Wilhite 1998; Hale *et al.* 1998; Garamone 1984; Wicks and Soley 2003). The competitiveness of the race is not only measured by the position of the candidates in the polls, but also by the total amount of money spent (Grossmann 2009; Peterson and Djupe 2005), as the higher spending campaigns are expected to be the most hotly contested (Peterson and Djupe 2005). Peterson and Djupe (2005) also measure the competitiveness of the race by looking at the number of quality candidates in the race. A quality candidate is a candidate that previously held office.

Walter *et al.* (2014) did not find evidence that a close race in a multiparty system, operationalised as a race where the gap between the two largest parties in the polls is small, heightens the overall use of negative campaigning. In Chapter Seven of this book, Bol and Bohl yield similar findings for the Swiss case; they suggest the reason why studies in Europe fail to reproduce this finding from mainly US studies is the absence of pre-electoral alliances.

Third, the probability of a candidate going negative varies over the course of the campaign (Ridout and Holland 2010; Damore 2002; Haynes and Rhine 1998; Freedman and Goldstein 2002; Nai and Sciarini 2015). Candidates are more willing to take the risk of going negative as the election nears (Damore 2002; Haynes and Rhine 1998). The general idea is that at the beginning of the race candidates mainly make use of positive campaigning as a means to build a base of supporters and then make use of negative campaigning to contrast themselves from other candidates (Peterson and Djupe 2005; Elmelund-Præstekær 2011). Dolezal *et al.* (*see* Chapter Ten) and Bol and Bohl (*see* Chapter Seven) fail to find that negative campaigning heightens at the end of the campaign.

Fourth, political system characteristics affect the likelihood that candidates or parties go negative. Four general characteristics of the political system affect the nature of election campaigns: the institutional structure, the electoral system, the party system and the media system (Bowler and Farrell 1992; Farrell 2005). The few studies paying attention to the influence of political system characteristics on negative campaigning has primarily focused on the party system (Walter 2014b; Ridout and Walter 2013; Walter *et al.* 2014; Elmelund-Præstekær and Svensson 2014; Elmelund-Præstekær 2010). As explained in the paragraph on negative campaigning as a strategic choice the party system affects the decision calculus, the cost benefit structure of negative tactics is different in two party and multiparty systems. The decision regarding the use of negative campaigning is considerably complicated in a multiparty system in comparison to a two-party system, as the objectives that parties strive for do not coincide in a multiparty system. Where in a two-party system parties that win the votes at the election, will also get the office and thus the opportunity to implement policy, in a multiparty system this is not necessarily the case. In a multiparty system parties can become part of the coalition government that lost at the elections and parties that gained can be excluded. As a result the costs of negative campaigning are higher in a multiparty system as it might jeopardise a party's chance of being part of the coalition government and the rewards are lower as a third party might win the voters that are put off by attacking your opponent. Walter (2014b) indeed finds that the level of negative campaigning is significantly higher in the UK than in Germany and the Netherlands. Ridout and Walter (2013) test the proposition in New Zealand. New Zealand exchanged single member first past the post for a mixed member proportional electoral system. As a result of the change in electoral system, the country witnessed party system change (Mair 2006), the almost ideal two party system became a multiparty system. The overall use of negative campaigning in advertising was higher in New Zealand when it had a two party system than a multiparty system. However, some scholars (Salmond 2011; Bohl and Bol, Chapter Seven) argue that it is not the party system, but the electoral system that matters; it is the difference between winner takes all single member district systems and proportional representation. PR generally coincides with a multiparty system, however there are exceptions to Duverger's law. Ridout and Walter (2013) try to make a convincing argument as to why it is the party system and not the electoral system that impacts the use of negative campaigning, nevertheless more work needs to be done to filter out what system characteristics affect negative campaigning and in what way.

Recent developments and the rise in negative campaigning

The decision calculus of candidates and parties of whether to make use of negative campaigning is affected by the context they operate in. In the previous paragraph we discussed context characteristics that cause the use of negative campaigning to fluctuate between different kinds of races/elections over the course of the campaign, over campaigns across time and geographical contexts. However, some scholars (e.g. Benoit 1999; Geer 2006; Abbe *et al.* 2001; Fowler and Ridout 2010) do not see the use of negative campaigning as a tactic which fluctuates from election to election; they argue that negative campaigning is on the rise. This rise in negative campaigning is considered a response to developments that are permanently changing the context in which negative campaigning takes place nowadays. Studies show that four general developments are linked to negative campaigning, respectively the professionalisation of election campaigns, the increasing electoral volatility, increasing polarisation of the party system and the mediatisation of politics (*see* Geer 2012; Walter 2014b). These developments are not independent of one another. In the next paragraph we will discuss these developments, their link with negative campaigning and assess the claim that negative campaigning is on the rise.

First of all, the use of negative campaigning is linked to the increasing professionalisation of election campaigns (e.g. Geer 2012; Walter 2014b). Scholars often use the term 'professionalisation' interchangeably with 'modernisation' and 'Americanisation' and they tend to use these terms to refer to a range of campaign practices (*see* e.g. Swanson and Mancini 1996; Strömbäck 2007; Plasser 2000). These terms all essentially describe a process whereby many tasks that were formerly ascribed to party members are instead given over to outside agencies (Lilleker and Negrine 2002). This development whereby campaigns are increasingly run by professionals (sometimes even US agencies) is likely to stimulate the use of negative campaigning. Despite the fact that substantive evidence is lacking, campaign consultants increasingly believe that negative campaigning works and regard it as a key to electoral success (Iyengar 2011). A candidate who wants to win the election cannot refrain from attacking their opponent (Perloff and Kinsey 1992; Lau and Pomper 2004; Lau and Sigelman 2000). As a result consultants would encourage candidates to go negative. Abbe *et al.* (2001) put this relationship between campaign professionalism and negative campaigning to the test. They find that a fully professional campaign that employs political professionals to perform all major campaign activities (such as campaign management, media advertising, PR, polling, issue and opposition research, legal advice and fund raising) is 19 per cent more likely to go negative in US House races. Francia and Herrnson (2007) demonstrate that candidates who wage 'professional' campaigns (those who employ at least one paid consultant) are more receptive to using negative campaign tactics and profess a greater willingness to attack an opponent on issues concerning an opponent's professional conduct or legal infractions. Over time tests and examinations of this relationship in non-US contexts are still absent.

The second development that is linked to the rise of negative campaigning is the increased electoral volatility that political parties similar to US candidates are witnessing, although the level of electoral volatility varies across countries (Walter 2014b). As voters have loosened their ties with parties, leaving more votes potentially 'up for grabs', parties have become more inclined to run an offensive campaign (Andeweg and Irwin 2009; Mair *et al.* 2004). Negative campaigning as a campaign practice fits better with an offensive campaign than a defensive campaign. The first is aimed at volatile voters and the opponent's adherents and the latter at mobilising a party's own adherents. This link between electoral volatility and the use of negative campaigning is indirectly assessed in the study of Walter *et al.* (2014) who assess the relationship between the size of the electoral market operationalised as the number of undecided voters and the use of negative campaigning in Germany, the UK and the Netherlands. They do not find evidence for this relationship, however, this study tests this relationship only since 1980 and the instability of the electoral market originated already decades earlier.

Third, the 'so-called' rise in negative campaigning is associated with an increasingly polarised party system (Geer 2006, 2012; Elmelund-Præstekær and Svensson 2014). They argue that when the ideological span in the party system widens, more differences between political parties arise, consequently political conflict increases and thus the use of negative campaigning. According to Geer (2006) candidates in the US tend to disagree more on policy than they did thirty years ago. He finds a strong correlation between polarisation and negative campaigning (r=0.88 in Geer 2006), but polarisation affects primarily issue negativity and not so much trait negativity. Ansolabehere and Iyengar (1995: 113) argue the opposite to Geer (2006) and Elmelund-Præstekær and Svensson (2014), they reason that negative campaigning fuels polarisation in American politics. Attack behaviour would drive the independent voter from the polls and thus generate a more partisan and hence more polarised electorate. The whole notion that polarisation and negative campaigning are strongly linked is contested by Buell and Sigelman (2008). They claim that party polarisation might not be that important as widely thought. They found that even though voting choices in 2000 reflected the highest degree of polarisation up to that point in American recorded history, the overall negativity of the 2000 contest ranked lower than that of any other race in our study except the one in 1976.

Finally, the use of negative campaigning is linked to what some call mediatisation (e.g. Geer 2012; Walter 2014b). Nowadays, parties increasingly have to compete with one another and with other actors in the public domain for the attention of the mass media. To increase the odds of being considered newsworthy it is likely that parties adapt their communication to the mass media's standards. Conflict is one of those criteria used for news selection and the practice of negative campaigning can be regarded as a way for parties to create conflict (Walter and Vliegenthart 2010; see also Chapter Sixteen). Thus the growing role of the mass media may be stimulating the use of negative campaigning. This process by which political institutions are increasingly dependent on and shaped by mass media is called mediatisation (Mazzoleni and Schulz 1999). The empirical evidence is somewhat mixed as a study of the 1992 Democratic nomination found that races that get more media attention are more likely to have a high level of negative campaigning (Haynes and Rhine 1998), whereas primary campaigns from 1998 with more media attention were no more likely to be negative (Peterson and Djupe 2005). Ridout and Smith (2008) find that negative advertisements are more likely to be covered than positive advertisements. Geer (2012) reports that 75 per cent of the stories on the nightly networks are about negative advertisements, and that this percentage has increased over time. Moreover, political consultants do point out that an attack can provide the attacking candidate the needed media attention (Swint 1998). The link between mediatisation and negative campaigning is scarcely explored.

Therefore, when trying to explain the use of negative campaigning it is important to assess the claim that negative campaigning is on the rise (e.g. Benoit 1999; Geer 2006, 2012; Abbe et al. 2001). As last decade's electoral volatility, campaign professionalism and mediatisation have increased, altering the context in which candidates and parties wage campaigns, consequently, one can expect a rise in negative campaigning. If no such rise in negative campaigning exists, these developments cannot be the (sole) explanatory factor(s) for the use of negative campaigning. So, is there empirical evidence for this claim of an ongoing increase in negative campaigning? We searched for empirical studies examining the so-called 'rise' in negativity. We selected all studies based on data from more than two election campaigns, as three points in time is generally the minimal requirement to be able speak of a trend. We do not claim that this selection is exhaustive; it is likely that there are more studies, in particular studies written in a language unknown to the authors of this chapter. Table 6.1 provides an overview of the found studies examining the rise in negativity. In total we found twenty-two studies examining the use of negative campaigning, of which nine studies focused on the US. All studies measured negative campaigning on the basis of content analysis of campaign sources, the majority focusing on television advertisements. The studies differ in the coding method used, selection of data and weighting procedure, which makes them not directly comparable. Overall, the studies draw mixed conclusions, thereby providing not much support for the claim that the use of negative campaigning is growing. However, six out of the eight studies examining the US report an upward trend supporting the claim that negative campaigning is increasing over time. The studies examining negative campaigning in other countries barely provide evidence for this claim. The only exceptions are Sullivan (2008) who argues that negativity might be on the rise in Taiwanese presidential elections and Scammell and Langer (2006) who argue there is no rise in negativity in the UK in general, but the Conservative Party increasingly makes use of this tactic. Holtz-Bacha (2001) and Schweitzer (2011) even provide empirical evidence for a downward trend in negativity in Germany. In addition, Samaras and Papathanassopoulos (2006) argue there is a decrease instead of increase in the use of negativity in Greek political advertising. Thus, for now the state of the art seems to suggest that the use of negative campaigning is not increasing, but that its level fluctuates from election to election, with exception of the US. As a result, negative campaigning is likely not (solely) the result of these general developments.

Conclusion and avenues for further research

This chapter set out to give an overview of the literature explaining the use of negative campaigning. Although several literature overviews on the effects of negative campaigning exist (e.g. Lau *et al.* 2007; Fridkin and Kenney 2012), not much attention has been given to the decision to go negative. To our best abilities we have reflected on the most important features mentioned in studies, trying to explain which candidates and parties are likely to make use of negative campaigning and the circumstances under which they do so. Not an easy task as this part of the field is transforming as we speak. However, the decision to go negative seems to be foremost a strategic choice, one that is affected by characteristics of the attacker, characteristics of the target and contextual characteristics. All these characteristics are part of the complex decision calculus of candidates/parties when they decide whether the benefits outweigh the risks of negative campaigning. If this is the case they will decide to run a negative campaign. In addition, when summing up the studies that assessed the claim of a rise in negative campaign tactics, we lacked convincing evidence. Some evidence supporting this claim has been found, although only for the US. A finding that might relieve critics of

Table 6.1: Overview studies examining level of negative campaigning across elections

Study	Country	Election	Source	Trend
1. Benoit 1999	United States	1952–96	Television advertisements	Upward
2. Buell and Sigelman 2008	United States	1960–2008	Newspaper articles	None
3. Druckman *et al.* 2010	United States	2002–06	Campaign websites	Upward
4. Fowler and Ridout 2010	United States	2000–12	Television advertisements	Upward
5. Geer 2006	United States	1960–2004	Television advertisements	Upward
6. Håkansson 1999	Sweden	1948–98	Party manifestos, election debates	None
7. Haigron 2012	United Kingdom	2001–10	Television advertisements	None
8. Holtz-Bacha 2001	Germany	1957–98	Television advertisements	Downward
9. Jamieson *et al.* 2000	United States	1952–96	Television advertisements	Upward
10. Kaid and Johnston 2001	United States	1952–96	Television advertisements	Upward
11. Lau and Pomper 2004	United States	1992–2002	Newspaper articles	None
12. Elmelund-Præstekær and Svensson 2014	Denmark	1971–2011	Letters, television advertisements, election debates	None
13. Ridout and Walter 2013	New Zealand	1969–2011	Television advertisements	None
14. Samaras and Papathanassopoulos 2006	Greece	1993–2000	Television advertisements	Downward
15. Scammell and Langer 2006	United Kingdom	1992–2001	Television advertisements	None*
16. Schweitzer 2011	Germany	2002–09	Online news releases, party websites	Downward
17. Sullivan 2008	Taiwan	1996–2004	Television and newspaper advertisements	Upward
18. Toros 2013	Turkey	1983–2011	Newspaper articles	None

Table 6.1 (*continued*)

Study	Country	Election	Source	Trend
19. Van Heerde-Hudson 2011	United Kingdom	1964–2005	Television advertisements	None
20. Walter 2014b	Germany Netherlands United Kingdom	1980–2006	Television advertisements, election debates	None
21. Walter and Van der Brug 2013	Netherlands	1981–2010	Television advertisements	None
22. West 2005	United States	1952–2004	Television advertisements	Upward

Note: All studies examining the US are presidential elections, with exception of Fowler and Ridout (2010) who study advertisements from Congress and Senate elections, Lau and Pomper (2004) who study advertisements from Senate elections and Druckman *et al.* 2010.
* With exception of the Conservative Party, their advertisements showed no increase in negativity.

negative campaigning that are concerned about its effects on the electorate and the political system (*see* Chapter Fourteen).

The overview illustrates the width of the field, the range of features that seem to impact the likelihood of running a negative campaign. However, it also shows its inconclusiveness on many aspects. There is need for research that not only looks for new theories, undefined explanatory variables, but that foremost assesses the current findings. The mixed findings in the field are most likely to be (partially) the result of different methodological choices made, one of them being the source of data collection. This issue also becomes more apparent with the more recent work in non-US settings and a handful comparative studies that is often not based on television advertisements, as these do not play a prominent role in the campaigns of these countries or they are subject to all kinds of government restrictions. Elmelund-Præstekær (2010) and Walter and Vliegenthart (2010) point at the importance of measuring negative campaigning over various campaign sources as the level, content and targets of negative campaigning significantly varies across them. Therefore, patterns of attack behaviour that are found should be validated on a variety of campaign sources.

Non-US studies on the use of negative campaigning will bring us closer to a general theory on negative campaigning, one that for instance also covers campaigns in multiparty settings, PR electoral systems or less established democracies. Several chapters in this section already work on this. Chapter Seven looks at negative campaigning in federal and cantonal election campaigns in the Swiss PR system, Chapter Eight examines negative campaigning in national and state level elections in the German multiparty system, Chapter Ten examines negative campaigning in parliamentary election campaigns the Austrian multiparty system, Chapter Eleven studies attack behaviour in two round presidential campaigns in the Brazilian multiparty system and finally, Chapter Twelve explores negative campaigning in national and local election campaigns in the Turkish multiparty democracy. Chapter Nine reflects on a different matter, namely negative campaigning in direct-democratic campaigns, a type of campaign that can happen in most countries, but is particularly an incremental part of Swiss politics.

Many findings in the field are based on studies that examine single or few election campaigns, comparative work can help to advance present theory. A larger number of elections across time and space would ascertain that the results are not idiosyncratic to the time and place of examination, for example during the recent US presidential election campaigns. In addition, this would allow us to understand better which contextual characteristics affect the use of negative campaigning. We would be able to assess the relationship between electoral volatility, party system polarisation, mediatisation and campaign professionalism with a dataset covering election campaigns for a considerable number of years. In addition, with a large dataset covering numerous countries we would be able to tease out the exact role of systemic variables, such as institutional rules, the media system, political system and electoral system. Research on the influence of systemic variables on the use of negative campaigning can also shine more light on why the US might be a peculiar case when it comes to attack behaviour and why negative campaigning is possibly solely on the rise in the US.

Finally, the work on the strategic use of negative campaigning would benefit from a more interdisciplinary approach. Most work on negative campaigning stems from the field of political science and communication science. Nevertheless, research on negative campaigning can benefit from theories and methods developed in economics, psychology, sociology and linguistics. Chapter Thirteen exemplifies the fruits of a more interdisciplinary approach. This study tests whether people that score high on certain personality are more likely to make use of attack behaviour. An approach that might help us move beyond the more clear visible candidate characteristics, such as gender, race and party affiliation, and their relationship with negative campaigning.

However, foremost it is clear that still much needs to be done if we want to solve the puzzle on the use of negative campaigning and come to a general theory on negativity. This section hopes to contribute to this endeavour.

Chapter Seven

Negative Campaigning in Proportional Representation (Yet Non-Coalition) Systems: Evidence from Switzerland

Damien Bol and Marian Bohl

During the last twenty years, many scholars have studied the causes of negative campaigning in American politics (for a full review, *see* Walter and Nai, Chapter Six in this volume). Unlike traditional party competition theorists, such as Downs (1957) or Strøm (1990), who assume that campaigns are bare channels for candidates and parties to communicate to voters about their own policy position, they argue that the reality of electoral campaign is also full of incentives pushing these candidates and parties to discredit their opponents (Geer 2006).

Along these lines, negative campaigning scholars working on American politics state that one of the key factors explaining the decision to go negative is the state of electoral competition. For example, various theoretical as well as empirical studies show that the closer the electoral race between candidates, the more these candidates attack each other (Lau and Pomper 2001b; Skaperdas and Grofman 1995). However, this argument originally developed to fit the United States' (US) context, is said to be of little relevance to explain negative campaigning in European proportional representation (PR) democracies. Recent evidence reveals that classic theories only poorly fit the reality of electoral campaigns in this context (Elmelund-Præstekær 2008, 2010; Walter *et al.* 2014).

In this chapter, however, we argue that the impact of the electoral competition on the decision of parties and candidates to go negative in PR democracies should not be discarded too quickly. The existence of some form of pre-electoral coalition agreements, and the necessity to effectively bargain with other parties to reach coalition agreements after election day, which are the norms in these countries, is likely to bring noise to the empirical tests of theoretical models. To bring new insight on the topic, we offer a test of the classic American-based theories of negative campaigning in four electoral campaigns in Switzerland: The 2011 Zurich federal and cantonal campaigns, and the 2011 Lucerne federal and cantonal campaigns.[1] Unlike other PR democracies, the Swiss federation and cantons are not entirely parliamentary governmental systems. The influence

---

1. Given the de-centralised nature of Swiss electoral and party competition, we regard the federal campaigns in these two cantons as separate campaigns (*see* next section).

of coalition bargaining on the composition of the executive is therefore limited. In the next sections, we first review the literature on the electoral determinants of negative campaigning; second, we describe the nature of electoral competition in Switzerland and more specifically in the four elections covered; third, we explain carefully our data collection; and last, we report our findings and the implications following from them.

The electoral determinants of negative campaigning

In the US, a growing body of evidence has formed that electoral competition influences the tone of campaigns. In the mid-1990s, Skaperdas and Grofman (1995), followed by Harrington and Hess (1996), elaborated a theoretical model of negative advertising in which electoral competition plays a crucial role. Both their modelling efforts start from the assumption that candidates, or parties, have a finite amount of resources available for their electoral campaign. They may decide to spend it for either negative or positive advertisements (often a certain mixture of the two). But these two strategies do not have the same impact on voters: While positive campaigning is supposed to turn a share of undecided voters into one's own camp, negative campaigning is assumed to turn a share of the opponents' voters into the undecided pool. Also, they postulate that adopting a negative tone is a costly strategy, as a certain amount of candidates' or parties' own voters does not appreciate it and may therefore (with a certain probability) decide to join the undecided group.

From these straightforward and quite realistic assumptions, the theorists derive a series of propositions. First and foremost, they argue that the candidate or party that is lagging behind should spend more resources to discredit the frontrunner, especially when the two are very close to each other. What is at the heart of this proposition is the perspective of winning the election. When a candidate or a party is certain to win, she must not engage into negative campaigning and on what appears as a risky strategy. In contrast, those that are close to winning, just as those that are close to losing, are expected to discredit their opponents to diminish opponents' support, and ultimately to steal just enough voters with the share of resource they continue to devote to positive campaigning. A central hypothesis about the impact of the closeness of the electoral race on the tone of the campaign has been derived from this theoretical foundation: The closer the electoral race between candidates or parties, the more they attack each other.

Another implication of this model is that additional 'spoiler' candidates or parties, i.e. those that are only supported by a marginal share of voters, should not engage in negative advertising. Assuming they have a long-term perspective, they should at this stage of their political life aim at securing the small amount of convinced supporters they already have instead of adopting a costly strategy, which might result in alienating considerable parts of their constituency.

These propositions are supported by empirical evidence coming from US Senate elections (Hale *et al.* 1996; Lau and Pomper 2001b), US presidential primaries (Haynes and Rhine 1998), Russian presidential elections (Sigelman and

Shiraev 2002), and even laboratory experiments (Theilmann and Wilhite 1998). Lau *et al.* (2007) also conducted a meta-analysis cross validating all these findings. However, without exception, these pieces all concentrate on elections held under single-member districts, and plurality or majority rules. In PR countries in contrast, little evidence supports the hypothesis according to which negative campaigning is driven by electoral competition. For example, the effect of electoral competition is low to nil in Denmark (Elmelund-Præstekær 2008, 2010), Germany and the Netherlands (Walter *et al.* 2014).

In this chapter, we argue that the absence of results in the aforementioned studies might be partly due to the necessity to bargain with other parties to form coalition agreements in PR democracies (as already noted by Elmelund-Præstekær 2011), which naturally inhibit negative behaviour within such a coalition. In these European PR countries with a tradition of coalition or minority governments, the designation of the government personnel depends as much on the electoral results than on agreements contracted between parties (at least if no party obtains a majority of the parliamentary seats, which rarely occurs under PR). Parties are therefore reluctant to attack their potential future coalition partners. These alliances between parties, that are sometimes secret, change the nature of party competition and, in consequence, a campaign's dynamics (Golder 2006). To address this problem of PR's influence blurred by coalition bargaining, we focus on four electoral campaigns in Switzerland. Although the legislative elections in the country rely on a very permissive version of PR, parties do not have strong incentives to sign pre- and post-election coalition agreements, given the very specific nature of the Swiss institutional setting, especially its presidential elements (*see* next section). The country is thus an interesting case study to investigate the effect of electoral competition on negative campaigning outside the single-member districts context.

Electoral competition in Switzerland

The nature of electoral competition in Switzerland is rather unique. Most parliamentary chambers (with the exception of the second chamber of the federal parliament, which works as a US Senate-like representation of the cantons) are elected through a multi-member district free-list PR system. However, there are so many institutional particularities that the dynamics at stake in the country do not really resemble those at stake in any other PR democracy. Yet, in this chapter, we take advantage of these particularities to test whether classic theories accounting for negative campaigning fit outside the single-member districts setting.

First, Switzerland is a federal country composed of twenty-six cantons, which have strong institutional autonomy and policy prerogatives. Although the names of the parties are similar at the federal and cantonal levels, most cantonal parties also enjoy large autonomy (Kriesi and Trechsel 2008). Besides, since the cantons are very different in terms of demographics and ideological preferences, the relative strength of each party is very different from canton to canton. Also, it is worth mentioning that the role of political parties is limited in some of these cantons where the legislative process is still dominated by a popular assembly of citizens. We take advantage of this variance within one country in our study.

Second, the Swiss institutional regime does not fit the classic distinction between parliamentary and (semi-) presidential systems (Cheibub 2007). On the federal level, the joint two chambers of the federal parliament elect each of the seven members of the federal government individually (for a fixed four-year term) at the beginning of the legislature. As to reflect the consensual nature of Swiss politics, the government is traditionally composed of all four main parties (all together, they represent between 80 per cent to 85 per cent of the popular votes). The largest parties are granted two government members while the others are granted only one. Changes to this informal rule have been extremely rare since the 1950s. However, while the partisan composition of the federal government remained perfectly stable from 1959 to 2003, two small changes have been operated these last ten years (since 2007/08, a sixth party joined the federal government as a result of a government member's defection). Also, unlike parliamentary regimes, the federal government is completely independent from the parliament. In particular, the deputies cannot force any member of the federal government to resign. Therefore, the office motivation of the parties is even more weakly linked to electoral performance than in single-member district elections.

In the vast majority of cantons, the population directly elects the cantonal government (composed of five to seven members) for a fixed four-year term using a two-round majority system. Although the election of the cantonal parliament and government (at least the first round) is held the very same day, they are institutionally separated from each other. In particular, the government is not politically accountable to the parliament. This also makes the cantons mixed political regimes, lying in between traditional ideal types of presidentialism and parliamentarism. Unlike most presidential systems however, the government is not forcefully dominated by a single party.

The unconventional Swiss institutional setting creates limited incentives to the cantonal and federal parties to bargain over coalition agreements. At the cantonal level, legislative election agreements between parties would not have any effect on the composition of the government since it is the population that directly elects this government.[2] At the federal level, the consensual tradition as well as the bargaining uncertainty is so strong so that parties have not been able to form any other alliance than the one consisting of all main parties. As a consequence, the Swiss federal and cantonal political systems are almost impermeable to the dynamics of coalition bargaining. The noise they bring into electoral explanations of negative campaigning is therefore limited, even more so in the cantonal systems with directly elected government officials than on the federal level, where (since

---

2.   Parties, support committees, and advocacy groups might endorse a government candidate. However, this endorsement is institutionally separated from the legislative election. In some instances, parties also agree on list apparentments to minimise wasted votes in the seat allocation process, but this is merely a mathematical move without consequences for policy or government composition.

the aforementioned defection of the SVP-member disrupting the old order in 2007) a growing amount of bargaining has to take place before the investiture vote of the members of government.

In this chapter, we concentrate on four campaigns: the 2011 Zurich cantonal and federal campaigns, and the 2011 Lucerne cantonal and federal campaigns. All in all, three elections and two cantons are thus covered. This concentration allows us to conduct a comparative analysis, while enabling us to control for regional idiosyncrasies, as well as periodic competition patterns. For example, at the beginning of the spring 2011 cantonal campaigns, relatively non-controversial economic issues related to the economic crisis in Europe and the world dominated the media, panel discussions and advertisements. However, the Fukushima incident gave rise to heated debates about nuclear phase-out strategies. The federal election campaign of fall 2011 reverted to the economic issues again, after the Fukushima topic had been defused over the summer by a quickly adopted nuclear phase-out strategy of the federal government backed by a great majority of the parties.

In 2011, fourteen party branches effectively competed in Zurich and Lucerne in both federal and cantonal elections, two sections per party. They were the four main parties: the Social Democratic Party (SP, socialist), the Christian Democratic People's Party (CVP, centre-right Christian-Democrat), the Swiss People's Party (SVP, far-right populist), and the Liberal Party (FPD, centre-right liberal). The rather long-established Green Party (GP, left-green) also presented party-lists, together with the much more recent Green Liberal Party (GLP, centre-right green) and Conservative Democratic Party (BDP, centre-right conservative). Other parties also formally competed, such as the Evangelical People's Party (EVP, centre-right Christian radical) or the Alternative List (AL, far-left). However, they are excluded from the present analysis as they only made hardly visible campaign efforts. At the federal level, the government is composed of the SP (two members), the FDP (two members), the SVP (one member), the CVP (one member), and the BDP (one member). The BDP joined the government *de facto* in 2008 after one of the two SVP's members defected and created this new party. Among non-micro parties, only the two green parties (GP and GLP) are thus excluded from the government.

The relative strength of these fourteen party branches is very different in the two cantons we cover. Table 7.1 reveals the parliamentary seat shares[3] obtained by all of them at the 2011 federal lower house and cantonal parliamentary election (and differences with the 2007 elections). In Zurich, a highly urbanised and modern canton, the competition is polarised between the SP (left-wing) and the leading SVP (right-wing), with the more centrist FDP as a moderator (these three parties also have two government members at the cantonal level each). In 2011, the parliamentary seat shares of the two first parties were over 30 per cent (SVP) and

---

3.   We are using seat shares, because they are the ultimate goal on the office- and vote-dimension in a non-parliamentary system. Polls are not considered here, because they are very stable over time and predict the vote-shares (almost) perfectly, but do not easily translate into exact seat share expectations the parties can work with.

Table 7.1: Results of the 2011 cantonal and federal elections in Zurich and Lucerne

Party	Zurich		Lucerne	
	Federal	**Cantonal**	**Federal**	**Cantonal**
SVP	0.32 (-0.03)	0.30 (-0.01)	0.20 (-0.10)	0.23 (+0.03)
SP	0.21 (+/-0)	0.19 (-0.01)	0.10 (+/-0)	0.13 (+0.02)
BDP	0.06 (+0.06)	0.03 (+0.03)	0.00 (+/-0)	0.00 (+/-0)
GP	0.09 (-0.03)	0.11 (+/-0)	0.10 (+/-0)	0.08 (+/-0)
FDP	0.12 (+/-0)	0.13 (-0.03)	0.20 (+/-0)	0.19 (-0.05)
GLP	0.12 (+0.03)	0.11 (+0.05)	0.10 (+0.10)	0.05 (+0.05)
CVP	0.06 (-0.03)	0.05 (-0.02)	0.30 (+/-0)	0.33 (-0.06)

Note: Entries are parliamentary seat shares. Changes to 2007 are in parentheses. The figures related to the federal election correspond to the Zurich and Lucerne districts respectively.

around 20 per cent (SP), while the FDP reached about 12 per cent. The other parties appeared as 'spoilers' even though the two green parties (the GP and the GLP) were also rather successful in 2011 with mostly over 10 per cent of parliamentary seat shares (the GP also has a government member at the cantonal level).

The situation is rather different in Lucerne, which is a more rural canton. The party competition reflects the traditional Swiss religious cleavage between Catholics and Liberals. As a result, the competition revolves around a dominant CVP challenged by the FDP, and to some extent by the SP. In 2011, their parliamentary seat shares in the canton were respectively around 30 per cent, 20 per cent and 12 per cent (these three parties also control the government at the cantonal level). Recently, the SVP made a breakthrough in Lucerne cantonal politics, while the traditionally dominant parties CVP and FDP had to accept considerable losses. In 2011, the party obtained around 25 per cent of the seats, making it the first challenger of the CVP. None of the other parties, including the green parties (the GP and the GLP) and the newly formed BDP are able to compete with them. In the light of the Swiss institutional givens, we will analyse the impact of party competition on the tone of the four campaigns in question with the following data and instrumentarium.

Measuring negative campaigning in Switzerland

Negative campaigning is defined as the material used during an electoral campaign to discredit one's opponents and which stresses the deficient nature of their manifesto, accomplishments, qualifications, associates, etc. The opposite is considered positive campaigning, a style that emphasises how good one's own manifesto, accomplishments, qualifications, programmes, *et cetera* are. In this sense, we rely on the Functional Theory of political advertisements developed by Benoit (Chapter Two in this volume). Although some scholars adopt more refined definitions in differentiating for instance uncivil negative advertisements from those that are not, this definition is the one that is the most often adopted (Brooks and Geer 2007). Besides, it would be hard to operate such a differentiation in our case study, since there are almost no uncivil statements in Swiss campaigns.

The data used in this paper were collected within the framework of the project Making Electoral Democracy Work (Blais 2010). For measuring negative campaigning in the Swiss context, we relied on data sources as little mediated, as easily adjustable for parties on short notice and as widely accessible for voters as possible. Earlier studies in other countries rely mainly on TV advertising to ensure those qualities (Benoit, Chapter Two in this volume). However, since political television advertising is banned in Switzerland, we turned to the form of campaign communication to the public most common in Swiss politics: Newspaper advertisements and letters to the editor by candidates. According to interviews with the cantonal parties' campaign planners and managers that have been conducted within the Making Electoral Democracy Work's project, on average roughly 20 per cent of the party sections' campaign budgets were spent on this type of advertising, the second largest average share of the campaign budget for one sort of activity, only exceeded by one-shot mailings like campaign letters or partisan election-newspapers.

The first quality criterion of this type of data is always to ensure that the content is as unmediated as possible. This is best fulfilled by newspaper advertisements. Since they are placed in paid-for space, the wording and content is under complete control of the payers (mostly parties or party-based support committees). Letters to the editors by candidates, however, are subject to an editorial process. But this process mainly involves selection and cutting, not changing the negative or positive tone of a contribution as severely as for example coverage of a campaign event.

Compared to this mild shortcoming, the advantage of adjustability over time justifies the inclusion of letters to the editor. As well as newspaper advertisements, a message via letters to the editor can be easily adapted and changed in tone over a relatively short amount of time, compared to billboards, manifestos or one-shot campaign newspapers. Via these channels, parties can easily react to polls, scandals, hot topics or other unforeseen events. In addition, these two channels can be expected to reach a high number of potential Swiss voters. Newspaper consumption in Switzerland is highest in Europe, except for the Nordic countries; the reported rate of non-readers for example is below 10 per cent (Elvestad and Blekesaune 2008).

During the three months before election day, we collected all newspaper advertisements and letters to the editors by parties in a sample of three leading newspapers, one federal and two cantonal respectively: the *Neue Zürcher Zeitung* (federal), the *Tagesanzeiger* (Zurich), and the *Neue Luzerner Zeitung* (Lucerne). It provided a total of more than 1,000 advertisements and letters to the editor.

These were coded as either relating to Zurich or Lucerne competition for the federal campaigns, or to the legislative or government election for the cantonal campaigns.

The coding-unit of negativity in an advertisement or letter is a quasi-sentence. In line with the definition presented above, quasi-sentences in statements attacking another party, candidate or office-holder were coded '1' whereas those about a party's own policy preferences, qualities or allies were coded '0'. Also, one would note that the sum of advertisements of all parties does not correspond to the overall number of advertisements in the campaign. Some parties sometimes 'share' an advertisement unit.

When looking at the number of negative quasi-sentences for each campaign covered by our study, we see huge differences between the federal and the cantonal level. Table 7.2 reports the mean proportions of attacks by campaign. It shows that the practice of negative campaigning was much more common during the 2011 cantonal campaigns in both Zurich and Lucerne. On average, newspapers advertisements of the federal campaigns contained 2 per cent to 5 per cent of attacks; while this average rises to 10 per cent for the cantonal campaigns, and even to 14 per cent when we concentrate on advertisements concerning legislative elections in these campaigns only (these differences are statically significant at a level of $p<0.01$). As to ensure the comparability of our analyses across elections, we focus on advertisements related to parliamentary elections of the lower house at the federal and the parliament at the cantonal level in the rest of this chapter. We thereby also can get rid of the bias induced by the fact that some parties did not run or endorse any candidate at the cantonal government elections.

These differences in terms of campaigns are in line with what we know about the incentives created by the cantonal and federal institutional systems in Switzerland. While all main parties are part of a traditional alliance that collaborates to vote in the government at the federal level, they do not have to agree on the composition of the government at the cantonal level since it is the

Table 7.2: Negativity by campaign

	Zurich		Lucerne	
	Mean (s.d.)	N	Mean (s.d.)	N
2011 federal campaign	0.02 (0.08)	325	0.05 (0.15)	278
2011 cantonal campaign	0.10** (0.21)	235	0.10** (0.21)	240
2011 cantonal campaign (legislative campaigns only)	0.14** (0.25)	156	0.14** (0.24)	178
All 2011 campaigns	0.05 (0.16)	560	0.07 (0.18)	518

Note: Entries are mean proportions of quasi-sentences in newspaper ads. Standard deviations are in parentheses. Difference of means t-tests: * $p<0.05$, ** $p<0.01$ (two-tailed); for region, the reference is the mean of the 2011 federal campaign.

population that directly elects it. Parties have thus more room to attack each other at the cantonal level. Also, it should be mentioned that the legislative elections are more negative than the government elections at the cantonal level, which should be due to the fact that, during the following term, the elected government members will have to collaborate more with each other than with the elected deputies. Finally, it is worth mentioning that there is no notable difference between Lucerne and Zurich in terms of the overall tone of the campaigns in these two cantons.

In Figure 7.1, we report the evolution of attacks during the 90 days preceding election day in each of the four campaigns covered. In the literature, it is said that campaigns get more negative as time passes. This is attributed to the so-called snowball effect of negativity, according to which a party that has been the object of negative advertisements is more likely to adopt this strategy in the rest of the campaign (Damore 2002). This trend however hardly exists in the federal and cantonal campaigns in Zurich and Lucerne. We do not find any statistically significant correlation between the proportion of negative quasi-sentence and the campaign day. This confirms that is it is the institutional setting, rather than a 'spiral of negativity' that explains the overall differences of negativity between campaigns reported above.

Figure 7.1: Evolution of negativity during campaigns

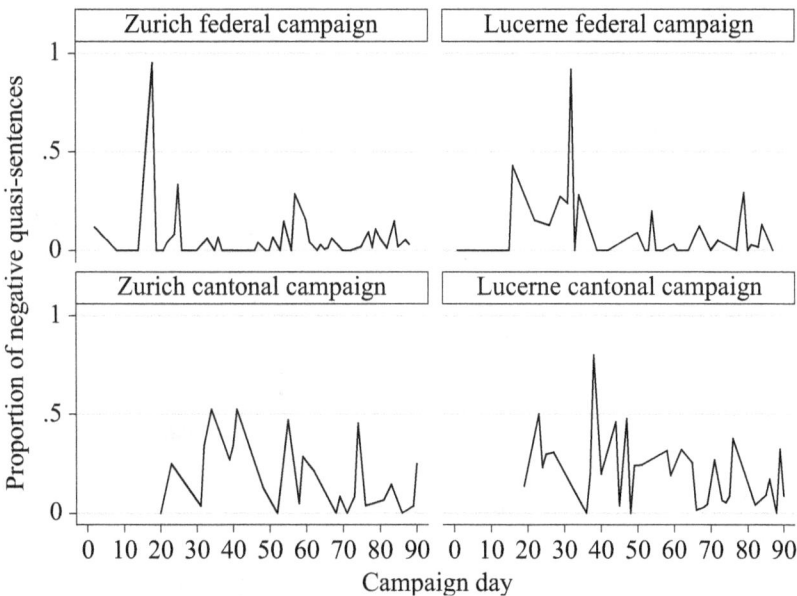

Note: Lines report mean proportions of negative quasi-sentences in newspaper advertisements per campaign/region day. No correlations between day and mean proportions are statistically significant.

The electoral determinants of negative campaigning

Table 7.3 reports the mean proportion of negativity/attacks contained in all newspaper advertisements released, arrayed by campaign and party. In Zurich, we observe that during the federal campaign, the second largest party (the SP) went relatively more negative than other parties. The party's proportion of attacks is 3 per cent (with a standard deviation of 13 per cent) compared to an overall mean of 2 per cent. At the cantonal level, it is the SVP who went more negative than others (with a mean of 16 per cent compared to a total average of 14 per cent). Even if these differences are not statistically significant, they are rather consistent with the theory regarding how electoral competition impacts negative campaigning. SP as the second in line resorts to more negative campaigning than the other parties to gain versus the frontrunner SVP. In the cantonal campaign, however, the picture does not support the theoretical propositions. In general, the results of Zurich should be taken with caution. SVP and SP Zurich are the by far best funded (with the FDP) and professionally organised party sections in Switzerland. They are the ones to be expected to most likely realise the potential

Table 7.3: Negativity by party

	Zurich		Lucerne	
	Mean (s.d.)	**N**	**Mean (s.d.)**	**N**
2011 federal campaign	**0.02 (0.08)**	**325**	**0.05 (0.15)**	**278**
SVP	0.02 (0.08)	98	0.09* (0.18)	71
SP	0.03 (0.13)	53	0.05 (0.16)	31
BDP	0.00 (0.00)	17	0.09 (0.24)	14
GP	0.00 (0.03)	35	0.03 (0.09)	25
FDP	0.02 (0.07)	79	0.02 (0.08)	62
GLP	0.08 (0.20)	7	0.03 (0.05)	15
CVP	0.00 (0.00)	40	0.03 (0.11)	70
2011 cantonal campaign	**0.14 (0.25)**	**156**	**0.14 (0.24)**	**178**
SVP	0.16 (0.20)	54	0.23** (0.29)	45
SP	0.08 (0.22)	21	0.13 (0.22)	26
BDP	0.23 (NA)	1	0.05 (0.12)	19
GP	0.04* (0.15)	16	0.19 (0.32)	28
FDP	0.15 (0.28)	64	0.05 (0.11)	25
GLP	0.20 (NA)	1	0.13 (0.18)	8
CVP	0.00 (0.00)	3	0.08 (0.16)	35

Note: Entries are mean proportions of quasi-sentences in newspaper advertisements. Difference of means t-tests: * $p<0.05$, ** $p<0.01$ (two-tailed); for Zurich campaign, the reference is the mean of the SVP, for Lucerne, the reference is the mean of the CVP.

gains of negative campaigning and to professionally apply this strategy, which had been highly uncommon in Swiss politics until the populist turn of the SVP in the early 1990s. Also, it is important to note that the number of advertisements for some parties in the 2011 Zurich cantonal campaign is so small that also these results should be taken with caution.

In Lucerne, in both campaigns, it is the SVP, the new challenger of the dominant CVP that showed a constantly higher mean proportion of attacks. In the federal campaign, the party's negativity share was 9 per cent (compared to an overall mean of 5 per cent, the difference is statistically significant at a level of $p<0.05$); while in the cantonal campaign, the share was 23 per cent (compared to an overall mean of 14 per cent, statistically significant at a level of $p<0.01$). By contrast, the dominant CVP showed a mean proportion of attacks lower than the overall average in both the federal and cantonal campaigns (of 3 per cent and 8 per cent respectively). This is again perfectly consistent regarding the classic electoral determinants of negative campaigning presented above.

However, it is important to note that the whole picture is not as clear as the presented results of the frontrunner parties. In both Zurich's and Lucerne's campaigns, some of the 'spoiler' parties showed a relatively high proportion of attacks. According to the theory, they should have remained positive in their advertisements as they had little chance to really compete with the leading parties. For example, the newly formed GLP was particularly negative in cantonal campaigns. This might be due to the fact that the party had to create its place in the Swiss political space. The GP was also rather negative in Lucerne's cantonal campaign. These findings suggest that electoral competition does not explain the *alpha* and the *omega* of negative campaigning. It nevertheless constitutes an important factor to be taken into consideration to investigate the phenomenon, especially when analysing party systems and competition patterns that have been stable over a long time.

In the non-coalition PR system present here, the positional explanation at least holds more value than the alternative 'fear of losing' explanation, stating that the party facing defeat (also the second party in majoritarian systems with SMDs) will resort to negative campaigning. These two approaches cannot be tested separately in SMD systems, because the second party is both trailing (positional), as well as fearing loss of seats (fear of defeat) at the same time. When we look at the losses of seats compared to 2007, it was not the parties severely losing (CVP and FDP in Lucerne) that resorted to negative campaigning, but rather the parties who were actually winning[4] (e.g. SP and SVP).[5]

To further test the classic theory of party competition with these findings, we will also look at the parties targeted by their opponents' attacks. Table 7.4 reports

---

4. Due to the stability of polls in Switzerland, it is valid here to operationalise expected losses with the tendency of actual losses.

5. SVP's losses in Zurich were mainly due to the technical reason of the now BDP deputies not being part of the SVP parliamentary group any more.

Table 7.4: Parties targeted by negativity

	Zurich		Lucerne	
	Mean (s.d.)	**N**	**Mean (s.d.)**	**N**
2011 federal campaign				
SVP	0.04 (0.19)	325	0.06 (0.23)	278
SP	0.02 (0.15)	325	0.04 (0.20)	278
BDP	0.02** (0.12)	325	0.03** (0.16)	278
GP	0.01** (0.11)	325	0.03* (0.16)	278
FDP	0.03 (0.17)	325	0.04 (0.20)	278
GLP	0.02 (0.16)	325	0.01** (0.10)	278
CVP	0.03 (0.16)	325	0.05 (0.23)	278
2011 cantonal campaign				
SVP	0.07 (0.26)	156	0.12 (0.33)	178
SP	0.18** (0.38)	156	0.08* (0.28)	178
BDP	0.17* (0.37)	156	0.04** (0.19)	178
GP	0.18** (0.38)	156	0.08* (0.27)	178
FDP	0.14* (0.35)	156	0.07** (0.26)	178
GLP	0.17** (0.38)	156	0.01** (0.07)	178
CVP	0.19** (0.40)	156	0.15 (0.35)	178

Note: Entries are proportions of advertisements targeting the party. Difference of means t-tests: * $p<0.05$, ** $p<0.01$ (two-tailed); for Zurich's campaign, the reference is the mean of the SVP, for Lucerne's, the reference is the mean of the CVP.

the proportion of advertisements targeting each party for each campaign. During the federal campaign in Zurich, the SVP was more often targeted than any other party (in 4 per cent of all advertisements, while it was 2 per cent or 3 per cent for other parties). Although small, this difference is statically significant at a level of $p<0.01$ for the BDP and the GP (two new 'spoiler' parties, against whom all major parties chose a strategy of ignoring). This is perfectly in line with the theoretical predictions stated above. The leading party is indeed more likely to be attacked than others. In contrast, it is also important to note that in the cantonal campaign in Zurich all parties were targeted more than the SVP. This theoretically counterintuitive result is probably due to the comparatively small number of advertisements during the campaign and to the fact that the SVP is responsible for a very large part of the overall negative advertisements.

The situation is even clearer in Lucerne's campaigns. The two largest parties (the SVP and the CVP) were clearly attacked more often than all other parties. During the federal campaign, they were the targets of 5 per cent to 6 per cent of advertisements (compared to an average of 3 per cent for the other parties); this proportion rises from 12 per cent to 15 per cent during the cantonal campaign (compared to an average of 5 per cent for other parties). Most of these differences are statistically significant. These findings give further evidence to the importance of the electoral determinants of negative campaigning, even in a PR system.

Conclusions

In the theoretical literature, electoral competition is said to be key to explaining negative campaigning. While this claim is supported by strong evidence from single-member districts democracies (and especially the US), studies focusing on PR democracies fail to find such a link. In this chapter, we argued that this unsatisfactory result might be explained by the existence of bargaining over coalition agreements between parties in most of these European PR democracies. To address this problem, we analysed four electoral campaigns in Switzerland (the 2011 federal and cantonal campaigns in Zurich and Lucerne) where the specific institutional setting gives little room for coalition bargaining. Although some variation between parties with regard to the tone of their campaign remained unexplained, we did find patterns that are in line with the electoral explanation of negativity. In particular, challenger parties appeared to conduct more negative campaigns than 'spoiler' parties. Also, the largest parties are more often targets of their opponents' attacks. Our chapter thus contributes to the literature on the subject in asserting the importance of the electoral determinants of negative campaigning, even outside the classic single-member districts context.

Chapter Eight

Do Female Candidates Feel Compelled to Meet Sex-Role Expectations or Are They as Tough as Men? A Content Analysis on the Gender-Specific Use of Attacks in German Televised Debates

Jürgen Maier

During the last decades, women have gained much ground in politics. According to the Inter-Parliamentary Union (2011: 4), in 2011 women held an average of 19.5 per cent of all seats in parliament. Compared to the situation six years ago, this is an increase of 8.2 per cent (Inter-Parliamentary Union 2011: 4). Compared to the situation after World War II, the percentage of female politicians represented in parliament has more than sextupled (Inter-Parliamentary Union 2014). In addition, women have a better chance to occupy a leading position in politics, such as head of parliament, minister, prime minister or president, or party leader, today than in the past.

Although women are still under-represented in this area, some scholars argue that the increasing number of female candidates is transforming politics (*see* e.g. Norris and Lovenduski 1989; Rosenthal 2002). On the one hand, a number of studies indicate that women have a different political agenda than their male colleagues. Females are more likely to address issues focusing on reproduction (e.g. social policy, infrastructural policy, environmental policy), whereas males tend to deal with issues highlighting production (e.g. economic policy, energy policy; *see*, e.g. Lovenduski and Norris 2001; Norris 1996). On the other hand, female candidates have different political attitudes. In general, they are more liberal and more supportive of the issues belonging to the mentioned 'female agenda' than their male counterparts within the same party (*see* e.g. Erickson 1997; Norris 1996; Welch 1985). Finally, US studies indicate that legislative behaviour of females differs from male candidates with respect to these policies (*see* e.g. Thomas 1994).[1] Differences between male and female candidates are usually traced back to socialisation effects and particular life experiences: 'most women's and men's lives continue to diverge sharply. Structural differences stretch from cradle to grave … these differences will lead to a distinctive women's perspective on many issues facing society' (Norris 1996: 90).

---

1. In parliamentary democracies, such gender effects are rare because of the strong impact of party discipline on legislative behaviour (Lovenduski and Norris 2001).

Based on this explanation we should expect gender differences not only in legislative behaviour but also in political campaigning. This expectation is further nurtured because male and female candidates differ in terms of perceived personality. Empirical studies typically find that 'male candidates are perceived as tough, aggressive, and assertive, while their female counterparts are described as warm, people-oriented, gentle, kind, passive, caring, and sensitive. Female candidates are also stereotyped as being more moral, hardworking, and honest than their male counterparts' (Banducci *et al.* 2012: 165). Moreover, a number of studies indicate that gender determines the style of campaigning, which also includes the use of negative campaigning (*see* e.g. Kahn and Kenney 2000; Lau and Pomper 2001b, 2004; Proctor *et al.* 1994).

Unfortunately, when taking a closer look, the findings turn out to be far from clear-cut (for a review, *see* Bystrom 2004; Walter 2012). Whereas some studies indicate that male candidates use attacks more often than females (*see* e.g. Herrnson and Lucas 2006; Kahn 1993; Kahn and Kenney 2004; Lau and Pomper 2001b, 2004), other studies indicate that females use negative campaign strategies as often or even more frequently than their male counterparts (*see* e.g. Benze and Declercq 1985; Bystrom and Kaid 2002; Bystrom and Miller 1999; Kahn 1996; Lau and Pomper 2001b, 2004; Panagopoulos 2004; Proctor *et al.* 1994; Robertson *et al.* 1999; Sapiro *et al.* 2011; Schulz and Pancer 1997; Sheckels 1994; Trent and Sabourin 1993; Walter 2012; Williams 1994). In addition, female candidates do not only often air more negative campaign spots and run more attacks in these than male candidates (Bystrom and Kaid 2002). Some studies show that women tend to attack the issues rather than the character of the political opponent (Benze and Declercq 1985; Bystrom and Kaid 2002; Kahn 1993). Another finding is that 'women softened their attacks ... whereas men used harsher attacks' (Bystrom 2004: 438–439). In contrast to this, other studies reveal no differences (*see* e.g. Proctor *et al.* 1994). These findings indicate that men and women follow the same principles when they produce attack advertisements (Bystrom 2004). This conclusion is supported by the analysis of Bystrom and Kaid (2002) who demonstrate that the campaign styles of male and female candidates have converged over time (also *see* Dabelko and Herrnson 1997; Sapiro *et al.* 2011).

Studies indicating that women are more hesitant than men to use attacks argue that female candidates try to avoid violating sex-role expectations (Herrnson and Lucas 2006), i.e. to contradict the general perception that they are 'warm, people-oriented, gentle, kind, passive, caring ... sensitive ... more moral [and] honest' (Banducci *et al.* 2012: 165). The reason for this behaviour is that voters tend to 'punish female candidates for appearing aggressive while rewarding their male counterparts for the same behaviour' (Herrnson and Lucas 2006: 71). In contrast, studies reporting a rather similar use of negative campaign strategies by males and females argue that women try to demonstrate that they are 'tough enough' or even want to '"out-tough" their male opponents' (Lau and Pomper 2004: 33). Especially for campaign instruments under control of the candidate, women make an effort to provide voters with impressions different from those presented by the mass media. The media very often portrays female candidates in the context of their traditional roles, emphasise their (physical) appearance, or focus on their personal lives (*see* e.g. Braden 1996; Witt *et al.* 1994). Therefore, it has been argued that television is more important for women than for men as a key source of campaign communication (*see* e.g. Bystrom and Kaid 2002).

Although there is a large body of research on male and female campaign styles, a number of issues still require further study. First, most research focuses on campaign advertising. Campaign spots are, of course, neither the only nor the most important televised messages under full control of their sender. For many reasons, televised debates seem to be more relevant. For instance, debates reach huge audiences and are accompanied by massive media coverage. In addition, a lot of studies indicate that televised debates have the power to persuade voters. In a nutshell, televised debates can be considered 'as the most important (single) event in the course of an election campaign' (Maier and Faas 2011: 76). Second, although televised debates have a long tradition, information about the use of attacks by male and female candidates are only occasionally available. In sharp contrast to advertising research, systematic analyses are lacking for this major campaign event. Third, a number of source-related (e.g. incumbency, party affiliation) and contextual variables (e.g. level of election, standing in the polls) influence the use of attacks in televised debates (*see* e.g. Benoit 2007). This makes it difficult to generalise gender-specific differences on the basis of a single debate. In addition, in bivariate analysis one needs to control for the impact of other variables to minimise the likelihood of spurious correlation. Furthermore, it is plausible that the use of attacks by male and female candidates is moderated by other variables. In any case, several analyses on legislative behaviour and campaign advertising point in this direction and report interactions with the candidate's political role (*see* Gordon *et al.* 2003; Proctor *et al.* 1994), party affiliation (Sapiro *et al.* 2011) as well as institutional constraints (Norris 1996; Walter 2012). To the best of our knowledge, no serious analyses have been done so far in the field of debate research. One reason for this might be that one needs data covering a large number of debates to run such an analysis. Data sets comprehensive enough for this are rare. Fourth, the nature of attacks varies. Debate research acknowledges this fact and distinguishes attacks focusing on policy from negative messages focusing on the character of the political opponent (*see* e.g. Benoit 2007). But attacks are, of course, more complex. For instance, the opponent can be criticised in an explicit or implicit manner. Finally, attacks can be formulated in a civil or an uncivil way. Whereas these variations are already an issue in advertising research (*see* e.g. Fridkin and Kenney 2011a), such differentiations are still lacking in the analysis of debate strategy. Fifth, most information on the use of attacks is based on content analysis of US debates. Studies in other countries are rare. The replication of US results in other nations still remains to be done.

The aim of this study is to analyse the use of attacks by male and female candidates in the context of televised debates. We will explore the extent (and the kind) of negativity, test for potentially relevant moderators, and control bivariate effects by other variables known as predictors for verbal aggression. Our analysis is based on data from a content analysis of candidate messages in all televised debates aired in Germany in the run-up to national or state elections. In the following section, we formulate more specific research questions and hypotheses on the relationship between negative campaigning and gender. After that, we provide a more detailed description of the data. We will then analyse the impact of gender on the use of negativity. Finally, we sum up our results and discuss our findings.

Hypotheses on the impact of gender on the use of attacks in televised debates

Because information on the gender-specific use of negative campaigning in televised debates is rare, our hypotheses lean on findings in advertising research. With respect to the utilisation of negative messages, the picture is far from being clear-cut. Whereas some studies suggest that male candidates attack more than females, other studies find no differences or indicate that women even outdo males in their use of attacks. Hence, we address the following research question:

RQ1: Is there a difference in the use of attacks between male and female candidates?

In addition, some studies in advertising research point in the direction that independent of the level of attacks, females tend to be less harsh. In contrast to this, other studies find no differences. We will investigate this aspect by measuring the explicitness and incivility of attacks. Therefore, our research question is as follows:

RQ2: Is there a gender-specific difference in the use of implicit and explicit attacks?

RQ3: Is there a gender-specific difference in the use of uncivil attacks?

Most studies indicate that female candidates attack the political opponent more on issues than on character. In contrast to this, men focus more on personality and less on policy. As a consequence, we formulate the following hypothesis:

H1: Female candidates attack more on issues and less on character than male candidates.

A large body of content-analytical studies has demonstrated that the use of attack in televised debates depends on the role of the candidates. In particular, challengers almost always attack more than incumbents (*see* e.g. Benoit 2007).

In addition, some studies indicate that the share of negative messages is a function of the level of election. Although US studies tend to show more negativity on lower-level elections (Airne and Benoit 2005a), it also seems plausible to expect a decrease of attacks if more is at stake. The argument for this assumption is that attacks are risky because voters do not like mud-slinging. Hence, attacking the political opponent can backfire to its source. As a consequence, negative campaigning should be less popular in national races than in lower-level elections. Furthermore, the position of a candidate as reflected in the polls seems to have an influence on campaign strategy. Studies on advertising research have revealed that candidates behind in the polls are willing to adopt more risky strategies (i.e. more verbal attacks) than candidates ahead in the polls (*see* e.g. Lau and Pomper 2001b, 2004). Finally, it seems reasonable that age and experience of a candidate might influence the strategic behaviour in televised debates. On the one hand, we often experience that younger people tend to behave more aggressively, whereas older people become more composed. On the other hand, even for politicians debates are a very special type of interaction. Therefore, older candidates or candidates with more debate experience might act differently than younger candidates or candidates participating for the first time in a televised debate. For all these variables, we want to investigate if there are significant interactions with gender. Hence, our research questions is:

RQ4: Is the impact of the candidate's political role, the level of election, the candidate's standing in the polls, the candidate's age, and the candidate's debate experience on the use of attacks moderated by gender?

Data and operationalisation

Our study covers all American-style televised debates ever held in Germany.[2] In total, our sample includes content analyses of forty-three televised debates between 1997 and 2013 (five debates on the national level and thirty-eight debates on the state level) running between forty-five and ninety minutes (mean: sixty-three minutes). Over this period of time, we identified ninety-two candidates (seventy-five male and seventeen female) participating in at least one televised debate. Some of the candidates appeared in more than one debate; some of them participated in debates on the national as well as on the state level.

---

2. Before the introduction of American-style televised debates there was a tradition of so-called 'elephant rounds'. They were aired in the run-up to every national election between 1972 and 1987 and included the leaders of all parties represented in the national parliament (*see* e.g. Schrott and Lanoue 1992). This format was (and still is) used at the state level. Because elephant rounds do not fit our definition of a televised debate – i.e. the live discussion between (typically two) top candidates who have the best chances of being elected as the head of the government (national level: chancellor; state level: prime minister, the governing mayor in Berlin, Bremen, or Hamburg) – we do not include them in our sample.

In a first step, we made a transcript of every debate.[3] In a second step, these transcripts were broken up into coding units (thought units).[4] Typically, coding units are separated by a change of speaker, strategy, content, or reference objects. A coding unit can contain several sentences as well as just a single word.[5] In the following, we also use the terms 'statements' or 'messages' even if the coding units involve more than a single sentence. In total, we identified 14,878 (functional and non-functional) candidate statements.[6] Third, each statement was connected to the speaker. Moreover, additional information about the speaker – e.g. age, sex, party affiliation, and political role[7] – was entered into the data set. Furthermore, we incorporated context variables like the setting (level of election, number of candidates participating in the debate, number of debates in the campaign, town hall meeting) and timing of the debate (days between the debate and election day) as well as the candidate's standing in opinion polls into the data set.[8] In a fourth step, in accordance with the Functional Theory of Political Campaign Discourse (*see* e.g. Benoit 2007), we coded three types of candidate strategies for every functional unit: acclaims, attacks, and defences. A statement was coded as an attack if the political opponent and/or his/her policy (as well as third persons or issues associated with the political opponent) were unfavourably portrayed or

3. Some transcripts can be downloaded via http://www.uni-koblenz-landau.de/komepol/publikationen/working_paper_series. For transcripts also *see* Maier and Faas (2003a, 2003b), Maier *et al.* (2006) as well as www.gles.eu.

4. The identification of coding units was done by two coders, while the coding of the strategy was carried out by five coders. In general, the codebook of the 2009 German televised debate was used as a reference guide to code the debates. The codebook and the data of the 2009 debate can be downloaded via the homepage of the German Longitudinal Election Study (GLES; *see* www.gles.eu).

5. This is in line with the definition of 'idea units' as a 'phrase, clause, or sentence that carries a claim' (Jamieson *et al.* 2000: 51). Hatfield and Weider-Hatfield (1978: 46) define a thought unit as 'the minimum meaningful utterance having a beginning and end, typically operationalized as a simple sentence'.

6. Non-functional units are statements that were so incomplete that they could not be understood. All non-candidate statements (i.e. statements from journalists, questions from the audience, video segments) are excluded from this analysis (N=6,784).

7. Most content analyses of televised debates distinguish between incumbents and challengers. This does not make much sense in parliamentary democracies where coalitions often have to be formed after an election. As a consequence, candidates joining a coalition may debate with each other at the end of a legislative period. This was the case in Germany, for instance, when Chancellor Angela Merkel and her Minister of Foreign Affairs, Frank-Walter Steinmeier, participated in a debate in the run-up to the 2009 national election. Steinmeier was unable to criticise Merkel very much because he was also responsible for the previous government's performance. As a consequence, the proper distinction for parliamentary political systems is between members of the government and members of the opposition instead of incumbents and challengers.

8. Survey data was retrieved from www.wahlrecht.de. This variable considers the difference in the share of votes between a candidate's party and the party of his/her opponent. In a debate with three candidates, for the front-runner we measured the difference between the first- and second-best party. For all other candidates we measured the difference between the candidate's party and the party of the front-runner.

challenged.[9] In addition, for each attack we examined if it was addressed in an explicit or an implicit manner.[10] Furthermore, we distinguished between attacks focusing on issues or on character.[11] Finally, for each statement we coded if a candidate had interrupted the political opponent or the journalist.[12] In addition, we combined this information with the identified strategy to find out if an interruption was used in order to voice an attack.

In a final step, we aggregated our data for each candidate and every debate. Hence, the sample of the following analyses is N=92 candidates. The dependent variables are the share of negative statements,[13] the share of attacks addressed explicitly or implicitly, and the share of attacks focusing on issues or on character. In addition, we have calculated the number of interruptions, respectively, the number of attacks introduced by an interruption. To be able to compare the degree of incivility between debates and candidates, we divided this information by the length of the debate. Hence, the information provided by these variables is the number of interruptions (respectively, the number of attacks introduced by an interruption) per minute. Finally, we take account of the fact that particular combinations of candidate personalities and a specific course of a debate might create a certain level of negativity. Therefore, we use regression analysis with clustered standard errors.

Results

The use of attacks

Our data indicates that the use of attacks by male and female candidates in German televised debates is quite similar (Figure 8.1). On average, 24.0 per cent of all statements uttered by women are negative. Compared to this, men opt for attacks in 25.9 per cent of their statements. This difference is statistically not significant (p>0.1). A closer look at the structure of attacks reveals that negative messages are predominantly addressed in an explicit manner. In addition, criticisms on policy

---

9. To assess intercoder reliability, about 25 per cent of all functional candidate messages were selected and coded independently by two coders. On average, intercoder reliability for strategy was 0.94 (Holsti's formula).

10. Explicit statements clearly refer to the political opponent. Implicit statements do not mention the political opponent. Nevertheless, the content of the statement can be assigned to him/her. Some statements could neither be classified as explicit nor implicit. The average intercoder reliability was 0.81 (Holsti's formula).

11. Issue statements focus on aspects of polity, policy, or politics. Character statements focus on candidate characteristics (i.e. competence, leadership, integrity, personality). Some statements could neither be assigned to an issue nor to candidate characteristics. The average intercoder reliability is 0.81 (Holsti's formula).

12. An interruption takes place if a candidate heckles another participant of the debate so that s/he is not able to complete his/her statement. The intercoder reliability is 1.00 (Holsti's formula).

13. The share of negativity was calculated as follows:
$$\frac{\text{(number of units coded as attacks)}}{\text{(number of all functional and nonfunctional units)}} \times 100$$

Figure 8.1: Use of attacks by male and female candidates in German televised debates, 1997–2013

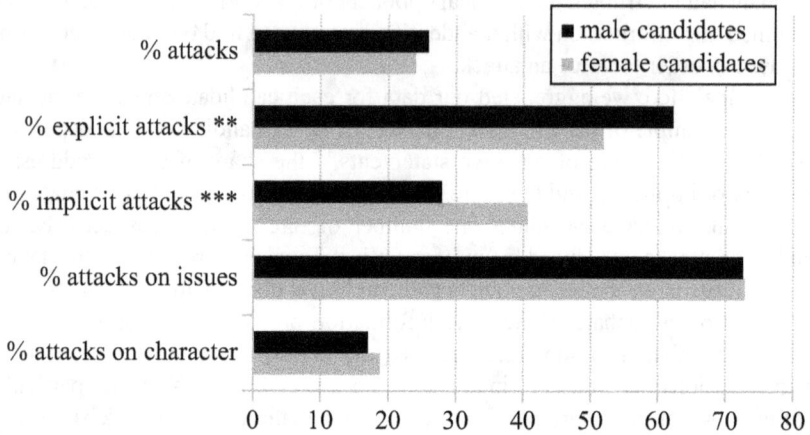

Significance levels: *: p<0.1, **: p<0.05, ***: p<0.01

clearly outweigh attacks focusing on the character of the political opponent. Whereas there is no significant difference between males and females in terms of the focus of attack (issues: 72.6 versus 72.9 per cent; character: 17.0 versus 18.8 per cent; p>0.1), male candidates use more explicit attacks than their female counterparts (62.2 versus 51.9 per cent, p<0.05). In contrast, attacks by females are more often implicit than negative messages uttered by males (40.6 versus 27.9 per cent, p<0.01).

The results displayed in Figure 8.2 indicate that males show more uncivil behaviour in televised debates than females. In general, men tend to interrupt more frequently than women. But the observed differences are neither significant for the interruption of the political opponent (0.18 versus 0.13 interruptions per minute; p>0.1) nor for the interruption of journalists (0.10 versus 0.06 interruptions per minute; p>0.1). In contrast to this, male candidates use interruptions significantly more often to utter an attack than females (0.08 versus 0.05 attacks introduced by interruptions per minute; p<0.1).[14]

With reference to our research questions and our hypothesis, we find that RQ1 (gender differences in the use of attacks) has to be rejected. This result corresponds

---

14. There is only limited evidence that female candidates are less likely to be the target of an (male) attack than male candidates. In general, male candidates do not behave differently if their opponent is male or female (p<0.1). The only exception is attacks on character. Our data indicates that men are more negative here if the opponent is a woman (male opponent: 15.6 per cent of all attacks focusing on character; female opponent: 24.0 per cent; p<0.05).

Figure 8.2: Interruption of the political opponent by male and female candidates in German televised debates, 1997–2013

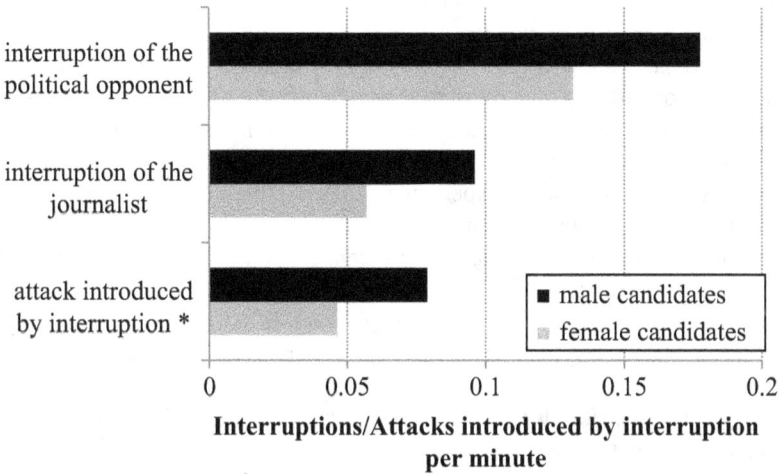

Significance levels: *: p<0.1, **: p<0.05, ***: p<0.01

to those findings arguing that female candidates try to demonstrate that they are 'tough enough'. In addition, H1 (female candidates' attacks focus more on policy and less on character than male candidates) must be rejected. In contrast, there a gender-specific difference in the use of implicit and explicit attacks (RQ2) as well as in the use of uncivil attacks (RQ3). Both results fit the explanation that women conform to sex-role expectations. The reason for this might be that women are afraid that voters could 'punish female candidates for appearing aggressive' (Herrnson and Lucas 2006: 71).

Gender as a moderator for the negative use of messages

The situation becomes more complex if we consider gender not only as a factor with a direct impact on the use of attacks but also as a moderator of effects caused by other variables. A number of studies have demonstrated that the use of negative campaign messages varies between, e.g., incumbents and challengers, national and lower-level elections, or between candidates ahead and candidates behind in the polls. The interesting question now is if male and female candidates respond in the same way to changing roles, institutional settings, or positions in the electoral race.

We have analysed the interaction between these variables and gender on all our dependent variables. In addition, we have investigated the moderating impact of gender on the political experience of a candidate measured by age and participation in previous debates. The result displayed in Table 8.1 indicates that only in four out of forty cases gender works as a moderator. In three cases, interactions are associated with the use of attacks (also *see* Figure 8.3). First, there are no gender-specific differences in the use of negative messages in state elections. In contrast, in national elections the share of attacks is higher for males than for females. Second, political experience has different consequences for the debate strategy chosen by women and men. On the one hand, younger male and female candidates show a rather similar use of attacks.[15] Older men, however, clearly use more attacks than older women. On the other hand, debate experience has no consequences for male candidates. It does not matter very much if a male candidate is a debate novice or more experienced: The level of negativity stays the same. In contrast, as debating experience increases, there is a sharp decline in the use of attacks for female candidates.

In one case gender serves as a significant moderator for the use of attacks focusing on issues (also *see* Figure 8.4). The positive regression coefficient indicates that a higher level of debate experience is associated with less use of issue-based attacks by male candidates and increasing criticism of issues by females.

Although it is difficult to find a reasonable explanation for all interactions, our results indicate that RQ4 is relevant. In some cases, gender serves as a factor moderating the impact of other variables on the use of negative messages. In the final step of our analysis we will investigate if the direct effects of gender as reported in the previous section and the interactions of gender with other variables described in this section still hold if we control for other important variables.

The impact of gender in multivariate models

Research on negative campaigning has revealed a number of variables responsible for the use of attacks. Elsewhere, we have assigned these variables to four broader categories: the candidate's personal profile, the candidate's political profile, the format of the debate, and the strategic context of a debate (Maier and Jansen 2013). The personal profile includes information about gender, age, and generation. The political profile consists of the political role of a candidate, his/her party affiliation, and political experience. The debate format captures the level of election, the number of candidates participating in a debate, the position of a debate within a series of televised debates, the timing of a debate, and the inclusion ('town hall meeting') or exclusion of an audience in a debate. Finally, the strategic context is represented by the standing of the candidates in the polls. We now extend our analysis by estimating the impact of all the mentioned variables on our dependent variables. In addition, we include those interactions that proved to be significant in Section 3.2.

---

15. For Figure 8.3, the age of the candidates was divided into two categories by calculating the median. For the analyses displayed in Table 8.1 and Table 8.2, age was included as a ratio scaled variable.

Table 8.1: Gender as a moderator for the use of negative messages

Gender x	% attacks	% explicit attacks	% implicit attacks	% issue-based attacks	% attacks on character	Interruption of political opponent	Interruption of journalist	Attack introduced by interruption
				Dependent variable				
Member of government	n.s.	n.s.	n.s.	n.s.	n.s.	n.s.	n.s.	n.s.
Level of election	14.45* (7.62)	n.s.	n.s.	n.s.	n.s.	n.s.	n.s.	n.s.
Standing in the polls	n.s.	n.s.	n.s.	n.s.	n.s.	n.s.	n.s.	n.s.
Age	−0.97*** (0.25)	n.s.	n.s.	n.s.	n.s.	n.s.	n.s.	n.s.
Debate experience	−8.07** (4.18)	n.s.	n.s.	12.88* (6.68)	n.s.	n.s.	n.s.	n.s.

Significance levels: n.s.: $p>0.1$, * : $p<0.1$, ** : $p<0.05$, *** : $p<0.01$. Displayed are unstandardised regression coefficients (in parenthesis: robust standard error) of an OLS regression with clustered standard errors including gender, the variable of interest, and the interaction between gender and the variable of interest.

Figure 8.3: Gender as a moderator for the use of attacks

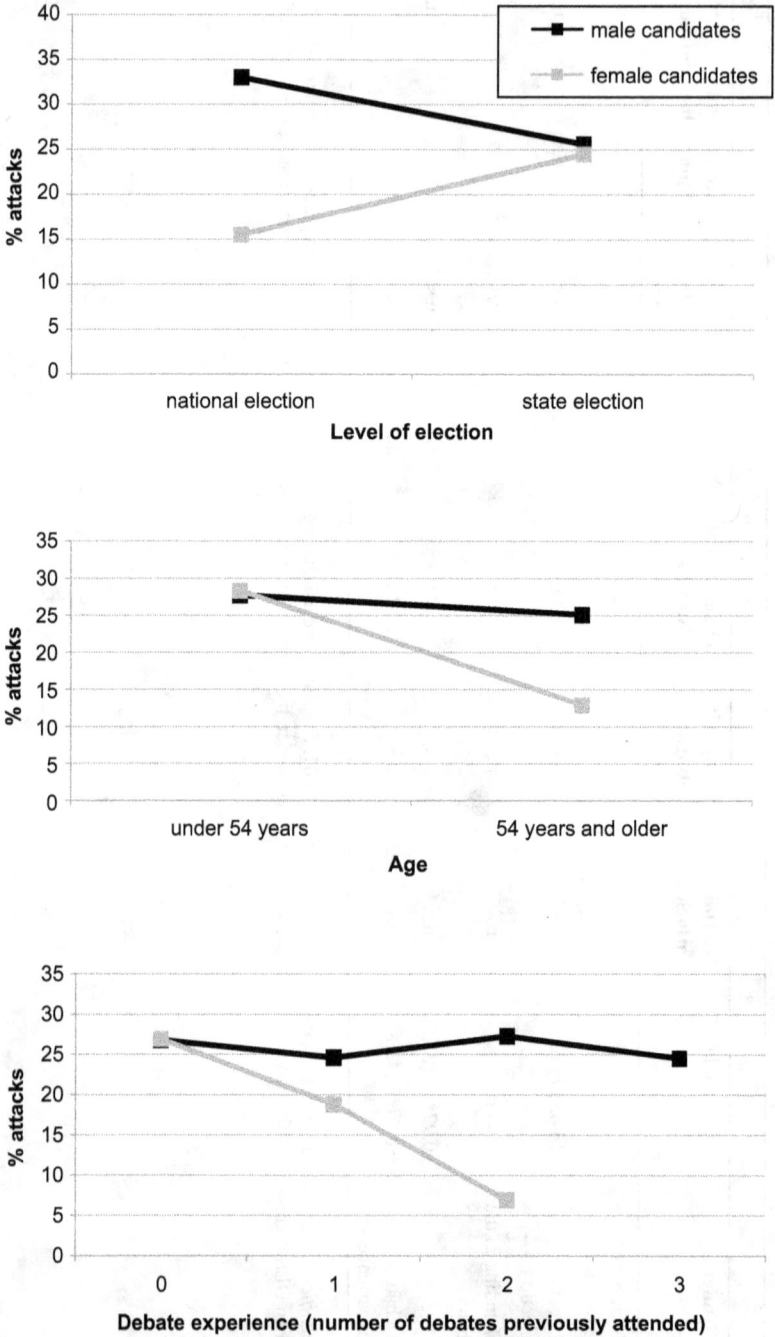

Figure 8.4: Gender as a moderator for the use of issue-based attacks

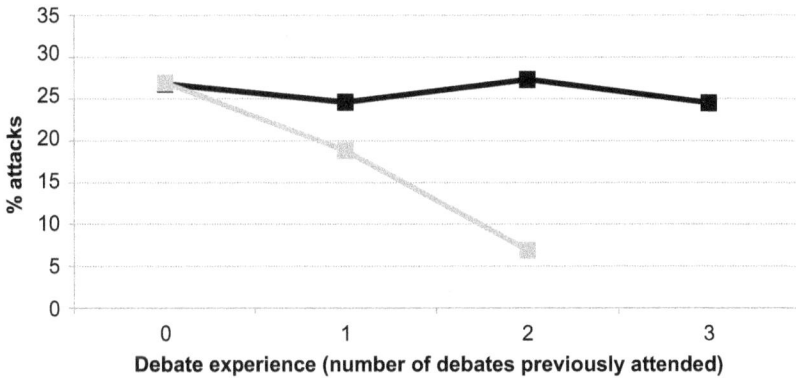

Our results indicate that gender only plays a minor role in explaining the use of attacks (*see* Table 8.2). In none of the eight models do we find a significant effect of gender. This leads to the negation of RQ1, RQ2, RQ3, and H1. In three out of four cases, the included interactions also fail to reach statistical significance. Only for the use of issue-based attacks we find a significant interaction between gender and debate experience. The results support the data already displayed in Figure 8.4: The more debate experience a woman has, the more she will focus on issues if she is attacking the political opponent. For male candidates, the relationship is reversed; increasing debate experience is associated with a declining use of issue-based attacks.

If we take a final look at which factors really drive candidates to attack each other, we find only few relevant variables. Probably the most important impact comes from being a member of the government or of the opposition. Being a member of the government decreases the likelihood to voice negative statements, to attack implicitly, and to make issue-based attacks. Instead, members of the government will use more explicit attacks and more attacks focusing on character than candidates belonging to the opposition. In addition, the level of election plays an important role for the use of attacks. Debates in the run-up to a national election show a significantly higher level of negativity than debates on the state level. On the other side, state debates seem to be rougher. Here we find significantly more interruptions than on the national level. In addition, interruptions are more frequently used in order to voice an attack. Furthermore, the standing in the polls has an impact on the use of attacks. The more a candidate is behind in the polls, the more s/he will show verbal aggression in a televised debate. In addition, the candidates with low public support tend to interrupt the political more often than frontrunners. Moreover, trailing candidates use interruptions of other participants of a debate more often to voice an attack than candidates with a more promising standing in the polls. The number of candidates invited to a debate also affects

Table 8.2: The impact of gender on the use of negative messages

	Dependent variable							
	% attacks	% explicit attacks	% implicit attacks	% issue-based attacks	% attacks on character	Interruption of political opponent	Interruption of journalist	Attack introduced by interruption
R^2	0.54	0.33	0.36	0.32	0.22	0.29	0.11	0.23
Personal profile								
Gender	n.s.	n.s.	n.s.	n.s.	n.s.	n.s.	n.s.	n.s.
Gender x								
Member of government	n.a.	n.a.	n.a.	n.a.	n.a.	n.a.	n.a.	n.a.
Level of election	n.s.	n.a.	n.a.	n.a.	n.a.	n.a.	n.a.	n.a.
Standing in the polls	n.a.	n.a.	n.a.	n.a.	n.a.	n.a.	n.a.	n.a.
Age	n.s.	n.a.	n.a.	n.a.	n.a.	n.a.	n.a.	n.a.
Debate experience	n.s.	n.a.	n.a.	19.21** (8.84)	n.a.	n.a.	n.a.	n.a.
Age	n.s.	n.s.	n.s.	n.s.	n.s.	n.s.	n.s.	n.s.
Year of birth	n.s.	n.s.	0.99** (0.45)	n.s.	n.s.	n.s.	n.s.	n.s.
Political profile								
Member of government	-12.04*** (2.63)	11.84** (4.45)	-14.38*** (3.74)	-15.30*** (3.45)	9.39*** (3.07)	n.s.	n.s.	n.s.
CDU/CSU	n.s.	n.s.	n.s.	n.s.	-25.68** (10.87)	n.s.	n.s.	n.s.

Table 8.2 (continued)

	Dependent variable							
	% attacks	% explicit attacks	% implicit attacks	% issue-based attacks	% attacks on character	Interruption of political opponent	Interruption of journalist	Attack introduced by interruption
SPD	n.s.	n.s.	n.s.	n.s.	−23.98** (9.57)	n.s.	n.s.	n.s.
Left party	11.54* (6.54)	n.s.	n.s.	n.s.	−24.74** (9.98)	n.s.	n.s.	n.s.
Debate experience	n.s.	n.s.	n.s.	n.s.	n.s.	n.s.	n.s.	n.s.
Debate format								
Level of election	−11.67*** (3.40)	n.s.	n.s.	n.s.	n.s.	0.20*** (0.05)	n.s.	0.06*** (0.02)
Number of candidates	n.s.	−23.11*** (7.45)	16.68** (6.55)	n.s.	n.s.	n.s.	n.s.	n.s.
Number of debates	n.s.	n.s.	n.s.	n.s.	n.s.	n.s.	n.s.	n.s.
Days until election day	n.s.	n.s.	n.s.	n.s.	n.s.	n.s.	n.s.	n.s.
Town hall meeting	n.s.	27.66** (12.64)	−18.59* (10.90)	n.s.	n.s.	n.s.	n.s.	n.s.
Strategic context								
Standing in the polls	−0.15* (0.09)	n.s.	n.s.	n.s.	n.s.	−.01* (0.00)	n.s.	−0.00*** (0.00)

Significance levels: n.s.: $p>0.1$; *: $p<0.1$, **: $p<0.05$, ***: $p<0.01$. n.a.: not applied. Displayed are unstandardised regression coefficients (in parenthesis: robust standard error) of an OLS regression with clustered standard errors. The 2000 Baden-Württemberg debate has been excluded from the analysis. N=90 candidates.

the degree of negativity. If only two candidates debate each other, the share of explicit (implicit) attacks is lower (higher) than in a three-candidate debate. The opposite effect can be observed for 'town hall' meetings. If there is an audience, the likelihood of explicit attacks is increasing whereas the share of implicit attacks declines. Occasionally, we also find significant effects for year of birth and party affiliation.

Interestingly enough, a number of variables have no independent impact on the degree of negativity in a televised debate. First, there is no impact of age. Second, debate experience has no significant effect. This means that candidates do not adopt or discard attack strategies as their political experience grows. Third, the timing of the debate has no influence. We see no effect if there is only one debate in a campaign or if there is a series of debates and – in this case – if a debate is the first or the second one. In addition, it has no consequences for the level of negativity if a debate is held at an earlier or later point in the campaign.[16]

Summary and conclusion

There is a lot of speculation if the increasing representation of women on all levels of the political system during the last decades will change politics. The core argument supporting this expectation is that female politicians do not only add a new perspective by, e.g., highlighting different issues than their male counterparts, but also that women have a different personality than men. If public perceptions of female personality really reflect the true personality of female politicians, then politics should become more 'people-oriented, gentle, kind, … sensitive … moral [and] honest' (Banducci *et al.* 2012: 165) to mention but a few. Furthermore, if females really have a unique access to the political process, this should be reflected in a different style of political campaigning.

The available studies dealing with this issue are rather inconclusive. This is particularly true for negative campaigning. A number of studies find no significant gender difference with respect to the use of attacks. Although there might be some gender differences in particular aspects of negative campaigning, more comprehensive studies give the impression that campaign styles of male and female candidates have converged and that both genders have adopted the same guidelines when producing negative campaign messages. Unfortunately, almost all empirical results focusing on gender differences in negative campaigning are based on studies of advertising in US electoral races. Hence, there is a considerable lack of research on other campaign events and in other countries.

---

16. About 85 per cent of the debates in Germany are aired during the last two weeks of a campaign. One major exception was the 2000 Baden-Württemberg debate, which was held about four months before election day. Because this debate has a major impact on the regression results (usually the variable 'days until election day' reaches statistically significance), we excluded this debate from the regression analysis. As a consequence, the number of candidates for this analysis is N=90.

The aim of this study is to make a contribution to close this gap. Based on a content analysis of candidate behaviour covering all German televised debates since 1997, our findings suggest that there is not much of a difference between male and female candidates in the use of attacks. Especially the multivariate analysis indicates that the impact of gender is very limited. The only effect we have found is an interaction between gender and debate experience with respect to the share of issue-based attacks. The direction of the interaction does not support the assumption that females will *per se* create more fact-based discussions. More criticism on policy can be expected if females are experienced; with increasing participation in political debates, women focus more on issues than males. In contrast, if females are debate novices, issue-based attacks are made as often as by inexperienced men.

In sum, our findings nicely match those results indicating that males and females obviously follow the same rules when it comes to negative campaigning (*see* e.g. Bystrom 2004; Bystrom and Kaid 2002): Our results point more in the direction that female candidates show as tough a behaviour as male candidates. However, there is no indication that women 'out-tough' their male colleagues. Conversely, there is not much evidence that women try to fulfill sex-role expectations and act more moderately in televised debate than men. In addition to the assumption that female candidates feel the urge to show the same kind of behaviour as their male colleagues do, we want to add another argument borrowed from organisational psychology. Eagly and Johnson (1990: 234) argue that male as well as female 'managers become socialized into their roles in early stages of their experience in an organization'. In addition, they 'have presumably been selected by organizations ... according to the same set of organizationally relevant criteria' (Eagly and Johnson 1990: 234). Therefore, 'leaders who occupy the *same organizational role* should differ very little' (Eagly and Johnson 1990: 234). This argument can be utilised for politics: Politicians usually start their career as a simple party member. To become a professional politician, candidates have to fulfill intra-party selection criteria at different levels. In general, those formal criteria do not differ for men and women. As a result, managers as well as top candidates 'of both sexes are presumably more concerned about managing effectively than about representing sex-differentiated features of social gender roles' (Eagly and Johnson 1990: 234). Hence, for candidates running for office as a chancellor, a prime minister, or a president the impact of gender on campaign style should be much smaller than the effect of roles determined by party organisations or the political system (e.g. incumbency).

We acknowledge that this study has several limitations. First, although the data covers all German televised debates, the number of cases is still small. Second, the presented results should be taken as the beginning rather than as the end of a more detailed analysis. In particular, this study provides no information concerning the topics that the candidates put on the agenda when their attacks focus on issues. In addition, it is desirable to obtain more detailed information about gender differences in character-based attacks: Which aspects are focused on in trait-based attacks? Third, this data provides insights into the behaviour of candidates in the context of the most important single campaign event in the run-up to German elections. Of course, candidates present many more campaign messages, and it would be interesting to compare their campaign communication for different channels. Finally, there is strong need for comparative research in order to find out if the results presented here can be considered typical or unusual. We hope that this study can serve as a springboard for further research on German elections but also for comparing negative campaign messages across nations.

Of course, our results should not be understood as support for the view that a fair representation of women in politics is not necessary because there are great similarities between the sexes in reference to negative campaigning. However, the findings suggest that the idealistic notion that more women in politics will automatically lead to a different if not better political discourse is by far unrealistic.

Chapter Nine

Going Negative in Direct-Democratic Campaigns

Laurent Bernhard

This chapter considers the political actors' use of negative campaigning in the context of direct-democratic campaigns. Such contests are characterised by three major features (Bernhard 2012). First, direct-democratic campaigns are typically waged in narrow scope, since they refer to issue-specific propositions. Compared to elections, campaign messages thus address above all 'issues' as opposed to 'images' of politicians (*see* Chapter Two by Benoit in this volume). Second, direct-democratic campaigns give rise to the confrontation of two opposing camps. This is attributable to the bipolar format of direct-democratic votes – propositions can in principle either be accepted or rejected. While supporters advocate for a change of the status quo, opponents wish to retain it. Third, direct-democratic campaigns tend to attract a large number of organisations, stemming from different backgrounds. Besides state actors and political parties, various economic interest groups (such as business associations and labour unions) as well as citizen interest groups (e.g. social movement organisations) usually go public. Participating in direct-democratic campaigns can be conceived of as the most appropriate means by which these political actors can exert an impact on the outcome of ballot propositions.

Once involved in a given campaign, a crucial decision for any political actor refers to the general tone to be adopted (Damore 2002). From a theoretical point of view, the main contribution of this chapter pertains to an encompassing message typology, which draws the distinction between the general campaign tone (i.e. positive or negative) and three forms of appeals – arguments, emotions, and heuristics. When reviewing the academic literature, it becomes obvious that negative campaigning is often understood in rather narrow terms. More specifically, most analyses have limited their considerations to attacks directed at political opponents. By contrast, this analysis proposes to take into account various elements of negative campaigning. In order to explain the use of this broad notion of negative campaigning, I will focus on two main hypotheses. Borrowing from Riker's theory of rhetoric, I will first argue that opponents (i.e. political actors who defend the status quo) are more likely to adopt a negative campaign approach than supporters (i.e. political actors who campaign for the passage of ballot propositions). Besides the structural position, the reliance on negative campaigning is expected to depend on the actors' competitive standing in a given campaign. Following game-theoretical models used in electoral studies (Skaperdas and Grofman 1995), trailing organisations as well as those that are involved in a competitive race are hypothesised to resort to more negative communication than frontrunners. To test this second hypothesis, I will for the first time systematically employ poll data about the competitive standing at the outset of direct-democratic campaigns.

As far as methodology is concerned, this contribution breaks new ground by making use of data obtained in the framework of interviews conducted with campaign managers. This stands in sharp contrast to the overwhelming majority of systematic empirical studies that rely on content analyses. I do not call into question the pertinence of this prevalent technique when it comes to measuring negative campaigning. However, interview data have the potential to complement studies based on content analysis by grasping the campaigners' general intentions to go negative. Hence, one major purpose of this analysis is to cross-check cumulative findings on negative campaigning that has been generated by extensive work of coding in the field of direct-democracy.

The empirical analysis deals with Switzerland. The importance of this context is all too evident, given that the Swiss case is considered the world's champion par excellence of direct-democracy (Schmitter and Trechsel 2004: 81). Indeed, more than 500 votes have taken place there since the founding of the Federal State in 1848 solely at the national level. Despite the worldwide rise in the use of referendums and initiatives in the last few decades (LeDuc 2003), Switzerland still stands alone in extensively employing these instruments (Gallagher and Uleri 1996). Hence, scholars interested in the practice of direct-legislation are well advised to pay attention to Switzerland's exhaustive experience in this regard. The selected cases revolve around eight salient votes that have taken place at the federal level from 2007 to 2013. As will be developed in the empirical part of this contribution, the structural position hypothesis will be supported. The empirical evidence for the competitive standing hypothesis, for its part, will prove to be less straightforward but nevertheless promising.

State of the art

There are only few empirical contributions dealing with the balance between positive and negative messages in the framework of direct-democratic campaigns. To my knowledge, the only comparative analyses have been conducted in the context of Switzerland so far. The most encompassing results stem from the examination of Nai (2013, 2014), which includes the entirety of seventy-five ballot propositions that occurred on the Swiss federal level between 1999 and 2005. Using press advertisement data, the study reports significant differences between the two opposing camps. The share of advertisements containing at least one explicit personal attack directed at the adversaries turns out to be more than twice as high for opponents (20 per cent) than for supporters (8 per cent). In other words, defenders of the status quo are much more likely to make use of negative campaigning. Besides this basic pattern, the analysis of Nai (2013, 2014b) suggests that the extent of personal attacks varies according to policy domains. More specifically, welfare state issues as well as security and foreign policies distinguish themselves by extraordinary high levels of negative campaigning.

In his detailed analysis of arguments political actors published in press advertisements in the framework of four campaigns, Marquis (2006) precisely focused on votes pertaining to the domain of Swiss foreign policy. The author detects the same finding as Nai (2013, 2014b). The defenders of the status quo are found to resort more to negative arguments (20 per cent) than the campaigners of the reform side (15 per cent), thus confirming that the structural positioning plays a major role when it comes to explaining the use of negative campaigning in direct-democratic campaigns.

Based on a content analysis of campaign documents (such as press releases and public statements) produced by those political organisations having participated in three federal direct-democratic campaigns from 2006 to 2008, the work of Hänggli (2010: 75) concludes that political actors only rarely make use of personal attacks. The campaigns are generally dominated by substantial aspects, i.e. by arguments in favour or against the propositions at stake. The biggest share of attacks is observable in the case of a ballot proposition dealing with the issue of naturalisations organised in 2008. It is noteworthy that, against conventional wisdom, the 'pro side' relied more on attacks than the defenders of the status quo in this particular campaign. In addition, this case reveals some notable differences in terms of actor types. Hänggli (2010) shows that interest groups on the 'no side' and political parties on the 'yes side' adopted a particularly offensive campaign approach.

Message typology

In the following section, I shall introduce an encompassing campaign messages typology. Political messages can either be positive or negative in nature. In either case, they can be expressed in three forms: arguments, emotions and endorsements (Tellis 2004). Arguments are considered the most elaborated option, followed by emotions and endorsements. The combination of the general direction of campaign messages and their degree of elaboration leads to the classification of messages presented in Table 9.1.

As is well known from socio-psychological theories, messages are either mediated by detailed processing of arguments, or by classical conditioning and mere exposure. Dual-process theories integrate both theories of systematic

Table 9.1: Classification of messages

General direction	Degree of elaboration		
	Arguments	**Emotions**	**Heuristics (actor-centred)**
Positive	Strength of one's arguments	Excitement/ enthusiasm	Endorsing
Negative	Weakness of opponents' arguments	Anxiety/stress/fear	Stigmatising/ discrediting/

processing and persuasion processes that are not based on systematic analysis of message arguments (Eagly and Chaiken 1993). Kriesi (2005) has shown that arguments provide Swiss voters with the main rationale when making up their minds in direct-democratic votes. Positive arguments refer to the strength of the own messages. Similarly, negative campaigning is concerned with putting emphasis on the weakness of the messages owned by the adversaries. The second possibility pertains to emotional appeals. Positive emotions refer to excitement or enthusiasm, while negative ones may evoke anxiety, stress, or fear. Until recently, the roles of emotions have been somewhat neglected in political science. Appeals to positive emotions seem to be particularly instrumental for the mobilisation of one's own constituency. They increase the interest in the campaign and the willingness to vote (Brader 2005). Appeals to negative emotions, by contrast, are well suited to destabilise the opponents' constituencies, as they signal people a need for closer scrutiny of the issue at stake (Marcus *et al.* 2000). Alternatively, campaigners may rely on actor-related heuristic strategies. Indeed, actor-centred heuristics such as following the recommendation issued by the government or the preferred party have proven to be influential with respect to the decision-formation process of citizens in Swiss direct-democratic votes (Kriesi 2005). Rather than studying the proposals in detail, voters often rely on signals from well-known opinion-formers. Given the importance of the source's credibility, campaigners might rely on actor-related heuristic strategies. Highlighting endorsements by prominent or prestigious actors are examples of positive heuristic appeals. Negative appeals include the discrediting the adversary or simply signalling unpopular actors who are aligned on the opponents' side.

Hypotheses

Structural positioning

By making reference to theories of decision making under risk, Riker (1996) argues that negative campaigning is pervasive in policy debates. Negative appeals are achieved by pointing out the danger implicit in the issue positions defended by opponents, while not emphasising the advantages of the campaigner's own programme. Riker's idea is that an important element of campaigning consists of exploiting voters' attitudes toward risk. Campaigners tend to emphasise dangers rather than advantages because they believe some voters to be extremely risk averse. The reformers offer an alternative to the status quo that is not completely understood and is vulnerable, therefore, to deliberate distortion by the defenders of the status quo. Although the reformers' campaign messages may be mostly negative, it has also to contain some positive elements. Thus, my hypothesis states that actors belonging to the reform camp less heavily rely on negative campaigning. Supporters of ballot propositions have, on the one hand, to point out the deficiencies of the current situation, and, on the other hand, to point out that the reform proposal constitutes an opportunity to do something about these deficiencies and that the proposed reforms will be effective. These actors find themselves in a similar situation as a protest movement that has to provoke a change in consciousness in its constituency. As Piven and Cloward (1977: 3f) argue, such a change in consciousness involves a loss of legitimacy of the status quo, a sense that change is necessary, as well as a sense of efficacy, i.e. a sense that one can do something about the unsatisfactory state of affairs. Accordingly, reformers typically use the *rhetoric of change* (Gamson and Meyer 1996), which also makes three types of arguments: they point out the urgency of reform (i.e. it attacks the deficiencies of the current situation), the opportunity for 'agency' (i.e. the window of opportunity), and the 'new possibilities' (i.e. the available solution). Following Riker (1996), I argue that elites are always able to 'go negative' by appealing to the disastrous consequences in the case of a victory of the other side. However, the magnitude of these attacks might depend on the actors' position in the campaign. Opponents (i.e. defenders of the status quo) have typically nothing to defend positively. The status quo is visible to all and not subject to transformation by rhetorical reinterpretation. They may thus devote almost all of their effort to negative arguments against the reform. To that end, they may use what Hirschman (1991) has called the *rhetoric of reaction*, which makes three types of negative arguments against reform: it points out the danger ('jeopardy'), futility and even perversity of the reform. According to this line of reasoning, it does not make a difference whether the defenders of the status quo are ideologically placed on the right or on the left. The asymmetrical incentives posed by the setting of the campaign induce all opponents to rely on a negative rhetorical strategy. This leads me to the first hypothesis:

H1: Opponents will employ a more negative campaign tone than supporters.

Following the logic of H1, I expect the defenders of the status quo to adopt a more negative orientation with respect to each of the three types of campaign messages. First, opponents should put more emphasis on the weakness of their opponents' arguments compared to the strength of their own arguments. Second, they are expected to rely more on negative emotions relative to positive ones. Third, opponents will be more likely to invoke the political organisations positioned on the opposite side as opposed to those from the same side.

Competitive standing

According to the game theoretical model of Skaperdas and Grofman (1995), the extent to which political actors rely on negative campaigning depends on their competitive standing in a given campaign. Those who lag behind in the 'horse race' are expected to adopt a more negative campaign tone than frontrunners. The rationale behind this hypothesis is based on risk considerations. Trailing actors have less to lose and should therefore be more willing to take the risky choice to engage in negative campaigning in order to overcome their initial handicap. By contrast, frontrunners should be more reluctant to do so. In light of a likely victory, these actors may consider extensive use of negative rhetoric an unnecessary risk. The literature on competitive positioning also states that political actors are more inclined to resort to negative campaigning as the race becomes closer (Skaperdas and Grofman 1995, Lau and Pomper 2004). In competitive campaigns, winning over undecided voters is of major importance. To persuade this segment of the population, the use of negative rhetoric can be regarded as an effective means to secure victory. It is well known from psychological research that people tend to be much more attentive to campaigns and to take into account alternative types of information when being exposed to negative messages (*see* Kahn and Kenney 1999b: 182f). With the hope of calling attention to pivotal voters, campaigners on either side are expected to adopt a negative orientation in competitive settings. Beyond this rather sophisticated line of reasoning, the political actors' more pronounced reliance on negative appeals can simply be attributed to decreasing degrees of risk aversion, which are induced by the conditions of a close race. As a consequence, campaign actors involved in competitive races will be generally more willing to bear the risk of resorting to increased amounts of negative campaigning (Lau and Pomper 2001), since negative campaigning can be considered a promising, but risky strategy. Based on these theoretical considerations, I formulate the second hypothesis as follows:

H2: Trailing actors and those involved in a competitive campaign are more likely to rely on negative campaigning than frontrunners.

In addition, I will apply H2 to arguments, emotions, and actor heuristics. Hänggli (2010) has been able to show that campaigners are more likely to address the arguments put forward by the adversarial side the closer a direct-democratic campaign beomes. Political actors tend to engage in so-called 'counterframing strategies' (Hänggli and Kriesi 2010). In line with this finding, the electoral studies conducted by Kahn and Kenney (1999b), Simon (2002), and Kaplan *et al.* (2006) have revealed that expected closeness tend to increase campaign dialogue. More specifically, candidates involved in close races are found to tackle the opponent's policy agenda and issue position more often than in non-competitive settings. A possible explanation for this pattern is that campaigners are obliged to put a lot of effort in to persuade undecided voters in neck-and-neck races. As far as emotions are concerned, psychological research (Marcus *et al.* 2002, Brader 2005) suggests that political actors who lag behind in the 'horse race' face a huge incentive to evoke negative emotions, since anxiety levels have been shown to encourage voters to reconsider their point of views. Frontrunners, for their parts, may prefer running on a positive emotional platform, given that satisfied voters stick to their initial attitudes. With respect to actor heuristics, I will also hypothesise that competiveness fosters a negative campaign tone. Beyond the theoretical considerations about the overall campaign orientation mentioned above, the use of negative actor-related heuristics can be regarded as particularly effective for campaigners. Since this type of message proves to be less sophisticated than arguments (and negative emotions), its use can be considered a cost-effective signal, which can easily be made available to citizens during campaigns.

Case selection, data, and operationalisation

For this examination, I have selected eight campaigns according to the direct-democratic institution and the policy domain in order to obtain a sample sufficiently broad to allow for generalisability (Seawright and Gerring 2008). With respect to direct-democratic institutions, the achievement of maximum variance is straightforward, as initiative and referendums represent the two basic variants in the Swiss context.[1] Regarding the second criteria, I rely on a wide range of policy domains. As is presented in Table 9.2 both a referendum and an initiative pertaining to the domains of immigration, welfare state issues, health policy, and economic liberalism are included into this study.

There is no doubt that these issues belong to the most salient in current Switzerland. Questions related to immigration, health politics and social insurances regularly rank top in the so-called 'barometer of concerns' (*Sorgenbarometer*), a survey published on a yearly basis by Credit Suisse, a Swiss bank. Probably for reasons of issue complexity, this is not the case regarding economic liberalism. However, neoliberal reform projects were high on the agenda of Swiss politics in recent years (Kriesi and Trechsel 2008). Occasionally they have given rise to particularly fierce referendum battles. The two propositions selected regarding immigration represent two typical cases of this policy domain: a referendum launched by the left against the tightening of the asylum law, and an initiative in favour of a more restrictive naturalisation policy launched by the conservative right. With respect to health policy, the cases included in this study are insofar typical for recently initiated reform attempts, as the referendum called for more market competition (constitutional healthcare article), while the initiative aimed at more state intervention (single health insurance). The referendum campaign in the realm of welfare state issues refers to the fifth reform of the disabled insurance

Table 9.2: Overview of the selected campaigns

	Immigration	Health	Welfare state	Economic liberalism
Referendum	Asylum (2013)	Healthcare article (2008)	Disabled insurance (2007)	Corporate tax (2008)
Initiative	Naturalisation (2008)	Unique health insurance (2007)	Old-age pensions (2008)	Right to sue (2008)

1. Initiatives are propositions 'from below', formulated by organisations representing groups of citizens, while referendums refer to propositions 'from above', i.e. legislative acts proposed by the government and adopted by parliament. Initiatives have an agenda-setting function, since they launch public debates on a given issue. Referendums, by contrast, concern legislative acts originating from the government and intervene only after the members of the parliament have taken their decision on the piece of legislation. The referendum therefore constitutes the final hurdle to be taken. Unlike the initiative, the referendum thus offers the possibility to block a reform project (i.e. to defend the status quo).

scheme. As is usually the case in this policy domain, the referendum challenge stemmed from the left. The second campaign envisaged lowering the retirement age in the context of the old-age insurance. The initiative, launched by the trade unions, was the left's sixth unsuccessful attempt in this regard. Finally, the two votes representing the domain of economic liberalism concern domestic liberalisations. The first campaign pertains to fiscal politics as it dealt with a corporate tax reform against which the left forced a referendum. The second campaign is politically unprecedented. The so-called 'right to sue initiative' was targeted at restricting the associations' possibilities to appeal against construction projects that are supposed to damage the environment. The proposition was launched by the Liberals (FDP) who only rarely make use of this instrument.

So far, the comparative studies on negative campaigning conducted in the domain of direct-democracy have relied on content analyses (Hänggli 2010, Marquis 2006, and Nai 2013, 2014b). As opposed to these contributions, the present analysis draws on *ex-ante* interviews that were held with campaign managers. This choice is motivated by the consideration that collecting information about the propensity to engage in negative campaigning at the level of decision-makers may constitute a promising alternative to content-analysing public-oriented campaign documents. The decision to go negative refers to intellectual considerations that are not publically available. As these thoughts are developed behind closed doors, it appears consistent to directly get in touch with those persons who decide on the campaign tone to be adopted. To avoid misunderstandings, I do not pretend that interview data are better suited to grasp the phenomenon of negative campaigning. I rather argue that such data have the potential to effectively complement findings obtained by means of content analysis techniques. More specifically, *ex-ante* interviews present the advantage of capturing the general intentions and plans for actions of campaign managers, whereas the analysis of documents is able to measure the actual use of negative campaigning during campaigns.

In the run-up to the eight votes under scrutiny, campaign managers of those political organisations that took part in the corresponding public debate were contacted by phone and asked to participate in a study that would analyse their campaign involvement. With some minor exceptions, these phone calls resulted in immediate acceptance. In some cases, a second call or formal request was in order. The process of obtaining these interviews was thus neither tedious nor time consuming. Altogether, only two persons refused to participate. The relevant organisations have been selected on the basis of various sources: the parliamentary debates, the campaign for the collection of signatures, voting recommendations, and the press, as well as websites more generally. In addition, cross-referencing was used with the people we interviewed to complete the set of organisations. Given this pragmatic procedure, I feel confident to have included the most important collective actors. To ensure that the responses were as accurate as possible, all respondents were guaranteed complete confidentiality. Overall, 238 respondents were interviewed. On the campaign level, the number of actors varies from twenty-five (disabled insurance) to thirty-four (healthcare article).

In the following, I shall outline the construction of the indicators. To measure the use of negative campaigning, I rely on a question about rhetorical strategies. Campaign managers were presented with a list of six aspects that corresponds to the appeal classification shown in Table 9.1. They were invited to indicate whether they intended to call attention to:

1. the strength of their own arguments;
2. the weakness of their opponents' arguments;
3. positive emotions;
4. negative emotions;
5. those organisations that are aligned on the same side; and
6. those organisations that are aligned on the opponent side.

By subtracting the number of affirmative answers referring to negative aspects (items '1', '3', and '5') from those dealing with positive ones (items '2', '4', and '6'), I obtain an ordinally scaled variable that theoretically ranges from '−3' to '3'. Thus, negative (positive) values delineate priority of negative (positive) messages. Critics may call into question the validity of the items used here by objecting that campaign managers do not necessarily answer truthfully. When it comes to negative campaigning, a bias towards positive campaigning is conceivable, since negativism can be assumed to be socially undesired. However, I need to mention that respondents frequently reported reliance on the negative dimension. While they indicated that they resort more to positivism regarding arguments (93 per cent versus 57 per cent) as well as actor-centred heuristics (48 per cent versus 26 per cent), campaign managers declared that they invoked more negative than positive emotions (32 per cent versus 24 per cent). These answers seem to suggest that campaign managers do not regard negative campaigning as something immoral but rather as a tool, which they use if required.

The first independent variable refers to the camp affiliation. I have created a dummy variable that equals '1' for the opponents of a given ballot proposition (i.e. the actors who wish to retain the status quo). The supporters – that is the political organisations campaigning for a reform – are coded as '0'. With respect to the competitive positioning of the various actors, I rely for the first time on early polling data. The Swiss Broadcasting Corporation (SBC) usually publishes the results of two surveys in the course of direct-democratic campaigns held on the federal level. The first is usually made available to the public around five weeks in front of ballot day, while the second is released about ten days before a given vote takes place. Since I am interested in the standing at the run-up to the campaign, I make use of the first poll results.[2] The first part of

---

2. The only exception concerns the corporate tax reform. In this case, I use the results of the only poll the Swiss Broadcasting Corporation commissioned for this vote. The poll was published two weeks prior to election day. Since another survey, which was taken a month prior to the vote, came to a similar result than the SBC poll (*see* Kriesi 2011), I feel confident to rely on a valid measure for this particular campaign.

Table 9.3 lists the shares of 'yes' and 'no' intentions as well as the proportion of undecided voters. For *referendums*, I consider those campaigns competitive which display a difference between the two opposing camps of ten percentage points at most. As is visible from Table 9.3, none of the referendum campaigns qualify for a close race. The supporters were well ahead in all four cases (asylum law, healthcare article, disabled insurance, and corporate tax reform). Hence, the organisations campaigning on the pro side are regarded as frontrunners, while the opponents qualify for trailing actors. As far as *initiatives* are concerned, it is well established that such campaigns often give rise to marked opinion reversals, which usually work at the disadvantage of the reform camp (Magleby 1984). Since vote intentions in favour of the supporters' positions tend to erode, supporters need a considerable advance at the beginning of a campaign in order to have realistic prospects of achieving victory. For this reason, I classify supporters as frontrunners if they enjoy an advantage of more than 20 per cent over their opponents. Lower advances are considered competitive races. Finally, supporters (opponents) are defined as trailing actors (frontrunners) if both sides are neck-and-neck or if the opponents enjoy an advantage from the beginning. Applied to the four initiative cases at hand, both the votes on naturalisation and the right to sue legislation qualify for a competitive campaign. The supporters (opponents) of the old-age pension proposition are considered frontrunners (trailing actors), while the opposite status applies to the political organisations having taken part in the campaign about the introduction of a single health insurance. Apart from these objective measures, I include a subjective indicator of competitiveness, which is based on each campaign manager's estimation of the various outcomes. Respondents were asked to predict the share of 'yes votes'. This information enables me to calculate the following measure for the expected closeness: 50– (percentage of yes votes −50).

Table 9.3: Standing in the race according to polling results by campaign

	Yes share	No share	Undecided	Supporters	Opponents
Asylum (ref.)	0.48	0.29	0.23	frontrunner	trailing
Naturalisation (i.)	0.48	0.37	0.15	competitive campaign	
Healthcare article (ref.)	0.62	0.18	0.20	frontrunner	trailing
Single health insurance (i.)	0.36	0.46	0.18	trailing	frontrunner
Disabled insurance (ref.)	0.43	0.32	0.25	frontrunner	trailing
Old-age pensions (i.)	0.52	0.30	0.18	frontrunner	trailing
Corporate tax (ref.)	0.46	0.31	0.23	frontrunner	trailing
Right to sue (i.)	0.42	0.40	0.18	competitive campaign	

Source: Swiss Broadcasting Corporation
Ref: referendum, i: initiative

The multivariate analysis also controls for a series of additional explanatory variables on both the actor-related and the contextual level. The literature on negative campaigning suggests that ideological orientations influence the decision to go negative (Lau and Pomper 2004). In this analysis, I account for the tripolar structure available in European countries (Kriesi *et al.* 2012) by using dummies for the left, the conservative right, and the moderate right. The assignment of the political organisations to these three groups is based on a self-reported left-right scale, which reaches from '0' (completely right) to '10' (completely left). The indicator for actors from the left takes the value of '1' for those organisations which marked values higher than '6'. Those organisations whose representatives opted for a location between '3' and '5' are considered belonging to the moderate right, while those who positioned their organisations below the threshold of '2' enter the category of conservative right actors. Furthermore, I control for actor types by drawing the distinction between political parties, economic interest groups, citizen groups, *ad hoc* committees, and state actors.

As far as the contextual level is concerned, I decided to include three types of control variables. First, I account for the direct-democratic institution by separating initiatives from referendums. Second, dummy variables for each policy domain (welfare state issues, health, economic liberalism, and immigration) are included. Finally, the decision to go negative may be driven by the actor configuration of a given campaign. The incentive to engage in negative campaigning may decrease the more organisations are positioned on the same camp relative to the opposing side. My measure for coalition size is obtained by dividing, for each campaign, the number of organisations I interviewed in the framework of my analysis on either side by the total number of selected actors.

Empirical analysis

As expected, supporters and opponents tend to sharply differ in their propensity to resort to negative campaigning. It appears that the reform camp exhibits a positive mean score in all eight campaign contexts. In other words, the 'pro side' generally seems to be reluctant to rely on negative campaigning. The average of the campaign tone indicator ranges from 0.23 (single health insurance) to 2.05 (old-age pensions). By contrast, the opponents put much more emphasis on negative aspects. In five campaigns, the mean values even turns out to be negative, which means that the political actors who stick to the status quo report to make more use of negative elements than positive ones. Positive average scores are obtained for the opponents of the old-age pension propositions and the two cases on immigration (i.e. asylum and naturalisation). The supporters nevertheless display higher average scores than the opponents in these three cases. In other words, the difference in campaign tone between pro and contra proves to be positive in all instances. As is visible from Table 9.4, the highest discrepancy between the two opposing camps is observable for the corporate tax reform (2.40), followed by the proposal on old-age pensions (2.13), while the lowest score comes about regarding the vote on naturalisations (0.36). When taking a closer look at Table 9.4, it becomes obvious that the fact that

Table 9.4: Difference in campaign tone between supporters and opponents by campaign and message type

	Overall	Arguments	Emotions	Heuristics
Corporate tax	2.40	0.55	1.19	0.67
Old-age pension	2.13	0.43	0.93	0.77
Healthcare article	1.82	0.68	0.92	0.22
Disabled insurance	1.36	0.88	0.10	0.39
Right to sue	1.01	0.38	0.52	0.11
Asylum law	1.00	0.72	−0.06	0.33
Single health insurance	0.87	0.38	0.58	−0.09
Naturalisation	0.36	0.43	−0.42	0.34

the disparity between pro and con turned out to be least pronounced in the latter campaign is primarily due to a counterintuitive pattern with respect to emotional messages. Indeed, the supporters of the naturalisation case went to a large extent more negative than the opponents. In the framework of the interviews, campaign managers of the reform camp reported their intention to evoke negative emotions. They were obsessed with pandering to their base by highlighting that Switzerland was subject to 'mass naturalisations'. This strategy was exemplified by campaign advertisements and posters that showed dark-skinned hands trying to get the red Swiss passport.

With respect to the second hypothesis, average scores tend to support the view that the competitive standing in the race influences the use of negative campaigning. When looking at all 238 political organisations included for this analysis, frontrunners are found to generally adopt a decisively positive campaign tone (mean of 1.30). This is in line with my theoretical expectations. By contrast, trailing actors seem to rely much more on negative campaigning (−0.11), while organisations involved in competitive races are located in between (0.39).

In order to test my hypotheses, I now turn to the multivariate analysis. Table 9.5 presents the results of four ordered probit models explaining the political organisations' use of negative campaigning. The first model refers to the overall balance indicator, while the three following ones separately look at the three message types (i.e. arguments, emotions, and actor-centred heuristics). For intuitional purposes, I decided to inverse the algebraic sign of the dependent variables. Thus, positive (negative) coefficients imply increasing (decreasing) effects on the use of negative campaigning. With respect to the structural positioning hypothesis (H1), the findings confirm the impression gained from the descriptive analysis. The four models show that opponents excel in terms of negative campaigning. In all cases, the positive association is statistically significant at least at the 0.1 per cent error level. This result lends support to my first hypothesis, which states that opponents tend to be more likely to resort to a negative campaign tone than supporters. Let us now consider the second hypothesis. The analysis reveals that trailing actors are generally not more likely to rely on negative campaigning than frontrunners. This result disconfirms the first part of the competitive standing hypothesis. However, campaigners who lag behind in the horse race tend to increase their level of negativity when it comes to actor-centred heuristics. Moreover, the first model of Table 9.5 lends support to the second part of the second hypothesis. Accordingly, political actors involved in close races tend to pursue a more negative general campaign approach than frontrunners. Yet, a closer look at the various message types reveals that this general pattern is limited to the evocation of emotions (third model). In addition, subjective considerations of competiveness seem to be of importance regarding the campaign tone political organisations adopt in direct-democratic campaigns. The alternative measure 'expected closeness' is positively associated with the extent of negative campaigning. Hence, the closer the political actors perceive the outcome of a given race the higher their propensity to engage in negative campaigning. This pattern applies to the encompassing indicator as well as to arguments and heuristics.

I now turn to the results of the control variables. Among the actor-specific indicators, the most consistent finding pertains to the ideological orientation. The multivariate analysis reports significant effects for collective actors from the conservative right. These organisations are more likely to rely on negativity than those belonging to the moderate right (which serves as reference category here). A more detailed analysis of campaign messages shows that the conservative right distinguishes itself from the remaining ideological camps only by a marked negative approach when it comes to emotional appeals. As far as actor types are concerned, solely one coefficient reaches statistical significance. According to the second model, citizen groups are more likely to pursue a negative approach when it comes to arguments than state actors. Regarding the contextual level, two main findings emerge from Table 9.5. First, campaigns on health politics seem to be characterised by an extraordinary high level of negativity. Indeed, the campaigns on the three remaining domains (immigration, welfare state issues, and economic liberalism) significantly display lower levels of negative campaigning. This result may be due to the fact that the healthcare domain is characterised by the participation of a multitude of actors. Apart from the 'usual suspects', (i.e. the federal authorities, parties, and economic peak associations), health insurances, the pharmaceutical industry, and numerous service providers (doctors, pharmacists, hospitals, nursing staff and so forth) usually get involved. These issue-specific players often defend heterogeneous and diverging interests. As a result, negative campaigning may be very prevalent during direct-democratic campaigns. Second, coalition size seems to matter. An increasing number of allies tend to prevent political actors from adopting a negative campaign tone. Put differently, isolation seems to favour the use of negative campaigning. This holds true for the overall indicator as well as for actor-centred heuristics. Finally, the estimation models establish that the direct-democratic institution does not systematically affect the campaign tone.

Table 9.5: Ordered probit regression models explaining the use of negative campaigning

	Overall (Model I)	Arguments (Model II)	Emotions (Model III)	Heuristics (Model IV)
Opponents	1.586***	1.150***	1.312***	0.771**
	(6.88)	(4.47)	(5.27)	(3.09)
Trailing	0.370	0.245	0.137	0.588*
	(1.59)	(0.90)	(0.54)	(2.24)
Competitive race	0.707*	0.300	1.131**	0.513
	(2.15)	(−0.77)	(3.10)	(1.37)
Expected closeness	0.045***	0.044**	0.015	0.037*
	(3.39)	(2.82)	(1.01)	(2.43)
Conservative right	0.671*	0.454	0.610*	0.404
	(2.56)	(1.44)	(2.07)	(1.37)
Left	0.048	0.007	0.064	0.021
	(0.28)	(0.04)	(0.33)	(0.11)
Parties	−0.031	0.553	−0.402	−0.085
	(−0.10)	(1.42)	(−1.21)	(−0.24)
Economic interest groups	0.185	0.658	−0.190	−0.022
	(0.60)	(1.67)	(−0.56)	(−0.06)
Citizen groups	0.215	0.819*	−0.120	−0.202
	(0.68)	(2.05)	(−0.35)	(−0.56)
Committees	0.323	0.804	0.021	−0.026
	(0.68)	(1.40)	(0.04)	(−0.05)
Initiatives	0.085	0.459	−0.428	0.324
	(0.41)	(1.76)	(−1.83)	(1.34)

Table 9.5 (*continued*)

	Overall (Model I)	Arguments (Model II)	Emotions (Model III)	Heuristics (Model IV)
Immigration	−1.124*** (−4.23)	−0.104 (−0.33)	−0.825** (−2.76)	−1.215*** (−4.13)
Welfare state issues	−0.496* (−2.37)	−0.234 (−0.95)	−0.967*** (−3.98)	0.056 (0.24)
Economic liberalism	−0.546* (−2.16)	0.180 (0.58)	−0.434 (−1.51)	−0.730** (−2.60)
Coalition size	−1.338* (−2.16)	0.794 (1.03)	−0.967 (−1.37)	−2.053** (−3.00)
Cut 1	−1.328** (−2.74)	2.148*** (3.33)	−0.398 (−0.74)	−1.744*** (−3.35)
Cut 2	−0.359 (−0.76)	4.252*** (6.25)	1.704** (3.08)	−0.109 (−0.21)
Cut 3	0.444 (0.95)			
Cut 4	1.551** (3.23)			
Cut 5	2.737*** (5.48)			
Cut 6	3.918*** (6.15)			
N	230	230	230	230
Pseudo R^2	0.167	0.190	0.160	0.159

* p<0.05, ** p<0.01, *** p<0.001
Z-scores in parentheses
Reference categories: frontrunner (competitive status), moderate right (ideological camp), state actors (actor types), and health politics (policy domain)

Conclusion

This contribution has been motivated by the fact that empirical studies on negative campaigning have only rarely focused on direct-democratic campaigns so far. I have examined the political actors' usage of negative communication by reverting to a broad conceptualisation of campaign messages. To that end, I have proposed a classification that draws the distinction between arguments, emotions, and actor heuristics, all of which can be expressed in positive or negative ways. As opposed to the empirical studies in the field, the present examination has relied on first-hand accounts. The data were gathered from interviews held with representatives of the most important political organisations involved in eight direct-democratic campaigns having taken place in Switzerland between 2007 and 2013. This approach has allowed me to make use of an alternative indicator of negative campaigning, which I have used in order to cross-check existing empirical evidence.

Two key findings emerge from the empirical analysis. First, opponents of ballot propositions (i.e. the defenders of the status quo) have been shown to outclass their rivals in terms of negative campaigning. This basic pattern holds true both for the general direction as well as for each of the three components of the message classification used here (arguments, emotions, and actor heuristics). This finding proves to be consistent with the empirical literature on negative campaigning in the framework of direct-democratic campaigns, which is based on content analyses. Thus, the structural position hypothesis seems to hold water at least in the Swiss context. As has been outlined in the theoretical section, the supporters of any ballot proposition face the burden of proof. Thus, these actors usually feel obliged to frequently highlight positive messages. By contrast, opponents do not have anything to defend positively. Consequently, the 'con side' heavily engages in negative campaigning to obtain a 'no majority'. Second, I have established that the propensity to go negative increases in competitive contexts. The fact that the *perception* of the competitiveness plays a crucial role when it comes to explain the decision to resort to negative campaigning, supports my approach to directly collect the data at the level of the campaign decision-makers who are in charge of elaborating the campaign strategies.

I am fully aware that this study has several limitations. Most obviously, this article has only dealt with eight campaign contexts. This small number gives rise to some cause for discomfort about the generalisability of the results presented here. It has to be kept in mind that the case selection turns out to be somewhat unbalanced, as I included six ballot propositions pertaining to the economic dimension, while only two refer to the cultural dimension (asylum law and naturalisation initiative). Another compelling criticism relates to the lack of interaction and dynamics. As this analysis focuses on the campaigners' general intentions, it is silent about their relationship with opponents during the whole campaign period. Yet, the literature on negative campaigning suggests that attacks are more likely when the election day approaches (Damore 2002, Marquis 2006) and that the rebuttal calculus matters a lot, since political actors are likely to respond negatively once they have been attacked (Damore 2002; Lau and Rovner 2009). Finally, this contribution did not address the fact that the use of negative campaigning also depends on the specific context in which messages are divulged. Recently, some empirical contributions on communication have found that the extent of negative campaigning strongly varies according to the communication channels political actors employ (Elmelund-Præstekær 2010; Walter and Vliegenthart 2010).

Chapter Ten

When Do Parties Attack their Competitors? Negative Campaigning in Austria, 2002–08

Martin Dolezal, Laurenz Ennser-Jedenastik and Wolfgang C. Müller

Which factors influence political parties' campaign strategies and, in particular, the extent, the targets, and the timing of negative campaigning? This chapter addresses these important research questions by focusing on Austria, a European parliamentary democracy with a multiparty system that has not yet figured prominently in this emerging field of research. Despite its being known for consensus politics, Austria has a considerable history of negative campaigning *avant la lettre*, especially in elections of the late 1940s, 1950s, and 1960s. These years gave birth to what became a typical feature of Austrian politics: the predominance of grand coalition government of the conservative People's Party (ÖVP) and the Social Democrats (SPÖ). A more recent development, by contrast, is the exceptional strength of the populist radical right. The consequences of both phenomena for negative campaigning have hardly been studied so far.

We define 'negative campaigning' as any attacks on political opponents, whether on policy or on character grounds. Our approach thus follows a 'directional' not an 'evaluative concept' of negative campaigning because it is based on the relation between an attacker and a target (Walter and van der Brug 2013: 369). It is also very similar to the one in Benoit's functional theory of political campaign discourse as presented in Chapter Two (this volume). Following the standard approach in the literature, we do not include the fairness or unfairness of attacks in our definition. Such an assessment would be too difficult as even distinguishing personal attacks from attacks on substance can be challenging if individual politicians are closely tied to particular policies. Rather than assessments by researchers, voters' perceptions of fairness and unfairness might be relevant and can, in principle, be measured. Unfortunately, we only have limited information on their views of parties' campaigns.

In addition to analysing a new country case we also present a new method for measuring negative campaigning based on a relational content analysis of party press releases. Carried out as part of the recently established *Austrian National Election Study* (AUTNES),[1] our data not only allow for applying standard approaches of research into negative campaigning such as identifying explanatory

---

1.   The authors gratefully acknowledge funding from the Austrian Science Fund (FWF), grant S 10903-G11. For details on this research project *see* http://www.autnes.at.

factors like the government–opposition divide. They also allow for exploring the dynamics of this strategy over the course of a campaign as we can record party behaviour on a daily basis.

The chapter proceeds as follows: In the next section we introduce the Austrian case and highlight what its analysis can contribute to the comparative study of campaigning and negative campaigning in particular. Next we present our research questions and several hypotheses. These include ones from the literature already tested in a few applications to European multiparty systems and ones that we test for the first time in such an environment. We then introduce our source material and explain how we collected our data. Then we present our results based on three recent national elections: 2002, 2006, and 2008.

The Austrian case in comparative perspective

Research on negative campaigning so far has primarily dealt with elections in the United States (US). Only recently have researchers broadened their focus to include several European countries (*see* the overview in Chapter Six in this volume). Two typical features of Austrian politics are of particular importance when analysing negative campaigning: the predominance of grand coalition government and the strength of the populist radical right.

Like most other European democracies Austria is a typical example of multiparty politics with a proportional electoral system and coalition government. Except for the period from 1966–83 when first the ÖVP (until 1970) and then the SPÖ managed to build single-party majority cabinets, all governments since 1945 have been coalitions. What makes the Austrian case specific, however, is the predominance of 'grand coalition' government by these two parties (Müller 2000). This type of government was not an exception reserved for reconstruction after World War II or for times of crisis (Mitchell and Nyblade 2008: 220), it rather became the rule: All but three coalitions (1983–87, 2000–03, and 2003–07) have been 'grand coalitions'. In sum, they cover almost two thirds of Austria's post-war history. During this long period, however, the two major parties have lost much of their support. Until the early 1980s the ÖVP and SPÖ controlled a vast combined majority of about 95 per cent of the parliamentary seats. Since then they have been facing more effective competition from both the left (mainly the Greens) and the populist radical right. This has resulted in a considerable reduction of the combined SPÖ-ÖVP vote and seat shares also in our period of observation. In 2002 both parties benefited from a crisis of the populist radical right and managed to temporarily increase their seat share again to 80.9 per cent. Since then, their combined share fell to 73.2 per cent in 2006 and to 59.0 per cent in 2008. Most recently, in 2013, they barely managed to win a majority with their seats combined (Dolezal and Zeglovits 2014).

Still, the main line of conflict and the contest for government leadership have remained between the two parties. Both have even experienced that they can do better in elections if they manage to stylise the voters' choice as one between their competing policy and leadership offers. The 'classic' example for such a strategy was the 1995 election following conflictual government termination over stark policy differences only one year after cabinet inauguration (Müller 1996). In 2008 internal conflicts again led to early elections, but this time without gains for the major parties (Luther 2009; Müller 2009).

Since the 1980s, the second characteristic feature of Austrian politics has been the strength of the populist radical right. Contrary to many other European countries its success is not restricted to single elections and it also has government experience which is still exceptional for this party family (Mudde 2013). While research on negative campaigning so far has rarely dealt with differences based on party ideology, the populist radical right should be a 'usual suspect' when looking for parties that follow such a strategy. Populism is not only a political style but also an 'ideology that considers society to be ultimately separated into two homogeneous and antagonistic groups, "the pure people" versus "the corrupt elite"' (Mudde 2007: 23). Attacks on representatives of the established parties should therefore be a core feature of their campaigns. Though the Austrian Freedom Party (FPÖ) – including a predecessor – has been represented in parliament since 1949, it has traditionally defined itself as belonging to the 'pure people'. Since the mid-1980s when Jörg Haider became party leader, the FPÖ managed to transform itself from a small national-liberal party into one of the most successful populist radical right parties in Europe (Luther 2011). In 1999 the FPÖ even gained a few hundred votes more than the ÖVP and subsequently accepted the role of junior partner in a government led by the ÖVP. This right-wing coalition not only provoked unprecedented waves of protest in Austria and diplomatic sanctions by many European governments. It also led to conflict within the FPÖ that struggled to adapt to its new role (Heinisch 2003). Early elections called by the ÖVP in 2002 resulted in a historic loss for the FPÖ (−16.9 per cent) and equally historic gains for the ÖVP (+15.4 per cent). Nevertheless, they renewed their coalition but in 2005 conflict within the FPÖ resulted in the splitting-off of the BZÖ (Alliance for the Future of Austria), including almost all leading FPÖ representatives in parliament and government. The ÖVP approved of this development and accepted the BZÖ as its new coalition partner for the rest of the legislative period, while the remainder of the FPÖ joined the opposition and in subsequent elections gradually recovered from this split.

The strength of the populist radical right, which peaked in 2008 with FPÖ and BZÖ taking a combined vote share of 28.2 per cent, is both a cause and a consequence of grand coalitions. Apart from anti-immigration and Eurosceptic stances, criticism levelled against the traditional parties' perpetual rule has been a strong element of its programme. But its strength also complicates coalition building and tends to tie SPÖ and ÖVP to each other. In general, Austrian parties abstain from the formation of pre-electoral coalitions and in recent years they mostly have chosen – contrary to, for example, Germany – not to inform their voters on their coalition preferences. The exception to this is that the parties of the left (SPÖ, Greens) have ruled out to join forces in government with the FPÖ since this party's transformation in the 1980s.

The country's long history of heated and largely negative campaigns followed by coalitions of the main contenders in these battles suggests that parties tend to see the campaign and government formation episodes only loosely connected. However, it is also worth looking at such relationships between different stages of the political process from the other end with a view of how coalitions terminated and elections were called. One might expect that the way a cabinet ends impacts on the subsequent campaign. Two of the three governments in our observation period ended in conflict and early elections: Apart from the first ÖVP-FPÖ coalition, the SPÖ-ÖVP government formed after the 2006 election also met this fate when the ÖVP provoked an early election in 2008. In addition to variation in cabinet terminations, the campaigns from 2002 to 2008 span three different cabinet compositions, thus allowing us to highlight some of the particularities of grand coalitions.

In addition to grand coalition governments and the strength of the populist radical right, another characteristic feature of Austrian politics deserves a mention. Elections are held in a particular media environment characterised by a strong role of the tabloid press and a high concentration of the newspaper market (Seethaler and Melischek 2006: 352–353). While the public broadcasting station ORF still dominates electronic media, private stations increasingly gain in importance. All these developments strengthen the general trend towards more sensationalistic reporting and provide a fertile soil for negative campaign strategies (Vliegenthart et al. 2011). Another particular feature of Austrian campaigns which is highly relevant in this regard is the exceptionally large number of television debates. Their unique format is such that each pair of party leaders goes through a one-hour debate on prime time television. In 2002, when four parties were represented in parliament, there were six such confrontations. After the schism of the populist radical right in 2005 five parties were represented in parliament resulting in no less than ten such debates before the 2006 and 2008 elections.

Despite this specific combination of contextual factors, research on negative campaigning in Austria is still in its infancy. In a long-term perspective covering the elections from 1945 to 1971, Hölzl (1974) described the campaigns until the 1960s as primarily driven by fear. In this period the SPÖ typically warned of a 'total power' of the conservatives and the ÖVP regularly cautioned against a potential drift towards Soviet socialism. In the early 1970s, by contrast, the parties changed towards more pragmatic and fact-driven strategies. Quite similarly, Dachs (1998) distinguished a period of 'aggressive polarization' (1949–66) and a subsequent period of 'pacification and convergence'. Yet this period proved to be only an *intermezzo*. Negative campaigning returned powerfully with increasing conflicts over economic policy between the main parties in the 1980s and the rise of the populist radical right. In the 1990s Plasser et al. (1995: 228–229) reported a general trend towards 'negativism' as a consequence of parties' campaign strategies but also the media's tendency of negative reporting. In all recent elections researchers observed instances of negative campaigning (e.g. Hofer 2007, 2008: 25–26; Lengauer 2012: 133–134; Plasser and Ulram 2007: 23–27; Plasser et al. 2003: 23–24). These pieces of information are valuable for understanding the sum of the recent campaigns but they do not add up to a systematic understanding of the relevance of this strategy and its determinants. We therefore aim to systematically explore for the first time the strategic use of negative campaigning in Austrian elections.

Questions and hypotheses

We analyse negative campaigning in Austrian national elections by asking three questions: Which parties resort to negative campaigning, whom do they target, and when in the campaign do parties 'go negative'? We therefore present three sets of hypotheses, often based on research on the US and its adaptations to multiparty systems (*see* Chapter Six in this volume). The first set is related to characteristics of the attacking party, the second refers to features of the targeted parties, and the third generates expectations about the timing of attacks during the campaign.

Starting with the characteristics of parties that engage in negative campaigning, government status is the factor most often discussed in the literature. Incumbents benefit from several advantages such as higher visibility, better name recognition, and a record from holding public office. Hence, they less often resort to negative campaign strategies than challengers. Transferring this logic to the European context of multiparty competition we formulate the following hypothesis:

H1: Opposition parties engage in negative campaigning more often than governing parties.

Another characteristic of the attacker is related to party family membership. The populist radical right, which is – as discussed above – especially strong in Austria, should be clearly associated with a negative campaign style. Recall that these parties were labelled 'protest parties' when they first emerged on the political scene. A protest party needs something to protest against and someone who is responsible for the alleged grievance. These are most typically the representatives of the political establishment (Betz 1994, Mény and Surel 2001, Mudde 2007). We therefore expect:

H2: Parties of the populist radical right engage in more negative campaigning than parties of all other party families.

The targets of negative campaigning, our second research question, have rarely been explored so far. This is due to the fact that in most presidential and congressional elections in the US, choosing the target of one's attack is rather easy: it is simply the opponent from the other main party. In one of the few analyses of a multiparty system Walter (2014b: 51–59) stresses four explaining factors: party size, ideological proximity, party location, and government status. Building on these results we put forward four hypotheses.

First, we assume government status to be a crucial explanatory factor. Blaming governing parties for their past behaviour should be a common strategy for opposition parties, and attacking governing parties should also lead to more media attention than opposition in-fighting. Walter (2014a) found empirical support for this prediction with regard to the Netherlands. While results obtained for Russian presidential election campaigns are less conclusive (Sigelman and Shiraev 2002) we nonetheless expect parties to primarily target governing parties:

H3: Parties target governing parties more often than opposition parties.

One of the corollaries of the notion that negative campaigning is structured along the government–opposition divide is that parties should not target each other when they share executive office (Elmelund-Præstekær 2008). Coalition partners have a common policy legacy that they cannot credibly distance themselves from. Any attack on the coalition partner would therefore serve to undermine a party's own record in government. Attacks between government parties should therefore be less likely. However, the peculiarity of the Austrian case also lets us expect that this coalition logic applies less for grand coalitions which are usually characterised by major policy disagreements in government and also pit the two parties against each other in competition for nominating the head of government in the next cabinet. Becoming (or remaining) the largest political party is thus only possible at the expense of the coalition partner. Our fourth hypothesis therefore is:

H4: Parties in coalition are more reluctant to attack each other than other party dyads, yet this logic does not apply to grand coalitions.

We also expect that parties are more likely to attack their larger competitors. Attacking large parties should have a greater impact on the election result and should also trigger more media attention irrespective of the parties' government status.

H5: Parties attack large parties more often than small ones.

In addition, ideology might be an important factor in the parties' calculations of whom to attack. Attacking an opponent can follow different logics: On the one hand parties can try to persuade voters to switch to them; on the other hand parties may try to mobilise their own base. When following the first logic parties should target ideologically similar competitors. If, by contrast, their focus is on mobilisation they should target clear opponents. Research on European elections has arrived at different empirical results: While Walter (2014a) concluded that Dutch parties in general attack opponents located nearby, Elmelund-Præstekær (2008) found Danish parties to primarily attack their ideological opponents. Due to the conflicting strategic rationales our hypothesis does not specify the direction of the relationship between ideological distance and targeting behaviour.

H6: The ideological distance between parties influences their selection of targets.

All hypotheses so far introduced refer to factors that vary only across parties and campaigns and therefore cannot explain variation in negativity over the course of a single campaign. To get a grip on how campaigns unfold we derive two additional hypotheses.

First, we assume that highly conflict-prone events will induce negativity in the communications of the parties involved. Within the Austrian context, this specifically refers to the series of televised debates. While these television debates are institutionalised, another type of high profile and high-conflict event has influenced some of the most recent campaigns: extraordinary plenary meetings of parliament. These are not only strategically called by the opposition to increase their visibility by attacking the government, but they can also be consequential in policy terms. For example, the breakdown of coalition discipline in 2008 allowed for the formation of unusual voting alliances across the government–opposition divide.

H7: Parties are more likely to attack each other in the immediate run-up to and aftermath of major political events.

Finally, we conceive of a campaign not only as a period in which parties communicate with the electorate but also as a series of interactions between the parties. We therefore explore how parties react to attacks by their competitors. Research on US presidential elections indicates that candidates' decision to go negative is often the result of prior attacks by the opponent (Damore 2002). In the hypothesis below we assume such a tit-for-tat approach:

H8: Parties that are attacked by other parties launch counterattacks in the short term.

Sources, methods, and data

Our analysis of negative campaigning in Austria is based on a relational content analysis of press releases issued by the parties. While press releases have often been used in research on agenda setting and issue emphasis (e.g. Dunn 2009; Harris *et al.* 2005, 2006; Hopmann *et al.* 2012; Rußmann 2012; Walters *et al.* 1996), only few scholars interested in negative campaigning and related questions so far have referred to this source (Cho and Benoit 2006, Lengauer 2012, Wilson-Kratzer and Benoit 2010). Compared to other kinds of (party) communication press releases are a valuable source to analyse negative campaigning for three reasons:

First, the content of press releases is under the direct control of their sender: the parties or party candidates. This is an obvious but important difference compared to several other sources typically used by scholars of negative campaigning. Some of these sources are not controlled by parties (e.g. media reports) while others grant party representatives varying degrees of freedom in their own communications (e.g. television debates). In addition, the competitive environment of a television debate but also mass media's interest in conflict might result in a strong bias towards negativity.

Second, press releases are issued daily, so that researchers can examine the dynamics of negative campaigning. Most other sources, by contrast, are static and are usually prepared rather at the beginning of or even prior to the actual campaign (advertisements in newspapers, posters, television spots, manifestos). The fact that the publication of every press release is traceable to the exact date (and even time) allows for the precise sequencing of campaign strategies. We therefore can analyse what actually happens during the campaign and how parties respond to relevant stimuli. So far, research on negative campaigning has rarely dealt with the actual dynamics during a campaign (Walter 2012: 69).

Third, press releases are a channel of communication that exists in all countries. Television spots, the main source for studies of negative campaigning in the US, for example, are highly regulated in many European countries. In Austria, which admittedly is an extreme example, they are *de-facto* forbidden. Until 2001 parties were entitled to free airtime in the ORF to 'inform' the viewers of their political programmes. The same law ruled out the purchase of airtime. In 2001 a regulatory change did away with free airtime but maintained the ban to purchase it. Apart from presenting their spots in cinemas and on the internet (e.g. on social platforms such as YouTube), Austrian parties are therefore only allowed to broadcast spots in private television channels. In view of this regulation, television spots do not feature prominently in parties' strategies (Plasser and Plasser 2003: 293). In the 2006 campaign, for example, the parties collectively spent only 5 per cent of their campaign budgets on this type of communication (Lederer 2010: 246).

Coming back to the press releases, critics might object that they are less visible than – for example – television spots, election posters, or television debates. However, from research on agenda-setting in the US we know that press releases strongly influence news coverage (Cho and Benoit 2006: 47–48; Dunn 2009; Flowers *et al.* 2003). With respect to European countries similar results have been obtained for example for Britain (Harris *et al.* 2005, 2006), Denmark (Hopmann *et al.* 2012), and also for Austria (Melischek *et al.* 2010).

Selection and coding

As a first step in the analysis we retrieved all press releases sent by parties and candidates within the final six weeks of each campaign and stored them in a local database. As source we used the website www.ots.at[2] that contains all press releases distributed in Austria and makes them freely available.

In a second step we selected all press releases issued by the parties that included some 'substantial' content. Thus, we manually de-selected all press releases that only informed about upcoming events (e.g. press conferences or

---

2.   OTS stands for *Originaltext-Service*.

campaign rallies)[3] or provided 'technical' information such as links to websites where visitors could download pictures of candidates or audio content. We also de-selected releases when they originated from low-ranking politicians (e.g. local representatives or members of regional assemblies who mostly focus on sub-national issues) as we were only interested in releases which mirror the national parties' official course. However, every candidate for the current election was per se regarded as a relevant actor. Table 10.1 (*see* below) shows the number of press releases finally selected.

All relevant press releases were subsequently manually coded using a relational method of content analysis that links 'subjects' (actors) to 'objects' (issues and/ or other actors). This method goes back to the work of Kleinnijenhuis and his collaborators (e.g. Kleinnijenhuis and Pennings 2001) and was also used by Kriesi and his colleagues (Kriesi *et al.* 2012, Kriesi *et al.* 2006, 2008). Within the *Austrian National Election Study* (AUTNES) we have developed this method further and use it not only to content analyse press releases but also party manifestos (Dolezal *et al.* 2014a), statements by leaders in mass media, and also online campaigning.

Two basic types of statements exist: In an 'actor-issue statement' an actor positions him- or herself towards a political issue. An 'actor-actor statement', by contrast, is a statement of one actor about another actor. A variable called 'predicate' connects the subject and the object and informs about the nature of their relation. We distinguish between positive (1), negative (−1), and neutral (0) relations. A critical statement by the FPÖ about SPÖ leader and Chancellor Werner Faymann is thus translated into the following code: FPÖ / −1 / Werner Faymann (SPÖ).

The coding is based on the title and subtitle of the press releases. Both the actors and the issues were coded with the help of a very comprehensive codebook. As regards the actors we coded all individuals and organisations; the list of issues includes about 650 categories. In the subsequent analyses, however, we exclusively focus on actor-actor statements. Negative campaigning relates to any statement that is critically directed at a political opponent. Our analysis thus covers statements with a negative predicate whenever the object is a competing party, a representative of this party, or the government. Table 10.1 shows the shares of press releases including such negative references in the three campaigns observed.

For each press release we coded up to three object-actors which is why a single press release can include zero, one, two or three attacks. However, if a party attacks two or three representatives of the *same* party in the *same* press release, we only count one attack against this party because we do not want to inflate our observations. As we are especially interested in the dynamic and interactive aspect of negative campaigning we also re-arranged our data into a dyadic structure based on pairs of parties and their daily relation. For this reason, the following analyses will be based not only on proportions (expressing the relative importance

---

3. However, whenever these events were announced with a thematic scope we selected the press release: e.g. a campaign rally with a motto such as 'fighting unemployment'.

Table 10.1: Press releases: Total numbers coded and shares of attack releases

		SPÖ	ÖVP	FPÖ	BZÖ	Greens	Total
Total number	2002	1,058	665	122	—[1]	189	2,034
	2006	1,040	477	258	290	167	2,232
	2008	835	694	397	303	223	2,452
Attack releases	2002	47.0%	40.0%	45.9%	—[1]	48.7%	44.8%
	2006	41.6%	49.9%	55.8%	47.2%	55.1%	46.7%
	2008	31.5%	48.4%	49.1%	52.8%	49.8%	43.4%

Notes: [1] The BZÖ was founded in 2005 (*see* main text).
Party acronyms: SPÖ (*Sozialdemokratische Partei Österreichs*), ÖVP (*Österreichische Volkspartei*), FPÖ (*Freiheitliche Partei Österreichs*), BZÖ (*Bündnis Zukunft Österreich*).

of negative campaigning as well as the relative importance of specific targets) but also on count data (referring to the daily number of attacks within each directed party-pair).

Analysis

According to the different types of hypotheses our analysis of negative campaigning in Austrian elections proceeds in three steps. Hypotheses about the general characteristics of attacking parties (H1 and H2) are tested by making comparisons across the fourteen party-election observations in our data, irrespective of who the target of each attack was. The expectations about targeting behaviour (H3 to H6) require an analysis at the level of directed party dyads, for which we calculate, for each attacker, the percentage of attacks directed at each other party. For the analysis of time-variant factors (H7 and H8), we examine daily attacks between directed party dyads, while holding all predictors constant that do not vary over a campaign.

Starting with the characteristics of attacking parties, we conduct simple t-tests between the shares of negative press releases for government and opposition parties (H1), as well as for populist radical right and all other parties (H2). Across the three years, we have fourteen party-election observations, with six instances of government participation (ÖVP in all years, FPÖ in 2002, BZÖ in 2006, SPÖ in 2008) and five observations categorised as populist radical right (FPÖ and BZÖ). The average level of negativity among opposition parties is 50 per cent, as opposed to 43.8 per cent for government parties. While this difference is in the expected direction, it is based on a small number of observations and thus reaches statistical significance only at the 10 per cent level (t-statistic: 1.888, p-value: 0.094). The results are similar when comparing the populist radical right and other parties. FPÖ and BZÖ score a mean share of 50.1 per cent negative press releases while all other parties' average is 45.8 per cent. The difference in the means is as expected, with slightly higher levels of negativity observed for the populist radical right, yet the results are not statistically significant (t-statistic: -1.479, p-value: 0.17). While we thus find tendencies in the data that conform to the expectations, we cannot confirm the two hypotheses, since it cannot be ruled out that the observed group differences are due to statistical noise.

In order to test the hypotheses that pertain to the *targets of negative campaigning*, we look at all directed party-pairs at the three elections and calculate the share of attacks that each sender directs to the other parties. As an example, if half of all SPÖ attacks in a given year target the ÖVP, the value of the dependent variable for that SPÖ-ÖVP dyad is fifty. Thus, we eliminate differences in the absolute number of releases (*see* Table 10.1) and attacks and focus on the distribution of targets for each sender. Furthermore, we log-transform this variable to make it conform to the normality assumption.

Four parties in 2002 and five parties (including the newly founded BZÖ) in 2006 and 2008 yield a total of fifty-two directed party dyads. Government status and coalition dyads are captured with simple binary indicators, party size is measured as the polling average during the campaign (which is highly correlated with the outcome of the election), and the distance measure is calculated by

Table 10.2: Explaining targeting strategies (2002–08)

	Model I	Model II	Model III	Model IV	Model V
Targeted party in government (H3)	1.215*** (3.86)				0.987*** (4.60)
Grand coalition (H4)		1.746# (1.98)			0.612 (1.22)
Centre-right cabinet (H4)		−0.750 (−1.18)			−1.434*** (−3.71)
Size of targeted party in polls (H5)			0.0740*** (7.58)		0.0653*** (8.27)
Left-right distance between parties (H6)				0.0486 (0.58)	0.0799# (1.75)
Constant	2.167*** (10.58)	2.672*** (14.82)	1.202*** (5.24)	2.498*** (6.95)	0.745** (2.78)
N	52	52	52	52	52
R^2	0.230	0.102	0.535	0.00678	0.749
Adjusted R^2	0.214	0.0656	0.525	−0.0131	0.721

Note: Figures are linear regression coefficients, with t-statistics in parentheses.
# $p<0.1$, * $p<0.05$, ** $p<0.01$, *** $p<0.001$

taking the absolute values of the parties' left-right distances from three waves (2002, 2006, 2010) of the Chapel Hill Expert Survey on party positions (Bakker et al. 2015).

The models show good support for H3, H4, and H5, but only a small effect of the left-right distance variable (H6). At 72.1 per cent, the overall explained variance in model V is extremely high, indicating that the predictors chosen for the models capture much of the relevant variation in targeting strategies.

Looking at individual variables, the estimates clearly show that parties in government are much more likely to be targeted than those in opposition. Holding all other variables at typical values (means for continuous, and modes for dichotomous predictors), the predicted share of attacks increases from 9.4 to 25.2 per cent as the government dummy changes from zero to one. The relevance of being in government as a predictor of being a target of negative campaigning is further underscored by the fact that 23 per cent of the variance in the dependent variable can be explained by this covariate. This result is especially interesting in combination with the weak finding for H1 (opposition parties attack more). It suggests that the government-opposition divide in negative campaigning is not so much a result of opposition parties making greater use of attacks, but a consequence of governing parties being targeted more often (not only by opposition, but also by other governing parties). While this differentiation is irrelevant in two-party systems, it is crucial to make in a multiparty context.

The coalition hypothesis (H4) is also borne out by the data, once other factors are controlled for. Model V clearly shows that parties attack each other less intensely when they share executive office, yet this holds true only for the centre-right cabinets that were incumbents in 2002 and 2006. The predicted share of attacks directed at a party increases from 6.7 per cent for centre-right cabinets to a whopping 51.9 per cent for grand coalitions (holding government participation and all other covariates constant). The fierce competition between the two major parties thus clearly trumps the coalition logic in 2008. What is more, the two party dyads SPÖ–ÖVP and ÖVP–SPÖ are, in fact, the 'most negative' in all three campaigns. Between 2002 and 2008, SPÖ and ÖVP directed between 70 and 89 per cent of all attacks at their main rival.

Party size arguably has the strongest effect on explaining attacking behaviour. Not only is this predictor highly significant, it also accounts for over half of the variance in the dependent variable. The predicted share of attacks rises from 5.5 per cent for parties polling at 10 per cent to 10.5 per cent for parties at 20 per cent, and further to 20.2 per cent for parties polling at 30 per cent. Substantively, this means that the majority of all attacks are targeted at the two major parties, SPÖ and ÖVP. This is true for all senders in all three campaigns, even in those cases when the SPÖ was in opposition (2002 and 2006).

Finally, the ideological distance predictor is positive and significant at the 10 per cent level in model V, thus indicating that parties are more likely to target distant competitors than close ones. Yet, we would classify this result as weak support for our sixth hypothesis at best. Neither is the effect very strong nor does it explain much of the variance in the dependent variable. Indeed, going from the

Figure 10.1: Number of attacks per day over the course of three campaigns

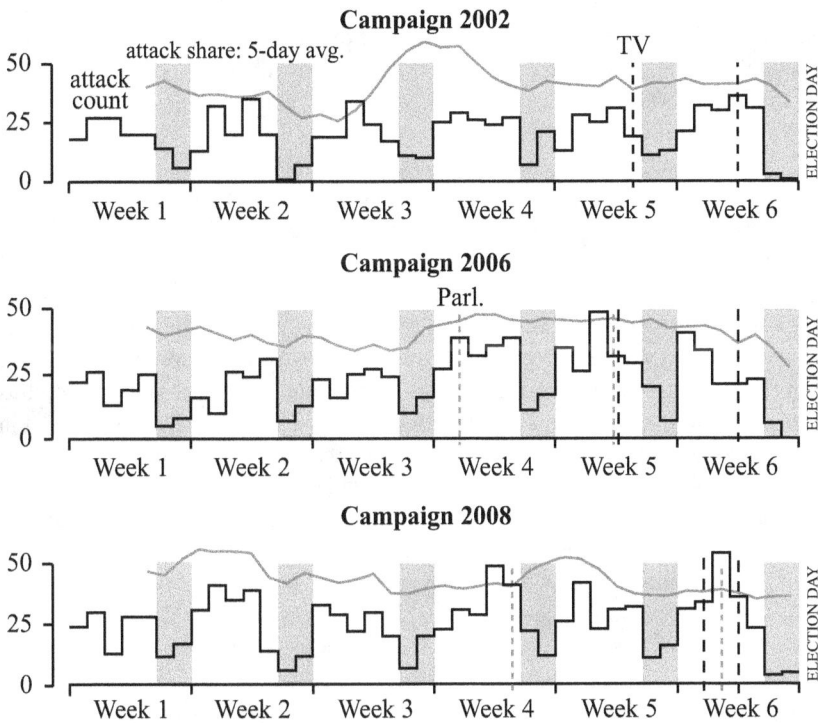

Note: Black step curves show absolute number of press releases with negative references to political opponent; grey rectangles indicate weekends; grey lines depict average percentage of attacks relative to total volume of press releases (five-day moving average); long-dashed vertical lines indicates dates of television debates (SPÖ versus ÖVP as well as debates of all party leaders); short-dashed vertical lines indicate plenary debates in parliament.

empirical minimum (0.64) to the empirical maximum (7.5) of the distance variable (while holding other predictors constant) increases the predicted share of attacks directed at the target by a mere 6 per cent.

Before turning to the analysis of negative campaigning dynamics during the campaign, Figure 10.1 provides a descriptive look at the relative and absolute numbers of attacks over time. The black step curve depicts the daily count of attacks. The grey lines indicate a five-day moving average of the share of press releases that contain attacks. This can be interpreted as a 'negativity barometer' over the course of each campaign. In 2002, for instance, negativity peaks around weeks three and four, before settling at around 40 per cent for the remaining two weeks. In 2006, the share of attacks is relatively constant, with a slight uptick after week three and a drop-off in the last few days. In 2008, there appears to be a slow decline throughout the campaign, with the exception of week five.

As to the impact of campaign events, the picture is not uniform (note, however, that not all television debates are shown in the graph). There appear to be peaks in the number of attacks issued around the parliamentary and the two most important television debates in 2008, but not so much for the other two elections. The overall picture that emerges from Figure 10.1 is thus one of relatively constant levels of negativity (with less overall activity on weekends) and some possible impact of individual campaign events.

For our test of hypotheses seven (H7) and eight (H8) we estimate count models of the number of attacks per day for each directed party dyad in each election year (*see* Table 10.3). Since the number of press releases per day and party-dyad is usually quite small (and often zero for dyads of small parties), the daily share of attacks for each party-dyad does not provide a meaningful measure. A check of the count time series reveals that neither the attack counts nor their first differences are auto-correlated over the course of a campaign. We therefore model the data with simple negative binomial models with fixed effects for each party dyad, thus eliminating all time-invariant factors from the analysis.[4] We observe six weeks in each campaign, which results in a total of 492 (twelve dyads × forty-two days – twelve dyads due to the inclusion of one time-lagged variable) observations in 2002 and, after the foundation of the BZÖ, 820 in 2006 and 2008 (twenty dyads × forty-two days – twenty dyads).

H7 is operationalised with a set of indicators for each party dyad and day on which a television debate between the two respective party leaders took place (we also code the following day with '1', so as to pick up reactions to the debate). We also include dummy variables that mark each day in the campaign during which a plenary debate in the lower chamber of the national parliament was held. We take these events to be focal points in the campaign around which there is heightened attention from the media and the general public. In addition, these events pit politicians against each other and thus serve as natural arenas for confrontation between parties.

For H8 we use the number of attacks at $t-1$ from the party targeted at t as a predictor. We thus examine to which extent attacks are directed at a specific party as a reaction to that party's behaviour on the previous day. Furthermore, we include a day counter and a dummy for Saturdays and Sundays (when press-related activity decreases significantly) as controls.

None of the central independent variables display significant effects in all three campaigns. H7 is supported by the 2008 data, but not for the other campaigns (although the coefficient for parliamentary debates is significant at the 10 per cent level in 2006).

In 2008, attacks were more likely to happen on days when parliament was in session, and around the time of television debates between party leaders. Attacks were around 38 to 40 per cent more likely on these days than on others.

---

4. Technically, there is variation in the party size variable, because the polls move slightly over the course of the campaigns. Yet, this variation is so miniscule that its impact is fully absorbed by the party dyad indicators.

Table 10.3: Explaining daily attack behaviour

	Model VI	Model VII	Model VIII
Year	**2002**	**2006**	**2008**
Television debate between party leaders (H7)	1.158 (0.87)	1.094 (0.58)	1.377* (2.38)
Parliamentary debate (H7)		1.268# (1.65)	1.400* (2.48)
Attacks from target at t−1 (H8)	1.016 (0.96)	0.991 (−0.52)	1.022 (1.54)
Day in campaign (count)	1.004 (1.12)	1.011*** (3.31)	1.000 (0.05)
Weekend	0.358*** (−8.65)	0.367*** (−9.63)	0.408*** (−8.94)
Party dyad dummies	Yes	Yes	Yes
Constant	0.136*** (−4.38)	0.397*** (−3.63)	0.508** (−2.73)
ln(α)	0.0691*** (−5.10)	0.0339*** (−3.85)	0.0522*** (−5.14)
N	492	820	820
Log likelihood	−586.2	−793.5	−883.5
McFadden's R^2	0.287	0.297	0.271

Note: Figures are incident rate ratios from negative binomial regression models; t statistics in parentheses
# p<0.1, * p<0.05, ** p<0.01, *** p<0.001

In 2006, the effect of parliamentary debates on the volume of attacks is in the expected direction, yet the coefficient is only significant at the 10 per cent level. The overall results for the event-related variables suggest that campaign events are not systematic determinants of attack behaviour but may be specific to each campaign.

The difference between the 2008 campaign and the other two may be due to the fact that the snap election of 2008 was called in response to massive intra-coalition conflict between SPÖ and ÖVP, as opposed to the FPÖ's intra-party difficulties that brought down the government in 2002 and the regular termination of the legislative period in 2006. Combined with the fact that negativity levels are much higher between the two major parties than between any other party pair, the presence of massive intra-cabinet conflict and the absence of coalition discipline after the government break-up in the summer of 2008 may help to explain why attacks are more responsive to highly mediatised campaign events such as parliamentary debates and leader confrontations on television. Still, the data only lend partial support to H7.

As for H8, we do not find any evidence that parties interact to a great extent. While this may come as a surprise to journalists and other close observers of Austrian campaigns, it may well be that our operationalisation fails to capture much of the expected effects. Daily counts of attacks and non-lagged counterattacks correlate at r=0.60 or higher in all three campaigns, indicating that parties often respond within a few hours or even less, and thus much of the interaction between parties happens in the very short term. Building on these insights, we are planning to tackle this problem with a more fine-grained research design in future publications.

With respect to the control variables, there are some significant though less surprising findings, with the number of attacks increasing over the course of the 2006 campaign, as well as a considerably lower incidence of attacks on weekends in all three years.

Conclusion

Negative campaigning is a highly relevant phenomenon also in Austrian elections. Parties had already engaged in negative strategies *avant la lettre*, thus before the term 'negative campaigning' was used in research on campaigning. The fact that parties attack their political opponents is therefore nothing new for observers of Austrian elections. However, this chapter is the first systematic analysis of negative campaigning that covers more than one election and combines a detailed analysis with a dynamic perspective.

Our chapter contributes to research on negative campaigning as Austria shares some typical features of most European countries, above all a multiparty system and coalition governments. Apart from these similarities we highlighted two specific characteristics of the Austrian case and their impact on negative campaigning: the predominance of grand coalition government and the exceptional strength of populist radical right parties. By examining several thousand press releases issued during three election campaigns in 2002, 2006, and 2008 we also presented a new method, which allowed us to contribute to this strand of research by evaluating a number of expectations about the senders, targets, and dynamics of negative campaigning. Considering these three dimensions of our analysis we sum up our results as follows:

With respect to the senders of attacks we expected opposition parties, the 'challengers', and parties belonging to the populist radical right to more often resort to negative campaigning. While the corresponding percentage differences were in the expected directions we could not confirm these hypotheses as the differences were not statistically significant.

As regards the targets of negative campaigning we could confirm that parties in government are much more likely to be targeted than those in opposition. In the context of multiparty competition it is therefore important to differentiate two aspects of the government–opposition divide which is so prominent in research on negative campaigning. Sharing government office decreases the level of negativity between parties but this is not the case for grand coalitions. SPÖ and ÖVP always attack each other, irrespective of their government status and the kind of coalition in office. An even stronger effect than for government status was found for party size as larger parties are attacked much more often. Contrary to these 'functional' characteristics of parties their ideological positions did not show a large effect.

The dynamic perspective, finally, showed that major events during the campaign such as television debates of party leaders or parliamentary debates tend to foster attack behaviour – but not in all elections. We also found little support for a tit-for-tat approach that would have parties primarily reacting to attacks by their opponents.

Naturally, this chapter is for the main part a first step into analysing negative campaigning in Austria. After the 2008 election, the last campaign covered by this chapter, another grand coalition was initiated. This time the parties managed to maintain their coalition throughout the extended legislative period. Nevertheless, the 2013 election was again dominated by attacks between the SPÖ and ÖVP (Dolezal *et al.* 2014b). Once more these attacks did not prevent the two parties from renewing their coalition. This most recent election has thus already confirmed some of our findings for the three elections examined in this chapter.

Chapter Eleven

The Strategy of Electoral Spots in Brazilian Presidential Campaign: The Decision on When and Where to Broadcast an Attack

Felipe Borba[1]

Televised political advertisements are the main strategy in the quest for votes in modern electoral campaigns. However, despite increased academic interest in the impact of political communication in voter decision, little is known with regard to how candidates strategically use spots in the course of the campaign and within the programming of television broadcasts. This implies the need for an approach where the aim is to analyse the timing of such commercials: when they are aired, during which attraction and their frequency. This set of information is crucial in order to understand the dynamics of elections as they reveal the strategies employed by candidates and the images they wish to project to the electorate.

The review of the literature suggests that this approach is found in academic investigations of elections in the United States (US), although do not yet comprise a solid research agenda. Still, the main trends suggest that there is a strong incentive for candidates to place spots in competitive states, in local television networks and in prime-time slots. Recently, researchers have detected advertisement migration to cable television networks, where the odds of reaching specific audience targets are considerably greater. A final finding is the trend of increasing the exhibition of spots as election day approaches (West *et al.* 1995; Freedman and Goldstein 1999; Johnston *et al.* 2004; Jamieson *et al.* 2010).

In Brazil, candidates must face a complex structure of incentives when deciding how to place their political advertisements. The reason for this is the legal benchmark for political advertising on television, which follows a distinct model and framework. Unlike the US model, where the placement of spots depends solely on the capacity candidates and their camps have to purchase television slots, in Brazil candidates vying for political posts must adapt their strategies to the scheduling system elaborated by the Superior Electoral Court (*Tribunal Superior Eleitoral*), which determines beforehand and according to a lot, the day and time when advertisements can be shown.

Despite this regulated context, this article aims to elaborate on a few behavioural hypotheses concerning how presidential candidates strategically insert advertisements in the attempt to secure the votes of Brazilian electors. To this

1.   The author acknowledges funding from the Research Foundation of Rio de Janeiro (FAPERJ).

end, I will present a study focusing on the 2006 and 2010 presidential campaigns, comprising both the first and second rounds of voting. The analysis builds upon a set of data that has remained untapped. This database contains all presidential advertisements exhibited in these two elections and, moreover, it contains information encompassing the number of spots produced by each candidate and the exact moment they were aired and the number they were repeated during the campaign.

In this article, the analysis of the strategic placement of advertisements is simplified and restricted to the behavioural decision of how candidates attack their adversaries on television. The decision to attack the opponent is empirically manifested in negative advertisements. This topic has been catching the attention of several researchers, especially in the US, who have been poring over the task of measuring the impact of negative advertisements in the democratic process. Even though findings are yet inconclusive, the literature has collected enough evidence to suggest that the tone of campaigns have an immediate impact on electoral participation, the level of information and voter decision (Ansolabehere and Iyengar 1995; Wattenberg and Brians 1999; Pinkleton 1997; Finkel and Geer 1998; Kahn and Kenney 1999a). Specifically with regard to the latter topic, there is significant evidence showing that negative advertisements are effective when it comes to causing the opponent to lose votes, although there is also some evidence suggesting this strategy can backfire (Garramone 1985; King and McConnell 2003; Fridkin and Kenney 2004).

This brings me to the empirical question: do candidates for federal executive branch posts follow a certain pattern when they decide to attack an opponent? As I intend to show in this chapter, the answer is yes. The candidates investigated pursued distinct strategies in the quest for elector votes, each of which obeying criteria on their turn influenced, most and moreover, by electoral campaigning rules, the position of candidates in the polls and the number of competitors. In this sense, the analysis seeks to further knowledge in two complementary ways. First, the case study of Brazil contributes to the debate concerning how elections play out in political environments other than the US by investigating the determinants of negative advertisements in multiparty environments and where there is a highly regulated system with the media, a reality analogous to that of most European countries (Walter 2014a; Kaid and Holtz-Bacha 1994). As pointed out by Benoit in the Chapter Two of this volume, studies that investigate the circumstances of negative advertisements encounter evidence that the decision to attack is influenced by the candidate's status (government or opposition), placement in the polls and competitiveness. One of the goals of this article, therefore, is to add to this list the number of candidates in dispute and the rules that determine access to television exposure. Secondly, the chapter seeks to further our comprehension by discussing how the decision to allocate resources can be an important factor in explaining how voter perception regarding candidates is formed. By broadcasting certain types of messages instead of others in distinct timeslots and moments in the campaign's evolution, candidates have a powerful tool to alter perceptions regarding themselves and their opponents. In an analysis of the 1992 presidential elections in the US, West *et al.* (1995), for example, found evidence that Bush's image was drastically influenced by how his team handled spots and became a 'negative campaigner'.

Given that in Brazil the quantity of studies on electoral advertisement is relatively modest, I shall dialogue with US political science literature, where the studying of this kind of advertising strategy has taken place since the 1950s. The next section engages in a brief review of the dynamic character of advertisements in US elections and how this model based on free competition can be useful in devising hypotheses applicable to the Brazilian case. On the other hand, the third section underscores the relativity of such hypotheses in view of the aforementioned reasons: the Brazilian regulated electoral advertising environment due to national electoral legislation and the Brazilian multiparty political system, and a double round voting system. Lastly, the methodology employed and results will be presented.

The dynamic character of spots in the US

The concept of strategy as it is defined in US political science literature is related to the degree that liberty campaigns can count on in terms of deciding when, where and how frequently they can exhibit an advertisement (West *et al.* 1995). A review of the literature, however, suggests that the topic requires further investigation. This deficiency probably reflects the lack of reliable data concerning the exhibition of spots (Freedman and Goldstein 1999). Although there are few of them, these studies show some interesting patterns. The main one is the strong influence of the US electoral system, which provides incentives for candidates to selectively allocate resources in geographic terms. In their analysis of the 2000 presidential elections Johnston *et al.* (2004) showed that due to the logic of the electoral college, George W. Bush and Al Gore all but ignored non-competitive states, regardless of size, concentrating the bulk of advertisements in the so-called swing states. So much so that the vast majority of spots were exhibited in local television broadcasts.

In the same way that advertisements are geographically concentrated in competitive states, the authors demonstrate that they are also determined by timing. The frequency of advertisements gradually increases as the day of the election approaches. This speeding up usually occurs after the last presidential debate. From the beginning of September until the third week of October, the total volume increased from an average of seventy-five spots per network to approximately 110. In contrast, at the end of October, the average of spots per network exceeds 175 weekly spots and in the last week prior to elections the volume soars to 250 commercials per week (Johnston *et al.* 2004).

The presidential elections of 2008 revealed a new pattern in the strategic use of electoral spots. A study conducted by Jamieson *et al.* (2010) noted the higher frequency of advertisements in cable television networks and radio. McCain and

Obama invested most of their resources in conventional television, primarily because of its wide reach, but when messages were aimed at a specific audience of a certain geographic region, the preferred vehicles for spots were alternative media. This strategy was implemented foremost by the Obama campaign and, according to the authors, was crucial in giving him the win.

Furthermore, electoral advertisements vary according to the time of the day they get aired. Freedman and Goldstein (1999) analysed the distribution of advertisements during the campaign for the seat of governor of the state of Virginia and reported that both candidates – incumbent democrat governor Don Beyer and his Republican challenger, Jim Gilmore – concentrated advertisements during daytime slots (10 a.m. to 4 p.m.) and prime access time (7:30 p.m. to 8 p.m.), neglecting the earlier morning hours (6 a.m. to 10 a.m.), night-time (8 p.m. to 11 p.m.) and weekends. However, the authors do not offer an explanation for this pattern. Unfortunately, there are no other studies indicating how presidential campaign advertisements are strategically distributed during the day.

Studies portraying strategic decisions taken by campaigns with regard to the application of negative advertisements are even more difficult to find. Freedman and Goldstein (1999) found little variation in the proportion of negative advertisements. During each part of the day, approximately five out of ten were intended to tarnish the opponent's image. Finally, West *et al.* (1995) outlined the innovative strategy used by George Bush in his 1992 run for presidency. In his shot at re-election, Bush aired positive spots in nationwide broadcasts and negative one in local networks.

The issues discussed above exemplify how dialogue with the theoretical benchmarks of the international literature can benefit our understanding of the elections in Brazil, and, by extension, in Latin America. However, the hypotheses derived from the US model need to be put into perspective if they are to be adapted to Brazilian institutions and political reality. The main difference is the existence of a legal benchmark for television advertisements in Brazil, which evolved as an alternative to the commercial exploitation of US television, where the broadcasting of spots is solely dependent of each candidate's capacity to purchase slots in television networks. In contrast, in Brazil, those vying for political posts must adapt their strategies to the media schedule map formulated by the Superior Electoral Court, who determines beforehand and by means of a lot system, the day and time when advertisements will be shown. Furthermore, Brazil sets the Superior Electoral Court apart from the US since it adopts a multiparty political system with a two-round voting system – a factor that strongly affects the incentive structure and favours distinct strategies compared to those pursed in bi-partisan models.

The description below provides a detailed account of how the Brazilian system of public political media advertisements – the Unpaid Electoral Advertisement Slot – and the multiparty, two-round elections political system influence the incentive structure for Brazilian candidates and offers a few behavioural hypotheses regarding how Brazilian candidates have adapted to this structure.

Empirical issues regarding the Brazilian model

In Brazil, political advertisements are aired on radio and television within a special slot designated as the 'Unpaid Electoral Advertisement Slot' (*Horário Gratuito de Propaganda Eleitoral* - HGPE). The HGPE is a time-slot guaranteed by law so that political parties can relay information to the electorate concerning their proposals free of charge. It is divided into two categories: advertisements aired in special block-slots and short, thirty-second commercials aired within regular broadcast programming. The first category requires television networks to reserve fifty minutes per day (twenty-five in the afternoon and twenty-five at night) so that candidates can air their proposals. These twenty-five minutes are distributed among candidates according to the following rule: one third of the time is divided equally among all candidates and the remaining two thirds in proportion to the number of seats occupied in the Chamber of Deputies.[2] Spots interspersed within programming are somewhat novel and started being aired after the 1998 presidential election, after the promulgation of the Electoral Statute (Law 9,504).

Each model has its own advantages and disadvantages, but Brazilian political analysts and academics have taken to argue against the block slot model, the main criticism being that its low influence does not justify the high budgets it requires from the campaign (Lavareda 2009). The thirty-second advertisements have received a more positive view mainly because they are considered to be in tandem with media strategies that articulate three characteristics: agility, penetration and unpredictability. The thrust of the argument is that spots are more dynamic and thus can reach all kinds of voters before they can redirect their attention, since they are caught 'off guard,' which is the opposite of what happens when advertisements are shown in pre-scheduled block slots, allowing the voter the prerogative of changing channels.

The Brazilian model for advertisements can be criticised, nevertheless, for being excessively regulated. In Brazil, advertisements are aired daily during a forty-five-day period that extends until two days before the date of the election. During this period, radio and television networks are required to reserve thirty minutes daily for the exhibition of advertisements, that must be divided equally among campaigns for presidency, state government, federal and state representatives and senator. This means that each post is allotted six minutes of thirty-second spots each day, i.e. twelve thirty-second advertisements daily. Among candidates, time allotment follows the same rules as in block-slot distribution: one third of the time is divided equally and the remaining time according to the proportion of seats occupied by parties or coalitions.

The problem with the Brazilian political advertisement model is observed in the articles defining the rules for the airing of commercials within network programming. The Superior Electoral Court elaborated a mechanism for television

---

2.   Although the electoral legislation was modified between 1989 and 2010, the rule for time allotment remains essentially the same. 1989 marks the year when the first presidential elections were held after end of the military regime (1964–85).

time that is faithful to the principle of equality among candidates, but in practice limits strategic use of advertisements, as it previously establishes, according to a lot, the date and placement of messages. The electoral rule determines that advertisements be distributed equally throughout the campaign period and that, during each day of the campaign, spots be distributed equally in four blocks designated according to audiences, in such a way that each candidate has a chance to air messages in times with more and less viewers.[3]

Based on this set of rules, the media schedule for the presidential campaign is processed as follows: first, the Superior Electoral Court divides the total of 540 advertisements by the number of days in the campaign period (forty-five days) in order to define the daily amount of advertisements (twelve). Next, this total is divided by four, which is the number of audience categories throughout the day, resulting in the three advertisements per block. Finally, the sequence of exhibition among candidates follows the lot drafted by the Superior Electoral Court. An important detail is that the slots are filled in reverse order, from end to start, meaning that all parties are guaranteed advertisements in the days closer to the election date, which, according to the Court's assessment, is when the there is greater popular interest in elections. It is important to point out that, in the second round, the number of slots is the same for both candidates, regardless of the number of seats occupied by their parties.

An additional problem with the Brazilian political advertisement model is the fact candidates are unable to decide during which programmes they can air their spots. The Superior Electoral Court determines the day, the audience block and the order of exhibition, but radio and television networks decide the specific time the advertisements will be aired within the blocks. Electoral law stipulates that networks keep a balance when spacing advertisements but makes no reference to the distribution of advertisements within scheduled programming. The rule only suggests that networks must avoid two or more spots during the same commercial break, which includes advertisements by the same candidate. The legislation, however, does not stipulate any rule regarding advertisements within programming, or any sanction if benefits are extracted from political favouring.

In addition to regulating allotment, the Superior Electoral Court also has the prerogative of regulating the content of spots. Electoral regulation forbids the use of 'external footage, montages, or gimmicking, computer graphics, animated cartoons or special effects,' in addition to prohibiting messages that can are intended to 'degrade or ridicule a party, candidate or coalition'. The violation of this article subjects the infracting party to the loss of the right to air advertisements and grants the opponent the so-called 'right to reply'. Although the concession of the right to reply is unusual in Brazilian presidential elections (Borba 2012), the existence of this possibility is a relevant factor in the elaboration of electoral tactics in the most

---

3. Audience blocks are defined as follows: Block 1, from 8 a.m. to 12 a.m.; Block 2, from 12 a.m. to 6 p.m.; Block three, from 6 p.m. to 9 p.m.; and Block 4, from 9 p.m. to 12 p.m. Advertisements are forbidden from 12 p.m. to 8 a.m.

part because of its psychological influence, as it warrants caution when attacking. It can be clearly noticed that the set of regulations in the electoral law stands in the way of strategic actions of candidates, who ultimately cannot decide when, where and how to air their spots. Thus, for example, a message directed to the electorate of a certain region ends up being viewed all over the country.

Furthermore, the Brazilian political system, which features multiple parties and presidential elections decided in two rounds of voting, influences both the volume of attacks, as well as the choice of whom to attack. In the multiparty system, the occurrence of attacks is lower due to the cost-benefit trade-off dilemma that parties must face, which greatly differs compared to the incentive structure of bipartisan, simple majority systems, as in the US. In disputes with more than two competitors, the benefits of negative advertisements are scattered in the sense that they could be divided among different parties and not benefit solely the one who launched the attack – while the cost of the attack is borne exclusively by the party that launched it (Hansen and Pederson 2008; Walter 2014a). In other words, in a plural dispute, the exchange of accusations among two candidates can, hypothetically, benefit a third party, a constraint that is non-existent in bipartisan systems, where disputes unfold as a zero-sum game, in which the lost of percentage points automatically translates into a proportional gain for the other candidate. Also, the existence of a run-off influences the decision to attack due to the fact that a candidate must reach out to those excluded for support in an eventual second round of voting. The consolidation of such an agreement can be hampered by attacks in the first round and thus increase the costs of prospective bargaining. This consideration is similar to the dilemma faced by European parties in parliamentarian democracies when choosing the enemy, in view of the need to form coalitions before elections (Walter 2014).

The multiparty system with two rounds of voting influences the choice of whom to attack. It is now uncommon in Brazilian majority elections, for candidates to initiate a dispute in third place in the polls and end up being elected. This kind of turnaround occurred in elections for mayor of Rio de Janeiro (in 2008) and São Paulo (in 2012). In these elections, candidates Eduardo Paes (Rio de Janeiro) and Fernando Haddad (in São Paulo) started their campaigns in third place and ended up being elected. Under such circumstances, what kind of behaviour is to be expected? Skaperdas and Grofman (1995) include the participation of a third candidate in their model and derive a few intuitive hypotheses: in competitions with three candidates, leaders attack less, no candidate attacks the weakest among the group and negative advertisements, when existent, are directed at the leader.

The problem with the Skaperdas and Grofman model (1995) is that it was conceived bearing only US politics in mind. Even if their hypotheses can be validated for the Brazilian cases, the simple majority system does not contemplate the possibility of competition for second place. We know that candidates are motivated by the prospect of acquiring power. In two-round elections, the first mission is to guarantee a place in the second one; the second one is to be elected. To this end, candidates must eliminate rivals ahead of them and keep those behind at a distance. This strategic premise entails a dispute between the candidates in second and third place for a chance in the second round. This scenario was observed, for example, in the presidential dispute between José Serra and Ciro Gomes in 2002 deciding who would compete against Lula in the second round. In competitive disputes, therefore, negative advertisements are not exclusively directed at the leader and the candidate in third place is not entirely ignored.

A regulated political advertisements system and a political system based on multiple parties and two-round elections together create particular incentives that lead us to a set of behavioural hypotheses regarding the communication strategies of political actors during electoral moments. In this case, the intensity of negative advertisements should be expected to be lower in the first than in the second round – which happens when no candidate alone attains more than 50 per cent of votes. This is because, as argued above, the disputes between two candidates eliminate the risks associated to the scattering of benefits and the cost of bargaining. Also, the volume of negative advertisements will be greater among candidates trailing in the polls. In other words, the decision to attack will be the main strategy among candidates at a disadvantage in a presidential race, facing pressure to close the gap between them and the leader. At the same time, we expect to observe the candidate placed second in the polls to attack the candidate in first, while the first candidate in the polls will attack the second to a lower degree.

The rule that stipulates the airing of spots distributed in four audience blocks consequently raises an inevitable question: is there a strategic pattern in the distribution of negative advertisements within the overall scheduling defined by the Superior Electoral Court? In this case, I argue that negative advertisements will preferably be exhibited in the last two blocks (prime time hours and late night), based on the assumption that in the morning the profile of the audience is composed of children, teenagers and homemakers, while at night this profile is substantially inverted. Consequently, one expects that candidates choose to launch attacks against opponents when the audience is more tolerant towards negative advertisements.

Lastly, this chapter will analyse the evolution of negative advertisements in the course of the campaign. In this case, it will be necessary to offer distinct explanations for two distinct situations. Concerning the first round, I made the suggestion that negative advertisements evolve as a normal curve: in the beginning negative advertisements are few, they grow in the course of the campaign and then wane towards date of the election. The dynamics of a campaign explains this bell-shaped curve. The initial phase serves to consolidate the candidate's image, the moment when her biography and proposals are presented. The intermediary phase is usually when time is devoted to deconstruct the opponent's image. Finally, advertisements take a step back as election date approaches and assumes a more intimate tone (Diamond and Bates 1992). However, it is important to point out that the negativity curve will have different tones for candidates trailing in the polls. Under pressure to close the gap separating them from the leaders, they anticipate attacks, while the leaders tend to postpone this decision.

On the other hand, my hypothesis is that this scenario changes in the second round. In this case, the strategy of using negative advertisements is employed from the beginning and remains stable until the end of the campaign. This reversal occurs for two reasons: First, because the time allotted for campaigns is reduced by half relative to the first round – in 2006, fifteen days, and in 2010, twenty-one days. This means that there is less time to reverse tendencies detected in the polls and it therefore becomes more necessary to use negative advertisements. Second, because there is no need to follow the campaign 'manual'. In the second round there is no need to build up an image or familiarise a candidate with the electorate. At this stage, the dispute pivots around the perception of what distinguishes candidates from each other, which is precisely where negative advertisements are crucial (Garramone *et al.* 1990). The following section describes the methodology used to carry out the analysis.

Methodology

To put the hypotheses outlined above to test, I resorted to the media schedule assigned to candidates elaborated by Doxa – The Public Opinion Laboratory at the Social and Political Institute of Rio de Janeiro State University (*Laboratório de Opinião Pública do Instituto de Estudos Sociais e Políticos da UERJ*) which contains data collected from advertisements aired on the Globo Television Network, Brazil's largest and most influential network, during the presidential elections in 2006 and 2010.[4] In these two elections, Doxa monitored all of the campaigns and recorded the exact times of spots and this contains all information necessary to investigate empirically the questions discussed above. Among the main categories of information, the spreadsheet contains the days, times, and programming in which spots were aired. It also contains information as to how many times each spot was repeated throughout the campaign.

The sample includes candidates considered competitive in each election, that is, those who have shown to stand some chance of electoral success. This criterion combined the number of votes obtained at the end of the first rand or filiation to a significant political party in the Brazilian context. Based on this rule, the final list encompassed an analysis of the campaigns of ten candidates and the coding of a total 2,993 spots (*see* Table 11.1).

The process of analysis was conducted basically in two stages. In the first one, we followed the theoretical arguments of Benoit described in Chapter Two of this volume and we classified the functions of the spots in three categories: acclaim (positive statements about the candidate), attacks (criticism of the opponent) and defence (rebuke of attacks). In the second one, we tried to relate the content of these messages to the moment they were launched. In the identification of negative messages, all kind of criticism were included, like candidate's personality, his political beliefs, his record as a politician and public administrator, his political party, his associates, family and friends, support group and his aids. By considering all criticism named to an adversary, I differ from those suggesting that negative campaigns are only those focusing on the personal attributes of

---

4.   Globo's viewer share is of approximately 60 per cent.

Table 11.1: List of analysed candidates

	Candidates	
Year	**First round**	**Second round**
2006	Lula (PT)	Lula (PT)
	Geraldo Alckmin (PSDB)	Geraldo Alckmin (PSDB)
	Heloísa Helena (PSOL)	
	Cristovam Buarque (PDT)	
	Dilma Rousseff (PT)	
2010	José Serra (PSDB)	Dilma Rousseff (PT)
	Marina Silva (PV)	José Serra (PSDB)
	Plínio Sampaio (PSOL)	

candidates (Mattes 2001).[5] This implies that so far no distinction has been made with regard to the tone of the attacks, as suggested by Kahn and Kenney (1999), who only consider negative advertisements as those 'below the belt.' In this sense, the classification proposed reflects a concern that is simply to know if candidates use allotted time with intent to highlight negative aspects of the opponent, instead of emphasising their own qualities.

The Functional Theory of Benoit furthermore suggests that spots must also be analysed relative to the veracity and the topic, which we have ignored in this text. The decision to restrict the analysis to the function of the message, although it might not contribute much to the understanding of the semantic structure of political communication in this context, nevertheless is coherent with the aims of this chapter. At this point, my focus is to evaluate whether or not spots are used strategically in the course of the campaign. The question I hope to answer is: is there a relationship between the decision to praise oneself or to attack the opponent and the incentive structure described above according to the rules of the electoral legislation.

Results

The analysis shows that positive messages were predominant in the communication strategies of presidential candidates in 2006 and 2010. Conflating the data for both elections, 62.3 per cent of the advertisements were self-praising, 34.9 per cent launched attacks and only 2.8 per cent of the messages were rebuttals to attacks. The percentage of attacks found shows that candidates used one third of their advertisements as attempts to steal votes from opponents. This percentage is considerably higher in comparison to the percentage for advertisements aired in block slots (Borba 2012) and suggests that in presidential campaigns candidates prefer launching attacks in spots interspersed within regular programming.

---

5. Mattes (2001), for example, argues that the criticism aimed at the opponent's political beliefs or positions should be classified as 'issue differentiation', rather than negative advertisement.

Table 11.2: Function of spots in per cent

Candidate	Position in the poll (all campaigns)	Positive	Negative	Defence	Total
Lula	First place	97.3	2.6	0.0	100.0
Geraldo Alckmin	Second place	58.5	41.5	0.0	100.0
Heloisa Helena	Third place	87.1	12.9	0.0	100.0
Cristovam Buarque	Fourth place	60.3	39.8	0.0	100.0
1st round 2006		72.5	27.6	0.0	100.0
					100.0
Lula	First place	42.1	57.5	0.0	100.0
Geraldo Alckmin	Second place	64.3	35.7	0.0	100.0
2nd round 2006		55.2	44.7	0.0	100.0
					100.0
Dilma Rousseff	First place	75.9	18.3	5.8	100.0
José Serra	Second place	61.7	38.4	0.0	100.0
Marina Silva	Third place	100.0	0.0	0.0	100.0
Plínio Sampaio	Fourth place	81.0	19.0	0.0	100.0
1st round 2010		71.7	25.9	2.4	100.0
					100.0
Dilma Rousseff	First place	38.6	52.5	8.9	100.0
José Serra	Second place	67.6	29.9	2.5	100.0
2nd round 2010		55.3	39.4	5.3	100.0

There are significant differences among electoral stages. The second round is, as predicted, more negative than in the first, as it is possible to observe with the decline of the percentage of positive messages. This result confirms a previous study, which compared the level of negativity of the advertisements, aired in the traditional block slot model and is related to the structure of incentives typical of elections with only two candidates, which follow a zero-sum logic (Borba 2012). In 2006, during the first round dispute 72.5 per cent of messages were positive, against 55.2 per cent in the second round. In 2010, the percentages are extremely similar: 71.7 per cent of the spots in the first round were positive, and 55.3 per cent in the second round.

The variations in campaign tactics of the candidates also followed the formulated hypothesis. The intensity of attacks and the choice of target were strongly influenced by the positioning of candidates in polls. It is possible to observe that the leaders in disputes attacked less than their adversaries. Lula used only 2.6 per cent of his time to attack, while Rousseff did so more frequently (18.3 per cent). Serra and Alckmin, the opposition candidates belonging to the PSDB and seconds in the polls, were less economical in criticising their opponents: 41.5 per cent and 38.4 per cent of attacks, respectively. In relation to other competitors, the data shows that Buarque was the most negative (39.8 per cent), followed by (19.0 per cent) and Heloísa Helena (12.9 per cent) – Silva did not launch attacks. In the second round, the strategies are reversed with leaders launching more attacks. Lula (57.5 per cent) and Rousseff (52.55 per cent) used more than half of their allotted time with negative advertisements, while Alckmin (35.7 per cent) and Serra (29.9 per cent) decreased the rate of attacks. This result contradicts the expected hypothesis that leaders attack less. A possible explanation is the political conjuncture at the time. In both elections, Lula and Rousseff ended the first round with declining numbers in the polls, while their opponents were on an upward trend. This suggests that the higher rate of attacks by the leaders aimed at curtailing this trend.

The choice to attack also seems to be influenced by popularity. Leaders in the polls usually only attack those in second, and those in second exclusively attack leaders. This is exactly what the behaviour of Lula and Rousseff (leaders in the polls), on one side, and Alckmin and Serra (seconds in the polls), on the other, indicate. The remaining candidates alternate strategies. In 2006, Heloísa Helena (the third in the polls) attacked either Lula or Lula and Alckmin simultaneously. Buarque, placed in fourth, chose to aim his attacks only at Lula. In 2010, Sampaio repeated Heloísa Helena's strategy. In addition to attacking Rousseff in exclusive spots, part of his advertisements were targeted at both Rousseff and Serra and also Rousseff, Serra, and Silva, simultaneously.

The main hypothesis that candidates will choose to launch more attacks in the night-time blocks was partially confirmed. Generally speaking, leaving aside variations among a few candidates, election years and rounds, it is possible to state there is a certain amount of stability in the percentage of attacks by audience block, although the night-time blocks tend to have a slightly higher rate of negative advertisements. The total averages are 23.1 per cent (B1), 24.7 per cent (B2),

Table 11.3: Target of attacks by position in the polls in per cent

	2006			2010			
	Leader	Second	Leader and second	Leader	Second	Leader and second	Leader, second and third
Leader	–	100.0	–				
Second	100.0	–	–				
Third	25.0	0.0	75.0				
Fourth	100.0	0.0	0.0				
Leader				–	100.0	0.0	0.0
Second				100.0	–	0.0	0.0
Third				81.0	0.0	9.5	9.5

Table 11.4: Objective of spots by audience blocks in per cent – 2006

Candidate	Position in the poll (all campaigns)	Block 1 (8h–12h)	Block 2 (12h–18h)	Block 3 (18h–21h)	Block 4 (21h–24h)	Total
Lula	First place	0.0	16.7	33.3	50.0	100.0
Geraldo Alckmin	Second place	20.8	26.6	27.3	25.3	100.0
Heloisa Helena	Third place	50.0	25.0	25.0	0.0	100.0
Cristovam Buarque	Fourth place	33.3	22.2	18.5	25.9	100.0
First round		22.5	25.7	26.2	25.7	100.0
Lula	First place	24.2	22.4	26.7	26.7	100.0
Geraldo Alckmin	Second place	12.6	21.0	33.6	32.9	100.0
Second round		18.8	21.7	29.9	29.6	100.0

26.6 per cent (B3), and 25.6 per cent (B4). However, there are some thought provoking variations in the comparison of elections. In the 2006 presidential contest there is clearly a slant towards night-time attacks. The percentages observed were 20.2 per cent (B1), 23.2 per cent (B2), 28.5 per cent (B3), and 28.1 per cent (B4). In contrast, the scenario in 2010 was relatively distinct, with morning blocks exhibiting higher rates of negative attacks: 25.6 per cent (B1), 26.0 per cent (B2), 24.9 per cent (B3), and 23.5 per cent (B4).

Candidates also fluctuated in their communication strategies. In 2006, Lula privileged the night-time block for attacks against opponents. It can be noted that the ex-president did not air any kind of negative advertisements in the morning blocks. Alckmin, on his turn, distributed his attacks more evenly, although it can be noted that block one had the lowest rate of attacks. Once again, other candidates sought unique strategies. Buarque mostly used negative attacks in blocks one and four, Heloisa Helena did not air attacks in the last audience block.

In 2010, Rousseff followed a different pattern than Lula in the previous election. Her negative advertisements were concentrated in blocks two and three. Serra's attacks, however, are based on the premise of less variation. The PSDB candidate distributed his messages evenly among all audience blocks, while Sampaio distributed his negative advertisements mostly in block one. In the second round this scenario changes, especially with regard to Serra. The PSDB candidate starts attacking more in blocks one and two, while Rousseff continues to concentrate negative advertisements in blocks two and three.

The final sections of this chapter investigate how negative advertisements evolved during the 2006 and 2010 presidential campaigns. For the sake of analysis, rather than examining the individual behaviour of each candidate, I will analyse

Table 11.5: Objective of spots by audience blocks in per cent – 2010

Candidate	Position in the poll (all campaigns)	Block 1 (8h–12h)	Block 2 (12h–18h)	Block 3 (18h–21h)	Block 4 (21h–24h)	Total
Dilma Rousseff	First place	24.0	26.6	28.0	22.0	100.0
José Serra	Second place	25.2	24.3	25.2	25.2	100.0
Plínio Sampaio	Third place	50.0	25.0	25.0	0.0	100.0
First round		25.4	24.9	26.0	23.7	100.0
Dilma Rousseff	First place	24.8	25.7	26.2	23.4	100.0
José Serra	Second place	26.9	27.5	22.2	23.4	100.0
Second round		25.7	26.5	24.4	23.4	100.0

collectively the evolution of negative advertisements for candidates seeking re-election and poll leaders (Lula and Rousseff), on one hand, and opposition candidates and candidates trailing in the polls, on the other one (Alckmin, Heloísa Helena, Buarque, Serra and Sampaio). The goal here is to observe the occurrence or non-occurrence of distinct strategies according to the political situation (government versus opposition) or the electoral scenario (leader versus trailers), which in both elections coincided. This decision would be problematic if the candidates of the opposition had exchanged mutual accusations, which was not the case. In both elections, all candidates assumed and cooperated in staunch anti-government stances, except for, obviously, pro-government candidates. In addition, this made it possible to circumvent the problem of analysing the behaviour of candidates who, according to the time allotment rule established by the Superior Electoral Court, had few spots to air. For example, Sampaio had a mere twenty spots during the forty-five-day campaign, meaning that he only aired spots on half of the days, which makes it difficult to analyse his strategy.

Figure 11.1 illustrates the evolution of negative advertisements relative to the first rounds of 2006 and 2010. It can be noted that, generally speaking, the curve is in line with the assumptions of this model. The negative advertisements are almost absent in the first days of the campaigns, increase in the intermediate stages of the competition, being that the peak usually occurs at the end of the second third of the campaign, and then dips towards the final stretch. It can also be noted that there is variation in the strategies adopted by the leaders and candidates of the opposition. Lula and Rousseff ignored their opponents in the first weeks of the campaign and waited until the final period of the campaign to launch attacks. Serra, Alckmin and the other opposition candidates, on the other hand, anticipated attacks, as predicted.

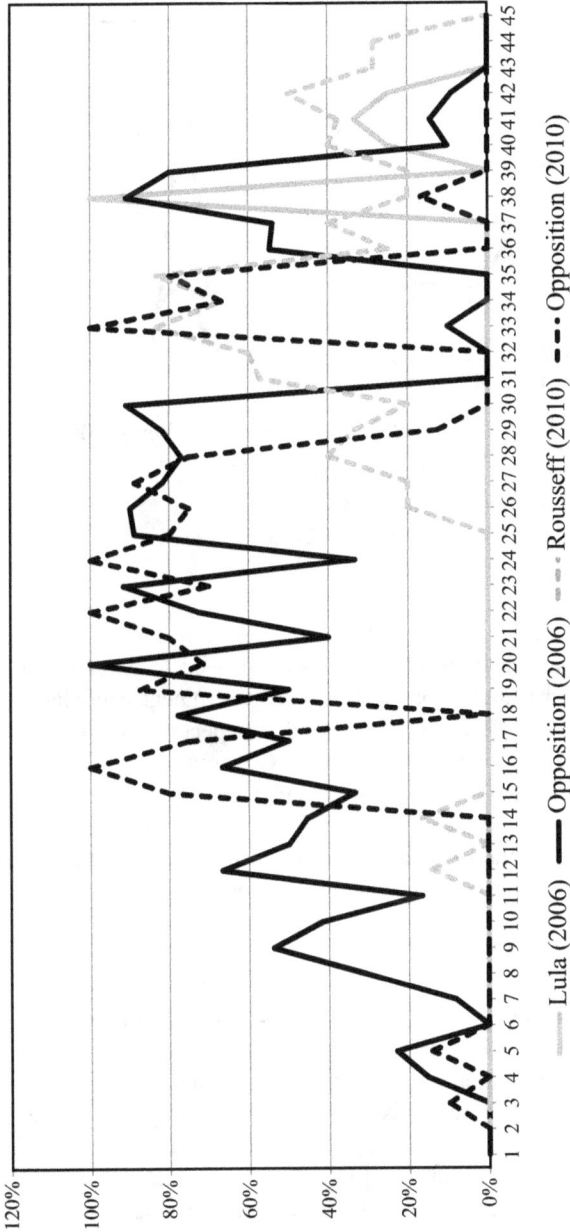

Figure 11.1: Evolution of negative advertisements in the first round (2006 and 2010)

Figure 11.2: Evolution of negative advertisements in the second round (2006 and 2010)

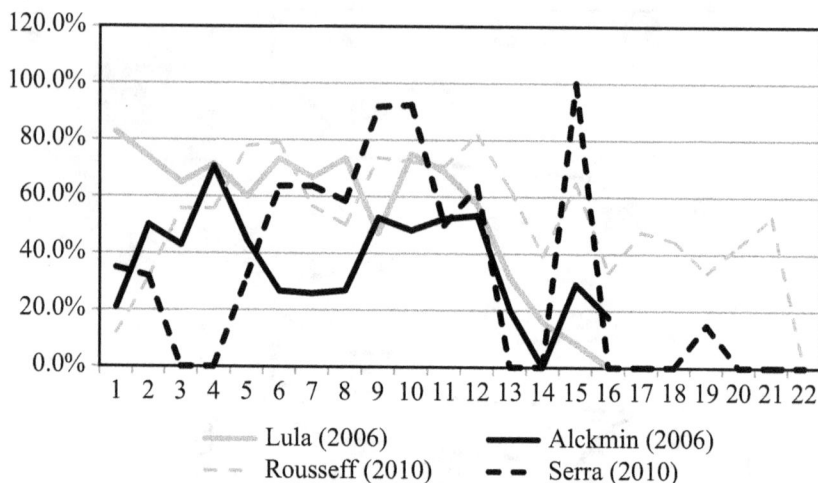

The 2006 presidential campaign lasted sixteen days.
The 2010 presidential election lasted twenty-two days.

In the second round, the pattern observed also follows the initial hypothesis. The election begins with high attacks rates. The need to reverse the scenario explains the high percentages, particularly for government candidates. Both in 2006 and 2010, the PSDB candidates upended expectations and attained vote percentages above those predicted by the polls. Government candidates, however, who expected to win elections in the first round, were forced into a second round facing declining numbers in the polls. Only after poll numbers stabilised, assuring them the win, did the tone of attacks soften and the number of messages with positive advertisements become once again prevalent.

Conclusion

This chapter set out to analyse the political advertisements aired during the 2006 and 2010 presidential elections. The purpose was to stimulate the debate concerning the strategic use of spots in presidential elections in Brazil and the impact of the electoral legislation and political system in the structure of incentives. The study sought to emphasise the regulated character of the Brazilian model of political advertising, which is significantly different than the US model, where the only regulation in place is the guarantee that all candidates can freely purchase television time. As a result, these differences complicate the task of making comparisons with the findings of studies carried out in other countries.

In Brazil, the electoral legislation stipulates a set of rules, which affects two features of party strategies. On one hand, it has a strong influence over the content of electoral messages. The restrictiveness of Brazilian legislation is noted in the articles that forbid spots from using montages or gimmicking, computer graphics, animated cartoons and special effects. Most importantly, it forbids the airing of messages that might 'degrade' or 'ridicule' a party, candidate or coalition, punishing violators with the removal of the message and the concession of a rebuttal. From the point of view of political communication, the regulation of the content of messages suggests an excessive degree of tutelage over the electorate and, what is more, has a direct influence on the quality of information available for the public concerning the political alternatives available.

The majority of studies carried out thus far to understand the logic of electoral competition in the US has supported the use and expansion of negative advertisements. The main point of this argument is that the tone of advertisements is merely secondary, what matters is knowing if the messages are correctly informing the public. These studies claim that negative advertisements contribute to the exercise of democracy and provide valuable contributions to the informational environment (Geer 2006). Negative advertisements are considered more informative since certain information about candidates wouldn't otherwise be publicised (Polborn and Yi 2006). Of course, no one expects candidates to speak openly about their problems, shortcomings and faults. This is what Mayer (1996) calls the questioning character of negative advertisements. This is what highlights the faults of characters, the skills and virtues they do not possess, the mistakes they made and the problems they do not confront and the topics they would rather avoid. For Geer (2006), negative advertisements are adequate sources of information because they approach subjects the public considers relevant, in addition to presenting evidence that confirms the content of messages.

Studies on the reception of messages also demonstrate that negative information stimulates learning, are retained longer in the memory and are helpful in electoral choices. Marcus and Mackuen (1993) report that the rhetoric of feat stimulates anxiety which, on its turn, catches the attention of voters and their helps them learn about relevant political issues Brader (2005) argues that negative advertisements are persuasive because they have the ability to shatter political predispositions. For Newhagen et al. (1996), the ability of voters to remember information longer helps in persuasion, as ultimately voters forget the source of attacks but do not forget the information they contain. Lastly, Garramone et al. (1985), argue that negative advertisements help electoral choice because it shows the significant differences that exist among candidates. Based on the conclusion of international studies, it could thus be said that the restrictions imposed by electoral legislation in Brazil do not help the Brazilian elector decide. In fact, the opposite is the case: there is less information and the quality of information is lower in campaigns.

On the other hand, electoral legislation interferes in party strategies by determining how candidates are supposed to air their spots within regular television and radio programming. Such a set of rules directly affects the dynamics of campaigns and the influence parties can have over the electorate by keeping candidates from deciding when and how to air their messages. Despite this complex incentive structure, this article sought to elaborate theoretically and test empirically a set of behavioural hypotheses concerning how candidates distribute spots within the schedule established by the Superior Electoral Court. This aim was simplified by examining how candidates distribute attacks against opponents in this context of a complex yet restricted incentive framework. The analysis uncovered some peculiar patterns. Certainly the most interesting was that despite the risk of punishment because of the 'right of rebuttal' rule, candidates do not shy away from attacking their opponents. It was possible to observe that the strategy of using negative advertisements is a resource used especially by candidates trailing in the polls. Lula and Rousseff, who in the elections analysed led the dispute for presidency by a wide margin, used attacks more sparingly, although in the second round, because of a different scenario, decided to use negative advertisements more frequently.

The results of this investigation indicate that candidates also make other strategic decisions. The analysis showed that candidates would rather attack in night-time slots than during the day, although there some points off the curve, as Buarque, who made most attacks in the morning. Lastly, the investigation found distinct patterns as to the evolution of negative advertisements during the campaign. The differences were observed between the rounds of the elections and the political situation of candidates in voter intention polls. In sum, the analysis has emphasised that a political campaign must be concerned with not only what and how to portray a negative message, but also when.

The final question is: how can studying campaigns in Brazil increase the understanding of elections elsewhere? I believe that this chapter contributes in two ways. First, by addressing the determinants of the negative campaign in a multiparty political system. The second contribution of this chapter was to debate the role of electoral legislation and its impacts on electoral strategies and voter decision. The hypothesis seems to be that the more liberal and open rules for the airing of advertising on television, the more impact campaigns will have on the electorate. In Latin America, for example, television advertisements are allowed during 117 days in Venezuela, fifty days in Uruguay, forty-five days in Brazil, twenty-eight days in Chile and only eight in Paraguay (Borba 2013). This perspective challenges us to compare different electoral legislations in democratic countries. However, I believe that the answer as to the endless debate over whether or not campaigns have 'minimal effects' can be found in this variable.

Chapter Twelve

Understanding Negativity Within and Among Different Levels of Governments: Evidence from Turkey

Emre Toros

The highly competitive and rapidly changing scenery of electoral activity throughout the world seems to be more chaotic than ever. In different contexts, political actors test various tools in order to influence voter preferences. Operating in this diverse environment, these actors still have to decide on one common and crucial aspect of their electoral campaigns: whether to prioritise their own assets or draw attention to the weaknesses of their rivals. This decisive choice is conceptualised under the categories of positive and negative campaigning in political science literature. Recently, the latter, namely negative campaigning, attracted an increased attention both from academic and non-academic circles.

The basic motivation behind this chapter is to test the negative campaigning theory within and among different levels of government. Considering the growing interest in negative campaigns, there has still been relatively little study of its a) situation among different governmental levels and b) usefulness and travelling capacity in the context of alternative democratic settings. In that sense, Turkey seems to be an interesting case. The Turkish Republic has been a multiparty democracy since the mid-1940s. Although it has been interrupted by three military coups, the party and election system in Turkey has brought real alternations in the government from the very early years of the multiparty system. Thus, it is plausible to argue that Turkish voters have a tradition of evaluating the performance of political parties, as in any other Western-type democracy. That is to say, the dynamics of the evaluation of political parties in Turkey follow a similar pattern to those of other contemporary democracies, being driven by both economic and political forces. Moreover, the elevated importance of local elections in Turkey since 1990 provides a suitable base for the comparison of negativity between different governmental levels.

Accordingly, this chapter investigates the level of negative campaigning in Turkish election campaigns both for national and local elections. It sets explanations to the following two questions: What is the level of negativity in Turkish electoral campaigns and is there a difference in the level of negativity when we compare the general and local elections?

The analysis will begin with a theoretical discussion and an operational definition of negative campaigning. The outline of data collection, operationalisation, method of analysis and empirical results will follow the theoretical part. The study will conclude with a discussion on theoretical and practical suggestions.

Negative campaigning

Although not being mutually exclusive in the perfect sense, it is possible to define four basic concentration points in the towering literature of negative campaigning. The first concentration point is *description*. Descriptive studies analyse negative campaigning in different contexts and outline its basic features. Although context-wise the research on negative campaigning heavily concentrates on the US electoral scene (Skaperdas and Grofman 1995; Klotz 1998; Lau and Pomper 2001b; Sigelman and Kugler 2003; Francia and Herrnson 2007; Fridkin and Kenney 2011b), research on the subject has expanded to other multiparty systems of Europe (Elmelund-Præstekær 2008; Hopmann *et al.* 2012; Nai 2013; Walter and Vliegenthart 2010; Walter *et al.* 2014) and beyond (Sullivan and Sapir 2012b; Sigelman and Shiraev 2002). The second focus is the *normativity* where studies of this kind aim to differentiate negative campaigning from 'mud-sliding' by focusing on unethical and misleading aspects of messages (Mayer 1996; Davis and Ferrantino 1996; Schweitzer 2010). The third focus is the *cause* where researchers analyse negativity as a part of a grand electoral strategy and focus on why political actors decide to attack (or not to attack) their opponents (Geer 2006; Lau *et al.* 2007; Ladd 2012; Mattes 2012; Walter 2012a). The fourth and last focus is the *effect* of negative campaigns. Two camps are visible here. The first camp evaluates negative campaigning in a pejorative way and criticises it for being the cause of lower turnouts, political efficacy, cynicism and biased opinion formation (Ansolabehere and Iyengar 1995, 1994; Thorson *et al.* 2000; De Vreese and Semetko 2002; Jamieson 1992). Alternatively, the second camp values negative campaigning and argues that this strategy may act as an efficient informational source for the voters (Criegler *et al.* 2006; Geer 2006) and consequently leads to a further sense of belongingness to the political system (Finkel and Geer 1998; Martin 2004).

Additionally, an important sub-branch of the descriptive dimension of negative campaigning literature focuses on the content of the messages. This literature usually classifies the content of the electoral messages based on traits or issues (Swint 1998; Geer 2006; Blais and St-Vincent 2011; Walter and Vliegenthart 2010; Fridkin and Kenney 2011b). Both in the US and Western European context, the trait attacks are more frequently used compared to the issue attacks (Walter 2012b: 17). This is due to a number of reasons including the increased personalisation of politics (McAllistar 2007) and decreasing party loyalty (Deschouwer 2004). It is plausible to think that the situation will be similar in the Turkish context since political leaders in Turkey have always been the salient actors, not only within the sphere of politics but also within the spheres of economics and international relations (Heper and Sayarı 2008). The actions of these leaders while shaping these spheres also contoured the principles of political culture in Turkey.

Not surprisingly the complex literature on negative campaigning did not produce a single definition. For the purposes of operationalisation, however, the early definition of Surlin and Gordon (1977) and the more recent and popular attempt of Geer (2006) and Benoit (2007) seems rewarding. In these conceptualisations negativity is defined as any kind of criticism which is directed at one political actor to another during a campaign. This definition has a number of advantages. First of all, since this definition excludes normativity, it provides a perfect ground for measurement and hence empirical analysis. By this definition it is possible to carry out longitudinal studies in different contexts and time periods that will set up opportunities for comparisons, which is one of the main aims of this research. Consequently this study will follow the above-mentioned definition in order to answer the research questions and it leaves the cause and normativity dimensions of literature out of its scope.

An synopsis on Turkish local and general elections and electoral campaigns

The political parties and the elections have always been the central components of Turkish political structure. With the transition to democratic politics during the mid-1940s their view of political structure expanded, and the political parties consolidated their position in Turkish politics. During the early years of the Republic, two parties, namely the *Cumhuriyet Halk Partisi* (Republican People's Party, CHP) and the *Demokrat Parti* (Democrat Party, DP) dominated the electoral scene. In the three elections held in 1950, 1954 and 1957, CHP and DP collectively received more than 90 per cent of the total votes, and controlled 98 per cent of the parliamentary seats (Sayarı 2002). Although these early years displayed similarities with basic characteristics of two-party systems of Western European countries, it lacked in alteration in power and displayed a high level of polarisation (Sayarı 2002).

Although the electoral campaigns of this period were not subjected to any kind of empirical analysis, there is evidence which may be enough to think that this highly polarised structure provided suitable ground for negative campaigning.

The military administration of 1960 outlawed DP and banned its leading figures from politics. However, it did not take too long for DP to reunite under the newly formed *Adalet Partisi* (Justice Party, AP). Even stronger than DP, AP won the 1965 and the 1969 elections in a landslide with 52.87 per cent and 46.55 per cent vote shares respectively. For the first time, the electoral campaigns of this period utilised mass media coupled with the traditional tools of face-to-face interaction. However, similar to DP, AP's tenure in office was cut by the military in 1971. As opposed to the 1960 coup, this time AP was not outlawed and its executives were not banned from politics. Up to the third military intervention of 1980, AP and CHP dominated the party scene; but a series of new developments were also visible within the system. Among those, the most important one was the rising role of the minor parties. With the introduction of the new constitution and the changes in legal framework, a number of new parties managed to find a place in the political spectrum. The Marxist *Türkiye İşçi Partisi* (Turkish Workers Party, TİP), the extreme right-wing *Milliyetçi Hareket Partisi* (Nationalist Action Party, MHP), the explicitly *Islamist Milli Nizam Partisi* (National Order Party, MNP) and its successor, *Milli Selamet Partisi* (National Salvation Party, MSP), and the Alevi-based *Birlik Partisi* (Unity Party, BP) were representative of the expanding ideological and political spectrum of the party politics in 1960s and 1970s (Sayarı 2002). This fragmentation was coupled with the ideological polarisation, which was basically fuelled by the cold war tensions. When this highly polarised and fragmented political system was accompanied by the economic crisis, the military once again stepped in and suspended parliamentary politics in 1980.

It is correct to argue that the Americanisation of the electoral processes started during the 1960s. Firstly, the electoral campaigns of the period significantly prioritised the party leaders in their messages and frequently used the news published in print media to convey their messages (Aziz 2007: 143). Secondly, for the first time news about the political parties started to appear on television broadcasts of Turkish Radio and Television (TRT). And lastly, within this period, political parties started to employ public relations professionals for their election campaigns. In line with the recommendations of the advising public relations company, the AP spent a considerable amount of money and published five million copies of hand brochures and twenty thousand tape-cassettes (Özkan 2002: 40–53).

Unlike the previous coups, the 1980 military intervention had a strong impact on the Turkish political system. As the executive body of the military, the National Security Council (NSC) banned all political parties, arbitrarily vetoed the political rights of the individuals who were involved with politics before the coup and permitted only three new political parties for the electoral competition in 1983. Among these were the centre-right *Anavatan Partisi* (The Motherland Party, ANAP) that managed to get 45.1 per cent of the votes and formed a single party government. ANAP's single party government continued after the 1987 elections although ANAP's votes declined to 36.3 per cent. The single party governments of ANAP during the 1980s were replaced by a number of coalition governments during the 1990s. The three parliamentary elections in 1991, 1995 and 1999 underscored the volatility of the electorate as parties experienced significant shifts in their popular appeal (Sayarı 2002). One of the significant developments of the 1990s was the victory of the Islamist *Refah Partisi* (Prosperity Party, RP) in the 1995 elections. The 1999 election was also marked by the rise of the far-right nationalist party MHP. So, by the 1990s the Turkish political system was fragmented again as it was before the 1980 coup: none of the three elections of the 1990s formed single party governments. During the 1990s, the Turkish political system also experienced some other important developments. *Fazilet Partisi* (Virtue Party, FP), which is the successor to the RP that was banned by the constitutional court in 1998, managed to obtain 15.4 per cent of the votes in the 1999 elections, and also maintained control at the local/municipal level, including the metropolitan ones such as İstanbul and Ankara. When the FP was also closed by another ruling of the Constitutional Court in 2001, the Islamist movement faced a major split for the first time in their history. While the conservatives formed the *Saadet Partisi* (Felicity Party, SP), a faction which was labelled as reformist formed the new *Adalet ve Kalkınma Partisi* (Justice and Development Party, AKP) under Recep Tayyip Erdoğan's leadership. Additionally, for the first time the pro-Kurdish parties entered electoral competition in 1990s. As the first example of these parties, *Halkın Demokrasi Partisi* (People's Democracy Party, HADEP) managed to receive around 5 per cent of the votes in the 1995 and the 1999 elections, and became the lead party in a number of Eastern and South Eastern provinces of Turkey.

The mediatisation and Americanisation of the electoral processes gained further ground during these years. Starting with this period, parties used the tools from American-style campaigning more frequently. For example, during the 1983 electoral campaign ANAP's leader Özal was displayed like a US presidential candidate in various forms. Additionally, all of the parties that competed in this period, starting with the 1983 general elections, hired professional public relations companies which have turned electoral competitions into PR wars (Aziz 2007). Moreover, starting from the 1983 elections, competing parties were allowed to publish political advertorials in print media, which contributed the mediatisation process. In 1987 this right was expanded to television broadcasts which have totally changed the nature of electoral campaigns: for the first time in history, parties produced political advertorials and aired these advertisements via TRT. The influence of television in political campaigns became more visible in the 1991 elections with the establishment of private television channels. Abusing the administrative and legal vacuum of the time, the media bosses of these channels, depending on their alliances with the alternative political parties, openly supported or opposed political parties in their broadcasts (Aziz 2007: 146). Although governments of the time applied a number of measures to prevent this 'race of mud-sliding' within the Turkish media, the situation continued in the 1995 and 1999 elections: The Turkish print and visual media, which was highly monopolised and guided by a number of media bosses, continued to display examples of strong negative tones.

The successive victories of AKP reshaped the Turkish political arena, starting with the 2002 elections. Following the victory in 2002, AKP won the 2007 and 2011 elections and became the only incumbent party which has increased its votes in three subsequent elections in Turkish political history. As with the rest of the world, the election campaigns of this decade in Turkey used the Internet as the new communication channel to reach the voter: Parties published their advertisements on popular search engines like Google and Yahoo; sent emails to voters and took advantage of Facebook and Twitter. Additionally, in order to contact the voter directly, parties sent short messages (SMS) to mobile phone users. Also in this decade, the saliency of local elections increased in Turkey (İncioğlu 2002; Eligür 2009; Çarkoğlu 2009; Toros 2012a) which in return forced political parties to run nationwide campaigns similar to the ones they plan for in general elections.

The local government structure of the Turkish Republic is tripartite: villages, municipalities, and provincial administrations. Mayors of municipalities are elected according to the plurality of votes and serve for five years. While the district municipalities are responsible for basic municipal services in their own areas, the greater city municipalities carry out bigger long-term projects. Even though the elections are held for all three of these components, the most significant race has always been at the municipal level. The local elections in Turkey followed a similar path as the general elections in the 1940s. However, their importance increased especially after the 1990s. Until then, the local elections in Turkey were characterised by low turnout rates coupled with the same results acquired for the parliamentary elections. This was mainly due to the legal framework of the time, which provides a very limited space for the self-government agencies to enact their own policies. However, the local government reforms which took place during the 1980s have changed the whole picture, as these reforms strengthened the municipalities financially and broadened their scope of policy areas. Moreover, this reform introduced a two-tier system that combines the district municipalities and a Greater City Municipality in big metropolises like Istanbul and Ankara. With the new laws introduced to the system, the greater city municipalities have access to an important amount of funds provided by central governments (Kalaycıoğlu 1989). As large cities like İstanbul, Ankara and İzmir continue to accommodate larger populations; the mayors became more and more significant to the political scene. The administration of these cities has become very important, in order for the political parties to consolidate their vote base. After their services as mayors in İstanbul, Bedrettin Dalan, Ali Müfit Gürtuna and Recep Tayyip Erdoğan formed new political parties and competed in national elections.

Unlike the pre-1990 period, political parties and their candidates engaged in intense political campaigns which attracted a lot of media attention and coverage (İncioğlu 2002). The content of the electoral messages also altered from national issues to local issues and projects. Most of the time candidates asked for voters to cast their votes on the basis of these projects, rather than the party competition happening at the national level. Although this is the case, the agenda of national politics highly shapes what happens at the local elections (İncioğlu 2002). When the increasing number of urban voters are causing concern, coupled with the calls of decentralisation and greater democratisation demands, the importance of local governments is likely to continue in the forthcoming years.

Data and coding

The coding scheme of this study was constructed after checking a number of available examples such as the 2001 British Electoral Study (Clarke 2003), and the 2006 Federal Election Study of Canada (Soroka et al. 2006) and Geer (2006).[1] Data collection was carried out by manifest and latent content analysis of the news texts.

---

1. Geer's (2006) coding method does not differ much from Benoit's (2007) coding method. The main difference is that Geer does not makes a distinction between attacks and defences as Benoit does, Geer just labels both as negative campaigning. In addition, Geer takes also the prominence of the positive or negative appeal into account. When the same appeal is repeated Geer counts them as separate appeals in contrast to Benoit who would see them as one message based on its content.

The analysis includes only the news about political parties and politicians with party affiliations. Opinion pieces, news on other political actors like leaders of civil society organisations or information produced by columnists were excluded from the analysis. In the first step, manifest content analysis was carried out to determine the nature of the quantitative distribution. This analysis included the name of the newspaper, election period, the date of the news, message sending party, message sending person, message receiving party and message receiving person. All of the manifest content was measured at the nominal level and coded according to the predefined categories of existent newspapers, election dates, political parties and politicians. For example, message sending and/or receiving party was recorded after determining the explicit name of the party within the reported news. Similarly, the message sending and message receiving politician was noted according to the politician's party affiliation which is present in the coded news.

Table 12.1: Variable characteristics

Content element	Short definition	Manifest or latent	Measurement level	Measurement categories
Newspaper name	The name of the newspaper in which the news is found	Manifest	Nominal	Newspaper names (i.e. *Hürriyet*, *Milliyet* etc.)
Election period	The election year that the news belongs to	Manifest	Nominal	Election dates as years (i.e. 1983, 1987, 2011 etc.)
Message receiving political party	The political party which receives a message with negative tone	Manifest	Nominal	Names of the political parties (i.e. CHP, AKP, MHP etc.)
Message sending political party	The political party which sends a message with negative tone	Manifest	Nominal	Names of the political parties (i.e. CHP, AKP, MHP etc.)
Message receiving politician	The politician who receives a message with negative tone	Manifest	Nominal	Names of the politicians who have political party affiliations.
Message sending politician	The politician who sends a message with negative tone	Manifest	Nominal	Names of the politicians who have political party affiliations.
The tone of the message	The categorised content of the news according to positive or negative tones	Latent	Binary	Positive or negative

Latent content analysis was then used in order to determine the contextual orientation of the text. For this purpose – a single variable – the tone was set. The tone of the message is a binary variable and captured by a proxy measure, which is common within literature. As previously mentioned, the coders recorded statements which are defined as any kind of criticism which is directed at one political actor from another as negative. The statements which fall out of this scope were coded as messages with a positive tone. Table 12.1 summarises the variables used for the analysis according to their basic characteristics (coding scheme available upon request).

As mentioned above, the newspapers are chosen as the source of information. This is because the way in which the campaigns are reported in the media is very often shaped by how citizens actually perceive and experience the campaign (Ridout and Franz 2008). Five national newspapers were subjected to content analysis for each local and national election. The newspapers were first stratified according to their ideological leanings as left, centre and right (Toros 2012b) and then were chosen randomly (one each from the left and right and three from the centre). The analysis covered the news that was published in the four weeks prior to the election day. In total the analysis covered eleven election campaigns, eight general, and three local elections starting from 1980.

The coders followed the below mentioned guidelines:

- Determine if there is an appeal; which is any kind of criticism that is directed from one political actor to another.
- If 'yes', count and record the number of appeals.
- Determine the date and actor of the appeal and note his/her characteristics according to the coding scheme.
- For each appeal, determine if the actor of the appeal is criticising any other party (negative campaigning) or presenting his or her own policy (positive campaigning).
- For each appeal determine the content: issue or character trait.

The inter-coder reliability was checked by using Krippendorf's Alpha Test. The questions of tone (positive or negative) and the content of the appeal (issues or traits) were checked and test results were reported as 0.78 and 0.71 respectively. As a result, the study produced a scale of negativity for each election, which varies from zero to 100, where zero represents an absolute positive and 100 means an absolute negative campaign.

Results

Before putting forward the results, it would be worthwhile to present the descriptive characteristics of the data. The research process provided a significant amount of data; in total the research team coded 4,779 cases from eighteen different newspapers. Table 12.2 summarises the general characteristics of the database according to the previously defined sampling characteristics.

Table 12.2: Code frequencies and percentages according to newspapers and election years: general elections and local elections, 1983–2011

General elections			Local elections		
Newspaper	f	%	*Newspaper*	f	%
Birgün	58	1.5	*Birgün*	23	2.7
Cumhuriyet	755	19.3	*Hürriyet*	308	35.8
Gözcü	100	2.6	*Milli Gazete*	82	9.5
Günaydın	45	1.1	*Vatan*	164	19.1
Güneş	85	2.2	*Zaman*	23	2.7
Hürriyet	865	22.1			
Milli Gazete	139	3.5			
Milliyet	203	5.2			
Ortadoğu	243	6.2			
Radikal	210	5.4			
Sabah	231	5.9			
Sözcü	119	3.0			
Taraf	99	2.5			
Türkiye	107	2.7			
Yeni Yüzyıl	106	2.7			
Yeniçağ	114	2.9			
Zaman	440	11.2			
Election year	f	%	*Election year*	f	%
1983	315	8.0	1999	315	36.6
1987	466	11.8	2004	235	27.3
1991	588	15.0	2009	310	36.1
1995	400	10.2			
1999	492	12.5			
2002	595	15.1			
2007	486	12.4			
2011	577	14.7			
	3,919	**100**		**860**	**100**
			TOTAL	**4,779**	**100**

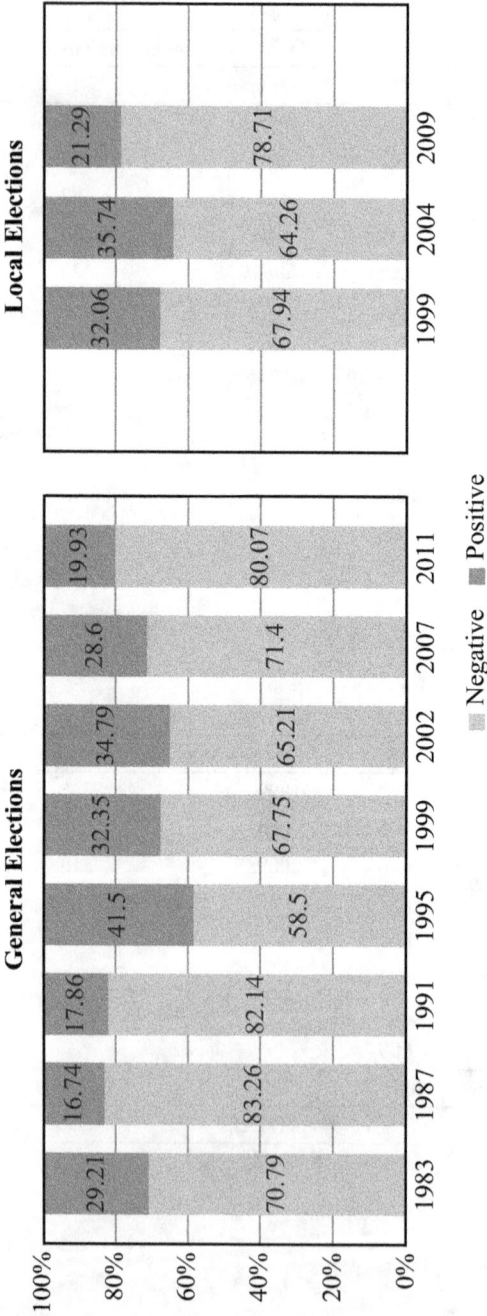

Figure 12.1: The tone of the election campaigns in Turkey, general and local elections 1983–2011 (newspaper articles)

Describing the situation of negative campaigns in Turkey

To recall, this study firstly searches for the answer to the following question: 'What is the level of negativity in Turkish electoral campaigns?' Figure 12.1 and Figure 12.2 display the findings related to this question. While the former illustrates the tone of the campaigns (negative or positive), the latter presents the degree of negativity for all of the elections.

As it is evident from Figure 12.1, for both general and local elections, the share of negative appeals is larger than the positive appeals. The statistical significance of this difference was tested separately for the different governmental levels with chi-square procedure and results ratified the statistical significance of the differences: for general elections $x^2 = 133,545$, $df = 7$, p<0.001 and for local elections $x^2 = 15,504$, $df = 2$, p<0.001. Accordingly, as the first conclusion for this research question it can be argued that for both of the general and local elections, the dominant tone of the election campaigns in Turkey is negative.

By checking the results of Figure 12.2 it is not possible to trace a major decreasing or increasing trend in the degree of negativity for elections in Turkey.[2] The scores vary between 58.5 and 83.3 per cent. On three occasions, in 1987, 1991 and 2011, the negativity score of elections exceeds the overall average of the negativity score, which is 72.9 per cent. On the other five occasions it falls below the average. One interesting point to mention is that the negativity scores display a steady increase after 2002: scores increased around 5 per cent on average for each election after the 2002 general elections. The peak scores, which are all over 80 per cent, were also recorded in 1987, 1991 and 2011. Since these scores were recorded during the single party governments of ANAP (1983 and 1987) and AKP (2007), as the second conclusion for this research question, it is possible to argue that negativity increases during the single party governments ($r = 0.83$, p<0.01). This also explains the rise in the 2007 elections when the AKP won the elections and established its first single party government after the 2002 elections.

When the campaign tone is in question, the local elections display a similar pattern with the general elections. The independent group's t-test ratified that general elections ($M=72.9$, $SD=8.8$) do not differ significantly from local elections ($M=70.3$, $SD=7.49$), $t(9)= 0.36$, p<0.72. Additionally, the increasing tendency in negativity after 2002 is also visible in local elections. Therefore, as the last conclusion, it is possible to argue that the tone of the electoral messages did not differ for general and local elections.

In light of the above arguments it can be concluded that although the negativity scores increase during the single party governments, it fluctuated during the elections and there is no visible increasing trend in negativity.

---

2.   At the time of preparing this chapter, the data for the remaining local elections, which dates back to 1987, was still in the process of coding. However, interpreting the data in hand and considering the theoretical link between local and general elections (Toros 2012a) it is still possible to argue that the similarity between local and general elections will sustain after the inclusion of this data.

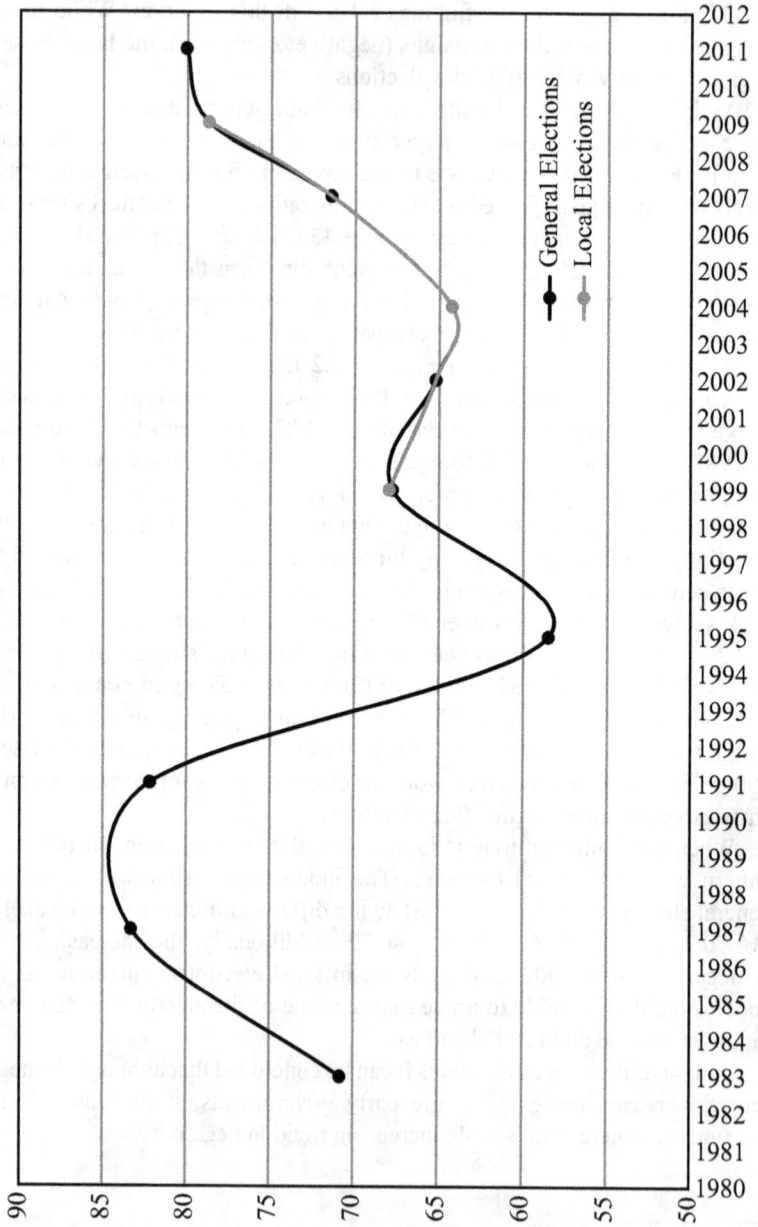

Figure 12.2: Level of negative campaigning in Turkish general and local elections 1983–2011 (newspaper articles)

When comparing the different governmental levels with respect to negativity, it would be worthwhile to check the content of the negative campaigns in Turkey. Parallel with existing literature, the research team coded the content of both positive and negative appeals under the categories of character traits and issues.

Figure 12.3 displays the fact that, where both positive and negative appeals are concerned, issues have more space compared to the character traits. Although according to Figure 12.3 the gap between the categories decreases for local elections, the differences are still statistically significant: for general elections $x^2 = 89,010$ $df=7$, p<0.001 and for local elections $x^2 = 21,266$, $df=2$, p<0.001. Accordingly, the first conclusion is that the content of the messages mostly refer to issues rather than the character traits in the Turkish setting.

However, unlike the similarity between general and local elections regarding the tone of the messages, general and local elections differ when the content of the messages are analysed. The independent groups t-test for the category of character traits, ratified that general elections ($M=27.87$, $SD=7.8$) differ significantly from local elections ($M=40.30$, $SD=9.5$), $t(9)=-2.226$, p<0.05. Hence the second conclusion is that the messages in local elections tend to be more character trait oriented compared to the messages of general elections. Going one step further, Figure 12.4 analyses the share of issues and traits only in negative appeals. It is evident that the gap reduces further and comparatively and character traits find more similarities within the messages. Therefore, as the last conclusion, it is possible to argue that for local elections the content of character traits is more common in negative appeals.

Discussion and conclusion

This study tested the theory of negative campaigning in the Turkish context and produced the following results: (1) The dominant tone of the election campaigns in Turkey is negative; (2) negativity of electoral campaigns increased during the single party governments; (3) the dominant negative tone of the electoral messages did not differ for general and local elections; (4) in general the content of the messages refers to issues rather than the character traits, but the messages in local elections tend to be more character traits-oriented compared to the messages of general elections; and (5) the content of character traits is more common in negative appeals.

First of all, the study revealed the fact that Turkey displays similar characteristics as European countries like the UK, Germany and the Netherlands, where negativity fluctuates over time. However, the level of negativity is quite high in Turkey when compared to these countries. This extraordinary level of negativity, which is 72.9 per cent on average, needs some further elaboration. Two explanations are possible. Firstly, it may be argued that this high score is related to the media outlet chosen for the unit of analysis. Newspapers, in accordance with the media bias explained in the theoretical part, highlight and prioritise news with polemics, which can attract readers' attention and hence cause this high level of negativity. This explanation, at the same time, signifies a weakness of this study. In order to reach more robust and substantial conclusions about the subject, these results should be supported with information collected from other mediums like party election broadcasts and alike.

Figure 12.3: Levels of issues and traits in electoral messages (both positive and negative appeals), Turkish general and local elections 1983–2011 (newspaper articles)

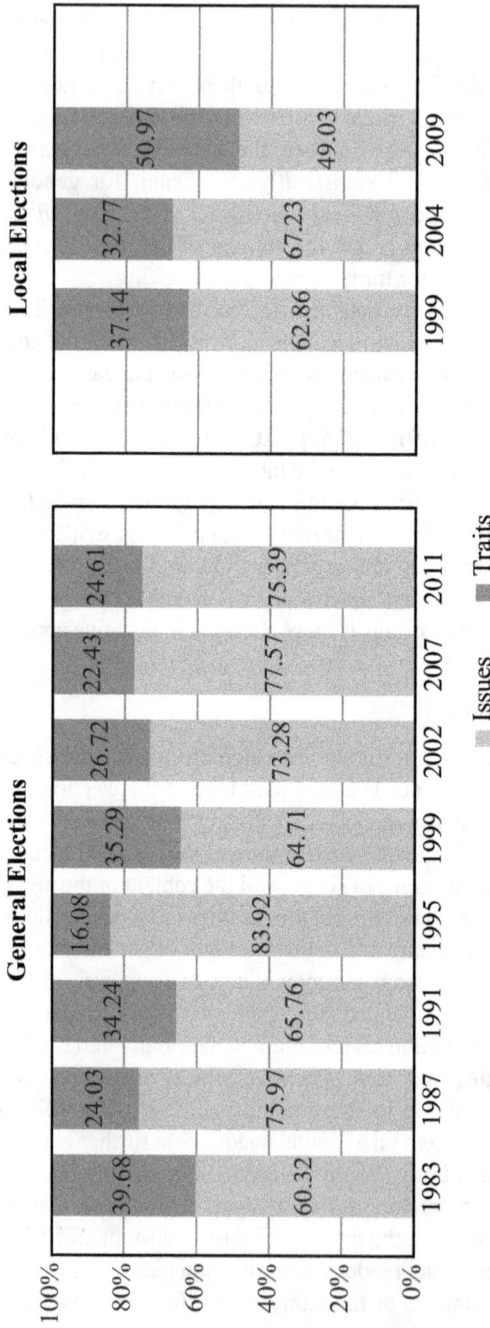

Figure 12.4: Levels of issues and traits in negative electoral messages, Turkish general and local elections 1983–2011 (newspaper articles)

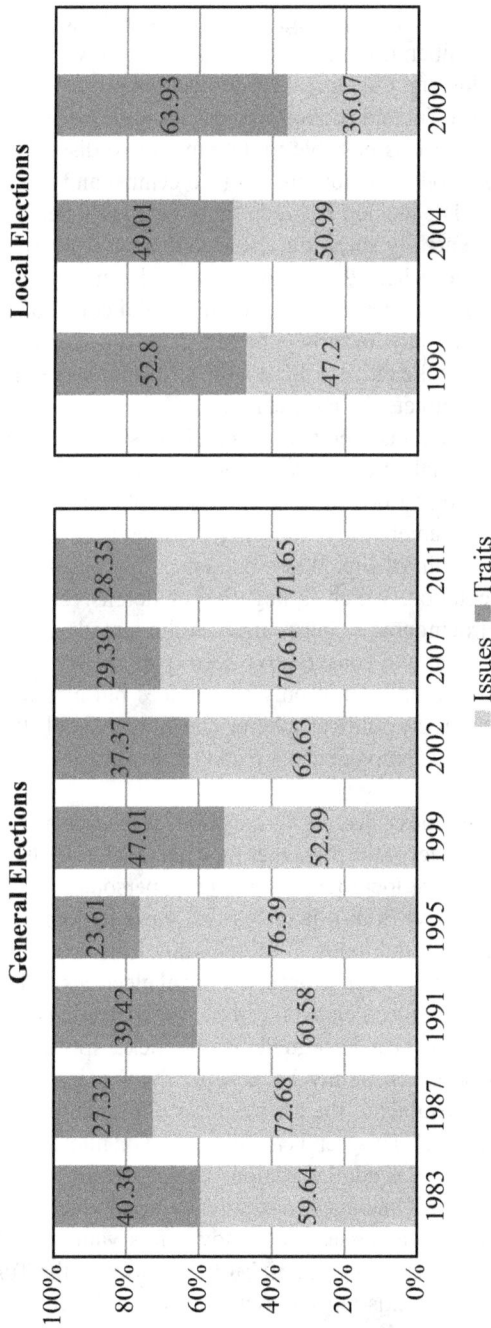

General Elections

	1983	1987	1991	1995	1999	2002	2007	2011
Traits	40.36	27.32	39.42	23.61	47.01	37.37	29.39	28.35
Issues	59.64	72.68	60.58	76.39	52.99	62.63	70.61	71.65

Local Elections

	1999	2004	2009
Traits	52.8	49.01	63.93
Issues	47.2	50.99	36.07

Issues   Traits

Second, and perhaps more convincingly, this high level of negativity is due to a specific character of Turkish political culture. The lines of division within Turkish politics which are shaped by ethical, religious and cultural motivations leave only a limited space for deliberation and consensus. As in any other top-down modernisation projects in history, the radical modernisation project of the Turkish Republic created political, social and economic blocks within the society. For the Turkish modernisation project it is possible to determine two distinct camps: the defenders of the Kemalist modernisation project (the centre) and the others (the periphery) (Mardin 1973). The tension between these camps shaped the political culture of Turkey today. Generally speaking, these camps have always perceived politics as a 'zero-sum-game' where there can only be winners or losers. In that sense politics has always been a 'battleground' rather than a constitutive activity. That is to say that political activity in Turkey did not shape the economic, cultural or sociological principles that the citizens agreed on. Instead it served as the main tool for gaining power to eliminate the rival camp.

The most visible, long-lasting and powerful line of division within the Turkish society, which is the secular-Islamic rivalry, became even more salient after the successive victories of the AKP. Looking at the Turkish political landscape today one can draw this as two diametrically opposing pictures that reflect the deep cleavages in almost every walk of life. When one takes into account the motive of the AKP's power orientation, which is negative or defensive, the AKP rule does not lead to a liberal democracy, 'but reinforces the already existing power orientations among the secular and conservative sectors of society' (Çınar 2011). This kind of governmental mind-set not only reproduces but also sharpens the division lines that exist within the political sphere. Thus it is probable that the high level of negativity in electoral campaigns is a result of this integral characteristic of Turkish political culture.

When the content of the messages are in question, it is expected that issues should be more likely the subject of the messages than personal traits at the national level campaigns. Conversely, at local level campaigns, personal traits should be more common than issues (Geer 2006). It seems that these hypotheses are valid for the Turkish case. Although the tones of the messages display similarity, the content of the messages varies between general and local elections in Turkey. This can be explained by the personalised character of the local elections compared to the general elections in Turkey. It can be argued that the 'ticket splitting' in Turkish local elections (İncioğlu 2002) is mainly because of the dominant tendency to vote by considering the credentials of the candidates, rather than the promises of political parties at the local level. This trend can be verified on numerous occasions in the past, where mayors of local administrations changed their political parties just before the elections and still managed to receive winning vote shares.

In general, even with its weaknesses, this study offers valuable information about the situation of negative campaigning in Turkey. It locates the Turkish case within literature by testing the existing theories with the help of an up-to-date database. However, there is a need for further research, especially for locating the Turkish case in cross-country comparisons. In that sense, it is hoped that this study constitutes a starting point and provides ground for further work in the field.

Chapter Thirteen

An OCEAN of Negativity: An Experimental Assessment on Personality Traits and the Chances to 'Go Dirty' in Debates on Political Issues

Alessandro Nai, Valentina Holecz, Mario Marchesini, Adrien Petitpas and Ben Sanogo-Willers[1]

This chapter deals with the personality underpinnings of negative discourse during political debates. Why are some people more likely than others to attack their adversaries – verbally, of course – when discussing political issues? Is this related to their inner personality traits, and how?

In doing so, we attempt to bring together two strands of recent literature: the first deals with how personality traits influence social and political behaviour, while the second deals with the causes of negative discourse during political debates (i.e. the use in campaign speeches or any form of political debate of verbal attacks towards opponents). Both strands of literature have received strong and increasing attention lately, but to our knowledge no one has yet attempted to bridge the blatant gap between the two.

On the one hand, a growing and undoubtedly 'trendy' literature deals with how personality traits drive our social and political life. Although several approaches do exist for the qualification and measure of personality traits (on this, *see* Ashton 2007: 42–46), one that has quickly established as the most prominent one (Gerber *et al.* 2011: 266) is the so-called 'Big Five Inventory' (BFI; John *et al.* 1991; John *et al.* 2008). Accordingly, personality can be summed up through five major individual traits: *Openness to experience, Conscientiousness, Extraversion, Agreeableness* and *Neuroticism* (aka OCEAN). Those 'Big Five' have recently been linked to a disparate range of social and political behaviours,[2] e.g. media use and political attentiveness (Mondak 2010), consumption of alcohol and tobacco (Mezquita *et al.* 2010), partisan identification and affiliation (Gerber *et al.* 2011; Vecchione *et al.* 2011), emotional intelligence (Van der Zee *et al.* 2002), political engagement (Mondak *et al.* 2010), stigmatisation against HIV/AIDS (McCrae *et al.* 2007), turnout and political participation (Anderson 2009; Vecchione and Caprara 2009).

1. We are very grateful to Professor Koviljka Barisnikov and Mrs Caroline Cheam (Department of Clinical Psychology, University of Geneva) for lending us their experimental laboratory and for their precious help on logistics. Our sincere thanks also go to all participants in our experimental sessions for their kindness and receptiveness.

2. For a review on existing literature, *see* the excellent article by Gerber *et al.* (2011).

The yet unanswered question in this literature is: are such personality traits also relevant for negative discourse, and how?

On the other hand, recent literature has shown that the use of negative discourse in political debates (usually referred to as 'negative campaigning'; Ansolabehere *et al.* 1994; Lau and Pomper 2004; Stevens 2009; Nai 2013) might depend on a variety of determinants as, e.g. ideological view of the speaker (Theilmann and Wilhite 1998; Lau and Pomper 2001b), gender (Fridkin Kahn 1993), prospect of electoral failure (Skaperdas and Grofman 1995; Harrington and Hess 1996; Walter *et al.* 2014), issue ownership (Damore 2002), anonymity of the speaker (Brooks and Murov 2012).

Again, the yet unanswered question in this literature is: what if the reasons to 'go negative' are also to be found within the personality traits of those who (verbally) attack their opponents during a debate?

The aim of this chapter is to show that the classification of personality traits according to the Big Five Inventory has a serious contribution to make to our understanding of the causes of negative discourse (and, thus, on the use of 'negative campaigning' during political debates). Our hope is to open up new research venues appealing to both scholars working on how personality shapes participation in social and political life, and researchers dealing with the roots of negative speeches in the political game.

Our data come from a series of experimental debate simulations run during the 2014 spring semester at the University of Geneva on a sample of fifty-four voluntary students. Small groups of participants were asked to discuss a chosen political topic (the power of television nowadays), during which a team of coders measured how participants used negative discourse. Those simulations were furthermore based on a double experimental treatment: some groups were exposed to an emotional video on the topic, whereas other groups were told to reach a consensual decision at the end of the debate. Those experimental treatments were designed to manipulate the contextual settings of the debate: increased emotionality of the topic, and increased competition (or cooperation) between participants during the debate. In line with recent research on the interaction between contextual and individual traits (*see* e.g. Mondak *et al.* 2010), we explore for a second time how those changing contextual situations moderate the relationship between personality traits and the use of negative discourse.

Negative discourse and where does it come from

Current attention to negative speeches, both within and outside the academic community, is driven mostly by two facts: first, nasty messages are unpopular (*see* e.g. Fridkin and Kenney 2011a), and a substantial part of the electorate thinks that today's campaigns are 'too negative'.[3] Second, we do not know precisely

---

3. The PEW January 2012 report shows that about 50 per cent of Americans find the early stages of the 2012 US Presidential Election campaign 'too negative', and 55 per cent find it even 'dull'. (http://www.people-press.org/2012/01/18/campaign-2012-too-negative-too-long-dull/).

what kind of effects such nasty messages have on the political game, which has lead to a rather interesting controversy in literature (*see* Chapter Fourteen in this volume). On the one hand, several scholars provide evidence of harmful effects: negativism may cause citizens' disaffection to vote (Ansolabehere and Iyengar 1995; Ansolabehere *et al.* 1994; Ansolabehere *et al.* 1999; Lemert *et al.* 1999), cynicism toward political elites (Thorson *et al.* 2000; Valentino *et al.* 2001) and the political system itself (Ansolabehere and Iyengar 1995), and even lead to increased ambivalence (Nai 2014a). On the other hand, a number of studies highlight a positive effect of negativism, which is said to increase issue salience and, therefore, citizens' turnout (Finkel and Geer 1998; Freedman and Goldstein 1999; Martin 2004), and to enhance the quality of the information delivered during political campaigns and, thus, of individuals' decisions (Geer 2006).

Whatever the effects of negative discourse might be, a growing strand of research has dealt with what might *cause* participants in a political debate to 'go negative' on their opponents. Although research on this issue is rather fragmented (*see* Chapter Six in this volume), two major types of factors might be isolated: situational and personal determinants.

On the one hand, *situational* determinants deal with the nature and progress of the political game, and the position the actors hold within it.

Thus, for example, the prospect of (electoral) failure has been shown to increase the chances to 'go negative' (Skaperdas and Grofman 1995; Harrington and Hess 1996; Damore 2002; Walter *et al.* 2014; Nai and Sciarini 2015). More willing actors bear the risk of 'backlash effect', i.e. the risk that negative advertisement might 'scare off' voters in the attacker camp (Pfau and Kenski 1990; Brooks and Murov 2012; Walter 2012), actors lagging behind have little to lose – and much to gain – from an offensive strategy. Similarly, the frequency of negative messages is stronger for opposition parties (Walter *et al.* 2014), and increases as the voting day draws near: 'at the outset of a campaign, it may be more effective for candidates to provide voters with information about who they are and what issues are important to them. If candidates attack early, they are unable to define themselves to voters because all they are communicating is negative information about their opponents' (Damore 2002: 672). By contrast, negative rhetoric is more likely to appear towards the end of the campaign, in order to increase citizens' support once voters are saturated with positive information (Damore 2002: 673; Peterson and Djupe 2005; Elmelund-Præstekær 2011). Actors perceived as more 'credible' have also been shown to make greater use of negative speeches: 'by waiting to go negative until after they have established themselves in the mind of voters, candidates may be perceived as more credible, which may increase the veracity of their attacks' (Damore 2002: 673), which is the reason why actors 'owning' the issue at stake are more likely to attack their opponents.

On the other hand, personal determinants, of higher interest for us here, deal with who the actors are.

Research on how personal traits affect the use of negative speeches is far less developed, for obvious reasons. Some scholars have however shown that the ideology of the person matters greatly for its use of negative discourse. Thus, in a US setting, Republican candidates are more likely to attack their opponents than Democrats (Theilmann and Wilhite 1998; Lau and Pomper 2001b), as are members of more 'extreme' political parties in other non-US settings (Elmelund-Præstekær 2010). Moving closer to our scope, some research points to the fact that personal attributes also matter for the use of negative discourse. Thus, candidates perceived as having less attractive personal attributes have been shown to be more willing to 'go negative' (Harrington and Hess 1996), and even that female candidates are more likely to use negative appeals than their male counterparts (Fridkin Kahn 1993).

But what about other personal attributes, such as personality traits? On this issue, literature is silent.

The Big Five approach and the personality underpinnings of negative discourse

Personality traits might be defined as 'internal psychological structures that are relatively fixed and enduring, that are susceptible to observation, and that predict behaviour' (Mondak *et al.* 2010: 2). Their relative stability over time has been confirmed in recent research (*see* Ashton 2007: 81–100), which comes from the fact that those traits might be partially determined by our genetic structure (McCrae *et al.* 2001; McCrae and Costa 2003; Hatemi and McDermott 2011).

Although several approaches do exist for the qualification and measure of personality traits (Ashton 2007: 42–46), the one usually seen as the most prominent one is the so-called 'Big Five Inventory' (BFI; John *et al.* 1991; John *et al.* 2008). According to this approach, personality can be summed up through five major individual traits: *Openness to experience, Conscientiousness, Extraversion, Agreeableness* and *Neuroticism.*

It is important to note that those five traits represent a 'framework enabling parsimonious representation of the bulk of trait structure' (Mondak 2010: 2); they should thus not be seen as depicting each variation in the complexity of human personality, but instead as 'broad domains, collectively organising and summarising the vast majority of subsidiary traits' (Mondak *et al.* 2010: 2).

First, *openness to experience* refers to a tendency to experience fresh situations, an eagerness towards everything that is new, challenging and stimulating. High openness to experience (versus closed-mindedness) is associated 'with increased creativity, curiosity, imagination and nonconformity, self-efficacy, and high-risk health behaviours' (Mondak and Halperin 2008: 342). We expect openness to experience to have no direct effect on the use of negative discourse. This personality trait has been shown to decrease self-reported anger and hostility, but no significant effect on verbal aggressiveness has been shown (Tremblay and Ewart 2005: 342–343).

Second, *conscientiousness* refers to a tendency to plan and organise all aspects of the individual and collective life, and is often associated with responsibility and conformity. Individuals high on conscientiousness 'are viewed as dutiful, organised, and reliable. For those who score low, adjectives such as lazy, impulsive and unreliable are considered befitting' (Mondak and Halperin 2008: 343). We expect conscientiousness to decrease the use of negative discourse. Individuals high in this personality trait have been shown to rate high on self-control (Roberts *et al.* 2005) and report lower levels of anger (Jensen-Campbell *et al.* 2007); in the same vein, conscientiousness decreases self-reported likelihood for physical aggression (Tremblay and Ewart 2005: 342–343), thus it seems logical to expect a similar effect on verbal attacks in a direct way.

Third, *extraversion* (versus introversion) refers to a tendency to enjoy a sociable and active life, to move away from withdrawal, passivity and shyness (Mondak and Halperin 2008: 344). Individuals high in extraversion are sociable, energetic, active and assertive. Concerning extraversion, we can anticipate both reasons to 'go negative' and reasons not to. First, extravert individuals effortlessly engage in social interactions, and seem to dispose of all the rhetoric tools to fit into place during discussions; extraverts show higher levels of tolerance (Mondak 2010: 57) and lower levels of hostility (Tremblay and Ewart 2005: 342–343). Thus, the likelihood for negative discourse should be lower. At the same time, however, extraverts easily show bold and energetic social interactions (Mondak 2010: 56) and a stronger tendency for risk taking (Eysenck 1976; Hoyle *et al.* 2000; Nicholson *et al.* 2005), which could lead to an increased use of negative discourse.

Fourth, *agreeableness* refers to 'co-operative, sympathetic and altruistic tendencies, and has been shown to predict membership in coalitions and strategic alliances, social trust, conflict avoidance and conflict resolution and health behaviours' (Mondak and Halperin 2008: 346). An individual higher in agreeableness tries to please them all and is thus expected to be the one who will make a lower use of negative discourse overall. This personality trait is often shown as opposite to any form of antagonism (John *et al.* 2008: 120), and has been shown to lead to increased kindness and sympathy (Mondak 2010: 58). Agreeable individuals tend to report lower levels of physical and verbal aggression (Tremblay and Ewart 2005: 342–343). For individuals higher in agreeableness, thus, the likelihood for negative discourse should be weak.

Finally, *neuroticism*, an inverse function of emotional stability, refers to a tendency to experience emotional distress and generally to be easily subject to negative feelings such as anxiety, sadness, tension, edginess, excitability, stress and instability. People high in neuroticism 'view many developments as unfair and often unsatisfactory' (Mondak and Halperin 2008: 345). We expect individuals high in this personality trait to show an opposite behaviour than those high in agreeableness, and thus to 'go negative' quite likely on their colleagues during debates. Individuals high in neuroticism are often referred to as tense, anxious and nervous (Mondak 2010: 61), which should affect their use of negative discourse. Indeed, Tremblay and Ewart (2005: 342–343) find neurotic individuals to score higher on anger and hostility scales, Stanford *et al.* (2003) find similar effects on IPAS (Impulsive/Premeditated Aggression Scales) scores, and Infante and Wigley (1986) show that neuroticism leads more likely to hostility, assertiveness, and argumentativeness.

The experiment

Data have been gathered through a series of experimental simulations held at the University of Geneva during the 2014 spring semester. Fifty-four voluntary students have participated in our experiments, during which they had to debate on an assigned topic (the power of television nowadays) in a small group setting. Overall eleven debate simulations were run, with an average of 4.9 participants (minimum three, maximum six) per debate; in order to take into account these differences, all analyses are controlled by the number of participants in the debate session.

Our sample of fifty-four participants is stratified as follows: 33.3 per cent females, 26.1 years old on average (SD=6.5), 57.4 per cent students at BA level, 29.6 per cent at MA level, 3.7 per cent at PhD level and 9.3 per cent signalled another occupation (just finished formation or reorienting); 63.1 per cent were French speaking native (although all participants expressed in perfect French during the debate). Attitudinally, our participants rate on average 4.1 on the 0–10 left–right scale (SD=2.7) and 5.6 on a 0–8 scale rating libertarian (0=authoritarian) values (SD=1.6).[4] Their average self-reported satisfaction is 3.6 on a 1–5 scale where one represents the lowest satisfaction and five the highest (SD=0.5).[5]

The sample of participants has no statistical representativeness – no random sampling was possible – which of course raises the problem of external validity, both for the general population and the sub-population of students. Our sample meets however the three criteria discussed in Druckman and Kam (2011: 44) for the assessment of external validity in non-representative experimental samples: 1) no prior work on this research agenda already exists on a similar sample (which means that the use of other samples is less pressing); 2) our sample seems relatively generalisable to the population of students; and 3) the goal of our study is more to generate new theoretical insights than to generalise existing ones.

Our experimental protocol was at the same time quite simple and rather complex. Quite simply, we asked participants to fill in a short survey, and then to freely discuss on an assigned topic in a small group setting. Some sessions were however more complex, based on up to two active treatments;[6] all in all, six different session types have been run. Participants have been randomly assigned to each session type (except when schedule conflict did not allow them to be present for a specific session).

---

4. Computed by adding responses to a question on gay rights ('gays and lesbians should be free to live their life as they wish') and on exclusion of extreme political parties ('ban political parties that wish to overthrow democracy', reverse coding), both ranging from '0' 'strongly disagree' to '4' 'strongly agree'.

5. Computed as the mean value on six variables ranging from '1' (not at all) to '5' (very much) on satisfaction with life in general, the state of the economy in a country, the quality of social relations, how democracy works in the country, the state of healthcare in country, and current occupation.

6. All protocol material (surveys, treatment videos, codebooks), data and syntaxes are available at http://www.alessandro-nai.com/#!big-five-and-negativism-an-experiment/c1rbm.

Participants in all session types were first introduced to the debate topic, the power of television nowadays. They were provided with pros and contra arguments for an increased public control on television content, and were told that they would have to debate on this issue during the session. All participants had first to fill a survey, used to measure personality traits (*see* next section). All groups where then told to freely debate on the assigned issue during a fixed time slot (30 minutes). Debates were run without the presence of any moderator, and were observed through a unidirectional mirror and camera-recorded for further coding. Coding of debates allowed us to measure the use of negative discourse.

This chapter looks mostly at the direct effect of personality types on the use of negative discourse. In the second part however, we also provide an exploration on how different contexts might mediate such effect. In order to test for such mediating effects, some session types were based on one or two experimental treatments. The first treatment intervened before the debate and aimed to increase the emotional saliency of the debate issue; participants in those groups have been shown a 20-minute clip about how television can be seen nowadays as a new legitimate authority (a replication of Milgram's experiment). A control group was confronted with a control clip of about the same length. The second treatment aimed at increasing the cooperation (or, inversely, conflict) between participants in the debate. Participants in groups submitted to this second treatment were told that they would have to reach a consensual decision at the end of the debate (provide a series of policy propositions). Figure 13.1 schematises the six session types and highlights which treatment (if any) the different groups were submitted to.

Two measures require special attention here: the use of negative discourse and personality traits. The first comes from the structured coding of debates, whereas the latter is based on survey data.

Negative discourse is defined in our study as *a speech act based on a voluntary attack personally raised against other participants in the discussion.* Occurrences of negative discourse are considered to be any forms of 'ad hominem attacks' (Tinkham and Weaver-Lariscy 1993; Eemeren *et al.* 2000; Walton 1998), may they be abusive (head-on personal attacks or invectives, for instance calling an opponent 'naive') or circumstantial (undermining the opponent's credibility, for instance pointing out that s/he's saying this or that because s/he has a hidden agenda). Within the framework of Functional Theory (e.g. Benoit *et al.* 2003b; Benoit 2007; *see* also Chapter Two in this volume) our definition and measure echoes Benoit's 'character attacks'. This definition of negative discourse is somehow more restrictive than the one used in the existing literature on negative campaigning, which also often considers criticisms to the opponents' ideas as 'negative' speeches (versus 'positive', 'advocacy' or 'acclaim' speeches; Pfau and Kenski 1990; Ansolabehere *et al.* 1994; Skaperdas and Grofman 1995; Lau and Pomper 2004). Such a narrower definition, used in recent work on negative campaigning and its effects (Fridkin and Kenney 2008; Nai 2013; Nai 2014a), is however probably more effective to isolate interpersonal attacks, such as those taking place in public debates. On the other hand, an excessively broad definition

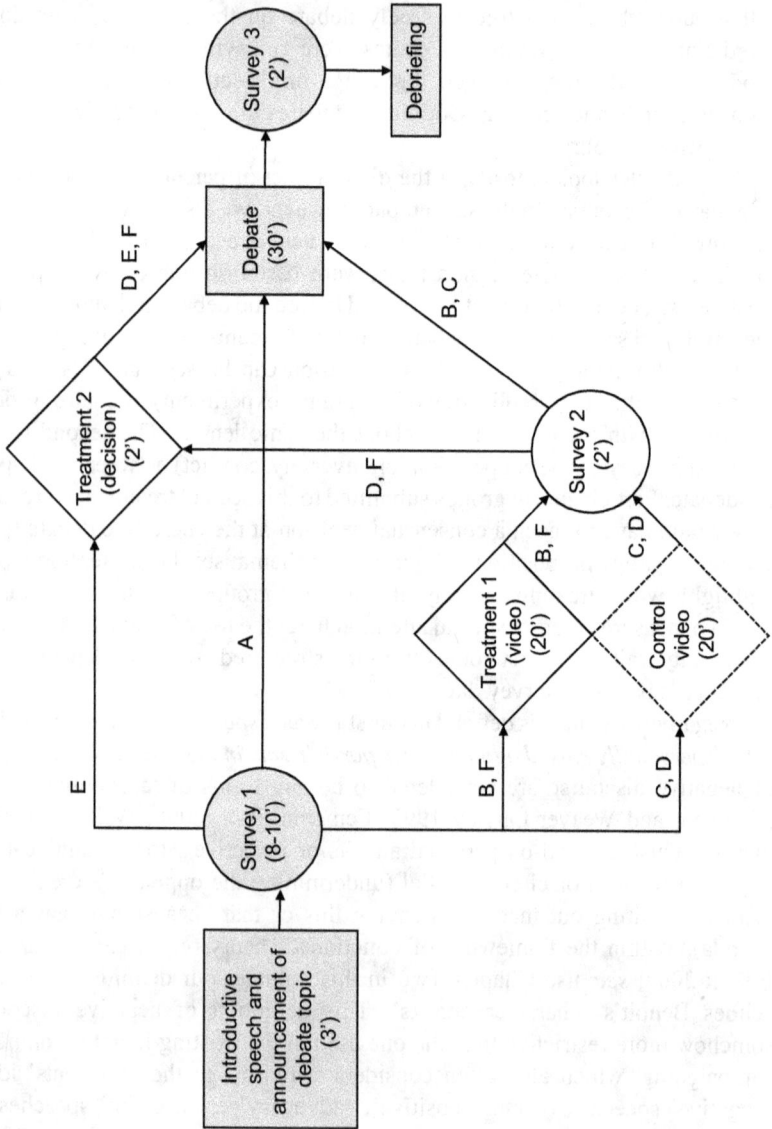

Figure 13.1: Experimental protocol

would encompass all forms of argumentative dissent, which are, after all, what debates are made of. A narrower definition of negative discourse (and, eventually, of negative campaigning) is besides more in line with the common appraisal of 'nastiness' in politics; if disagreeing with someone during a discussion would be enough to be qualified as 'nasty', who would not be qualified as such? In a nutshell, dealing with personal, 'ad hominem' attacks instead of controversies on ideas seems sounder for our main question: who 'goes dirty' during debates on political issues?

A team of four trained coders[7] measured the use of negative discourse during the debates. For each participant in the debate the coders assessed the total number of unique negative speech acts during a joint coding session. Each occurrence of negative discourse was discussed among the four coders; only the occurrences that were qualified as negative by all coders consensually were used in our study.

The total number of negative speech acts for a given participant varies between zero and twenty-three, and on average our participants made 1.7 negative speech acts (SD=3.8) during the debate. Results presented in the next section assess the effect of personality traits on the use of negative discourse in absolute terms (total number of attacks). Participants were free to intervene during the course of the debate, and speech times vary considerably among them (which is also a function of personality). Speech time and negative discourse are however only weakly correlated, which means that assessing the use of negative discourse in absolute terms (instead, e.g. in terms of attacks per speech minute) is not spurious.

The five personality traits – *openness to experience, conscientiousness, extraversion, agreeableness and neuroticism* – were measured for each participant through a series of forty-five[8] questions in survey one, which set out the so-called 'Big Five Inventory' (BFI; John *et al.* 1991; John *et al.* 2008). To be sure, numerous batteries of items exist for the measure of those five personality traits, from the very lengthy NEO-Personality Inventory-Revised (NEO-PI-R; Costa and McCrae 1992) based on dozens of items to the much shorter Ten Item Personality Measure (TIPI; Gosling *et al.* 2003). If lengthy items batteries have the advantage of higher internal reliability, they are at the same time very time-consuming to administer; on the other hand, shorter inventories are easier

---

7. Intensive training was offered to all the coders, during which they all had to recognise negative speech acts in a TV debate.

8. Note that the original BFI is based on forty-four questions. The most recent French adaptation of the inventory (Plaisant *et al.* 2010) introduces however a forty-fifth question ('I am someone who easily looks for trouble', our translation from French) to increase validity on the measure of agreeableness. We used this revised version in order to provide comparable results with the French BFI. In our data the measure of agreeableness differs only marginally with or without this additional item; the two measures correlate at Pearson's R=0.989***, and have virtually identical effects in our analyses (alternative models based on the 'shorter' measure of agreeableness are available upon request).

to administer but might lack reliability (Gerber *et al.* 2011: 267). The forty-five items BFI seems thus an excellent compromise between validity, reliability and efficient administration.[9]

The forty-five questions we used for the measure of personality traits asked the respondents how much they agree with a series of qualifying sentences (e.g. 'I am someone who is talkative', '... who has a great imagination', '... who is easily distracted'); possible answers range on a five-points scale from 'totally disagree' to 'totally agree'. The responses to those forty-five questions are then used to compute five continuous scales, one for each personality trait (John *et al.* 1991; John *et al.* 2008). We used in our survey the French wording of the BFI questions (BFI-Fr), validated through PCA factor analyses in Plaisant *et al.* (2010). Descriptive statistics for the BFI factors in our data are shown in Table 13.1.

Negative discourse and personality traits

Our first set of analyses show the direct effect of personality on the use of negative discourse during debates. Table 13.2 presents the correlation between each of the five traits and the use of negative discourse in absolute terms (number of unique attacks). Our analyses show that, as expected, openness to experience is not directly related to negative discourse. Surprisingly, this is also the case of conscientiousness, which has a non-significant effect on negative discourse where a negative effect was expected. Expectations for the direct effect of extraversion were unclear, both reasons for an increase and a decrease in negative discourse could be justified. Our results show that an increase in extraversion leads to an increased use of negative discourse; the effect is however only significant at p<0.1. According to these results, extraverts are

Table 13.1: The five traits of personality in our data

Personality traits	Mean	SD	Min	Max	Pearson's Correlations				
					O	C	E	A	N
O Openness to experience	3.86	0.51	2.20	4.90	.				
C Conscientiousness	3.54	0.72	1.67	4.89	0.05	.			
E Extraversion	3.43	0.84	1.63	4.88	0.09	0.05	.		
A Agreeableness	3.68	0.64	1.80	4.80	0.17	0.11	−0.03	.	
N Neuroticism	2.71	0.92	1.38	4.83	0.07	−0.14	−0.29*	−0.41**	.

n=54, *p<0.05, **p<0.01,***p<0.001, [†]p<0.1

---

9. *See* Mondak *et al.* (2010: 8–9) for a concise albeit excellent discussion on the merits and pitfalls of lengthy versus short items batteries for the Big Five measures.

Table 13.2: The five traits of personality and negative discourse during debates

	Personality traits	Negative discourse (total number of attacks)
O	Openness to experience	0.15
C	Conscientiousness	−0.08
E	Extraversion	0.23[†]
A	Agreeableness	−0.27*
N	Neuroticism	0.16

Note: coefficients are Pearson's Correlations (partial correlations, controlled by the number of participants in the debate).
$n=54$, *$p<0.05$, **$p<0.01$, ***$p<0.001$, [†]$p<0.1$

thus more likely to engage in bold and energetic social interactions, which then leads to an increased likelihood to attack colleagues during a debate; even if the effect shown in Table 13.2 is not excessively strong, it contrasts with the lower hostility in extraverts shown in Tremblay and Ewart (2005) through self-reported measures. We then expected individuals high in agreeableness to adopt the less negative discourse. Our results confirm this expectation. Finally, we anticipated individuals higher in neuroticism to be more likely to 'go dirty' on their colleagues during debates; Table 13.2 shows that the correlation coefficient goes in the expected direction, but the effect is not statistically significant.

Note that additional analyses controlling for the presence or absence of the two experimental treatments (partial correlations, results not shown) yield very similar results (although significance levels are somehow lower). A regression analysis where the direct effect of each personality trait is controlled by the other traits also shows similar magnitudes and directions (*see* Table 13.3).

Situational influences

Personality traits do matter for the use of negative discourse. Different debate situations, however, naturally create different dynamics. We thus might expect that the direct effects shown beforehand differ when the context changes. In order to explore such intuition, our experimental protocol manipulated the situational context via two independent treatments: the first aimed at increasing the emotional charge of the topic discussed, whereas the second imposed a consensual decision.

These two conditions simulate two major characteristics of debates on political issues:

Discussions about 'hot' issues are what most political debates are made of, be it among friends, during a TV show, or in a formal setting such a parliament. At the same time, in many situations citizens debate not for the sake of good rhetoric but

Table 13.3: OLS regression analysis

IVs		B	S.E.	95% B Confidence Interval		Tolerance
				Lower bound	Upper bound	
O	Openness to experience	1.22	1.05	−0.89	3.31	0.92
C	Conscientiousness	−0.30	0.75	−1.81	1.21	0.90
E	Extraversion	1.10	0.68	−0.26	2.45	0.83
A	Agreeableness	−1.40	0.94	−3.29	0.49	0.73
N	Neuroticism	0.48	0.67	−0.87	1.82	0.71

Note: dependent variable is the use of negative discourse (total number of attacks, continuous variable); model controlled by the number of participants in the debate.
n=54; R^2=0.16

in order to take informed decisions. Once again, this happens in several different venues, from meetings of parties' executive committees to social movements assemblies and parliamentary deliberations.

It is quite hard to develop precise expectations for how personality traits affect negative discourse in each situational condition. We can however anticipate some tendencies.

First, a debate with a decisional finality creates a conflict between cooperation and confrontation. In such a situation, individuals high in *openness to experience* might voluntarily decide not to verbally confront their colleagues; those individuals 'do not impose rigid restrictions on their own thoughts of behaviours, or those of others. Given a choice, the person who is open to experience would opt for "anything goes" rather than "my way or the highway"' (Mondak 2010: 51). Similarly, individuals high in *conscientiousness* are more likely to be in favour of status quo and usually tend to be risk averse (Mondak 2010: 54); thus, we expect that during situations where a collective decision has to be taken, those individuals are even less likely to 'go negative' on those they are discussing with. Conscientiousness 'facilitates task- and goal-directed behaviour' (John *et al.* 2008: 120), and has been linked to obedient behaviour (Bègue *et al.* in press). Thus, when a collective decision has to be taken, conscientious individuals deal with the task dutifully and with diligence, which probably implies that they will restrain from attacking their colleagues. We also expect *extraverts* to 'go negative' when a collective decision is needed. When the stakes are high, extraverts might push their sociability a little too far, and get carried away in the discussions that take place. Furthermore, *agreeableness* has been linked to cooperation (LePine and Van Dyne 2001), submission and docile behaviour (Digman 1990), and obedience to authority (Bègue *et al.* in press); we thus expect agreeable individuals to make use of negative discourse even less when they have to take a consensual decision with their colleagues. Finally, LePine and Van Dyne (2001) show that *neuroticism* is inversely correlated with cooperative behaviours;[10] we thus expect individuals high in neuroticism to 'go negative' on their colleagues even more strongly during debates with a decisional finality.

Second, a debate with a higher emotional charge might create the conditions for a bolder discussion. Intuitively, this makes sense; 'hotter' discussions usually do not happen on consensual or 'quiet' topics, whether in a bar among colleagues or in a parliamentary deliberation. When the emotional charge of the issue is higher, we might expect extraverts to make a higher use of negative discourse. Given their predisposition for social intense interactions, extraverts might 'forget' their inner predisposition of consensual social interactions and adopt a bolder and energetic rhetoric. As well, neuroticism is often presented as an inverse function of emotional stability (John *et al.* 2008); we thus expect that individuals high in neuroticism are even more likely to (verbally) attack their colleagues when the emotional charge of the debate issue is high. In this case, the emotional charge of the issue resonates with their inner disposition to 'get emotional', and be carried away.

Table 13.4 and Table 13.5 show the effects of personality traits on negative discourse under the two different contextual situations. It is first important to note that personality traits do not differ significantly or substantially across groups (i.e. some personality traits are not higher, for instance, in groups exposed to 'treatment 1'); any variation between groups on the relationship between personality traits and negative discourse is thus imputable to the different nature of those groups.

Table 13.4 compares groups according to 'treatment 1'. First, we expected extraverts to 'drop their gloves' when the discussion is emotionally charged; in such a situation, we anticipated extraverts might push their sociability a little too far, 'forget' their inner predisposition of consensual social interactions, and get carried away in the discussions that take place. Our results show that extraversion correlates more strongly with negative discourse in individuals exposed to the emotional video than in those not exposed to any video, but the difference between the two groups is not statistically significant.

We then expected individuals higher in neuroticism to attack their colleagues even more during discussion on emotionally charged issues. Our results show that neuroticism is positively and significantly associated with negative discourse in groups exposed to 'treatment 1'. As for extraversion, however, Fisher r-to-z transformations (Kenny 1987: 274; *see* last column of Table 13.4) show that the difference between the experimental and control groups is not statistically significant.

Table 13.4 highlights then that when exposed to 'treatment 1' individuals higher in agreeableness are less likely to attack their colleagues (difference between the two groups is statistically significant at p<0.1). We did not have explicit

---

10. Note, however, that Hirsh and Peterson (2009) find that individuals high in neuroticism are significantly less likely to defect (and, thus, more likely to cooperate) in 'prisoner's dilemma' simulations. This type of decision-making is however radically different from the consensual decision making tested in our experiments.

Table 13.4: The five traits of personality and negative discourse during debates; comparison for 'treatment 1' (emotional video)

Personality traits	Control group	Control video	Emotional video	Sig. diff.[a] (p–values)
O Openness to experience	0.05	0.45	0.09	0.44
C Conscientiousness	−0.24	−0.62[†]	0.21	0.07
E Extraversion	0.14	0.31	0.25	0.35
A Agreeableness	−0.20	−0.03	−0.54*	0.11
N Neuroticism	0.16	−0.11	0.45*	0.16
Group n	24	9	21	

Note: coefficients are Pearson's Correlations and refer to the correlation between the personality trait and the presence of negative discourse (partial correlations, controlled by the number of participants in the debate). Control group has not been submitted to any treatment. Control group contains participants in session types 'A' and 'E', control video group contains participants in session types 'C' and 'D', and emotional video group contains participants in session types 'B' and 'F'.

[a] Values refer to the significance of the difference between correlation coefficients in first (control group) and third (emotional video) columns; p-values are computed through Fisher r-to-z transformations (Kenny 1987: 274).

*p<0.05, **p<0.01, ***p<0.001, [†]p<0.1

Table 13.5: The five traits of personality and negative discourse during debates; comparison for 'treatment 2' (decisional finality of discussion)

Personality traits	Control group	Decisional finality	Sig. diff.[a] (p-values)
O Openness to experience	−0.43*	0.37[†]	0.00
C Conscientiousness	0.27	−0.28	0.03
E Extraversion	0.04	0.34[†]	0.14
A Agreeableness	−0.08	−0.35[†]	0.16
N Neuroticism	−0.06	0.19	0.19
Group n	28	26	

Note: coefficients are Pearson's Correlations and refer to the correlation between the personality trait and the presence of negative discourse (partial correlations, controlled by the number of participants in the debate). Control group has not been submitted to any treatment. Control group contains participants in session types 'A', 'B' and 'C' and decisional finality group contains participants in session types 'D', 'E' and 'F'.

[a] Values refer to the significance of the difference between correlation coefficients in first (control group) and second (decisional finality) columns; p-values are computed through Fisher r-to-z transformations (Kenny 1987: 274).

*p<0.05, **p<0.01, ***p<0.001, [†]p<0.1

expectations on the behaviour of agreeable individuals in such conditions, but the results are not surprising given the direct effect of agreeableness on negative discourse. Agreeable persons are furthermore less likely to attack their colleagues when a decision has to be reached at the end of the discussion, as expected (*see* Table 13.5), even if the difference between control group and the group exposed to 'treatment 2' is not statistically significant. This partially supports previous research linking agreeableness to cooperation (LePine and Van Dyne 2001), submission, and docile behaviour (Digman 1990).

Table 13.5 also shows an interesting effect for openness to experience controlling by the decisional finality. Although the direct effect of this personality trait on negative discourse is not significant (*see* Table 13.2), the difference between the effects found in the two groups (i.e. negative for control group and positive for decisional group) is statistically significant at $p<0.01$. Contrary to our expectations, individuals high in openness to experience are more likely to 'go negative' when a collective decision has to be taken.

Finally, Table 13.5 highlights that higher neuroticism and extraversion are both related to an increase in negative discourse when a collective decision has to be taken, even if the difference between experimental and control groups is not statistically significant.

In a nutshell, our results highlight that adopting a negative discourse is, first, more likely for individuals higher in extraversion and lower in agreeableness; these effects exist directly, when the debate issue is emotionally charged and when individuals have to take a collective decision. Secondly, higher neuroticism somehow increases the use of negative discourse, but especially when the issue is emotionally charged and (partially) when a collective decision has to be taken. Third, conscientiousness is surprisingly not related to negative discourse, but neither is openness to experience, as expected (with the exception of debates with a decisional finality, where this trait unexpectedly increases negativism).

All in all, this provides a preliminary confirmation that research on the roots of negative discourse was missing an interesting element: personality traits.

Discussion

In his study on the causes of negative campaigning in Danish elections, Elmelund-Præstekær (2010) notes that his explanatory models work well for advertisements and manifestos, but explain very little variance for political debates. This, he concludes, might be related to the fact that communication within this particular channel is probably shaped by 'the individual presenting it [... and by] non-systematic idiosyncrasies' (Elmelund-Præstekær 2010: 150). The point he tries to make, but unfortunately without having the data to test it, is that individual traits might matter greatly when searching for the reasons to 'go negative'. We believe him to be on the right(eous) side of the street. Our contribution provided a first empirical assessment on precisely this interrogation: is negative discourse directly related to the personality traits of those who attack? Our data, coming from experimental debate simulations, showed that, indeed, this seems to be the case.

Results from an experimental protocol with fifty-four voluntary students showed that some personality traits do matter for the use of negative discourse during debates on political issues. Our analyses highlighted that this type of discourse is more likely for individuals higher in extraversion and lower in agreeableness, that higher neuroticism somehow increases the use of negative speeches (and especially when the issue is emotionally charged and a collective decision has to be taken), and that conscientiousness is surprisingly not related to negative discourse, but neither is openness to experience (except when a collective decision has to be taken).

Our contribution opens up new research venues on two – previously unconnected – strands of recent literature. First, research on how personality shapes participation in the social and political life. To be sure, some existing research already points to how personality traits affect (verbal) violence. Those studies are however based on self-reported measures, such as the Buss and Perry Aggression Questionnaire (AQ; Tremblay and Ewart 2005) or the Impulsive/ Premeditated Aggression Scales (IPAS; Stanford et al. 2003); on this, our contribution innovates by measuring actual behaviours in experimental settings.

Second, our research contributes to the growing literature dealing with the roots of negative speeches in the political game (aka, negative campaigning). Our results suggest that personal traits other than ideology or gender also play a key role on the likelihood to 'go negative' during debates. Of course, participants in our experiment were students, and not political candidates or public figures. Having said that, we cannot think of fundamental reasons why personality traits should affect the use of negative discourse for common people and not for public figures. For sure, during high-profile debates candidates are undoubtedly less free to speak with their heart (or, their inner traits) than students in simulated debates; in this sense, our results should not be overestimated. This being the case, political figures and leaders become visible in the public space also through their personality. Recent research suggests that voters appraise political figures according to some basic personality traits (Caprara et al. 2002; Skarzynska 2004; Caprara et al. 2007), which means that such traits are not entirely hidden behind the mask of social acceptability expected from public figures. Further research is currently underway in order to replicate the (direct) effects shown here on a sample of political figures having recently participated in televised debates on political issues.

PART THREE

THE EFFECTS OF NEGATIVE CAMPAIGNING

Chapter Fourteen

How Negative Campaigning Impinges on the Political Game: A Literature Overview

Alessandro Nai and Annemarie S. Walter

Assessing the impact of negative messages echoes more general questioning about political campaign efficacy, an issue that has received extensive attention during the last decades. Preliminary results from the early Columbia studies (e.g. Lazarsfeld *et al.* 1944) were disappointing, as the researchers found almost no effects at all, which resulted in formulating the 'minimal effects hypothesis'. However, the interest of the scientific community for political campaigns did not fade; improved procedures to measure both the content of campaigns and their effects forced them to reconsider this pessimistic premise. Nowadays, we know that political campaigns *do* have effects on voters' attitudes and behaviour (e.g. Iyengar and Simon 2000; Schmitt-Beck and Farrell 2002; Claassen 2011; Arceneaux 2006). The magnitude of these effects is questionable and harshly debated. However, it seems safe to say that no academic would claim that political campaigns do not have an effect whatsoever.

The notion that campaigns somehow have the power to shape individual opinions and attitudes is shared outside the academic community. Citizens and civil society actors often rant about the persuasive political information flow from the elites and militate against what they call 'political propaganda'. Just think about the existence of watchdog organisations such as the Center for Media and Democracy (CMD), whose primary mission is to 'report on spin and disinformation'.[1] Would they complain if they thought that propaganda did not have any effects? In addition, 'modern' political elites are nowadays willing to spend large amounts of money on communication campaigns (Swanson and Mancini 1996). Why would they do this if they did not think they could turn the tide? Undeniably, 'all campaigners have in common a desire to influence events; they also have in common a belief that they can have influence, that their campaign can matter' (Schmitt-Beck and Farrell 2002: 13).

Today's academic literature offers a multitude of studies that demonstrate how political campaigns affect voters' attitudes, opinions and behaviour. Although it is not our goal to present an exhaustive overview of this issue (*see* e.g. Farrell and Schmitt-Beck 2002; Brady and Johnston 2006), it is worthwhile to mention a couple of examples that have paved the way for research on the effects of negative

---

1. http://www.prwatch.org/cmd.

campaigning. Starting from the late 1980s, several studies show that campaign messages have under certain circumstances, the ability to alter the argumentative structure that voters employ to justify their choices. The idea of a 'priming' effect (Iyengar and Kinder 1987; Krosnick and Kinder 1990; Iyengar and Simon 1993), although contested (Lenz 2009), assumes that 'media coverage leads voters to attach more importance to a given consideration in deciding their vote' (Gidengil *et al*. 2002: 76). The theory stems from the presumption of 'cognitive minimalism' (Sniderman *et al*. 1991; Sniderman 2000): given that individuals have limited cognitive abilities to process the immense and complex amount of information they are confronted with, they are forced to pay attention to information selectively. Thus, the 'priming' effect exists when the content of media information – and more specifically, political campaigns – is 'framed' in such a way that voters tend to pay attention to specific messages and not to others. As a result, voters will start to think differently about a matter, a candidate or a reform.

Furthermore, academic work has shown that political campaigns can increase voters' issue knowledge. Media exposure is directly linked with political knowledge (Delli Carpini and Keeter 1996; Norris and Sanders 2003), and intense campaigns are intended to enhance voters' attention, learning and knowledge (Bartels 1988; Norris and Sanders 2003; Kriesi 2005; Jerit *et al*. 2006; Marquis and Bergman 2009). As a result, political campaigns affect voters' electoral choices. The 'straightforward goals of maximising vote shares, electoral/referendum victory and taking control of government' (Schmitt-Beck and Farrell 2002: 15) are the main reason political actors campaign in the first place. Since the early Columbia studies, countless research has shown that political campaigns affect candidates and parties' electoral gains (*see* for the US – Jacobson 1990; Japan – Cox and Thies 2000; Spain – Fernandez-Albertos and Martinez i Coma 2014; the UK – Whiteley and Seyd 2003; Switzerland – Lachat and Sciarini 2002; Germany – Finkel and Schrott 1995; Canada – Carty and Eagles 1999).

In a nutshell, political campaigns in general have a wide range of effects, both intentional and unintentional, at different levels. The question central to this chapter is: Do *negative* campaigns have effects and if so in what way? This is not an easy question to answer. First of all, a multiplicity of phenomena is affected by negative messages, for example voters' opinions, attitudes, feelings and behaviour. They are logically a result of a complex interaction between predispositions and the content of (political) information that voters encounter along the way. Even more profoundly however, the current debate on negative campaigning and its effects is characterised by a deep fracture between the partisans of an overall detrimental effect of negative campaigning and those advocating positive consequences.

This chapter aims neither to propose a general theory on how negative campaigning works, nor to provide a full account on all the phenomena it affects. More modestly, its goal is to give an overview of research on the effects of negative campaigning, to show its inconclusiveness and that the found effects can be caused by different mechanisms.

This chapter is structured as follows: we begin by presenting evidence in support of the 'negativity bias', i.e. the tendency to retrieve, process, sample and remember negative messages better than positive messages. Then, we provide a general account of the literature showing the three ways negative campaigning might impinge on the political game. This threefold classification has the advantage to boil down the process of information exposure into separate and subsequent phases. This classification bears close resemblance to the one proposed by Lau *et al.* (2007) or Fridkin and Kenney (2012). First, negative campaigning might have an effect on the psychological foundations of electoral behaviour, and actually affect how voters think about candidates, how they learn relevant political information and how they shape opinions on the issues at stake. Second, negative campaigning might directly affect electoral attitudes such as affect towards candidates, vote choice, and turnout. Third, negative campaigning might have an effect on more general political attitudes ('systemic effects'; Lau *et al.* 2007), such as views on the political system, sense of political efficacy, institutional trust and so on.

These phenomena are often intertwined: for instance, voters' attention to a message (psychological mechanism) is most likely not independent from voters' 'systemic' attitudes such as the sense of political efficacy, and the latter in turn is likely to affect political attitudes such as affect for candidates and turnout. Most research tends to focus on a particular psychological mechanism; this research generally performs well in controlling for intervening factors. A complete overview of the mechanisms at work – from unconscious psychological sparkles to general systemic attitudes – is however still absent in the literature.

The primacy of negative messages

Negative messages are more likely to be retrieved, processed, sampled, and remembered than positive messages. Negative messages 'stick' to the mind of those who are exposed to them. In their meta-analytic re-assessment, Lau *et al.* (2007) find a small but significant effect showing that negative messages have, indeed, higher memorability, a finding supported by Lau and Redlawsk's analysis in this book (*see* Chapter Fifteen).

Decades of research on social and cognitive psychology showed the existence of a negativity bias (Rozin and Royzman 2001; Ito and Cacioppo 2005): 'negative information produces a much stronger psychophysiological response than does positive information; [...] people are more reactive and attentive to negative news than they are to positive news' (Soroka and McAdams 2010: 2). As exemplified by Rozin and Royzman (2001: 296), 'brief contact with a cockroach will usually render a delicious meal inedible. The inverse phenomenon – rendering a pile of cockroaches on a platter edible by contact with one's favourite food – is unheard of'. Negative objects, issues, events, and phenomena have the capacity to arouse attention more quickly than their positive counterpart, and are more likely to receive cognitive treatment and to be stored in memory for further use. Evidence also exists that voters 'devote more cognitive energy to thinking about bad things than to thinking about good things' (Soroka and McAdams 2010: 3), that describing a person's negative traits influences impression formation more than describing a person's positive traits, and that negative first impressions are more stable than positive first impressions (Lau 1982: 355). More generally, 'negative information may be more likely than comparable positive information to be noticed and processed, thereby having the opportunity to get its message across' (Lau and Pomper 2002: 47), which comes from the fact that 'negative stimuli are preferentially detected – that is, detected at lower levels of input or exposure than are positive stimuli' (O'Keefe and Jensen 2008: 53).

The reasons for this negativity bias are multiple. In an attempt to uncover how negative biases are manifested, social psychologists Paul Rozin and Edward Royzman, propose four principal mechanisms (Rozin and Royzman 2001: 298–299): *negative potency* (i.e. the fact that negative entities – objects, images, phenomena, events – have a higher saliency than their positive counterparts of identical objective magnitude), *steeper negative gradients* (negative events develop more rapidly – for instance, in time – than positive events), *negative dominance* (when positive and negative events exist simultaneously, the resulting perception of the overall event is more negative than the objective 'sum' of the involved components[2]), and *negative differentiation* (negative stimuli are generally a more complex and elaborate phenomena and have a wider range of response repertories).

In a similar way, John T. Cacioppo and colleagues (Cacioppo and Bernston 1994; Ito and Cacioppo 2005) developed a theory that posits a tendency for individuals to start with positive evaluations of elements of objects (*positivity offset*) when information input is weak, and then shift towards negative evaluations (*negativity bias*) when information input increases in frequency and intensity. Thus, 'as negative and positive input increases, the negative system responds with greater relative increase in motivational output per quantum of activation than does the positive system' (Ito and Cacioppo 2005: 2). During the course of a campaign, which naturally increases in intensity as the vote draws near, the balance between how positive and negative messages are perceived by voters is thus likely to favour negative messages.

Whatever the underlying reasons for a negativity bias, when it comes to getting the message across, nowadays it seems common wisdom that 'bad is stronger than good' (Baumeister *et al.* 2001). Negative messages 'may be a kind of guilty pleasure [... for voters] - they claim to dislike them, but inadvertently are drawn to them in much the same way that shoppers find themselves drawn to the tabloids in the checkout aisle' (Martin 2004: 546). According to political psychologists negative messages are more likely to stick to the mind of those who are exposed to them. In addition, recent research seems to point towards the fact that such a bias is likely to affect conservatives more than liberals (Hibbing *et al.* 2014). Consequently, the question to ask is: how do negative campaign messages affect the subsequent attitudes, opinions and behaviour of the voters exposed to them?

---

2. For instance, if we consider two identical advertisements (whatever this might mean), one perceived as 'positive' and the other as 'negative' the overall perception would not be 'neutral' but rather negative. This, furthermore, might explain why observers systematically feel that political campaigns are almost exclusively negative.

Negative campaigning and cognitive processes

Political communication – even the 'negative' kind – affects voters' electoral and political attitudes. This happens, bluntly, because voters acquire the content of political information, translate it according to their own political vocabulary, frame it in line or in contrast to their current political predispositions, and accordingly adapt their views and opinions. In other terms, a 'black box' of psychological mechanisms links information to attitudes and behaviour.

Decades of research in cognitive and political psychology opened the lid of this 'black box' and unveiled part of the mechanisms and processes that occur within peoples' minds when confronted with a decisional task (e.g. Petty and Cacioppo 1986; Eagly and Chaiken 1993). The field of political psychology has recently produced several studies that show how and why negative messages affect psychological processes during political tasks. The discipline is vast and constantly evolving, behaving like a 'living organism' (Marcus 2013: 3), and thus providing a simplified overview is demanding. In this section, we focus on three types of psychological and cognitive mechanisms on which negative messages have shown to have an effect: (1) opinion formation and treatment of political information; (2) learning and knowledge of the issues at stake; and (3) consistency of the 'cognitive map' that voters' use as basis for their political decisions. These three mechanisms somehow represent the different stages of the cognitive processes underlying individual decisions, as shown for instance in Petty and Cacioppo's Elaboration-Likelihood Model (ELM, Petty and Cacioppo 1986): how the information is acquired and treated and what its effects are on issue knowledge and cognition.

First of all, is the way voters make up their minds, or put differently, the cognitive processes they activate influenced by negative campaign messages? Recent research suggests that voters react to negatively charged political communication by lowering the cognitive effort they put in opinion formation; when campaigns go negative, they simply are less eager to provide consistent effort to make up their minds. This finding has been found in Switzerland during direct-democratic votes, where the use of systematic reasoning, i.e. a 'comprehensive, analytic orientation to information processing in which perceivers access and scrutinise a great deal of information for its relevance to their judgment task' (Eagly and Chaiken 1993: 326–327), a mental process in which 'all things are considered' (Barker and Hansen 2005), is significantly lower during negative campaigns (Nai 2014b). When political campaigns go negative, voters become less attentive to what political elites have to say in general, for instance they make less use of information sources (Nai 2014c). Similarly, Pinkleton et al. (2002) report experimental data that shows that negative advertisements are perceived as less useful for forming opinions than positive advertisements. Other research shows that exposure to negative advertising decreases voters' campaign interest (Kahn and Kenney 2004; Brader and Corrigan 2006; Brooks and Geer 2007) and that voters perceive negative campaigns as less fair or useful (Sides et al. 2003; Brooks and Geer 2007). Consumer research suggests that negative advertising induces negative frames about the product for individuals low in need for cognition (Zhang and Buda 1999).

Although negative campaigns can contain arguments that are easy to process and remember, evidence exists that negative campaigning has detrimental effects on opinion formation and general attention to the political elites. Thus, the priming of negative messages comes with a price, namely a decrease in cognitive engagement.

Negative campaign messages, especially those containing personal attacks can increase anxiety and other negative emotions. Indeed, 'one of the primary goals of negative campaigning is to paint the opponent in the worst possible light. These efforts may raise fears [or anxiety] about the individual candidate, especially among partisans' (Martin 2004: 550). These negative emotions, in turn, have demonstrated to increase the reliance of peripheral-route cognitive processes; Malhotra and Kuo (2009) argue that strong negative emotions facilitate the activation of heuristics used in peripheral routes, whereas weak emotional reactions enhance central-route processing.

Other research suggests that exposure to negative campaigning results in increased attention to the message itself. This is one of the core ideas of the *Affective Intelligence Model* (Marcus and MacKuen 1993; Marcus *et al.* 2000; Marcus 2002). The AIM shows that 'two fundamental systems operate in parallel to produce emotional appraisals that in turn shape the choices and actions of voters. The disposition system generates enthusiasm/satisfaction or depression/ frustration as incoming information reports that the execution of one's plans either matches or does not match expectations (or success). The surveillance system generates anxiety/unease or relaxation/calm as incoming information suggests it is either safe or potentially unsafe to go about one's business as usual' (Brader 2006: 60). The point is that some negative emotions are easily associated with increased issue attention.[3] Thus, 'anxiety [...] causes individuals to become more aware of their surroundings, in particular novel or threatening circumstances [... and] stimulates a desire to fully understand and analyse the source of a potential threat, thus promoting active learning and reasoned thinking and decreasing reliance on habits and dispositions' (Steenbergen and Ellis 2006: 111). Are you anxious about something that you have heard about your preferred candidate? If yes, denial and ostrich behaviour will not solve this, but increased attention towards new information probably will. Conflicting expectations on how emotional arousal mediates the link between (negative) messages and interest perfectly represents the embryonic stage of research on the psychological effects of negative campaigning.

Second, are negative campaign messages more likely to increase issue knowledge? Are voters 'learning' from negative messages? As we discussed before, scholars agree that negative messages are more easily remembered than positive messages. But then, do these negative messages increase what voters *know* about issues? It is common wisdom that fear appeals are widely used in

---

3. Interestingly, Malhotra and Kuo (2009) show that experiencing negative emotions might decrease cognitive engagement.

health communication to increase awareness on potentially harmful behaviour. An excellent example is the anti-drug 'fried egg' TV commercial[4] (*see* e.g. Witte 1992). Does this also work for political advertising and more specifically for negative political advertising?

Once again, the field is split into two camps. On the one hand, negative messages are reported to lower attention and to be perceived as less informative. For example, experiments with US undergraduate students highlight that negative campaigns are perceived as less informative and less useful for opinion formation and are globally evaluated more negatively (Pinkleton *et al.* 2002). On the other hand, exposure to negative advertisements increases voters' levels of 'issue information', most likely via increased attention towards (and saliency of) the issues covered in these advertisements (Ansolabehere *et al.* 1994). Therefore, negative political information might not be harmful, but useful (Geer 2006). The rationale for such a positive effect comes from the fact that negative advertisements contain 'more facts, more on issues, more on the subjects that people care about, more information that draws on the candidates' records and, overall, more that allows voters to make an informed choice by pointing to what candidates disagree about [than positive advertisements]' (Allen and Stevens 2013: 6). The finding that negative campaign messages tend to contain more issue-information than positive campaign messages might explain why the former are often perceived as having a greater impact (Stevens 2012).

Third, do negative message change the 'cognitive map' (i.e. the set of feelings and opinions related to the issue at stake) that voters use to justify their behaviour such as vote choice? James and Hensel (1991) predict that the effectiveness of negative messages on opinion change (i.e. the implementation of a 'central route to persuasion', Petty and Cacioppo 1986) is lower when the messages are perceived as too extreme (James and Hensel 1991: 61), in other words excessive negative advertisements are unable to reframe voters 'cognitive map'. However, negative advertising has been shown to encourage the use of counterarguments when pondering pros and cons of a given option or decision to take (Wilson and Muderrisoglu 1980; Belch 1981). Therefore, negative campaigning might increase the tension between conflicting arguments. Recent research on direct-democratic voting supports this finding. Nai (2014b) reports that high levels of negative advertising during direct democratic campaigns in Switzerland lead to an increase in ambivalence, i.e. strong support for arguments in favour and against policy changes (or strongly rejecting both types of arguments). In a similar vein, negative direct-democratic campaigns reduce the likelihood of 'consistent' decisions, i.e. vote choices in line with voters' opinions on issue arguments (Lanz and Nai 2015).

---

4.   The commercial, promoted by the Partnership for a Drug-Free America and aired nationwide in US in 1987, shows a man standing right in front a frying pan. He takes an egg ('this is your brain'), points to the frying pan ('this is drugs'), puts the egg into the hot frying pan ('this is your brain on drugs'), and shows us the obvious result ('any questions?').

Negative campaign messages are more likely to be acquired and processed. However, this does not necessarily mean that they positively influence the cognitive structure of those who process them. Evidence exists that negative messages decrease cognitive efforts (Nai 2014b) and increase confusion and support for conflicting arguments (Nai 2014a; Lanz and Nai 2015). However, these studies are quite specific and we should be cautious generalising their findings; they study a specific political setting, Switzerland, which deals with direct-democratic campaign dynamics and legislative issues instead of elections with competing candidates. At the same time, negative campaigning has been linked with increased learning, issue knowledge and increased attention. Furthermore, Lau and Redlawsk (*see* Chapter Fifteen) show surprising results on the effects of negative messages on correct voting. Correct voting is at its lowest when both candidates go negative, but also when both candidates stay positive; campaigns where one candidate stays positive and the other goes negative are more likely to score high on correct voting.

Research on the cognitive effects of negative campaign messages is still at an early stage, if we exclude research on the presence of a 'negativity bias'. Existing literature is in particular in need of research that digs deeper within the black box of psychological processes. New technologies allowing exciting advances in brain imagery such as 'clarity' (Chung et al. 2013) or optogenetics (Deisseroth et al. 2006; Mancuso et al. 2010) can help scholars to come to a better understanding of what is really going on there.

Negative campaigning, candidate affect and turnout

Evidence exists that negative campaign messages can alter the psychological foundations of political attitudes and behaviour. Lau et al. (2007) call this 'intermediate effects'. Much more has been written on the direct effects of negative campaigns on electoral attitudes and behaviour than its psychological foundations. This section discusses research on two of these attitudes, respectively (1) affect towards a candidate and (2) the decision to cast a vote (turnout). We begin with the attitude that bears the stronger link with psychological considerations (affect) before discussing the attitude with larger systemic implications (turnout).

First, a classical question from the perspective of campaign strategists, spin doctors and other political masters of puppets is 'are attack messages effective'? In other words, does negative campaigning produce a net gain for the attacker or a net loss for the target? Do attacks undermine the targets' credibility and more generally voters' affect for the target? At the heart of these questions lie two conflicting dynamics. On the one hand, negative campaigning is likely to increase support for the attacker. Negative campaign messages are easily remembered and recalled, and point toward the target's weaknesses which naturally decreases its popular support. As a result attack behaviour can produce a loss of support for the target and thus a net gain for the attacker. Evidence for such a positive effect can be found in studies by Kaid (1997), Fridkin and Kenney (2004), Arceneaux and Nickerson (2005) and Coulter (2008).

On the other hand, attacks can backfire. Attackers might wrongly point to weak issues, in which case rebuttal from the target is an easy task. Furthermore, when asked about negative campaigning, voters describe negative messages as vile, a form of discursive practice that does not honour the democratic principles of respect and civil debate. Therefore, the use of negative campaigning can potentially undermine the credibility of the sponsor; this is also why the share of negative advertisements sponsored by 'anonymous' third parties such as superPACS is constantly growing (Brooks and Murov 2012; see also Nai and Sciarini 2015). In this situation the attacker loses support, which creates a net gain for the target. Evidence for the 'backlash effect' (Roese and Sande 1993) is abundant (*see* for instance Basil *et al.* 1991; Hitchon and Chang 1995; Lau and Pomper 2002).

The decision to 'go negative' thus faces two opposing potential outcomes, which are likely to exist simultaneously: a decrease in the (intended) target's support and an unintended decrease in the attacker's support. The question is, which one prevails? Is the net advantage in favour of the attacker or the target? As Dassonneville (2010: 6) points out, 'the size of [the] backlash determines the effectiveness of a negative campaign'; such 'size' matters less in first-past-the post systems where a positive net gain suffices, than in PR elections, where each vote lost weakens the power both in parliament as in the government coalition after the election.

Lau and his colleagues provided two meta-analyses of existing research on the effects of negative campaigning. The first meta-analysis (Lau *et al.* 1999) is based on forty-seven studies examining affect for the target, affect for the attacker and net affect, shows no effect of negative campaigning whatsoever. The authors revised this conclusion in their second-meta analysis. This study (Lau *et al.* 2007) based on eighty-one studies reports mixed findings, namely a 'modest tendency for negative campaigning to undermine positive affect for the targeted candidates' (Lau *et al.* 2007: 1182). De Nooy and Maier (*see* Chapter Seventeen in this volume) also find that negative campaigning in German televised debates does not affect the audience's response significantly. Viewers tend to evaluate the candidate independent of the candidate's strategy (i.e. attack or acclaim) or their partisan attachment.

Second, does negative campaigning affect turnout? This is the question that received by far the most attention in the literature, most likely because of the systemic implications of low turnout. Scholars from an elitist tradition (e.g. Schumpeter 1979) do not consider low turnout a problem but simply an indication of 'citizens' basic satisfaction with the performance of the political system, which means that they can concentrate on their personal matters' (Anduiza Perea 2002: 645; *see* also Rosema 2007). However, most scholars support the idea that abstention (or non-participation) from the electoral process is a concerning development in today's democracy, as political participation can compensate for socioeconomic inequality and avoid exclusion of already underprivileged social groups (e.g. Verba and Nie 1972). Low turnout, described as democracy's principal 'unresolved dilemma' by Lijphart (1997), affects the electoral process negatively.

The literature is again inconclusive. Seminal work of Stephen Ansolabehere, Shanto Iyengar and their colleagues has laid the foundation for the 'demobilisation' theory (Ansolabehere and Iyengar 1995; Ansolabehere *et al*. 1994; Ansolabehere *et al*. 1999). They argue that negative campaigning is one of the major causes for voters' feelings of disaffection towards the political elite. Voters 'become fed up with the mudslinging and decide to stay at home on Election Day. Attacks that last the length of a long campaign may spill past assessments of the candidates and alter citizens' views of the political system. [...] Citizens may begin to readjust their attitudes toward politics in general, become less trustful of government, less politically efficacious and less interested in politics' (Fridkin and Kenney 2012: 178–179). All this makes that voters become 'disenchanted with the business of politics as usual' (Ansolabehere *et al*. 1994: 835), which discourages turnout. Negative campaigning can also depress political participation outside the electoral arena and increase overall political alienation. Researchers have consistently found support for this effect in recent years (e.g. Wattenberg and Brians 1999; Lemert *et al*. 1999; Lawton and Freedman 2001). However, these findings are again contested by others (e.g. Brooks 2006, Finkel and Geer 1998; Freedman and Goldstein 1999). First of all, a large share of research shows negligible or null effects of negative campaigning on turnout (Garramone *et al*. 1990; Thorson *et al*. 2000; Brader and Corrigan 2006; Brooks 2006; Krasno and Green 2008). Moreover, recent research points toward opposite findings, i.e. negative campaigning produces higher turnout, (e.g. Finkel and Geer 1998; Freedman and Goldstein 1999; Kahn and Kenney 2004; Niven 2006; Jackson and Carsey 2007). The rationale behind a 'mobilising' effect is threefold (Martin 2004: 549–551): first of all, negative campaigning puts issues forward that polarises the electorate and thus stimulates the republican duty of voting. Second, negative campaigning arouses anxiety, which has shown to stimulate attention and involvement. Third, from a rational choice perspective, negative campaigning can be perceived as an indicator of a close race, in which the marginal utility for individuals to participate in the electoral process is higher. Research shows that the presence of a mobilising or demobilising effect depends on the type of the attack (issue-based versus person-based; Kahn and Kenney 1999a; Min 2004) and/or focus of the campaign (defending status quo versus defending policy change; Nai 2013).

To summarise, the literature consists of contradicting theories. Even more so, the underlying narrative to justify mobilisation instead of demobilisation relies on distinct paradigms; if demobilisation theories 'rely on a reading of the cultural tastes of the mass public, [...] the mobilisation arguments rely on a reading of the psychology of negative information' (Martin 2004: 547). As for the outcome, efforts have been made to extract from existing literature the 'average' net effect of negative advertisements on turnout. Meta-analyses from Rick Lau and colleagues (Lau *et al*. 1999, Lau *et al*. 2007) found no significant effect on (intended or actual) turnout, which results in the general conclusion that existing research cannot be summed up to a mobilisation or demobilisation effect. However, this does not imply that systematic empirical assessments of the literature are not worthwhile. On the contrary, the finding that such a wealth of research adds up to no significant 'average' result opens up avenues for further research that aims to disentangle the dynamics at work.

Negative campaigning and general political attitudes

This last section discusses how negative campaigning affects more general political attitudes. The main research question is 'are negative campaign messages producing systemic effects on public opinion'? All in all, existing research shows little support for such findings (*see* Lau *et al.* 2007). This is partly due to the research designs implemented. The vast majority of effect studies rely on surveys or experiments, which are relatively ineffective methods to find long-term effects (Fridkin and Kenney 2012: 181). To our knowledge no comprehensive longitudinal analysis has been conducted to examine the stability of those systemic effects over time. The literature does not address the general issue of political 'disaffection', but focuses on three principal issues, namely (1) political trust; (2) sense of political efficacy; and (3) interest in politics. All in all, empirical evidence suggests that citizen's trust and sense of political efficacy are only limitedly affected by negative campaigning, whereas it can enhance political interest.

First of all, research both based on experimental as well as survey data suggests a decrease in voters' political trust after exposure to negative campaigning (Wanta *et al.* 1999; Pinkleton *et al.* 2002; Brader 2005). This makes also sense intuitively if we consider both possible outcomes of attack advertisements on citizens' affect for candidates. If attacks are successfully lowering the affect for the target, political trust can be negatively affected. However, if attack advertisements 'backlash' the sponsor loses credibility and popular support (or affect), which can lower trust in politics (or politicians). Negative advertisements tend to emphasise someone's weaknesses and these weaknesses are either believed or not by the general public; in both cases the credibility of the candidate takes a blow and political trust for politicians and the political system weakens. Although some studies suggests a harmful effect of negative campaigning on political trust (Wanta *et al.* 1999; Pinkleton *et al.* 2002; Brader 2005), other studies found no significant effect (Lau and Pomper 2004; Geer 2006) or a spurious relationship between negative campaigning and political trust when one controls for basic political predispositions (Martinez and Delegal 1990).

Moreover, a rationale for the opposite effect of negative campaigning on political trust is easily formulated. Citizens might feel that highlighting of the opponent's flaws demonstrates the nastiness inherent to the whole political system. However, negative campaigning might make politics easier to understand for the ordinary voter, which, at the end, enhances political trust. Studies suggesting that negative advertisements are perceived as more informative than positive advertisements (Ansolabehere *et al.* 1994; Geer 2006) support this view.

Second, some scholars argue that negative campaigning shrinks the (reported) feeling of political efficacy (e.g. Alsolabehere *et al.* 1994; Ansolabehere and Iyengar 1995; Finkel and Geer 1998; Craig and Kane 2000; Brader 2005). Negative messages, these scholars argue, reduce the faith that individuals have in the political system itself. As a result of negative campaigning those voters feel that their vote does not count, that politics is just a game that they have little say about and that politicians do not care about them. The rationale behind a decrease in political efficacy as a result of negative campaigning comes from a decline in political trust. Voters do not appreciate negative campaign messages, which increases cynicism towards political elites, which in turn increases distrust and yields a 'perceived lack of ability to produce a desired outcome or effect' (Pinkleton *et al.* 1998: 36).

Although to our knowledge no study has shown the opposite (i.e. that negative messages *increase* voters' sense of political efficacy), several studies report that negative campaigning and political efficacy are empirically unrelated phenomena. For instance, the work of Wattenberg and Brians (1999), Rahn and Hirshorn (1999), Pinkleton *et al.* (2002), Goldstein and Freedman (2002), Lau and Pomper (2004) or Jackson *et al.* (2005) shows few or no significant effects of negative campaign messages on the reported feeling of internal or external political efficacy. To sum up, no consistent conclusion can be drawn on declining political efficacy as a result of negative campaigning.

Third, evidence exists that negative campaigning increases general political interest (*see* Pinkleton and Garramone 1992; Bartels 2000; Brader 2005 and Brooks and Geer 2007). These authors argue that an increase in political trust comes from an increase in attention for negative messages and saliency for messages framed with a negative tone. Thus, under some conditions a negative campaign 'becomes a colorful, exciting display that reminds voters that politics isn't boring and dull. Just as people are drawn to celebrity disagreements in tabloids or the viewing of car accidents on freeways, it may be that malicious, personal politics garners interest from people who would not otherwise notice the electoral process' (Brooks and Geer 2007: 19). Furthermore, this attention-grabbing effect seems larger for messages with person-based attacks (Dassonneville 2010).

Wrapping up our review on political interest, we go back to our initial disclaimer: the outcomes discussed here are often intertwined. Political interest strongly defines how voters are exposed to media and campaign information, and directly influences attention to its content (Lupia and Philpot 2005; Strömbäck and Shehata 2010).

Conclusion: Exiting the stalemate?

The wealth of existing research on how negative campaigning affects the political game makes providing an overall conclusion a difficult task. Is negative campaigning harmful or is it just a way to get the message across? Regardless which perspective scholars support they will not have a hard time finding supporting empirical evidence. This being said, some final issues deserve close attention. The apparent stalemate between 'optimists' (i.e. those who see potentially positive effects) and 'pessimists' (those who do not see positive effects or even see negative effects) can potentially be solved by looking more closely at the definition of negative campaigning, its measurement and the source of negative campaigning.

First, scholars do not have a similar understanding of what constitutes a 'negative' message (*see* Chapter One in this volume). Most research defines negative campaigning in terms of acclaims (positive statements about a candidate) versus attacks (critique towards the opponent) versus defences (refutation of attacks and criticisms) according to functional theory (Benoit 2007; *see* also Benoit's Chapter Two in this volume). However, some scholars focus in their work on the use of ad-hominem attacks (e.g. Fridkin and Kenney 2008; Nai 2013; Nai 2014a), thus adopting a more narrow definition of negative campaigning. Negative campaign messages vary in substance, for instance what is attacked (the candidate's personality or his policy propositions) and in what terms (civil or uncivil), but also in the emotional charge they carry (Brader 2006). Thus, 'it is very different to question an opponent's honesty by pointing out that "he didn't keep the promise he made to his community" as compared to saying that he "turned his back on everyone in his community, by deceiving them with lies and deceptions." Both are negative messages. Both are negative trait messages. But one crosses the line of civility, while the other does not' (Brooks 2006: 694). In addition, unwarranted attacks are not the same as rebuttal attacks and are perceived quite differently (Whaley and Holloway 1997; Wicks and Souley 2003; Roese and Sande 1993).

Second, the method used to test the effects of negative campaign messages on turnout matter. As Martin (2004) points out, empirical evidence suggesting voter demobilisation comes generally from research employing an experimental design, whereas evidence suggesting voter mobilisation tends to stem from survey research. Both methods have clear advantages and disadvantages in terms of external and internal validity, such as the possibility to control for spurious effects or generalisability. Studies that combine both types of data are still rare in the literature, notable exceptions are Martinez and Delegal (1990) and Ansolabehere and Iyengar (1995). However, although combining experimental and survey or aggregate data is undoubtedly time-consuming and expensive, this might be necessary to move forward.

Third, what is also likely to matter for the effect of negative campaigning on attitudes and behaviour is the identity of the attacker. The same attack made by two different actors is likely to be perceived differently. In Switzerland, Nai (2013) found that negative campaigns defending the status quo ('no' campaigns) are likely to lower actual turnout in contrast to campaigns defending policy changes ('yes' campaigns) that tend to enhance turnout. Nai argues that this could be related to the mediatory effect of increased aversion felt by voters towards 'no' campaigns, which are almost always negative by nature, and increased enthusiasm experienced by voters towards 'yes' campaigns. In addition, evidence exists that US challengers are more likely to benefit from negative campaigning than incumbents (Kahn and Kenney 2004). The point is, everything else being constant – the electoral setting, the nature and content of the attack – effects might differ depending on who is going negative.

Where to go from here? First of all, as argued, scholars linking campaign tone to attitudes and behaviour should be attentive to *what* is measured (issue-based criticisms, personal or 'ad-hominem' attacks, incivilities), *how* it is measured (experimental manipulations, survey data, mixed protocols), and *who* looms behind the attack (who goes negative).

Second, future research should make use of longitudinal (panel) survey data and repeated experimental protocols and examine whether negative campaigning has long-lasting effects on voters' (systemic) attitudes. For instance, research should examine whether voters are also better able to remember negative advertisements than positive advertisements in the long run. In addition, recent results from a study combining observational and experimental data (Krupnikov 2014) show that while keeping everything constant, the timing of exposure to negative advertisements produces unique effects. Early exposure to negative advertisements while still evaluating the candidates mobilises voters, whereas exposure to negative advertisements after deciding which candidate is preferred demobilises voters.

Third, regardless of the wealth of existing research on negative campaigning and its effects, the field has not yet provided an integrated framework that combines unconscious psychological responses (e.g. memory), behaviour (e.g. turnout) and structural political attitudes (e.g. efficacy). These intertwined phenomena form a complex causal network that defines how we respond to stimuli and translate them into political actions. Recent research focusing on personality traits (e.g. Mondak 2010; Gerber et al. 2011; Vecchione and Caprara 2009; Vecchione et al. 2011) and the genetic foundation of social behaviour (e.g. Fowler and Schreiber 2008; Hatemi and McDermott 2011) complicates this relationship further.

Chapter Fifteen

The Effects of Advertising Tone on Information Processing and Vote Choice

Richard R. Lau and David P. Redlawsk

Every election season media attention is drawn to the presumed power of 'negative' or 'attack' political advertisements. In recent years we have heard how Barack Obama wants to teach kindergartners about sex, and how John McCain is mentally unfit to be president. Candidates have been accused of being atheists (Kay Hagan, 2008 North Carolina Senate race), or even of worshipping an 'Aqua Buddha' (Rand Paul, 2010 Kentucky Senate Race.) And, as we all know, Mitt Romney had no concern whatsoever for the average person, and was even accused of being responsible for the death of the wife of a worker who was laid off when Romney's company, Bain Capital, 'restructured' his employer. According to conventional wisdom (e.g. Ansolabehere and Iyengar 1995; Jamieson 1992; Johnson-Cartee and Copeland 1991; Lau *et al.* 1999) advertisements like these and others have an unusual ability to convince voters about the undesirable characteristics of the target (we are being gentle here), which by comparison makes the sponsor of the attack seem like a statesman with the backbone to point out his opponent's weaknesses. Attack advertisements get noticed, they are more memorable, and while such advertisements are not liked, they typically provide a significant net benefit to candidates who employ them, both in terms of relative popularity ratings and at the ballot box. At least that is the conventional wisdom.

In fact, there is little consistent empirical support for many of these 'facts' about negative political advertisements. Recent meta-analyses of all existing studies of the effects and effectiveness of negative political campaigns (e.g. Lau *et al.* 2007) found significant support for only one aspect of what candidates who employ negative advertisements are trying to accomplish: a lowering of affect for the opposing candidate, the target of the attacks. But this effect was counterbalanced by an opposite and even larger (and more often significant) backlash against the sponsoring candidate. Thus the *net* effect of differential change in candidate affect tends to be negative – that is, counter to what the candidate sponsoring the negative advertisements wants to achieve. Studies that look at intended or actual *vote* have on average found a similar result, that negative campaigns are counter-productive for the candidate sponsoring the negative advertisements (although the vote effects are rarely significantly different from zero). There are some suggestions in the literature (most of which, until very recently, has been conducted in the US) that Republicans view negative campaigning as more acceptable than Democrats (e.g. Ansolabehere and Iyengar 1995), which could mean that Republicans who go negative are less likely than Democrats to suffer backlash effects from their own supporters – but then also less likely to make any headway with their opponent's supporters (Perloff and Kinsey 1992). Negative advertisements are a little more memorable than positive advertisements (a common explanation for why negative advertisements are more effective), although the average effect is not as large as one might expect (an average delta of only 0.28). And most recently, Mattes and Redlawsk (2015) build on Geer's (2006) informational argument to show that *without* negativity, the campaign environment would be incomplete and voters would fail to have all the information they need to make informed choices.

There is no denying that negative advertisements are a major part of modern political campaigns, however, a part which has clearly grown over the past three decades or so.[1] They were also a part of the general election campaigns of every one of the mock election studies run by us in our book *How Voters Decide* (Lau and Redlawsk 2006). These studies made use of a unique dynamic information processing technique that allows the researcher to observe voter decision making while the decisions are being made. Hence we can look to see whether negative advertisements, in the context of our mock presidential election campaigns, were any more effective in decreasing evaluations of (or voting for) the target of the attacks. We have no particular reason to think they will be any more powerful than the norm, but this is the question that is of primary concern for most people who study campaign advertisements, and we will look.

The strength of this methodology is not in addressing such global outcome questions, however, but in the ability to study *process*. Thus the primary focus of this chapter is a question that few have had the data to ask before: Do negative advertisements impact on the information processing and decision strategies employed by voters? If persuasive messages of any type are to be effective, they must be received, processed, and (unless they are delivered immediately before a choice must be made) somehow stored in memory. Most experiments are somewhat unrealistic in modelling media effects in that they pretty much insure that everyone receives the message. But this will be equally true of positive and negative advertisements. With the dynamic process tracing methodology we should be able to say something about whether those messages are differentially processed once they are received, and thus be able to test hypotheses about differences in advertisement-related information processing resulting from positive and negative advertising campaigns.

---

1. While this often-repeated statement is somewhat difficult to document empirically, as there are few records of the nature of political advertisements at any level save the presidency which extend much before the 1990s, and almost no evidence on how *frequently* different advertisements were aired in any campaign before 1996, John Geer (2006) has recently provided the clearest documentation of this increase.

Method

Dynamic process tracing methodology

Dynamic process tracing builds off of a classic information board (Carroll and Johnson 1990) that has been a major research tool in the study of decision-making for many years (*see* Payne *et al*. 1993, for a review). With a traditional information board, the decision environment is an alternatives (the columns) by attributes (the rows) matrix, where decision-makers must click on an entry of the matrix to learn the desired information. For example, Jacoby and colleagues (Jacoby *et al*. 1974a; Jacoby, Speller, and Kohn Berning 1974b) used this approach to determine the effects of increasing information availability on the ability of consumers to choose from among detergents, rice, or frozen dinners. This classic technique has also been used to examine decision-making and information search in various political environments (Herstein 1981; Huang 2000; Huang and Price 2001; Mintz *et al*. 1997; Redd 2002; Riggle and Johnson 1996; Taber and Lodge 2006).

There are, however, some definite drawbacks in using the traditional information board to track political decision-making, which is what led us to examine an alternative approach we call 'dynamic process tracing' (Ditonto *et al*. 2014; Lau and Redlawsk 1997, 2001, 2006; Redlawsk 2001, 2002, 2004; Civettini and Redlawsk 2009; Redlawsk, Civettini, and Emmerson 2010). In its original design, the information board is *static*, allowing constant access to all attributes for all alternatives under consideration. In the context of an election, this would be as if a voter had the ability to access any piece of information about a candidate – be it a position on a particular issue or a personal characteristic – at any time they want, allowing easy comparisons between candidates on any attribute. In a real election, however, information is much less organised, somewhat more chaotic, and the time allowed for learning and information gathering is limited by election day. During a campaign, information comes and goes, and candidates do not always make it easy for voters to learn where they stand on policy issues. Clearly the classic information board does a poor job of modelling these prominent features of modern political campaigns, or of any decision or judgement task that must be completed in a similar dynamic environment for several reasons. In many ways the classic information board represents an 'ideal world' for decision-making that can be contrasted to voting in an actual political campaign.

We have revised the traditional static information board, modifying it in a way that better mimics the flow of information in any dynamic social environment such as a presidential campaign. Where the static board allows subjects to have access to all available information at all times, our revised dynamic board emulates the ebb and flow of a political campaign by making only a relatively small and ever changing subset of the total information set available at any point in time. The essential feature of the static information board – the ability to trace the decision-making process as it happens – is retained while information about candidates comes and goes. Where standard information boards are easily managed by the subject, our election simulation overwhelms subjects with information. Where standard information boards allow all information to be available whenever a subject wants it, information during a real election campaign contains a 'here today, gone tomorrow' quality, as does our simulation. And, where the standard information board would make all types of information equally accessible, from positions on arcane issues to party identification and poll results, our simulation models the relative difficulty of finding certain kinds of information at different times during a campaign.

We accomplished this by designing a radically revised information board in which the information – or rather the attribute labels that describe what information is available for access – scroll down a computer screen. Thus there are only a limited number of attribute labels visible on the computer screen at any one time. Most labels include a candidate's name and the particular information that would be revealed if this label were accessed. The rate of scrolling is such that people can read two or three labels before the position changes. Subjects access the information behind the label by using a mouse to click on the label. The scrolling continues in the background while the detailed information is read, however, creating a cost in terms of missed information and mimicking the dynamic nature of election information flow. This scrolling format allows only a small subset of a very large database of information to be available at any one time, and it makes the task of processing campaign information much less manageable for the subject. In addition, the relative likelihood of any particular piece of information becoming available is controlled, so that some information (e.g. party identification) is much easier to obtain (i.e. appears much more often) than other types of information (such as detailed policy positions). Finally, at periodic intervals the computer screen is taken over by a political advertisement for one of the candidates, providing all voters with a fair amount of 'free' information they did not actively choose to learn. All of these features make our dynamic information board a much better experimental analogue to a political campaign – or to any dynamic social situation.[2]

A mock presidential election campaign

Our experiments using the dynamic information board have at their base a mock US presidential election campaign with eight potential candidates – four Democrats and four Republicans – of whom six are usually used in any given study. Most of our experiments have involved both primary and general election campaigns, where two or four Democrats and four or two Republicans are competing for their party's nomination in the primary, and eventually one of the Democrats faces one of the Republicans in the general election. All of the candidates are fictitious, although they are realistic in terms of prior political experience, ideological appropriateness for their party, and so on. This allows the benefits of political experience or expertise to be manifest, while still giving us complete control over

---

2.   The DPTE system is now freely available to researchers around the world. Visit http://www. processtracing.org to learn more about the programme and/or obtain a researcher ID.

what information about the candidates is available to voters, and what subset of that total pool of information they choose to consider in making their decision. Subjects 'register' as a Democrat or a Republican before the campaign begins, and can learn anything they want about any of the candidates during a primary campaign which typically lasts twenty to twenty-five minutes, but must choose only among the candidates running in their party. During the general election one Democrat opposes one of the Republicans, and of course voters may support either of those two candidates. We are able to randomly manipulate many different theoretically interesting features of the campaign, including the advertising strategies candidates pursue. In the end we have a very detailed record of those decision strategies, as we know what information subjects accessed about the candidates, how long they looked at it, how deeply they processed it (which can be inferred from an unexpected memory task), and so on.

While we describe many of the results of these experiments in our book (Lau and Redlawsk 2006) and in various research papers, we have previously ignored the effects of the advertisement tone in our studies. We present those results now.

Campaign advertisements

We must be careful to define just what we mean by positive and negative advertisements, because for most people a negative advertisement is anything they do not like. Following Lau and Pomper (2001a, 2001b, 2002, 2004) and functional theory more generally (*see* Chapter Two of this volume), positive advertisements or 'acclaims' are when the candidate talks about him- or herself, her policies, or her party. Negative advertisements or 'attacks' are when a candidate criticises the opponent, his or her policies or party (*see* also Mattes and Redlawsk 2015).

To produce our mock candidates' advertisements, we borrowed short video clips from several collections of advertisements of recent Congressional candidates, being careful not to use advertisements from any candidate from New Jersey or bordering states which might have actually aired in New Jersey since our studies were carried out there. Sometimes the clips included a 'man on the street' speaking, complaining about high taxes, or a lack of jobs, or poor healthcare; and when they did, we retained the audio portion of the clip. However each of our mock candidates had their own official spokesman who often did a voice-over during the borrowed video clip. Each advertisement was twenty seconds long, including fifteen seconds of video images and the last five seconds with the candidate's name and picture on the screen while the candidate's official spokesman repeated the candidate's 'tag-line' (which always included the candidate's name – e.g. 'Now is the time for the rest of us. Terry Donald for President').

Our manipulations required us to produce five general election advertisements for every candidate, although only three of them were shown during any given 'campaign.' Our positive campaigns consisted of three positive advertisements, while our negative campaigns consisted of one positive and two negative advertisements. The advertisements were presented in random order during the general election campaign.

1. Each candidate had a positive advertisement about healthcare. This positive healthcare advertisements was always shown – that is, it was the single positive advertisement shown as part of a negative campaign. Although we used the same fifteen-second video clip for every Democrat's advertisement and the same clip for every Republican's advertisement, the voice-overs differed somewhat across candidates to make sure the advertisement was consistent with the thrust of each candidate's more detailed 'healthcare policy' which could be examined during the broader campaign. The final five seconds of each advertisement differed, of course, depending on which particular candidate was running in the general election.

2. We produced a positive Democratic advertisement calling for more jobs that was identical for every Democratic candidate (except for the candidate-specific last five seconds). Likewise we produced a positive Republican keep-our-defence-strong advertisement, which was identical for every Republican candidate, except for the last five seconds.

3. We produced two similar 'feel good' positive advertisements (one for each party) with little policy content: 'Times are good, the world's at peace, vote Democratic/Republican. Thus a positive campaign by a Democrat included this generic feel-good advertisement, a positive advertisement about healthcare policy, and a positive advertisement about jobs. The positive campaign by the Republican included a generic feel-good advertisement, a positive advertisement about healthcare policy, and a positive advertisement about defence spending.

4. We produced a generic negative advertisement for each party, attacking the opposite party's candidate's health policy ('policy attack'; Benoit et al. 2003b; Benoit 2007). These advertisements worked against any specific candidate's policy. The Democrat's advertisements started 'to hear Republicans talk you would never know there is a healthcare crisis,' while the Republican attack advertisement started 'While no one doubts there is a healthcare crisis, Democrats want you to believe that only big government can solve the problem.'

5. We also produced generic attack advertisements aimed at all Democrats (or all Republicans). For example, the Democrat's advertisement started with 'Who really benefits from a Republican president?', while the Republican's advertisement started with 'Let's take a look at the Democratic record: High taxes, increased welfare costs, soft on crime ...' ('character attack'; Benoit et al. 2003b; Benoit 2007).

Thus a negative campaign by the Democratic candidate included the generic attack on Republicans, a negative advertisement specifically targeting the opponent's healthcare policy, and a positive advertisement about the candidate's own healthcare policy. A negative campaign by the Republican included the generic attack on Democrats, an advertisement attacking the Democratic candidate's healthcare policy, and a positive advertisement about the candidate's own healthcare policy.

Manipulations

All of the advertisements aired during the primary campaign of our experiments were positive. But each general election campaign included a manipulation of the positive or negative nature of the candidates' advertisements. In most experiments we randomly manipulated the nature of both the out-party's *and* the in-party's general election advertisements, resulting in a fully crossed two by two design.[3] In our first experiment, however, only the nature of the out-party's advertisements was manipulated, while the in-party candidate always ran a positive campaign. As discussed above, all of the advertisements addressed broad policy goals or tried to establish general 'feel-good' themes; none addressed the personal characteristics (ethics, qualifications, etc.) of either the sponsoring or target candidate.

Subjects

All subjects (N=414) were recruited from the central New Jersey area with only three provisos: they were American citizens, at least eighteen years of age, and *not* currently attending college. Most subjects were paid volunteers who were donating their subject fee to some voluntary organisation to which they belonged. These subjects are not a random sample of anything, but they are broadly representative of the type of people living in central New Jersey. Fifty-four per cent were female, 16 per cent were non-white, forty-seven per cent were college graduates, and their average age was forty-five.

Results

Candidate evaluation and vote choice

We begin by asking an obvious and straightforward question. Did the candidates' advertising strategies influence how much they were liked and/or the vote choice in our general election campaigns? For simplicity we will present the results from all studies combined, although we analysed each study separately to make sure this combined approach was not distorting the results.[4] Our primary hypotheses is that negative (attack) advertising will not be any more effective that positive (advocacy) advertisements, and if anything may prove to be counter-productive. For candidate affect and the vote choice, the results were very consistent across studies. Whether the dependent variable is liking for the in-party candidate, liking for the out-party candidate, or net liking of the in-party candidate minus liking of the out-party candidate, we observe an interaction between the nature of the out-party's campaign strategy, and party.

---

3. 'In-party' and 'out-party' are defined by voter registration in for our primary election campaign, and it is not always consistent with party identification. In particular, it includes independents (by the standard party identification measure) as 'members' of one party or the other. It also includes a handful of subjects who 'cross-registered' with the party opposite of the one with which they identify.

4. Such analyses always included dummy variables representing the effects of the different studies.

(The nature of the in-party candidate's campaign strategy does not seem to affect evaluations of the candidates.)

Democrats like their own candidate more when he or she is attacked by the opponent (80.8 versus 76.3) and they like the opposing candidate less when he or she attacks (53.9 versus 56.2), which combine to make a greater net preference for their own candidate over the opponent of over six and half points when the opponent attacks compared to when they stay positive. Thus going negative is doubly counter-productive for Republicans. On the other hand, while Republicans seemed immune to the advertisements of their opponent, liking their candidate equally well regardless of whether the Democrat has a negative or a positive campaign (81.1 versus 80.7), they actually like their Democratic opponent a lot less when he or she ran a positive campaign (51.7 versus 58.9). This is the opposite of the usual 'backlash' effect. Thus in terms of *net* preference, they like their own candidate relatively more than the opponent when the Democrat ran a positive campaign, but this is due entirely to the Republicans' reaction to the Democratic sponsor of the advertisements, rather than to any effect of the Democrats'

Figure 15.1: Net affect for in-party candidate, by party and opponent's campaign strategy

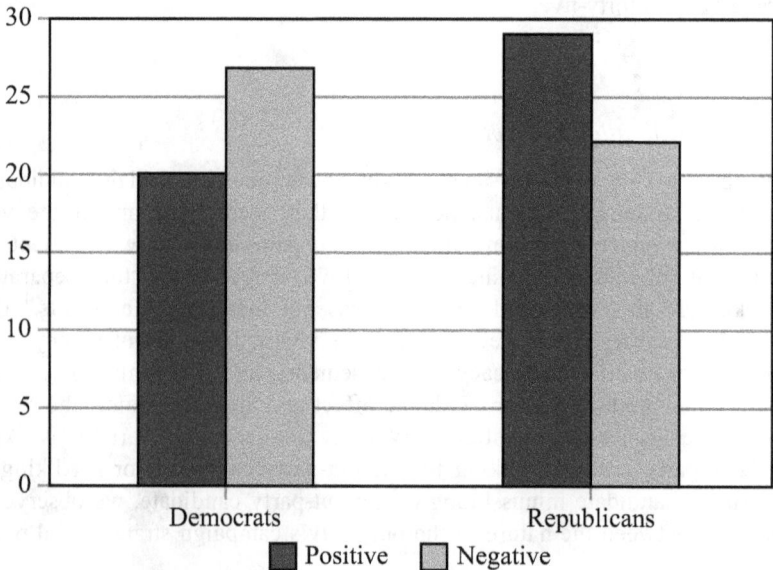

Note: Table entries are the feeling thermometer rating of the in-party candidate minus the feeling thermometer rating of the out-party candidate. N=405.

advertisements on their Republican targets. Figure 15.1 illustrates this difference for net preference for the in-party over the out-party candidate.

These mean differences in evaluation of the candidates also translated into the vote decision. As would be expected in any election, our voters strongly supported their own party's candidate in the general election irrespective of campaign strategies (and anything else), voting for him or her over two-thirds of the time. But as shown in Figure 15.2, voters' willingness to defect from a party was in part of function of the candidates' advertisements campaigns to which they had been exposed. Democrats were most likely to defect when both candidates stayed positive in their advertising, whereas Republicans were most likely to defect when both candidates went negative. The three-way interaction reflected in Figure 15.2 is statistically significant (p<0.05).

These data paint a mixed picture about the effectiveness of attacking the opponent as a campaign strategy – but then, that is exactly the nature of the literature as a whole (Lau *et al.* 1999, 2007). It seems as if Democrats react defensively when their candidate is attacked, and rally in stronger support of the party's standard bearer. Thus 'going negative' is a poor strategy for Republicans to choose, judging by their

Figure 15.2: Defection of party voters by campaign strategy

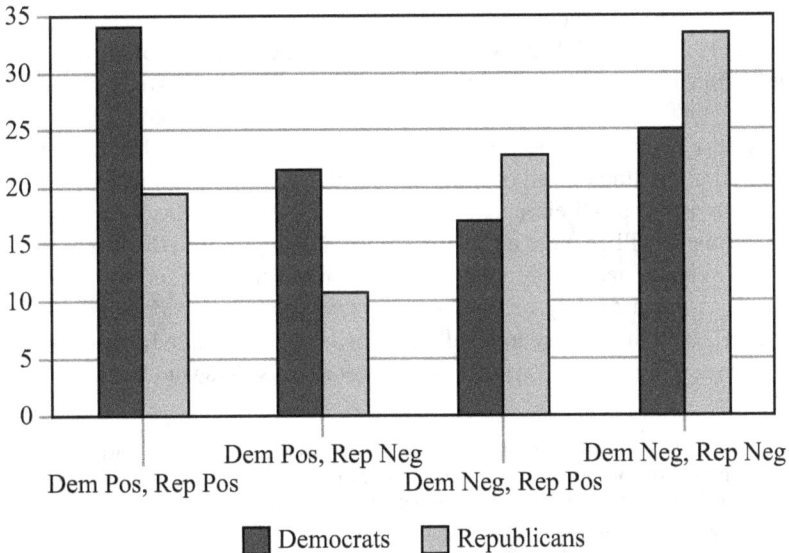

Note: Figure shows per cent of party voters defecting to the opponent as a function of the nature of both candidate's campaign strategy. N=407.

success at winning converts from the opposition.[5] Republicans, on the other hand, seem to be much more tolerant of negative campaigning, and do not react particularly defensively when their candidate is attacked by a Democrat. In fact, they seem to like a Democrat more who *will* attack them – or perhaps more accurately, really dislike a Democrat who will *not* attack. Ironically, this translates into attacking the opponent being a relatively more successful strategy for Democrats to follow.

These findings on the effectiveness of negative campaigning are based, we remind readers again, on a mock presidential election campaign, and we doubt we could get rich trying to peddle these results to campaign consultants of either party. Still, these findings are similar enough to most other studies of negative campaigning to suggest to readers that they really should pay attention to where our studies have something new and unique to add: the effects of negative campaigning on information processing.

Information processing

While there are a large number of studies examining the effectiveness of negative advertisements, there is very little research exploring the process by which presumed differential effectiveness of negative advertisements is produced. The one big exception to this statement is memory. There are a good number of studies addressing memory for different types of advertisements (twenty, seven years ago – *see* Lau *et al.* 2007), and greater memorability is a very good explanation for effectiveness. If an advertisement is to have any type of effect at all, it must first be noticed and processed in some way, and memory is a good indicator of such processing. Certainly the voters in our experiments *saw* all of the candidate's advertisements (again – one of the least realistic aspects of studying any type of advertising campaign experimentally), and they certainly could have 'stood out' against a generally more positive background.[6] But how deeply they were processed in the flood of all of the other campaign information that was coming at subjects is not at all clear. Nonetheless, we clearly hypothesise that negative advertisements will be more easily remembered than positive advertisements.

After subjects had voted in the general election campaign and were instructed to recall as much as they could about the two general election candidates, we explicitly asked them to try to recall as many of the political advertisements that they had seen.[7] Figure 15.3 reports the percentage of voters who had any memory

---

5. Another goal of negative campaigning in actual elections is mobilising one's own partisans, and negative campaigning could be much more successful on this front. Our studies do not address turnout, however, so we cannot address this point empirically.

6. Only in the *negative-negative* condition were a majority of the general election campaign advertisements negative, and even here they always followed a primary election campaign in which all ten to twelve advertisements were positive. A 'figure-ground' hypothesis is one of the leading explanations for a *negativity effect* in information processing (Lau 1985).

7. We did not ask a separate question about memory for campaign advertisements in the first experiment, although subjects could (and a few did) report as memories in describing what they remembered about the two general election candidates.

Figure 15.3: Effect of campaign strategy on memory for advertisements

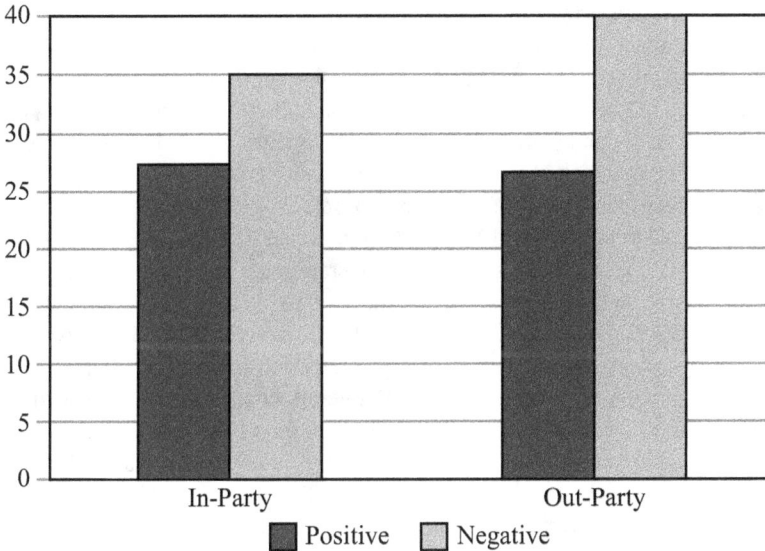

Note: Data are the per cent of respondents remembering each type of advertisement N=213.

of any of the advertisements shown by the in-party or the out-party candidate, in the positive and negative advertisements conditions. In our data, the negative advertisements campaigns did prove to be about 8–13 per cent more memorable than the comparable positive advertising campaigns. In the case of in-party advertisements, this difference is not statistically significant, but in the case of out-party advertisements, it is significant.[8] The results are essentially the same if we eliminate memory for the one (positive) advertisement, which was shown in both the positive and negative advertisement conditions. So here is some empirical support for the conventional wisdom: Negative advertisements are a bit more memorable.

---

8. There are no party differences on memory for advertisements. These statements about statistical significance come from ordinal regressions, which also included age and political expertise as covariates. Future meta-analysts will probably prefer learning the simple bivariate results, however. For in-party advertisements, positive advertisement conditions, there were 72.8 per cent with no memory of any advertisements, 23.9 per cent could remember one advertisement, and 3.3 per cent could remember two advertisements. In the negative advertisement condition, the comparable figures were 65.3 per cent, 28.1 per cent, and 6.6 per cent. This yields a $X^2(2)$ of 1.92, and a tau-c of 0.08, with an approximate t of 1.29 (p< 0.20), and a delta of 0.19. For out-party advertisements, the numbers are 73.3 per cent, 21.7 per cent, and 5.0 per cent in the positive advertisement condition, and 60.2 per cent, 31.2 per cent, and 8.6 per cent in the negative advertisement condition, yielding a $X^2(2)$ of 4.21, and a tau-c of 0.13, with an approximate t of 2.04 (p<0.05), and a delta of 0.28. N=213.

But now we go on to ask whether a positive or negative advertisement campaign alters information processing in any detectable way during the campaign. Another way that advertisements could be effective is by inspiring more discretionary information search about the topic of the advertisement. An advertisement promoting a candidate's own policy on some issue, or attacking the opponent's, at the very least conveys the message that the candidate thinks this is an important issue, and could inspire the voter to learn more about those policies being promoted or attacked on her own. (Our advertisements were never as specific as the more detailed information available by selecting the candidate's policy from the dynamic information board.) So we hypothesised that negative advertisements are more likely to result in subsequent discretionary information search about issues addressed in the advertisement, compared to positive advertisements.

Our results suggest that indeed they do, in several interesting ways. First of all, we observed a significant two-way interaction between the nature of each candidate's advertisement campaign and overall depth of search. The deepest search (about 8 per cent deeper than the remaining three conditions) occurs when both candidates attack their opponent. There are no party differences on depth of search, so it cannot explain any of the observed differences in the effectiveness of the advertisements across party. But there are party differences on the comparability of search across candidates by advertising campaign. As shown in Figure 15.4, there is a significant two-way interaction between party and the

Figure 15.4: Effect of in-party campaign strategy on comparability of search across candidates

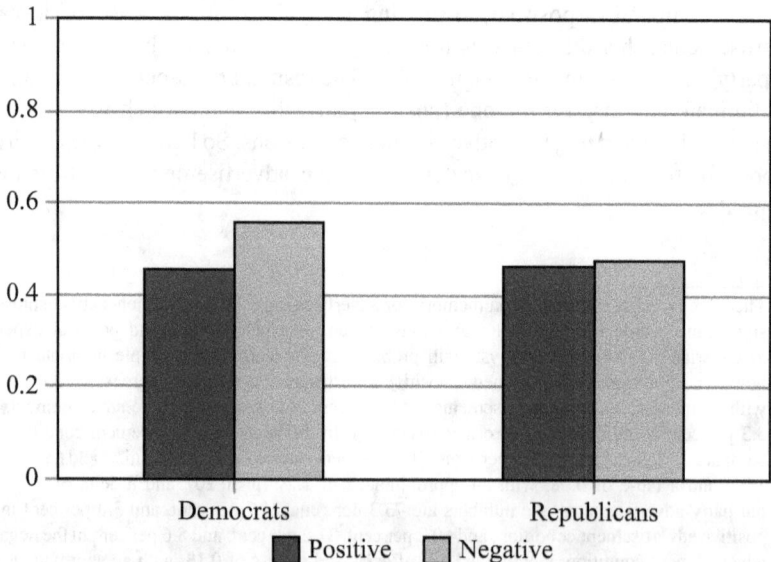

Note: Comparability of search measure has been rescaled to range between 0 and 1. N=403.

nature of the in-party's campaign advertisements. Democrats go out of their way to more carefully consider the Republican candidate when their own candidate attacks. It is as if Democrats are not sure they approve of such tactics, and want to assure themselves the attacks are justified. And they apparently received that assurance, judging by their subsequent vote choices.

Our overall depth and comparability of search measures are pretty broad, however. We can more narrowly hone in on the specific policies addressed in our various general election campaign advertisements by considering search directed at those specific policies. So we looked specifically at those policies addressed by each candidate's advertisements (healthcare and unemployment programmes, in the case of the Democrat's positive advertisements, healthcare and more general economic policies, in the case of Democrat's negative advertisements; healthcare and defence spending, in the case of the Republican's positive advertisements, healthcare and taxes and welfare, in the case of the Republican's negative advertisements). As shown in Figure 15.5, for each party there is significantly more advertisement-specific search resulting from negative advertisements compared to positive advertisements. These effects are huge – greater than 100 per cent increase in advertisement-specific search in the negative advertisement conditions – and highly significant ($p<0.001$). And they are clearly limited to the themes addressed in the advertisements themselves. That is, the nature of the Republican's advertisements has no effect on search for policies addressed in the Democrat's advertisements, and the nature of the Democrat's advertisements has no effect on search for policies addressed in the Republican's advertisements.[9]

Notice that the results on advertisement-specific search perfectly mirror those on memory for the advertisements, and thus can help provide a new explanation for the greater memorability of negative political advertisements. There may well be something about a negative advertisement that makes it more memorable than a comparable positive advertisement, all else equal; but in the context of a dynamic political campaign where voters have the opportunity to seek out additional confirmation of the claims made in advertisements, our results suggest that voters are much more likely to actively seek out such confirmation in response to negative advertisements compared to positive advertisements. This discretionary advertisement-specific search is an indication of deeper processing, which should also lead to greater recall.

---

9. On the other hand, the search is not limited to the candidate who is the target of the advertisements. The data in Figure 15.5 show total search across both candidates for the policies addressed in the advertisements, irrespective of whether the advertisement is attacking the opponent's policies or praising the sponsor's policies. The same general pattern is observed if we limit the dependent variable to count only search of policies of the targeted candidate – that is, search for the sponsor's relevant policies in the case of positive advertisements, or the target's relevant policies in the case of negative advertisements. In the latter case the means are lower across the board because we are only considering search for one candidate's policies rather than two.

Figure 15.5: Effect of campaign strategy on advertisement-specific discretionary search

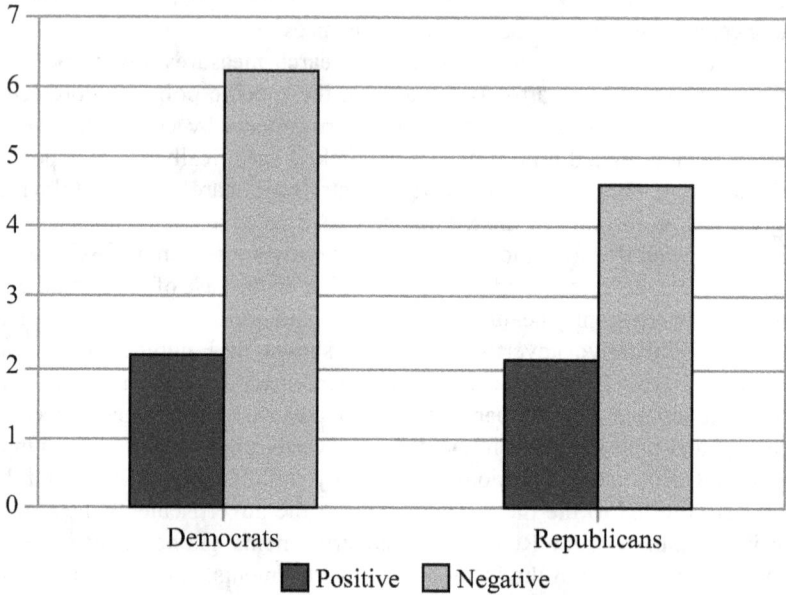

Note: Dependent variable is the number items relevant to the theme of the advertisement's respondents chose to examine during the general election campaign. N=407.

Correct voting

We have seen that the nature of candidates' advertisement campaigns can affect both the depth and comparability of search across candidates. These two measures of information-processing are used by decision researchers to infer which decision strategies are being employed by the decision-maker to make a choice (Ford *et al.* 1989; Lau 2003; Redlawsk and Lau 2013). We have also seen that the advertisement strategies affect accurate memory for the advertisements. As reported by Lau and Redlawsk (2006), both decision strategies and memory are associated with *correct voting* – the extent to which voters, under conditions of incomplete information (as exist in any election), nonetheless manage to select the candidate or party who most closely shares their own values and priorities (Lau and Redlawsk 1997). This leads us to consider whether the candidates' advertising strategies themselves affect correct voting. We specified a basic general election model for predicting correct voting, including a number of demographic control variables, long-term political orientations, political sophistication, indicators of four different decision strategies (varying the depth and comparability of search across candidates[10]), an indicator of accurate memory, and our manipulations of the two candidates' advertisement strategies (and the interaction between them).

The full logistic regression results are provided in Table 15.1. Here we focus on the effects of the two campaign advertisements manipulations and their interaction. The 'main effects' of each candidate attacking the opponent is to increase the probability of a correct vote, although only the effect of the out-party's campaign approaches statistical significance. Each of these coefficients can be interpreted as the effect of one of the candidate's going negative when the opposing candidate runs a positive advertising campaign. But the interaction between the two manipulations – that is, campaigns where both candidates go on the attack – is statistically significant and strongly negative. Thus the two conditions that have the lowest probability of a correct vote are when both candidates stay positive (63 per cent correct voting), or both candidates go negative (64 per cent correct voting). Campaigns where one candidate stays positive while the other attacks (and it does not really matter which candidate takes which strategy) are much more likely to result in correct voting (75 per cent correct, on average). Figure 15.6 shows the observed differences. Given that candidates tend to mirror the tone of their opponent's campaign strategy in real elections (Lau and Pomper 2001b), the positive-positive and negative-negative campaigns are the most likely to actually occur.

How can we explain this surprising difference? We cannot – at least, theoretically. We certainly did not predict this finding. We saw some reasons that negative advertisements could lead to more correct voting (they are associated with greater memory, at least about the advertisements themselves), and other reasons why it could lead to less (more likely to result in a Model 1 rational decision process, which we have previously found to be less effective [Lau and Redlawsk 2006]), and expected these two forces to cancel each other out. We were wrong. And the observed differences, in the neighbourhood of a 10 per cent difference in the probability of a correct vote, are quite substantial.

The best we can do, after the fact, is to report that depth of search tends to be greater when the two candidates match advertising strategies than when they choose different strategies ($p < 0.07$). This is particularly true of Republicans (interaction $p < 0.09$). Comparability of search also tends to be greater for Republicans (but not Democrats) in the match strategies condition (interaction $p < 0.10$). This translates into Republicans (again, but not Democrats) being about 12 per cent more likely

---

10. Model 1, *Rational Choice*, is indicated by relatively deep information search, evenly distributed across the competing candidates. Model 2, *Confirmatory Decision Making*, is indicated by relatively deep information search that is skewed in favour of the in-party. Model 3, *Fast and Frugal Decision Making*, is indicated by relatively shallow information search, evenly distributed across the alternatives. And Model 4, *Heuristic-Based Decision Making*, is indicated by relatively shallow information search, unevenly distributed across the candidates or parties.

Table 15.1: Effect of campaign advertisement manipulations on correct voting

	B	S.E.
Age	0.251	(0.568)
Education	0.064	(0.543)
Income	0.173	(0.365)
Female	−0.003	(0.239)
Strength of party ID	1.011**	(0.347)
Conservative ID	0.654	(0.539)
Political sophistication	−0.514	(0.798)
Perceived difficulty of choice	−0.429	(0.1,131)
Model 1 (Rational choice)	0.115	(0.853)
Model 2 (Confirmatory decision-making)	0.908*	(0.865)
Model 3 (Fast and frugal decision-making)	0.678@	(0.914)
Model 4 (Heuristic-based decision-making)	1.021*	(0.871)
Net accurate memories	1.494@	(0.907)
Negative in-party advertisements	0.553	(0.403)
Negative out-party advertisements	0.461@	(0.270)
Negative in-party advertisements X out-party advertisements	−1.138*	(0.508)

Correctly classified	70.1%
Nagelkerke Pseudo R2	0.12
Model X^2 (df)	34.49 (18)
Significance	p<0.02

@ p<0.09; * p<0.05; **p<0.01
Note: Table entries are logistic regression coefficients. Model also includes dummy variables representing the different studies (N=402).

Figure 15.6: Effect of campaign strategy on correct voting

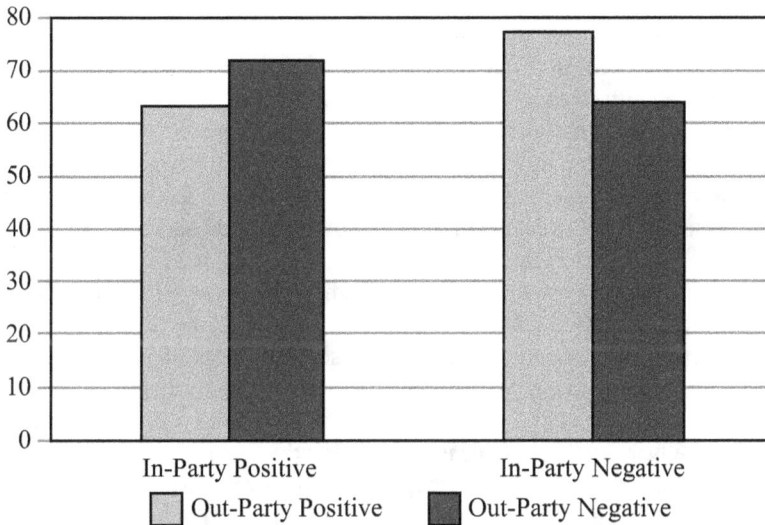

Note: Figure shows per cent voting correctly in each condition. N=402.

to utilise a Model 1 decision strategy in the two matched strategies conditions. Why this should be, we are at a loss to say, but it is true, at least in these data. Perhaps it relates to our earlier findings (Lau and Redlawsk 2006) about Model 1 decision-making. Those who try to be 'rational' in the sense of learning as much as they can about all of their options in fact do worse than voters who use more intuitive strategies. Thus such a rational strategy is not one that often leads to a high probability of correct voting. So here is a partial (and not very satisfying) explanation for this unexpected finding.

If we look back at Figure 15.2, we also see that defection from party is greatest when both candidates run positive campaigns (especially true of Democrats) or both candidates run negative campaigns (particularly true of Republicans). This is another partial explanation for this finding, as party is a factor in determining correct voting.

Discussion

To quickly summarise the major results reported in this chapter, we found that attacking the opponent was a much more effective strategy for Democrats to use against Republicans than for Republicans to use against Democrats. Democrats do not believe the attacks, and react very negatively against a Republican who attacks their party's candidate. Republicans, on the other hand, are much more accepting of negative campaigning, both in their own candidate and from their opponent. Indeed, they seem to respect a Democrat more if he or she attacks their own Republican candidate than if s/he refrains from attacking. These effects were also reflected in vote decisions.

But the strength of our methodology is in explicating information processing. We found, first, that the negative advertisements were a bit easier to remember than the positive advertisements. Overall, subjects searched for more information – a greater depth of search in our terms – when both candidates ran a positive campaign or both candidates ran a negative campaign. But the strongest processing effects, by far, were for advertisement-specific search – that is, for the policies or themes addressed in the advertisements. Negative advertisements seem to inspire about twice as much advertisement-specific search as positive advertisements.

This is important new evidence in the study of campaign or media effects. The positive or negative nature of candidates' advertisement campaigns inspire different levels of subsequent information seeking about the two candidates' policies, particularly those policies related to the ads themselves. Those attacks better be accurate, because information processing about both candidates was affected equally. Nonetheless, this is the type of evidence on the effects of political advertisements that no one that we are aware of has ever reported.

We ended with an intriguing but unexpected finding. The tone of candidates' advertising strategies is related to correct voting, but not in any straightforward manner. If ever the oft-repeated bromide about 'more research being necessary' is called for, now would be the time. We are pretty confident in this finding, in that it was replicated over several experiments and survived a wide range of statistical controls. But it was unexpected, and we do not feel like we have a good explanation for it.

Chapter Sixteen

How the News Media Amplify Negative Messages

Travis N. Ridout and Annemarie S. Walter

Negative advertising, i.e. political advertising that attacks the opponent on issues or traits (Geer 2006; Benoit 1999), is a common feature of political systems around the globe, as the various chapters in this volume attest. Yet in order to understand the influence of negative advertising, it is important that we look beyond people's direct exposure to the advertisements themselves. We must also examine to what extent the news media cover political advertising and how they cover that advertising – two factors that may serve to amplify or mitigate the effects of negative advertising. News coverage allows more citizens to be exposed to the messages contained within the advertisements (Min 2002), and how reporters write about the advertisement messages may affect voters' perceptions of the candidates or parties sending them. Moreover, the effects of advertisement coverage might be particularly powerful in settings where the density of advertisement airings is low. In this chapter, which compares print media coverage of televised political advertising in New Zealand, the United Kingdom (UK) and the United States (US), we find that the volume of coverage varies considerably across countries, and we find that negative advertising is amplified to a much greater degree in some places than in others. These findings suggest that, given the large variation in media amplification of negative campaigning, the potential impacts of negative campaigning on voters are much greater in some countries, namely, the US, than elsewhere.

Media coverage of advertising

At least in the US, one frequent element of campaign coverage is coverage of political advertising – generally, television advertising. Geer (2009) reports that the media started paying considerable attention to political advertising during the 1988 presidential race. Between 1984 and 1988, the number of stories in the *New York Times* and the *Washington Post* rose from under 100 to 200 – and it has remained at that high level ever since (Geer 2009). Geer's observations are consistent with the findings of Ridout and Franz (2011) who noted similar rises in the share of campaign coverage that concerned advertising. In both 2000 and 2008, over 10 per cent of articles about the presidential campaign in the *Washington Post* discussed television advertising. West (2005) finds that political advertising is covered by the news media most often in competitive races.

The media's focus on advertising is even greater in local and regional news outlets. One study found that 30 per cent of coverage of US Senate races across several local newspapers mentioned advertising (Fowler and Ridout 2009). That same study found that 20 per cent of coverage on local television stations mentioned political advertising.

Not only do the news media in the US give substantial coverage to political advertising, but they tend to focus on coverage of negative advertising. Geer (2009) shows that in each presidential election year between 1996 and 2008, over 75 per cent of the advertisements that were discussed on the networks' nightly news programmes were negative. Ridout and Smith (2008) show that the average positive advertisement received only 0.16 media mentions, compared to 0.58 mentions for the average negative advertisement and 0.67 mentions for the average contrast advertisement (those advertisements that mention both the sponsoring candidate and the opponent).

Clearly, the American news media devote substantial coverage to political advertising, and when they do mention specific political advertisements, they disproportionately focus on negative advertisements. It is unclear, however, whether these conclusions extend to other countries with different campaign environments and different media systems. To be sure, scholars have written anecdotally about advertisements aired in countries other than the US that drove media coverage. Still, to our knowledge there are no studies that systematically examine media coverage of televised political advertising comparatively or in the UK or New Zealand specifically.

Consequences of media coverage of advertising

Scholars have started to examine the effects of media coverage of political advertising, focusing both on citizen attitudes and the behaviour of campaigns. One line of research looks into the effects on citizens of a very specific form of media coverage called 'ad watches.' 'Ad watches' are media stories that subject political advertisements to scrutiny, with journalists acting as arbiters of what is true. The consensus finding of this research is that 'ad watch' coverage has an unintended effect because audiences better remember the attacks than the reporters' attempts to debunk those attacks (Ansolabehere and Iyengar 1995; Pfau and Louden 1994). Thus, the news media may be unintentionally enhancing the effectiveness of the advertisements (Kaid 2004; Min 2002). Still, findings are not unanimous in this regard. Min (2002) found in an experimental setting that when an 'ad watch' covered an advertisement negatively, voters were less likely to vote for the candidate that broadcasted the advertisement. Candidates have responded to the practice of 'ad watches' by not only documenting their claims more carefully (West 2005), but also by developing advertisements that would deliberately elicit 'ad watch' coverage (Iyengar 2011).

Another line of research looks at how media coverage of advertising affects citizens' perceptions of the tone of a race. For instance, Fowler and Ridout (2012) ask whether people perceive campaigns as more negative when the media emphasise coverage of negative advertising. This research finds that the relationship is not direct – more discussion of negative advertising does not automatically lead citizens to perceive a race as more negative. Rather, increased coverage of negative advertising – only when framed in a strategic fashion – leads to increased perceptions of campaign negativity.

Media coverage of campaign advertising and, in particular, attack advertising, may also influence the behaviour of candidates. Geer argues that the news media have 'altered the incentives of candidates to produce and air negative advertisements' (2009: 12). Geer suggests that many negative advertisements in the US, especially at the presidential level, are nothing more than 'press releases' designed to cater to the news media. But in order to win the attention of the media gatekeepers, one must offer up conflict and controversy, which is most easily done through a negative advertisement.

Why media cover (negative) political advertising

There are several reasons for the media to cover political advertising – and negative political advertising in particular. First, it is cost effective in that it takes little effort in terms of discovery (Fowler and Ridout 2009). Reporting on the latest political advertisement that is released by a campaign requires little entrepreneurial reporting. The reporter can simply rehash the arguments made in the advertisement while using the video provided. Indeed, campaigns in the US often promote the release of new advertisements to the news media in hopes of receiving news coverage.

Second, negative political advertising as a story appeals to three important news values. The first is the use of a game or contest frame (Lawrence 2000; Bartels 1988; Patterson and McClure 1976; Robinson and Sheehan 1983). Negative advertising can be used to illustrate a conflict between competing candidates or parties. What is more, citizens are more attracted to campaign news when it uses a game frame or focuses on conflict (Iyengar et al. 2004). Thus, it may be in the economic interest of news organisations to cover political advertising as it can attract larger audiences. The second news value is negativity, which has risen over the past decades in several countries around the world (Lengauer et al. 2012). Therefore, we should expect negative advertisements to attract more news than positive advertisements. A third news value is personalisation, where the news tends to report on individuals and present the news in a personalised way (Galtung and Ruge 1965). Walter and Vliegenthart (2010) find that the news over-reported trait attacks in the 2010 Dutch election campaign. As a result, personalised advertisements and, in particular, negative trait advertisements may be especially newsworthy.

Third, covering negative political advertising is consistent with the media's watchdog role, their responsibility to help provide citizens in a democracy with accurate information. Therefore, providing coverage of advertising, particularly 'ad watch' coverage that helps voters interpret political messages, can be considered part of a journalist's job.

Variations in (coverage of) political advertising across countries

Yet coverage of political advertising – and especially negative advertising – should not be equally prevalent across the globe. The characteristics of the political system influence the characteristics of election campaigns and their effects on citizens (Bowler and Farrell 1992; Schmitt-Beck and Farrell 2002; Farrell 2005). These characteristics of the political system include a country's institutional structure, its electoral system, its party system and its media system (Bowler and Farrell 1992). Strömbäck and Kaid (2008) argue that these characteristics not only affect the conduct of election campaigns but also the news coverage of these campaigns. Although the limited number of countries in our study prevents us from drawing iron-clad conclusions about the influence of these political system characteristics on coverage of negative campaigning, we will still theorise how some of these system characteristics are related to the coverage of advertising and, in particular, negative advertising.

First, coverage of political advertising, including negative advertising, is linked to the institutional structure of a country. One aspect of the institutional structure is the electoral laws that govern the conduct of elections before they take place. Laws that matter in this respect are regulations on broadcasting political advertising (and negative advertising in particular) and campaign finance regulations, which may affect the supply of advertising to cover. In the US, for instance, there are no restrictions on how much may be spent on advertising, and rules concerning how money must be raised have been loosened in recent years, resulting in massive campaign budgets. As a result, candidates, parties and outside groups may release a new advertisement almost every day for several months before election day, thus frequently supplying new stories for the news media. Most other countries, by contrast, have tighter regulations on advertising spending or only allow for government-allocated advertising. Thus, only a few advertisements – maybe up to a dozen – may be released over the entire length of the campaign. Some countries also have rules that might limit the supply of negative advertising. In France, for instance, using derisive language about candidates in political broadcasts is prohibited (Kaid and Gagnère 2006: 85). We expect that the larger the supply of advertising, including negative advertising, the greater the volume of advertisement-related coverage.

Second, media coverage of negative advertising might be related to a country's party system. The extent to which advertisements are negative varies across countries (e.g. Elmelund-Præstekær 2010; Hansen and Pedersen 2008; Van Heerde-Hudson 2011; Walter *et al.* 2014; Kaid and Holtz-Bacha 2006; Salmond 2011; Schweitzer 2009), thus constraining the supply of negative advertising for the news media to discuss. Although direct comparisons of levels of campaign negativity across countries are rare (e.g. Walter 2014b; Walter and Van Praag 2014; Kaid and Holtz-Bacha 2006; Salmond 2011), the evidence suggests that countries with multiparty systems tend to have less negativity than two-party systems (Elmelund-Præstekær 2010; Hansen and Pedersen 2008;

Walter *et al.* 2014; Ridout and Walter 2013). The first reason given for this is that negative campaigning might poison the well, hindering the potential for parties in multiparty systems to both form governments after the election and govern effectively in coalitions (Andeweg and Irwin 2009; Brants *et al.* 1982; Kaid and Holtz-Bacha 2006; Sjöblom 1968; Walter and Van der Brug 2013). The second reason for the higher level of campaign negativity in two-party systems is that attacks that serve to disqualify an opponent generally benefit the attacker, as voters have no other viable choices. But in a multi-party system, attacks are just as likely to benefit some other third party as they are to benefit the attacker (Elmelund-Præstekær 2010; Hansen and Pedersen 2008; Walter and Van der Brug 2013). This is because voters may identify with more than one party (Schmitt 2002; Tillie 1995; Van der Eijk and Niemöller 1983). This is especially true in multiparty systems where it is likely that a number of fairly ideologically similar parties compete. In line with these research findings, we expect less negative advertising in multiparty settings, which provides the news media with less opportunity to write about negative advertisements.

A third factor that is likely to influence the level of media coverage of negative advertising is the country's media system. Although media systems are shaped by several factors, including the degree of political parallelism, the development of journalistic professionalism and the degree and nature of state intervention (Hallin and Mancini 2004: 21), our primary focus here is the degree to which the media system is commercialised. The more commercialised the media system, the more economic pressure that news organisations face. As a result, news organisations feel pressure to tailor the content of their stories to presumed audience preferences (Semetko *et al.* 1991). Consequently, these news organisations have high incentives to produce conflict-based or game-framed coverage, with which coverage of negative advertising fits nicely. Therefore, we expect more coverage of negative advertising in more commercialised media systems. Using the typology of Hallin and Mancini (2004) we would expect that the most coverage of negative advertising would be found in countries following the liberal model, which is characterised by the relative dominance of market mechanisms and commercial media.

Competitive pressures on the media vary both across media systems and across media organisations (Semetko *et al.* 1991). It also matters how the media inside the country are organised, whether the media have clear segmented audiences or whether they must compete with one another for the same audience. In addition, their funding matters. Commercial news organisations, which must attract large audiences in order to ensure profitability, should face more pressure to focus on conflict than publicly-owned broadcasters. Moreover, news organisations that have corporate owners should face more pressure to turn to conflict coverage than independent news organisations (Dunaway 2008). Studies have found that tabloid newspapers focus more on conflict than broadsheet newspapers (Vliegenthart *et al.* 2011). Thus, there may be variations across news outlets in the extent to which they cover negative political advertising.

The cases: New Zealand, UK and US

We measured coverage of televised political advertising in fifteen newspapers during the two most recent national election campaigns in each of the three countries we examined, namely, New Zealand, the UK and the US. The three countries are somewhat similar in that they are all English-speaking established democracies. At the same time, they differ in various respects, including in the three political system characteristics that we linked theoretically to coverage of negative advertising. We will first discuss some generic differences between the cases and then focus on the three characteristics that we believe matter, namely, rules on party political broadcasting, the party system and the media system.

We examined national elections (as opposed to lower-level elections) as these serve to highlight the main political debates in each country. These 'first-order elections' (Reif 1985) are presidential elections in the US and parliamentary elections in New Zealand and the UK.

For each election, we examined newspaper articles sixty days prior to the day of the election. The length of the election campaign differs across the three countries. In the UK, the length of the official campaign is determined by the Electoral Commission, and it is normally four to five weeks (Scammell and Langer 2006). The length of the official campaign is similar in New Zealand (Mulgan 2004: 266). In the US, there is no formal campaign period, but traditionally, the presidential campaigns have ramped up after Labour Day, which marks the beginning of an intense period of eight to nine weeks of campaigning (Semetko *et al.* 1991:11).

Regulations on political advertising also differ between the three countries. In the US, television advertisements are the most prominent form of campaign advertising, and almost one billion dollars was spent to purchase television advertisements in the 2012 presidential race (Fowler and Ridout 2012). Parties, candidates and independent groups are free to purchase advertising time on television with few restrictions.

In the UK, however, paid political advertising is completely prohibited on television, but major parties do receive free broadcasting time on public and commercial television. These advertisements are labelled party election broadcasts (PEBs) during official campaign periods (Kaid and Holtz-Bacha 2006: 10; Scammell and Langer 2006: 65). These time slots for political broadcasting are divided among the British political parties on the basis of a formula that takes into account the number of seats they contest and the votes they secure at the elections (Leach *et al.* 2011). PEBs once were a major part of the televised election campaign and were broadcast simultaneously on all channels. This ended in 1987 when the number of channels expanded, making the previous practice unworkable (Scammell and Semetko 2008). This, and other factors, has led to a decrease in the importance of PEBs (Scammell and Langer 2006: 72).

At the same time, PEBs in the UK have become more professional with the hiring of marketing professionals. A few party election broadcasts have had enough impact to generate news stories that had a measureable effect on voters' party support (Leach *et al.* 2011). One particularly well-known PEB, which was aimed at generating news coverage, was the 1992 Labour advertisement called Jennifer's Ear. The advertisement showed the story of a little girl who had to wait for an ear operation due to the Conservative government's neglect of the National Health Service. This led to a counter-campaign by the Conservative Party, and the names of the parents of the girl were anonymously leaked to the press, which generated to a media hunt for the source of the leak (Scammell and Langer 2006).

New Zealand also has restrictions on advertising; the country does not prohibit paid political advertising like the UK does, but it does place limits on their purchase. Registered political parties may not spend more than the amount they were given in public funding on broadcast political advertising. Parties are also allocated some free airtime on Television New Zealand (Stewart 2006). Table 16.1 makes clear that the supply of advertising is the largest, by far, in the US – ten to twenty times larger than in the UK or New Zealand. In the US in 2012, for instance, 258 unique advertisements aired, compared to just twenty-two in New Zealand in 2011 and fourteen in the UK in 2010.

The party system also differs among the three countries. The US has had a stable two-party system for well over a century, with either Republican or Democrats holding the presidency. The UK has a two-and-a-half party system, which means that typically one party, either the Conservatives or Labour, governs. On occasion, however, a considerably smaller third party, the Liberal Democrats, has helped form a coalition government. The most recent instance of this was after the 2010 elections. New Zealand used to have a two-party system, but after a reform of the electoral system in the mid-1990s, New Zealand became a multiparty system without a dominant party. Since that time, election coalitions or minority governments have formed. In general, the Labour or National Party has ruled in coalition with a smaller party (or by receiving the support of a smaller party).

Table 16.1: Number of unique advertisements aired by country by election campaign

Country	Election campaign	Number of advertisements
New Zealand	2008	16
New Zealand	2011	22
United Kingdom	2005	12
United Kingdom	2010	11
United States	2008	222*
United States	2012	258*

Note: UK data come from a collection maintained by Walter, which is limited to Labour, Conservative and Liberal Democratic advertisements. New Zealand data come from a collection maintained by Ridout. US data for 2008 come from the Wisconsin Advertising Project, while 2012 data come from the Wesleyan Media Project.
*US figure includes just those advertisements aired in the six weeks prior to election day.

The last two elections resulted in minority governments led by the National Party. On the basis of these party system characteristics we expect that the most negative campaigning will be found in the US, followed by the UK and New Zealand.

The media system of all three countries could be classified as liberal under Hallin and Mancini's (2004) scheme. But there are still some differences across these three countries in the degree to which their media systems could be classified as liberal. The media system in the US is highly commercialised. Public broadcasters are poorly funded, capturing only 2 per cent of news audiences (Iyengar 2011: 30). Publicly-traded companies own almost all news organisations in the US, and independently-owned newspapers are almost extinct (Bennett 2005). Clearly, the behaviour of news organisations in the US is strongly driven by market incentives. In contrast to television, competition is lower among newspapers as they are organised along local and regional, rather than national, lines. Because of this, most American newspapers now enjoy a monopoly or semi-monopoly position in the cities that they serve (Semetko et al. 1991).

Many scholars view the UK as having a media system that sits between the free market liberal model of the US and the more regulated democratic corporatist media system model that most Northern European countries follow (Scammell and Langer 2006; Semetko et al. 1991). Like the US, the UK media system holds to the principles of free market competition, freedom of speech and media self-regulation. However, the UK has (like most Northern European countries) highly partisan newspapers and regulated television markets dominated by well-funded public service broadcasters (Scammell and Semetko 2008). Newspaper circulation is relatively high in comparison to the US, and the press is characterised by commercial ownership and national circulation (Scammell and Langer 2006). Newspapers can be divided along the lines of elite versus tabloid press and partisanship. During election campaigns newspapers often openly support one of the main parties (*see* Leach et al. 2011: 163 for an overview). In contrast, television news in the UK is highly regulated and is required by law to be impartial (McNair 2003; Scammell and Semetko 2008). Due to the fact that they seek to serve fairly distinct audiences, competition between the quality press and the tabloid press is minimal (Leach et al. 2011; Semetko et al. 1991). However, competition among the tabloid newspapers is fierce and is strengthened by the national distribution of newspapers. (Semetko et al. 1991). Ownership of the British press is concentrated in the hands of a few major groups.

While New Zealand's media system has become more commercialised since the early post-war era, the extent of the change has depended on the medium. As public broadcasters have faced more private-sector completion, television coverage of politics has become less focused on substance and has given way to game-framed, conflict-focused coverage (Rudd and Hayward 2005). The same is not true, however, for newspapers. Indeed, the amount of substantive, issue-based coverage in the country's largest newspaper, the *New Zealand Herald*, rose from the mid-1970s to the early 2000s (Rudd and Hayward 2005). The newspaper industry in New Zealand is characterised by local monopoly, as New Zealand does not have national daily newspapers. Each major city has at least one daily newspaper. Although upmarket broadsheet newspapers and mass circulation tabloid newspapers compete with each other in many countries, this sort of competition does not exist in New Zealand (Mulgan 2004: 294). The bulk of the country's major newspapers are owned by two companies, namely, Fairfax and APN News and Media. The television market also lacks media diversity as two companies dominate the news media.

Data collection

We examined coverage of televised political advertising in the five national newspapers with the largest readership whose coverage was accessible in the Lexis-Nexis or ProQuest electronic databases (*see* Table 16.2 for an overview). In New Zealand, these were *The New Zealand Herald,* the *Wellington Dominion Post,* the *Christchurch Press,* the *Waikato Times* and the *Southland Times.* The British newspapers were *The Sun,* the *Daily Mail, The Daily Telegraph, The Daily Mirror* and *Daily Express.* Newspapers examined in the US were the *Wall Street Journal,* the *New York Times, USA Today,* the *Los Angeles Times* and the *New York Daily News.* Among the sample of newspapers were five tabloids, *The Sun, Daily Express,* the *Daily Mail* and the *Daily Mirror* in the UK and the *New York Daily News* in the US. Although some 'community newspapers' do exist in New Zealand, the country does not have any daily tabloid newspapers.

Although we focus on coverage of televised political advertising in this study, we acknowledge that negative campaigning is not restricted to televised political advertising and that the importance of televised political advertising varies across countries.

We searched the Lexis-Nexis and ProQuest electronic newspaper databases for articles that mentioned televised political advertising. Our search terms varied somewhat by country given the different terms that journalists in different countries used to describe advertising.[1] We eliminated from the search results those articles that did not concern campaign advertising, leaving us with 498 articles from US newspapers, seventy-six articles from UK newspapers and thirty-four articles from New Zealand newspapers. The articles were coded manually on the basis of a coding scheme available upon request. The coding unit was the article. We coded all articles for whether they referred to television advertising generally – or a specific advertisement – as negative in tone. We also had coders provide a description of each advertisement mentioned specifically. This allowed us to match up those advertisements with databases that catalogue all advertisements

---

1. In New Zealand we searched for: (advertisement *or* advert* *or* commercial *or* broadcast) *and* (election *or* campaign). In the US in 2008, we searched for: (advertisement *or* advert* *or* commercial) *and* (Obama *or* McCain). In the US in 2012, we searched for: (advertisement *or* advert* *or* commercial) *and* (Obama *or* Romney). In the UK, we searched for: (party election broadcast *or* election broadcast).

Table 16.2: Readership numbers and type of newspaper studied

Country	Newspaper	Type	Readership
New Zealand	*New Zealand Herald*	Quality	147,369
New Zealand	*Dominion Post (Wellington)*	Quality	73,397
New Zealand	*Christchurch Press*	Quality	68,011
New Zealand	*Waikato Times*	Quality	30,844
New Zealand	*Southland Times*	Quality	24,688
United Kingdom	*The Sun*	Tabloid	2,082,899
United Kingdom	*Daily Mail*	Tabloid	1,715,915
United Kingdom	*The Daily Mirror*	Tabloid	963,685
United Kingdom	*The Daily Telegraph*	Quality	523,279
United Kingdom	*Daily Express*	Tabloid	487,543
United States	*Wall Street Journal*	Quality	2,378,827
United States	*New York Times*	Quality	1,865,318
United States	*USA Today*	Quality	1,674,306
United States	*Los Angeles Times*	Quality	653,868
United State	*New York Daily News*	Tabloid	516,165

Note: Source: New Zealand Numbers: Source is the New Zealand Audit Bureau of Circulations. http://www.newspaper.abc.org.nz//audit.html?org=npa&publicationid=%25&mode=embargo &npa_admin=1&publicationtype=19&memberid=%25&type=%25 (accessed 28 July 2014). Numbers cover the 1 April 2013, to 31 March 2014 time period.
UK numbers: 'ABCs: National daily newspaper circulation June 2014,' http://www.theguardian.com/media/table/2014/jul/11/abcs-national-newspapers. Numbers are taken from the Audit Bureau of Circulations, 2014 (accessed 28 July 2018). Numbers cover 1 January to 1 June 2014 time period.
US numbers: 'Top 10 Newspapers By Circulation: Wall Street Journal Leads Weekday Circulation,' Huffington Post. http://www.huffingtonpost.com/2013/05/01/newspaper-circulation-top-10_n_3188612.html (accessed 28 July 2014). Numbers are taken from the Alliance for Audited Media and are based on both print and online circulation from October 2012 through March 2013.

aired in each year.[2] Thus, we could compare the tone of those advertisements mentioned specifically with the tone of those advertisements not mentioned. The data for the UK are limited to national political parties that were represented in the House of Commons during this time period. As a result, regional political parties, such as the Scottish National Party (SNP), Plaid Cymru and Sinn Féin, are not included. The advertisements from this database were coded manually for tone

---

2. The US databases come from the Wisconsin Advertising Project and the Wesleyan Media Project. *See* Ridout and Walter (2013) for a description of the New Zealand data and Walter (2014b) for a description of the UK data.

and various other characteristics. Following Geer (2006), advertisements were coded as negative if they mentioned an opposing candidate or party; otherwise, they were considered positive. This approach has the advantage of making tone codes comparable across countries, but the disadvantage is that it may overstate levels of negativity in the UK where advertisements (PEBs) are typically much longer than in the US or New Zealand. A single mention of an opponent makes an advertisement negative under our classification, even if that mention was only five seconds long.

Results

To what extent do the print media in New Zealand, the UK and the US cover political advertising? Table 16.3 shows that coverage of political advertising is most common in the US, with 498 articles. This is followed by the UK, with

Table 16.3: Number of articles mentioning advertising by source per year

Country	Newspaper	2008	2011	Total articles mentioning advertisements
New Zealand	*New Zealand Herald*	11	10	21
New Zealand	*Dominion Post (Wellington)*	5	2	7
New Zealand	*Christchurch Press*	3	0	3
New Zealand	*Waikato Times*	1	2	3
New Zealand	*Southland Times*	0	0	0
NZ Total		20	14	34
		2005	**2010**	
United Kingdom	*The Sun*	3	6	9
United Kingdom	*Daily Mail*	5	8	13
United Kingdom	*The Daily Telegraph*	13	8	21
United Kingdom	*The Daily Mirror*	7	9	16
United Kingdom	*Daily Express*	12	5	17
UK Total		40	36	76
		2008	**2012**	
United States	*Wall Street Journal*	27	80	107
United States	*New York Times*	86	138	224
United States	*USA Today*	28	29	57
United States	*Los Angeles Times*	27	41	68
United States	*New York Daily News*	30	12	42
US Total		198	300	498

seventy-six articles mentioning advertising, and New Zealand, with thirty-four articles. Recall from Table 16.1 that the supply of advertising was also the greatest in the US. Interestingly, although there are more unique advertisements aired in New Zealand than in the UK, the UK print media devote more coverage to advertising than do the New Zealand media. In sum, our data suggest that American voters are the most likely to be exposed to political advertisements, both directly and indirectly through the news media.

Table 16.3 also speaks to differences across media outlets in the extent to which they report on political advertisements. For instance, the *New Zealand Herald* published twenty-one articles referring to political advertisements during the campaign in contrast to the *Southland Times*, which did not mention a single political advertisement. In the UK, advertisements were given the most coverage in *The Daily Telegraph*, the only quality newspaper in the sample, while the tabloid *The Sun* provided the least coverage. In the US, the *New York Times* provided the most advertisement coverage, while the tabloid *New York Daily News* provided the least. Even without statistical tests, we can see that tabloid newspapers tend to discuss political advertising less than quality newspapers.

However, we are not just interested in the coverage of political advertising in general, but in the coverage of negative advertising in particular. Table 16.4 displays the percentage of articles about political advertising that describe that advertising as negative. Table 16.4 shows considerable variation across election campaigns in the degree to which negative advertising is referenced. For example, in the 2005 British parliamentary election campaign, 7.5 per cent of the articles mentioning advertisements had references to negativity in contrast to the 2010 election campaign where 28.9 per cent of the articles referred to negativity.

Still, when one combines the two elections within each country, a remarkable result occurs: the degree to which negativity is referenced in articles about political advertising is very similar. New Zealand had the highest percentage of articles referring to negative campaigning at 23.5 per cent, followed by the UK at 22.4 per cent and the US at 21.4 per cent. At first glance, then, the data suggest that there is not much variation across countries in the degree to which negativity is used as a theme in articles about political advertising.

Table 16.4: Per cent of articles referencing advertisement negativity by country

Country	1st election	2nd election	Total
New Zealand	35	7.1	23.5
United Kingdom	7.5	28.9	22.4
United States	18.7	23.2	21.4

Source: NZ N=34, UK N=76 and US N=498 Second election refers to the most recent election.

Perhaps it is the case that tabloids more often describe political advertising as negative. We found no support for this idea. Combining data from the US and UK (recall there were no New Zealand tabloids in our sample), we found that the percentage of articles mentioning negativity in the five tabloids was 17.5 per cent compared to 22.4 per cent in the five quality newspapers.

Of course, the media do not only write about political advertising in generic terms but also mention specific advertisements. Table 16.5 shows the number of specific advertisement mentions in the election news coverage and the percentage of these advertisements that were negative. In New Zealand only eight specific advertisement mentions appeared in the thirty-four articles written about political advertising, but when advertisements do get mentioned, they tend to be negative advertisements (75 per cent). One negative advertisement from New Zealand that got some media attention in 2008 was a Labour advertisement in which a mother talked about how she trusted Helen Clark, the Labour party leader, but did not trust the National Party leader. She stated, 'You may know a few things about money and trading, Mr Key, but when it comes to my family's future, I just can't trust you.' In 2011, the New Zealand media focused on a series of Labour advertisements that attacked the National Party for wanting to sell state assets.

In the UK, sixty-nine out of seventy-six articles mentioned specific advertisements. Seven articles referred to advertisements from a party not included in our database, such as the Scottish Nationalist Party and the United Kingdom Independence Party. Within those remaining articles, when a specific advertisement was mentioned, 37.6 per cent of the time it was negative. But that percentage varied considerably across elections. In 2005, only 15.4 per cent of the specific advertisements mentioned were negative, but the comparable figure for 2010 was 71.4 per cent.

In 2005, coverage of advertising focused primarily on the first Labour advertisement aired during that campaign (59 per cent), which was a positive advertisement. This advertisement showed both Prime Minister Tony Blair and Chancellor Gordon Brown, known for their disagreements with each other, as a united front. Coverage of this advertisement either highlighted Labour Party campaign strategy or questioned the truthfulness of the event displayed.[3] The negative advertisement most frequently mentioned in 2005 was the last Labour advertisement of the campaign in which celebrities urged a vote for Labour to prevent Conservative Party leader Michael Howard from becoming Prime Minister.

If one in ten Labour voters don't vote Michael Howard becomes Prime Minister. Then low mortgage rates are at risk. A free and fair NHS is at risk. A rising minimum wage is at risk. Tax credits for families are at risk.

---

3.   *See* articles such as 'The five-minute show of friendship', *The Daily Telegraph*, 11 April 2005 or 'Brown a perfect partner in the Labour "marriage"', *Daily Mail*, 11 April 2005.

Table 16.5: Specific advertisement mentions and tone by country

Country	Number of specific advertisement mentions	Per cent negative	Number of specific advertisement mentions	Per cent negative	Total number of specific advertisement mentions	Total per cent negative
	1st election	*1st election*	*2nd election*	*2nd election*		
New Zealand	4	100	4	50	8	75
United Kingdom	40	15.4	29	71.4	69	37.6
United States	121	77.7	169	76.3	290	76.9

Source: NZ N=34, UK N=76 and US N=460 Second election refers to the most recent election. For the UK the percentage of negative advertisements references is calculated on the basis of only Labour, Conservative and Liberal Democratic advertisements.

In 2010, 71.4, per cent of the advertisements mentioned were negative, though no one specific advertisement stood out from the rest. The most mentioned negative Labour advertisement featured a warning for voters from former EastEnders actor Ross Kemp:

> Of course Labour aren't perfect - and no one's saying they are. This election isn't a beauty contest ... A vote for Nick Clegg is in reality a vote for Tory cuts that would hurt you and your family. Be careful. If you get into bed with Nick Clegg you might just wake up with David Cameron.

Another advertisement that received substantial coverage in 2010 was from the Conservative Party, which switched its strategy half way through the campaign. Instead of attacking Labour, they decided at the last minute to attack the Liberal Democrats:

> The great plan of Nick Clegg's is becoming clear. He's only interested in one thing and that is changing our electoral system so that we have a permanent hung parliament – a permanent coalition ... We never have strong and decisive government. It's now becoming clear he wants to hold the whole country to ransom - and just to benefit the Liberal Democrats.

The most mentioned 'advertisement' in the US in 2008 was a thirty-minute 'infomercial' aired by the Obama campaign just days before the election. It was less the tone than the novel format that seemed to pique the media's interest. The second most frequently mentioned advertisement in 2008 was a negative one sponsored by the McCain campaign that accused Obama of favouring sex education for kindergarten students. The third most frequently mentioned advertisement in 2008 was from the Obama campaign and concerned immigration. This attack advertisement tried to tie John McCain to comments from a conservative radio host who called Mexicans 'stupid and unqualified.' In 2012, the most mentioned advertisement was one by the Romney campaign that claimed that President Obama had outsourced US auto industry jobs to China. This was criticised as a lie by many news organisations. The second most mentioned advertisement was also from the Romney campaign. This one courted women voters by stressing that Romney was not opposed to birth control or abortion in all instances.

Is the focus on specific advertisements just a reflection of the tone of advertisements overall, or do the news media put more emphasis on negative advertisements? Table 16.6 addresses this. In New Zealand, the tone of advertisements mentioned was more negative than the tone of advertisements aired, suggesting that news values of negativity and conflict are important in New Zealand. In the UK in 2005, the media underreported on negative campaigning, as the advertisements mentioned were primarily positive. However in the 2010 campaign the tone of the advertisements mentioned was more negative than the tone of the advertisements aired. It is worth noting, however, that coverage in 2005 was driven by a positive advertisement – the

Table 16.6: Tone of advertisements mentioned and tone of advertisements aired

Country	Year	Per cent of advertisements mentioned that are negative	Per cent of advertisements aired that are negative	Per cent of advertisements mentioned that are issue-based	Per cent of advertisements aired that are issue-based
New Zealand	2008	100	32.6	100.0	75.0
New Zealand	2011	50	15	100.0	100.0
United Kingdom	2005	15.4	58.3	100.0	66.7
United Kingdom	2010	71.4	45.5	100.0	90.0
United States	2008	77.7	73.5	82.6	77.4
United States	2012	76.3	83.6	92.6	89.4

Note: Only advertisements sponsored by Labour, the Conservatives and the Liberal Democrats are included in the UK data.

one featuring Blair and Brown in a united front – that allowed the media to bring up past conflicts between the two. In the US, the percentage of advertisements mentioned that were negative was actually quite similar to the percentage of advertisements aired that were negative. Here, it seems, the supply of negativity – which is quite high – is reflected in the coverage. The link between advertisement negativity and increased coverage, then, is a weak one and seems contingent on the particular election context.

Table 16.6 also shows the percentage of advertisements in each election that are issue-based (as opposed to trait-based) and the percentage of advertisement mentions that are coded as issue-based. The vast majority of advertisements, regardless of country, are issue-based – at least two-thirds in each election. But the specific advertisements mentioned are even more likely to be issue-based. Not a single trait-based advertisement was mentioned in the UK or New Zealand, for instance, and in the US, the percentage of advertisements mentioned that were trait-based was similar to their proportion in the entire population of advertisements.

Our final analysis predicts the number of times each advertisement in our database is mentioned by the news media. Over 72 per cent of the advertisements in our database had no mentions in the news. The most-discussed advertisement had twenty-five mentions. Table 16.7 shows that advertisement negativity fails to predict the number of times an advertisement is mentioned, nor does an advertisement's being trait-focused, as opposed to issue-focused, help predict the number of times an advertisement is mentioned. The country-specific dummy variables, however, do help predict the number of mentions, with advertisements from New Zealand less likely to be mentioned than advertisements from the US and advertisements from the UK more likely to be mentioned. Again, the message seems to be that the media cover the advertisements that are made available to them as opposed to seeking out particularly negative advertisements – or advertisements that focus on personalities as opposed to issues.

Table 16.7: Predictors of number of media mentions of an advertisement

	B	S.E.	Z	p
Negative advertisement	-0.130	0.267	-0.490	0.626
Trait-based advertisement	-0.397	0.322	-1.230	0.217
New Zealand	-1.026	0.508	-2.020	0.043
UK	1.487	0.488	3.050	0.002
Constant	-0.431	0.248	-1.740	0.082
N=480				

Note: Table reports negative binomial regression coefficients.

Conclusions

We examined coverage of political advertising in election campaigns in fifteen prominent national newspapers in the US, UK and New Zealand in the most two recent campaigns. Our findings reveal considerable variation in the coverage of advertising both across countries, as well as across newspapers. Certainly, the supply of advertising seems to be one factor explaining the extent of coverage, with the US sometimes supplying at least ten times as many unique advertisements as the other countries – and considerably more news coverage as well. Yet, variation within the media system does less well in explaining the volume of coverage. Although tabloid newspapers tended to supply less media coverage than quality newspapers, there was still considerable coverage of advertising, including negative advertising, within the tabloids.

Remarkably, though, there was not that much variation across countries in the extent to which advertising was described as negative. In all three countries, 20 per cent of the articles that mention advertising describe it as negative. Even though journalists frame the tone of advertising similarly across the three countries, there was a great divergence in the tone of the advertisements that they decided to emphasise. While three-quarters of the advertisements mentioned in the New Zealand and US media were negative, less than 40 per cent of those mentioned by the British media were negative. Still, the sample sizes, especially in New Zealand and the UK, are quite small.

Citizens gain their perceptions of campaigns both directly from the messages that the candidates and parties send and indirectly through the news media. One important direct source of those messages is political advertising, and this seems to be especially true in the US where the volume of advertising is overwhelming at times. Campaigns in the UK and New Zealand are less dependent on advertising to get their messages out, but because of that media coverage of campaigns (perhaps ironically) takes on added importance. Thus, it is essential to examine not just the political advertisements that campaigns produce but the media coverage of those advertisements as well.

Whether the news media distort the tone of advertising in their coverage also varies by country. Although the numbers are small in New Zealand, they are consistent with a story of reporters seeking out negativity and conflict. In the UK, however, the media's emphasis on negativity depended, to a large extent, on the election year, with an over-emphasis on negative advertising in 2010, but an under-emphasis in 2005. Perhaps surprisingly, a disproportionate emphasis on negativity was not evident in the US. Why this is the case may have something to do with the dearth of positive advertising. The media did not have to work hard to find negativity and conflict given that the vast majority of advertisements in the last weeks of the presidential races were negative. Indeed, a positive advertisement may have provided something novel to cover. How can we square this with other findings from the US that suggest that the media privilege negative advertisements (Fowler and Ridout 2009; Ridout and Smith 2008)? The difference may stem from the fact that previous work examined sub-presidential races, such as those for Congress and for governor, which featured much more positive advertising.

In sum, the idea that the media privilege negativity in their coverage is not generally backed by our data. Although there are considerable mentions of negativity in news coverage – and negative advertisements draw considerable discussion – the amount of discussion they receive is generally on par with their proportion of all advertising.

Chapter Seventeen

When Do Attacks Work? Moderated Effects on Voters' Candidate Evaluation in a Televised Debate

Wouter de Nooy and Jürgen Maier

Televised debates between candidates are the centrepiece of election campaigns in several modern democracies (e.g. *see* Norris 2000: 153). Due to the high exposure among voters, debates are usually the most important single campaign event in the run-up to an election (Holbrook 1996). Hence, it is no surprise that many scholars have analysed the impact of televised debates. There is a body of evidence for the US (and increasingly also for other countries) that viewing televised debates increases viewers' knowledge about political issues and character traits of the candidates and strengthens subsequent attention to campaign information (for an overview, *see* e.g. Racine Group 2002; for a meta-analysis, *see* Benoit *et al.* 2003a). The impact on viewers' candidate preferences and voting intentions, however, is more contested. The influence of debates on voting behaviour is often deemed minimal in the US (McKinney and Carlin 2004: 210), whereas non-US studies indicate that instant evaluations of candidate messages have significant and substantive effects on post-debate perceptions of the debate winner, influencing candidate preferences and vote choice (for Germany *see* e.g. Maier and Faas 2011: 77; Maier *et al.* 2014, 42–3).

The latter result raises the important question which candidate messages create favourable impressions. Although there is a vast body of research on the impact of televised debates, only few studies are able to provide an answer to this question. This is because nearly all previous studies have investigated net responses to debate statements comparing aggregated pre- and post-debate candidate evaluations or comparing the debate audience with voters not exposed to the debate, focusing on average evaluations for all viewers (e.g. Lanoue 1991; McKinney *et al.* 2001) or for groups of partisan viewers (e.g. Benoit *et al.* 1998). Even studies based on real-time response (RTR) data, i.e. spontaneous reactions recorded on a second-by-second basis, usually analyse individual responses to candidate statements on a highly aggregated level (e.g. Jarman 2005) or they restrict the analysis to selected moments within the debate (e.g. Maurer and Reinemann 2003). Net responses and selected moments, however, do not disclose the full picture of debate effects because responses to candidate statements may cancel each other out due to the balanced nature of the information proffered in the debate (*see* e.g. Zaller 1996: 36).

This chapter investigates the impact of negative candidate statements, i.e. negative messages about the opponent's 'undesirable attributes or policy missteps' (*see* Benoit 2007: 36), on viewers of the 2009 German televised election debate using RTR data. Previous studies analysing RTR data provide mixed results on the impact of attacks. Whereas some studies conclude that negative messages increase the support for the attacker among its supporters (Nagel 2012, 193–4; similar results are provided by Maurer and Reinemann 2003; Maurer and Reinemann 2009; Reinemann and Maurer 2005; Reinemann and Maurer 2007), other studies did not find significant effects (Maier 2009; Nagel 2012: 196; Spieker 2011). We refine the analysis of RTR data in three important ways. First, we compare the effect of attacks to other debate strategies distinguished in the Functional Theory of Political Discourse, acclaims and defences in particular (*see* e.g. Benoit 1999; Benoit *et al.* 1998a; Benoit *et al.* 2003b, and Chapter Two in this volume), which has rarely been done in the analysis of televised debates. Second, we simultaneously consider characteristics of the speaker and characteristics of the viewers using a multilevel statistical model. Third, this model allows us to analyse the interplay between statement and viewer characteristics in great detail. Attacks are often presupposed to have the same effect on all voters. We argue that this is unlikely to be true. If we consider attacks in the broader framework of affective relations between candidates and voters, we should take into account voter partisanship as a long-term affective tie with a party (Campbell *et al.* 1960). Effects of attacks are likely to depend on which candidate is launching the attack in combination with the viewer's partisanship.

In the next section, we develop hypotheses on the relations between attack messages, candidates, and affective ties of voters to parties. Next, we describe the 2009 debate, our data, and statistical model. Then we present the results. Finally, we sum up our findings and discuss their implications.

Partisanship, affective relations, and negative campaigning

The absence of a substantial short-term effect on candidate evaluation and vote intention in the presence of high exposure among the electorate is puzzling. It has been suggested that this is due to selective perception and biased processing (e.g. Lord *et al.* 1979) that is also found in the processing of political information (e.g. Lanoue 1992). An important source of bias is partisan beliefs as reflected by e.g. party identification. In this approach, selective perception and biased processing of information are explained by a tendency for voters to avoid information on issues or candidate character that is not in line with their beliefs, in other words, that is cognitive dissonant (Festinger 1962 (1957): 292). One major consequence of this kind of biased processing of information is that campaigns tend to strengthen prior preferences of voters (for a review, *see* Iyengar and Simon 2000). As a consequence, public opinion in an electorate will become more polarised as the campaign continues.

Recent studies found that selective information processing in televised debates is not as strong as expected. The reason for this is that – in contrast to political advertisements, which are short, one-sided, and often focusing on one message – information is balanced in televised debates because candidates of both sides have the opportunity to present themselves favourably. Considering the length of a debate as well as the complex interactions between the candidates, the opportunities to process the whole debate selectively are limited. In line with this, it has been suggested that selective perception works only for the preferred candidate but fails to a large degree for the political opponent (Faas and Maier 2004).

Party identification was originally defined in terms of affect rather than cognition. In the Michigan school, partisanship was viewed as a long-term affective tie with a particular party (Campbell *et al.* 1960), stressing that the affective tie was the practical reason to vote for a party rather than cognitive evaluation of issue positions. Although the presence and the strength of party identification tend to decrease over time (*see* e.g. Dalton 2008), voters still react affectively to campaign information. Recently, Iyengar *et al.* (2012) presented a strong case highlighting the role of affect in citizen responses to political information. They show that polarisation among voters in the US is an affective matter related to group identification, separate but not disconnected from opinions on policy issues. Affects are likely to play a role in responses to candidate statements apart from the cognitive role of issue positions and issue ownership.

Psychology focuses on affect as a state in which a human being is, distinguishing between valence, that is, how a person evaluates the state she is in on a positive-to-negative scale, arousal as a bodily response, and motivational intensity as a tendency to act physically (Harmon-Jones *et al.* 2013). We focus on valence, that is, the positive versus negative evaluation by a person but we prefer to conceptualise it as relational: Affect is directed at something or someone outside the person. In our approach, affect valence (henceforth for short: affect) is the positive to negative quality that a person attributes to its relation with something or someone else, in other words, the positive or negative valence of a person's stance towards an issue or another person. We assume that the valence of a candidate as a political leader is at stake during election campaigns, including televised debates. In the end, a voter entrusts a candidate with her mandate to govern, so she must have a positive feeling about the candidate's ability to govern the country. We see this as an affective relation between voter and candidate, which need not necessarily originate from cognitive arguments on the part of the voter.

In preliminary analyses of the data, we found a positive overall effect of the speaker on his or her evaluation among all viewers (similar results are provided by Maurer and Reinemann 2003). If viewers identifying with the other party block increase their evaluation of the candidate while s/he is speaking, the issue position proffered in the statement is unlikely to be the cause of an overall evaluation change unless the statement addresses uncontroversial issues, issues strongly owned by the speaker's party block, or the valence of the speaker (e.g. leadership qualities). The latter two options, we posit, address the affective relation between the speaking candidate or its party block and the viewer because they imply a positive evaluation of the candidate's or the party's competence in leading the country and solving particular problems.

The fact that candidates are interacting with the viewer – perhaps expressed more precisely, acting towards the viewer – while they are speaking seems to strengthen the affective bond between candidate and viewer. This is in line with Intergroup Contact Theory, which predicts that negative affections, stereotyping, and misunderstandings among groups decrease if people from different groups interact or see people from different groups interact (Allport 1954). In essence, the general assumption is that interaction improves positive affect but interaction is rare between members of different groups, and therefore they tend to have negative affective relations. This effect is deemed to be present also if the interaction is taking place in or through the media (Schiappa *et al.* 2005).

H1 – Speaker effect: Viewers improve their evaluation of the candidate who is speaking.

Intergroup Contact Theory predicts that more contact yields a more positive affective bond but it does not differentiate between persons who already have a positive bond and the ones who do not. In contrast, Social Identity Theory stresses the difference in responses to in-group versus out-group members (Tajfel and Turner 1979). Identification with a group implies that one's self-esteem is linked to the social standing of the group, which must be evaluated positively. The in-group's standing is a relative matter, so it is higher if the standing of other groups is lower. Therefore, group members are inclined to evaluate members of other groups negatively. On the assumption that identification with a party is comparable to in-group identification, we can formulate two hypotheses on partisanship effects from this theory, a main effect and an interaction effect with the candidate who is speaking.

H2a – Partisanship I: Viewers improve their evaluation of the candidate with whom they identify.

H2b – Partisanship II: Viewers improve their evaluation of the candidate with whom they identify while s/he is speaking.

Human beings adjust their affections to the affections displayed by other people; people tend to evaluate a person or item more positively if they notice that other people like it. This self-strengthening effect of positive evaluation is known as the Matthew effect in sociology (Merton 1968). The tendency to imitate other people's affections is also in line with the concept of emotional contagion in psychology (Hatfield *et al.* 1994). Our viewers were not allowed to interact and publicly express their appraisals during the debate, so they could not take into account each other's appraisals. However, they could notice appraisals among the candidates in the debate, so we focus on these appraisals.

This brings us to the type or strategy of debate statements. According to the Functional Theory of Political Campaign Discourse, the three major messages are acclaims, attacks of another candidate, and defences (*see* e.g. Benoit 2007).[1] In an acclaim, the speaker only refers to herself and the valence is positive because the candidate stresses her advantages and benefits (Benoit 2007: 36). This type of statement does not entail an appraisal of another candidate but it serves to enhance the candidate's 'preferability' among voters (Benoit 2007: 36), so it is expected to appear a lot. In contrast, a statement attacking (or praising) another candidate represents an appraisal.[2] Attacks, that is, 'stressing an opponent's undesirable attributes or policy missteps' (Benoit 2007: 36), are assumed to improve the relative valence of the candidate making the statement unless attacks become too frequent or harsh.

Combining the assumption that human beings adapt their evaluations of a person or item to evaluations expressed by other people with the interpretation of an attack as a negative appraisal of a candidate by another candidate, we could have deduced the hypothesis that debate viewers lower their evaluation of candidates when they are attacked. However, we posit that the affective relation between the viewer and the attacking candidate is an important moderator of this effect, which gives rise to our last hypothesis on partisan bias. We deduce this hypothesis from a precursor of Cognitive Dissonance Theory, namely Balance Theory (Heider 1946; Heider 1958). The basic axiom of Balance Theory is much like the axiom of Cognitive Dissonance Theory except that it refers to affects instead of cognitions: A person feels more at ease if its affects towards another person and a third person or topic are balanced such that she agrees with a friend and disagrees with an adversary.

A voter who identifies with a party is assumed to have positive affections for this party but negative affections for the other party. In this situation, an attack between candidates of the two parties creates a balanced triple, which is more comfortable according to Balance Theory because an attack is the 'natural' type of interaction to occur in the eyes of the partisan viewer. An attack by the preferred candidate on the opponent is perfectly in line with the partisan's negative affect for the opponent, so it will contribute to a positive evaluation of the attacker for this viewer (no backlash effect) and to a more negative evaluation of the opponent. The same applies to an attack by the opponent on the preferred candidate, which will also benefit the attacked candidate because the positive affection for the attacked candidate's party will be reinforced by the attack of a negatively valued opponent. In other words, negative information from detested sources turns into a compliment for the partisan viewer. This hypothesis is in line with results from Meffert *et al.* (2006). Summing up, partisan voters are predicted to evaluate their

---

1. In addition, our data include praise for another candidate and self-criticism. We found only one statement of praise for the political opponent in the 2009 German chancellor debate, so we cannot test hypotheses about the effect of this type of statement but we did analyse the impact of self-criticism.

2. Praise reduces the relative valence of the candidate making the statement, so it is not expected to occur often. *See* the previous footnote.

candidate more positively if an attack statement is made, regardless who is the source or the target of the attack. This translates into an interaction effect of party identification and statement strategy regardless of who is speaking.

> H3 – Partisan bias: Viewers identifying with a candidate evaluate this candidate more positively if an attack statement is made by or directed at this candidate.

The German 2009 election debate and statement characteristics

We investigate responses of viewers to the televised election debate between the two main candidates for the Chancellorship in the 2009 German national election campaign. The data comprise information about the statements made in the debate collected with content analysis, information about the viewers collected with a questionnaire, and information about the evaluation of the candidates by the viewers while the debate was originally broadcasted collected with electronic RTR devices.[3]

The American-style televised debate is a fairly recent campaign format in Germany. It was first used in 2002 in a national election campaign. The 2009 German televised debate featured incumbent Chancellor Angela Merkel (Christian Democrats, CDU/CSU) and her Foreign Minister and Vice Chancellor, Frank-Walter Steinmeier (Social Democrats, SPD) with four moderators. This was the only televised debate between the two candidates during the campaign; it took place two weeks before election day. The ninety-minute discussion was aired by the four major German TV stations and was watched by 14.2 million citizens. Before the debate, polls showed that a Conservative coalition consisting of CDU/CSU and the Liberal Party (FDP) was clearly ahead of an alliance of left-wing parties (SPD, Green Party, Left Party). The fact that both candidates belonged to the cabinet may have tempered the tone of the debate. Without good prospects for a left-wing majority, the challenger may have wanted to moderate his attacks not to spoil a coalition with the other candidate. However, the dominant frame of the campaign was a choice between a Conservative and a left-wing coalition, so attacks were to be expected during the debate.

All statements of the debate were coded. A statement ends if the speaker, the content, the object, or the strategy changes. To match the content of the statements with recipients' RTRs, the exact starting and end time of each statement was recorded. The candidate's strategy was coded for all comprehensible and meaningful statements (functional statements). A message was counted as an acclaim if a candidate praised its past political record or future political plans or if s/he provided favourable information about his/her character or the character of affiliated persons, parties, and so on, while negative utterances on these aspects were coded as self-criticism.

---

3. The data were collected for the German Longitudinal Election Study (GLES) and can be downloaded at http://www.gesis.org/wahlen/gles/daten-und-dokumente/daten (ZA-Nr. 5309, 5310, and 5311).

A statement was coded as an attack if the political opponent, his/her policy, or other persons and issues associated with the political opponent were unfavourably portrayed or challenged. A statement was categorised as a defence if a candidate explicitly responded to an attack with self-justification or a rejection of the attack. To assess reliability of the coding, two coders coded 19 per cent of all functional candidate messages independently; intercoder reliability was 0.91 (Holsti's formula).

In total, we have 178 acclaims, sixty-eight attacks, forty-four defences, and ten self-criticisms (N=300). Steinmeier launched relatively many attacks and used slightly more defensive statements than Merkel (*see* Figure 17.1). The latter proffered relatively many statements in which she presented herself and her issue positions. This pattern is in line with research on the use of different strategies in US debates: Incumbents use acclaims much more often than challengers. Conversely, challengers attack more often than incumbents. In addition, incumbents as well as challengers try to avoid defences (*see* e.g. Benoit 2007).

Statements lasted from one to sixty-two seconds with an average of 12.7 seconds. Statements by Steinmeier (M=13.4, SD=9.5) tend to be slightly longer than statements by Merkel (M=12.0, SD=8.3, p=0.181). In the analyses, duration is divided by ten to obtain estimates with digits in the first three decimal places; duration, then, is measured in tens of seconds. It is centred on its grand mean in the analyses.

Viewer characteristics

Based on a quota sample meant to recruit equal numbers of males and females, age groups, educational groups, and political camps, 449 citizens were invited to take part in the study. The final sample contained slightly fewer females

Figure 17.1: Statement strategy by speaker

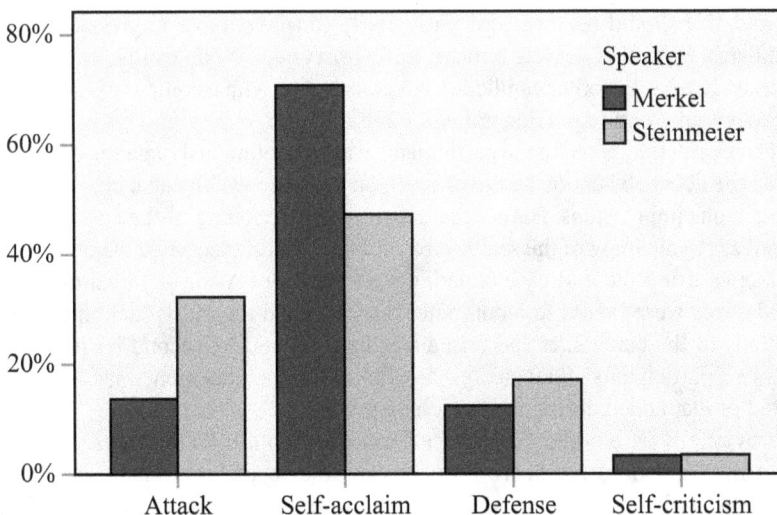

(45.9 per cent coded as '1') than males (54.1 per cent coded as '0', 3.1 per cent missing), about equal percentages of lower education ('*Realschule*' or lower: 45.8 per cent coded as '0') and higher education ('*Fachhochschulreife*' or '*Abitur*': 54.2 per cent coded as '1', 1.3 per cent missing), and more or less equal numbers of young adults (eighteen to thirty-nine years: 53.2 per cent) and older adults (forty years and up: 46.8 per cent, 1.3 per cent missing). In the analyses, age was centred on its grand mean. With respect to party identification three groups were created: viewers who identify with the Conservative-Liberal Party block (CDU/CSU, FDP, 33.8 per cent), viewers supporting the left-wing parties (SPD, Green Party, Left Party, 44.4 per cent), and viewers attached with neither of these party blocks (21.8 per cent).

The participants watched the debate live on a large screen in a university lecture auditorium in five different cities. The viewers are more or less equally distributed over the locations with one group only hearing the debate while the other groups also saw the debate. Immediately before and after the debate, participants were asked to fill out detailed questionnaires covering their social profile, political knowledge, attitudes, and their voting intentions.

Response characteristics

For 225 participants immediate reactions during the debate were recorded. Each subject was given a hand-held dial input device with seven positions. The centre-position of the scale ('4') was defined as the neutral position; this was the position of the dial at the start of the debate. Subjects were instructed to select this position if they experienced neither a positive nor a negative impression towards any of the two candidates. Subjects were told to choose positions below '4' if they had a positive impression of Steinmeier or a negative impression of Merkel. Positions above four should be used if subjects had either a positive impression of Merkel or a negative impression of Steinmeier. The far ends of the scale ('1' and '7') should be saved for particularly (un)favourable impressions of the candidates. With this device, a move in the direction of one candidate implies a move away from the other candidate, which is in line with a comparative approach to leader evaluation (e.g. Gidengil *et al.* 2002: 81–2).

The instruction given to the participants was to continuously rate the candidates during the debate by choosing the position on the scale which came closest to their spontaneous impressions. Before the debate, the functioning of the control device as well as the meaning of the scale were explained; all subjects had the opportunity to practice using the dial by evaluating participants of a non-political talk show. The devices were linked to a computer that recorded the individual participants' reactions to the candidates' performances on a second-by-second basis. For our analyses, participants' RTR scores are linked to the statement that was being uttered or that ended during the preceding second.

Previous RTR studies analysed effects on absolute RTR scores, assuming that a higher score or a score more favourable to the candidate uttering the statement indicates that the statement is more successful (e.g. Maier 2009;

Maurer and Reinemann 2003; McKinney *et al.* 2001; Reinemann and Maurer 2005; Spieker 2011). In our opinion, this approach ignores the dependencies between observations over time that are inherent to using an RTR device in the so-called latched mode (Baggaley 1987): The chosen position of the dial, that is, the rating of the statement, will last as long as the controller is not moved to another position. If a respondent moves the controller to a position favouring a particular candidate, this interpretation of the RTR scores would suggest that all subsequent statements create support for this candidate until the respondent makes a new move. So even if the respondent does not pay attention to subsequent statements by the candidate, previous RTR analyses will consider them effective because the RTR dial is still in a position favouring this candidate (for a critique of use of absolute RTR scores to assess the effectiveness of candidate statements and a more detailed discussion of the approach proposed in this chapter, *see* Maier 2013).

As the level at which a statement is rated clearly depends on the level at which previous statements were evaluated, the absolute score of a statement does not necessarily reveal its effectiveness. One solution is to correct for autocorrelation (Nagel 2012; Nagel *et al.* 2012) but this approach still assumes that viewers respond to every statement and that the absolute value of the response matters. We assume that viewers do not respond to all statements. We may be confident that they respond to a statement when they change the dial during that statement (or during the next statement but we will not consider lagged effects), not when the dial is at rest. We propose that a statement is effective if it increases support for the speaker. In contrast, a statement is counterproductive if it decreases support for the speaker. Finally, an utterance is ineffective if support for the speaker does not change at all.

With 225 viewers responding to 300 statements, there are 67,500 viewer-statement combinations, most of which (77.3 per cent) do not witness a dial change. In a majority of the remaining cases, the RTR dial was changed only once even if the statement took more than one second. The maximum number of changes during a statement was seventeen. If a viewer changed the dial more than once during a statement, the net change was calculated and used as the response to this statement.

Figure 17.2 presents a graphical overview of the RTR dial changes for the three partisan groups during statements by one of the candidates. Arc width and greyscale express the number of moves over the span of the entire debate. It is obvious that minimal changes (going to an adjacent category) occurred most often and that moves involved the categories in the middle much more than the extreme categories. Voters identifying with the left-wing party block tend to move more often between the categories favouring their party block's candidate (Steinmeier) but some of them are more on the side of the opponent (Merkel). A similar but reversed pattern can be seen among viewers identifying with the Conservative block. Overall, changes are nearly equally divided between changes in favour of Steinmeier (48.5 per cent) and changes in favour of Merkel (51.5 per cent).

Figure 17.2: RTR dial changes by partisan group during candidate statements

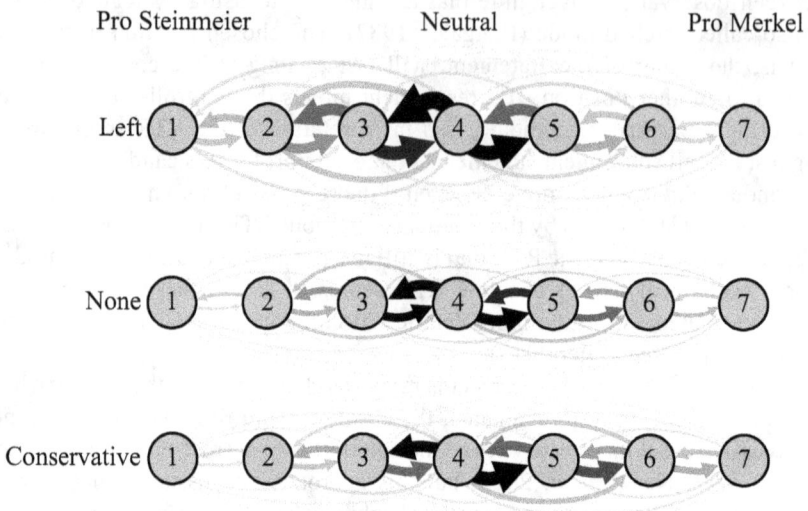

Statistical model

Although the size of changes varies, we decided to analyse only whether the dial changed and the direction of the change (favouring Steinmeier versus Merkel) because the major contrast in the data is the difference between cases that do not witness a change (77.3 per cent) and the ones that do (22.7 per cent). Our dependent variable, then, consists of three categories – change in favour of Steinmeier, no change, and change in favour of Merkel – which can be estimated with a multinomial regression model. Due to estimation problems related to the complex multilevel structure of our model, we present separate logistic regression models predicting changes in favour of Steinmeier and Merkel respectively (coded '1') in contrast to no change (coded '0').[4]

In both models, we use viewer and statement characteristics as predictors. This design requires a multilevel model with responses cross-nested within statements and viewers because each statement may elicit a response from each viewer. We first test a model without cross-level interactions (Models 1a and 2a), for which the effects can be interpreted as main or overall effects. Next, we test a model including interactions (Models 1b and 2b) to modify our interpretation of the main effects.

---

4. We excluded cases in one of the extreme positions, which could not change to a position more in favour of the candidate. For example, a change in favour of Steinmeier is not possible when the dial is in position '1.'

To avoid spurious relationships we include the recipients' social profile (gender, age, education) in our models as controls. Because the probability that an RTR score changes increases with the length of a statement, we also control for the duration of every candidate statement. The effect of statement duration may vary among viewers, so we included a random slope for duration. Finally, we also control for the impact of the experimental design by adding a dummy variable for audio versus video treatment.

All models are based on a maximum of N=67,500 observations but some observations had to be dropped due to missing values. We use MCMC estimation in MLwiN to obtain reliable estimates and standard errors (Browne 2004).

Results

Table 17.1 summarises the results of the logistic regression models. Let us interpret effects that are more or less the same for changes in favour of Steinmeier and changes in favour of Merkel first. Older and female viewers tend to change candidate evaluation less often than younger and male viewers, although the difference between male and female viewers is statistically significant only for changes in favour of Steinmeier. Hearing but not viewing the debate yields fewer changes on average but, again, this effect is statistically significant only for Steinmeier. Level of education has no effects at all. Statement duration has nearly the same positive effect on the evaluation of both candidates. The effect is highly significant and sizable if one realises that the average duration is twelve seconds: Ten additional seconds increase the odds of a change in favour of the speaker by 84 per cent ($e^{0.61}=1.84$) on average. In addition, the effect of duration varies between viewers as indicated by the highly significant variance of the random slope (0.04, p<0.001 respectively 0.02, p<0.01). The intercept-slope covariance is positive and significant indicating that the effect tends to be stronger for viewers having a stronger predisposition to change their evaluation. In other words, a longer statement is more likely to provoke a positive response, especially among viewers that are overall more responsive. Further research may look into the characteristics of viewers that explain their responsiveness. Likewise, the highly significant variance in response odds among statements (random intercept varies between 0.46 and 0.48, p<0.001) suggests that there are unexplored characteristics of statements that affect the evaluation of candidates, calling for further research.

Does the strategy of the message matter? Although attacks tend to have a positive main effect in comparison to defensive statements, it is not statistically significant in all models and the effect size changes among models. Similar main effects were found for acclaims and self-criticisms, so defensive statements seem to work out worse for a candidate. However, these effects require a more elaborate discussion because the predictors that are central to this chapter – speaker, strategy, and party identification – interact. We cannot understand their effects without taking into account the other effects.

Let us start with the effect of the speaker, that is, the candidate who is speaking at the time viewers consider changing their evaluation. Models 1a and 1b feature

Table 17.1: Predicting responses in favour of Steinmeier or Merkel

	Pro-Steinmeier				Pro-Merkel			
	Model 1a		Model 1b		Model 2a		Model 2b	
	Parameter	S.E.	Parameter	S.E.	Parameter	S.E.	Parameter	S.E.
Fixed Part								
Constant	-2.59***	0.209	-2.58***	0.217	-2.87***	0.201	-3.01***	0.201
Viewer characteristics								
Age	-0.01***	0.003	-0.01***	0.003	-0.01**	0.003	-0.01**	0.003
Female (ref. cat. male)	-0.24*	0.119	-0.25*	0.117	-0.18	0.117	-0.19	0.121
Education high (ref. cat. low)	-0.08	0.117	-0.07	0.112	0.01	0.117	0.00	0.119
Audio (ref. cat. video)	-0.25*	0.121	-0.25*	0.123	-0.13	0.130	-0.15	0.130
Party identification (r.c. none)	**		*		*n.s.*		*n.s.*	
- Left	0.31*	0.141	0.30	0.183	0.04	0.153	0.34	0.178
- Conservative	-0.12	0.152	-0.08	0.196	0.25	0.163	0.40*	0.193
Statement characteristics								
Duration	0.61***	0.051	0.60***	0.051	0.61***	0.05	0.61***	0.049
Speaker (Steinmeier or Merkel)[+]	0.43***	0.094	0.50***	0.107	0.72***	0.088	0.70***	0.105

Table 17.1 (*continued*)

	Pro-Steinmeier				Pro-Merkel			
	Model 1a		Model 1b		Model 2a		Model 2b	
	Parameter	S.E.	Parameter	S.E.	Parameter	S.E.	Parameter	S.E.
Strategy (ref. cat. defence)	*n.s.*		*n.s.*		*n.s.*		**	
- Attack	0.22	0.154	0.02	0.179	0.38**	0.146	0.55**	0.169
- Acclaim	0.22	0.132	0.24	0.154	0.24	0.127	0.44**	0.145
- Self-criticism	0.29	0.268	0.39	0.319	0.08	0.266	0.41	0.312
Cross-level interactions								
Speaker * Party identification			*n.s.*				*	
- Speaker * Left			-0.14	0.074			-0.07	0.075
- Speaker * Conservative			-0.05	0.083			0.12	0.078
Strategy * Party identification			*				*n.s.*	
- Attack * Left			0.31**	0.12			-0.27*	0.126
- Acclaim * Left			-0.01	0.106			-0.27*	0.11
- Self-criticism * Left			-0.16	0.228			-0.36	0.241
- Attack * Conservative			0.10	0.133			-0.18	0.13
- Acclaim * Conservative			-0.09	0.117			-0.27*	0.114

Table 17.1 (continued)

| | Pro-Steinmeier | | | | Pro-Merkel | | | |
| | Model 1a | | Model 1b | | Model 2a | | Model 2b | |
	Parameter	S.E.	Parameter	S.E.	Parameter	S.E.	Parameter	S.E.
- Self-criticism * Conservative			-0.10	0.247			-0.58*	0.256
Random part								
Level: Viewer								
Random intercept	0.67***	0.079	0.69***	0.078	0.72***	0.083	0.73***	0.082
Intercept-slope covariance	0.07**	0.022	0.07**	0.022	0.04*	0.020	0.04*	0.019
Random slope: Duration	0.04***	0.009	0.04***	0.010	0.02**	0.007	0.02**	0.007
Level: Statement								
Random intercept	0.48***	0.048	0.48***	0.048	0.46***	0.047	0.46	0.047
Level: Case								
Variance	1	0	1	0	1	0	1	0
-2*loglikelihood:								
DIC	37,494.5		37,493.5		38,191.17		38,178.8	
pD	545.3		552.1		529.15		537.3	

Table 17.1 (*continued*)

| | Pro-Steinmeier | | | | Pro-Merkel | | | |
| | Model 1a | | Model 1b | | Model 2a | | Model 2b | |
	Parameter	S.E.	Parameter	S.E.	Parameter	S.E.	Parameter	S.E.
Units: Viewer	218		218		218		218	
Units: Statement	300		300		300		300	
Units: Case	56,587		56,587		56,144		56,144	

Notes: Models with main effects had 50,000 runs, models with interaction effects had 100,000 runs. Chi-square Wald test: * $p<0.05$; ** $p<0.01$; *** $p<0.001$, *n.s.* not significant. Significance of joint effects for dummy variables is printed in the first row of the effect.
[+]In the analysis of responses in favour of Steinmeier, Merkel is the reference category, while Steinmeier is the reference category in the analysis of responses in favour of Merkel.

302 | New Perspectives on Negative Campaigning

the effect when Steinmeier is speaking instead of Merkel, whereas Models 2a and 2b show the effects of Merkel speaking instead of Steinmeier.[5] Clearly, there is a large, highly significant positive effect of being the current speaker on receiving a more positive evaluation. The odds of a change in favour of Steinmeier increase by 54 per cent (Model 1a: $e^{0.43}=1.54$) when he is speaking and the odds double for Merkel when she is speaking (Model 2a: $e^{0.72}=2.05$). These results offer strong support for H1 predicting that viewers improve their evaluation of the candidate who is speaking rather than their evaluation of the candidate who is not speaking.

The overall speaker effect for Steinmeier is more or less the same for viewers with different party identifications. On average, viewers identifying with the left-wing party block change slightly less in favour of Steinmeier than non-partisan viewers (Model 1b: $e^{-.14} = 0.87$ or 13 per cent decrease) and a similar but weaker effect is found for viewers identifying with the Conservative Party block (Model 1b: $e^{-0.05}=0.95$ or 5 per cent decrease). However, the interaction effect is not statistically significant. In contrast, partisanship does matter to the speaker effect for Merkel. We find a significant joint effect of the interaction dummy variables ($p<0.05$). Because none of the two comparisons with the non-partisan viewers is significant and these two effects have opposite signs (Model 2b: −0.07 and 0.12), the significant difference must be for the excluded contrast, namely between left-wing supporters and Conservatives. For Conservatives, the odds of changing in favour of Merkel are 21 per cent higher (Model 1b: $e^{0.12-(-0.07)}=1.21$) than for left-wing voters. The second partisanship hypothesis (H2b), predicting that viewers improve their evaluation of the candidate with whom they identify while s/he is speaking, only holds for Merkel but not for Steinmeier.

For the first partisanship hypothesis (H2a), stating that viewers are more likely to improve their evaluation of the candidate with whom they identify than with a candidate with whom they do not identify, we look at the models without interaction effects first. Controlling for the other predictors, party identification has a statistically significant effect for Steinmeier (Model 1a: $p<0.01$) but not for Merkel. Left-wing viewers are more inclined to change in favour of Steinmeier – regardless of who is speaking or the type of statement – than non-partisan viewers (Model 1a: $e^{0.31}=1.36$) and Conservative viewers (Model 1a: $e^{0.31-(-0.12)}=1.54$). The differences in odds are substantial, a 36 per cent and 54 per cent increase, respectively.

The results are more complicated if we take into account the interaction effects (Models 1b and 2b). Now, the party identification dummies represent effects for the reference categories of the speaker and strategy variables, that is, for defensive statements by the opponent. To facilitate interpretation, we estimated the probabilities of improving the evaluation of Steinmeier or Merkel for all subgroups on the speaker, strategy, and party identification variables while keeping other predictors at their sample average or reference category. Figure 17.3 displays

---

5.   The speaker variable was coded in opposite ways in the models predicting change in favour of Steinmeier versus the models predicting a more positive evaluation of Merkel.

Figure 17.3: Predicted probabilities for speaker-strategy-party identification combinations

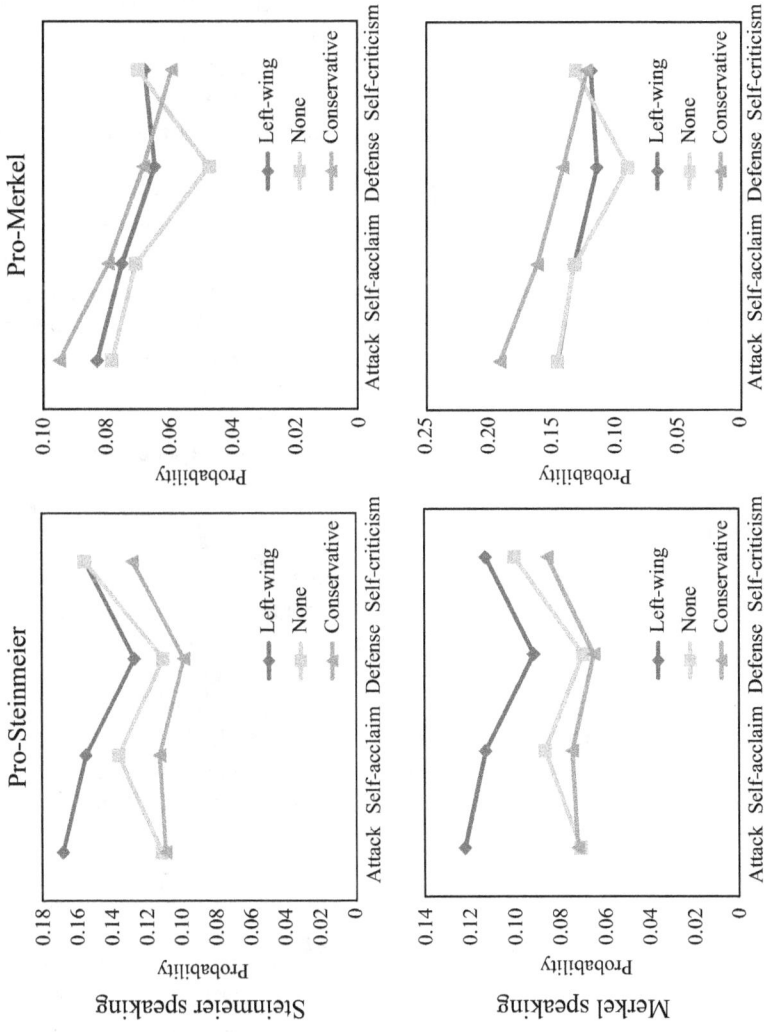

the predicted probabilities with effects on changes in favour of Steinmeier on the left and effects on changes in favour of Merkel on the right. Lines that are clearly not parallel indicate interaction effects.

The main differences among effects in favour of Steinmeier (Figure 17.3 left panels) occur between left-wing and other viewers responding to attacks. In comparison to their responses to defensive statements and acclaims, left-wing viewers respond more often positively to attacks while non-partisans tend to respond positively less often. The speaker does not seem to matter here because the pattern of lines is nearly the same when Steinmeier or Merkel is speaking. The higher probability for left-wing viewers to change in favour of Steinmeier in the case of attacks by or on Steinmeier sustains the partisan bias hypothesis (H3), predicting that viewers who identify with a candidate evaluate this candidate more positively if an attack statement is made by any of the candidates.

For evaluations favouring Merkel, the results hardly support the first partisanship hypothesis or the partisan bias hypothesis. Conservative viewers have significantly higher odds to evaluate Merkel more positively than non-partisan viewers in the case of defensive statements, regardless of who is speaking (Model 2b: $e^{0.40}=1.49$, p<0.01) but this effect does not apply to other types of statements or to comparisons with left-leaning viewers. Note that the statistically significant interactions between strategy and party identification are negative and more or less cancel out the positive effects for defensive statements.

Conclusion and discussion

This chapter presented an analysis of the effects of a televised debate on candidate evaluation among viewers, which is unprecedented in its scope and level of detail. Each response by an individual viewer to each single candidate statement during the debate was treated as a separate observation. This design enabled us to analyse effects of viewer and statement characteristics concurrently. As a consequence, we could control for effects of viewer attributes while determining the effects of statement characteristics and *vice versa*, which is crucial for disentangling the two types of effects. In addition, we could estimate interaction effects of viewer and statement characteristics, for example, partisanship as an interaction effect of the viewer's party identification with the candidate uttering the statement.

We formulated an affect-based approach to negative campaigning, conceptualising an attack between candidates as the expression of negative affect. The RTR scores were measured on a very favourable to very unfavourable scale, which also relates to affects. Finally, a viewer's party identification refers to a strong and durable affective bond between a voter and a political party (Campbell *et al.* 1960). Party identification suggested that the candidate making the statement in the debate should also be included in the model. Surprisingly, the speaker of the statement had the most general and strongest effect on candidate evaluation: Viewers tend to evaluate the candidate who is speaking more positively regardless of the strategy of the statement or the viewer's party identification.

We explained this effect from Inter-group Contact Theory, arguing that the speaking candidate is interacting with the viewer and interaction enhances positive affect. The speaker effect has interesting implications. If exposure to candidates of rivalling parties in a televised debate yields more positive evaluations for both candidates, it is to be expected that televised debates contribute to the acceptability and legitimacy of any candidate as the future chancellor – a depolarising effect. This would be contrary to the polarisation and decrease in support for future US presidents that is attributed to political advertisements (Iyengar and Simon 2000). As the televised debate is much more important than political advertisements in Germany, acceptance of the elected chancellor would be relatively high among all citizens.

The other hypotheses were not fully supported by the results. With regards to the general effect of partisanship, viewers were not more likely to improve their evaluation of the candidate representing the political block with which they identified irrespective of who was speaking and the type of statement. In some special situations, effects were found, e.g. conservative viewers responded more in favour of Merkel than non-partisan viewers in the case of defensive statements. These effects appear to be exceptions rather than a rule, so we concluded that partisanship by itself does not have an effect. The other partisanship hypothesis, predicting that viewers improve their evaluation of the candidate with whom they identify while that candidate is speaking, held for Merkel but not for Steinmeier. Conservative viewers are more inclined to improve their evaluation of Merkel while she is speaking than left-wing viewers.

Left-wing viewers responded more often in favour of Steinmeier in the case of attacks, either initiated by Steinmeier or targeted at him, as predicted by the partisan bias hypothesis derived from Balance Theory. Their affective bond with the left-wing party block and their disgust of the Conservative Party block or its candidate Merkel seem to be strong enough for them to interpret both attacks by and on Steinmeier as a positive feat for this candidate. The partisan bias hypothesis was not supported for evaluations of Merkel among Conservative viewers.

The differences between pro-Steinmeier and pro-Merkel effects open a new avenue for further research. Why do left-wing viewers evaluate their candidate more positively if he attacks and less positively if he defends himself, whereas these effects do not appear for the Conservative candidate? It seems likely that the challenger versus incumbent distinction is relevant here but personal characteristics of the candidates – the Merkel effect? – or the nature of party identification – stronger or more polarised within the left-wing party block? – offer alternative explanations. Comparisons with debates featuring a left-wing incumbent chancellor and another Conservative candidate than Merkel are needed to distinguish between these explanations.

The sizable and statistically significant random intercepts at both the viewer and statement level indicate that there may well be additional characteristics of viewers and statements that explain candidate evaluations, for example, non-verbal characteristics of the candidates accompanying statements (Nagel 2012: 219).

A cognitive explanation of candidate evaluation suggests including ideological beliefs and policy preferences of viewers and the issue addressed in the statement, taking into account issue ownership (Petrocik 1996).

We conclude this chapter with some of its limitations. We have not yet included cognitive aspects of candidate evaluation. In addition, the current dataset is based on a non-random self-selection sample. As a result, the sample probably includes citizens that are more interested in politics than the average citizen. Because citizens who are more interested in politics tend to be more critical towards statements that conflict with their political predispositions (Zaller 1992), partisanship effects may be stronger than in a random sample or in the entire population. The inflation of partisanship effects, however, may be corrected by the fact that viewers are more attentive to the debate due to their task to rate statements. Attention seems to dampen effects of partisanship (McKinnon *et al*. 1993: 116).

Chapter Eighteen

Feeding the Negative? Referendum Votes in Ireland

Theresa Reidy and Jane Suiter

The growth in the use of referendums to make major political decisions has brought renewed interest in the factors which underpin voting behaviour at these types of plebiscites. Offering a binary choice to voters, referendum contests pit 'yes' and 'no' campaigners against each other. The dynamic is unusual in many European countries in that a contest between directly opposing forces is not the norm in elections. Proportional electoral systems, multi-party systems and long traditions of coalition government deliver crowded, competitive election environments where negative campaign techniques have not become as prevalent as has been documented in two party systems and/or presidential systems. Consequently, referendums in Europe offer an unusual electoral environment in which to consider campaign techniques which place political forces in direct opposition to each other. Partisan dynamics play a lesser role in referendum campaigns (LeDuc 2002) and the primary purpose of each campaign is to a) sell its own arguments and b) plant doubt about the motivations and effects of the arguments of the other side. This dynamic should create greater incentives and opportunities for negative campaigning.

This chapter will examine negative campaigning at two referendums in Ireland. Allegations of lies and scaremongering, and campaigns which are often described as providing more heat than light, are the common refrain of 'the Irish referendum experience'. Using pre-referendum opinion poll data and a post referendum survey, this chapter will explore whether negative campaigning is a feature of referendums, how far it is used by both 'yes' and 'no' campaigners and which types of voters are most likely to be influenced by negative campaign messages.

Before we proceed we need to agree on a definition of negative campaigning. Benoit (2007) provides the theoretical frame for this volume and he argues that campaign messages have three functions; acclaims, attacks and defences. This research is primarily focused on attacks. Further, in classifying campaign messages we draw on Lau and Pomper (2002) who point to the importance of distinguishing between negative campaigning and unfair campaigning and they define negative campaigning as 'talking about the opponent, his or her programmes, accomplishments, qualifications, associates, and so on, with the focus, usually, on the defects of these attributes'. Hansen and Pedersen (2008) define a negative campaign message as an 'explicit critique of the political opponent'. Benoit (2007) goes on to discuss that campaign messages can focus on two topics, issues or image.

Image covers the character of the candidate and should feature less prominently at referendums than at general elections while, issues can be expected to dominate. Combining these insights, this chapter considers referendum campaign messages and classifies them as positive or negative.

The chapter is organised as follows, we draw on the international literature on negative campaigning to develop three hypotheses in section two. We provide a brief overview of the referendum context in Ireland in section three before presenting our data and methods in section four. Section five documents the results from our analysis and we present our concluding remarks in section six.

Literature

Farrell and Schmitt-Beck open their 2002 volume referring to the extensive literature on voters and how they make their decisions about which parties or candidates to support but they argue 'with few exceptions there has been little analysis of how these factors are connected with the communication activities of political parties and other campaign organisations'. The intervening decade has seen an increase in the study of campaigns internationally and the general consensus is that campaigns do matter (Campbell 2000; Box-Steffensmeier et al. 2009). However, there are still wide gaps. The literature remains concentrated on the US experience with just a small number of studies looking at European multi-party contexts. Campaign effects remain largely a mystery in Ireland where there has been no substantive study at either a general election or referendum.

The geographical disparity is even more pronounced in the negative campaign literature. Negative campaigning has been a long-standing concern of US political science but occupies the fringes of election studies in Europe. The theoretical foundations of negative campaigning are derived from social psychology research and the research on negative campaigning can be clustered into a number of sub-strands. Two of the primary concerns are the effectiveness of negative campaign measures (Lau 1995; Freedman and Goldstein 1999; Fridkin and Kenney 2011a) and the campaign strategy of candidates and parties including when, how and why parties and candidates make decisions to employ a negative campaign strategy (Damore 2002; Peterson and Djupe 2005).

The effectiveness and impact of negative campaign techniques have been widely considered in the US context but the literature yields mixed results. Freedman and Goldstein (1999) have argued that voters give greater weight to negative information. A more extensive treatment of negativity in politics is provided by Soroka (2014) where he explores the social psychology underpinnings of why voters are more likely to respond to negativity. Fridkin and Kenney (2011a) indicate that the tone, context and delivery of the negative message will all condition its impact and they conclude specifically that harsh negative messages can have an impact on voter decision-making. Lau and Pomper (2002) say they cannot give a clear answer on the effectiveness of negative campaigning but the general indication of their work is that negative campaigning does work and is relatively effective for challengers in a race. All that being said, Lau et al.

(2007: 1,185) were most unambiguous in their conclusion 'to state the matter bluntly: There is no consistent evidence in the research literature that negative political campaigning "works" in achieving the electoral results that attackers desire'. They acknowledge that hundreds of millions of dollars have been spent on negative campaign techniques at US elections over past decades and thus there is a disconnect between the theory and practice of negative campaigning. In a European context, the literature is more limited but several studies do exist, and their number is rapidly increasing (*see* for instance several contributions in this volume).

Referendums present a discrete challenge in the study of campaigns. As LeDuc (2002) outlines voters are presented with a different set of choices than at elections. There are no candidates or parties on the ballot and while these actors may be involved in the campaign, their functions differ from elections. The way that voters arrive at their final decision also varies and a great deal depends on the type of referendum question. LeDuc (2002) presents a framework for understanding voter behaviour at referendums where he posits that referendum questions which draw on fundamental values of the electorate are more likely to be stable in that the underlying cleavage structure of the polity will largely drive the vote. Volatile referendums, at the other end of the spectrum, are those that may pose questions on new or uncontroversial political issues. Voters may not have given a great deal of thought to these questions and consequently, the campaign plays an essential role in educating voters and shaping their position in relation to the referendum question. The centrality of the campaign for voters at volatile referendums raises the possibility that voters may change their opinions in the course of the campaign, thus increasing the stakes for campaigners on both sides and, potentially increasing their motivation to use overtly negative messages. Following on from LeDuc (2002) we argue that the importance of the campaign at volatile referendums raises the stakes for campaign participants and without the usual complexities of coalition politics to be found at general elections, referendum campaigns provide much greater potential for negative campaigning. This leads us to our first hypothesis: Negative campaign techniques are used at referendums.

Returning to the strands of research in negative campaigning, the question of who is likely to use negative campaigning, and when, is one of central importance. Skepardas and Grofman (1995) suggest that candidates with lower levels of support are more likely to opt for a negative tactic, arguing that in a way these candidates had less to lose. Kahn and Kenney (1999b) found that challengers were more likely to go negative in their campaigns, a decision in part, they put down to the greater campaign resources that would be available to incumbents, while Walter (2014a) concludes that large parties, parties that are close to each other ideologically and, those that are close to the median voter, are most likely to be the target of campaign attacks at Dutch elections. However, in a referendum campaign it is not always clear which side is the challenger and which is the incumbent, as both have claims to either side. For instance, the 'yes' side is always a challenge to the status quo. Yet, at least in Ireland, it is always the incumbent government which proposes the referendum and leads the 'yes' campaign. Likewise, the 'no' side is arguing for the status quo or incumbent position, yet it is generally supported by the opposition or non-government parties. Hence it is not always possible to extrapolate to referendums from the literature on negative campaigning at general elections. It is clear that both sides have an incentive and opportunity to use negative campaigning. This leads us to our second hypothesis: At referendums in Ireland, both sides of the campaign will use negative campaign techniques.

LeDuc (2002) has argued there are a multitude of factors which influence voter behaviour at referendums and specifically, that the campaign matters most when voters do not have an existing predisposition on the issue in question. There is evidence in the elections and referendum literature that negative campaign messages can have an effect on voters' preferences. Kaid (1997) and McKinnon and Kaid (1999) have considered the effects of negative campaigning on voter choice at elections while de Vreese and Semetko (2002 and 2004) consider media framing and its impact on voter choice at referendums. Elenbaas and de Vreese (2008) using data from a Dutch referendum demonstrate the effects that strategic and negative news framing can have on young voters and point out that it leads to greater political cynicism. Furthermore, they found that political cynicism exerted a positive effect on voting 'no'. Grabe and Kashawi (2006) report that women respond more strongly to positive news while men react more to negative news but risk aversion among women is widely reported in the business literature (Borghans *et al.* 2009) perhaps making them more likely to support the status quo position. Soroka (2014) in his examination of education related effects and negativity reports evidence that goes against existing beliefs about the relationship between education and voting. He concludes that negativity is significant for more educated voters. The question of which voters respond to negative campaigning is comparatively less researched than other areas of negative campaigning and there is a clear need for more work in this area. We argue that the campaign matters but in a variable manner leaving us with a final hypothesis: Negative campaign messages will have a heterogeneous impact on voters.

Referendum elections in Ireland

Ireland makes frequent use of referendums and this makes it an ideal case to examine the conduct of campaigns. In all, there have been thirty-seven referendums since 1937 and up to five more are planned by the current government for 2015. A wide range of issues have been the subject of referendums. EU treaties have contributed a growing number since 1987, social/moral questions though infrequent, tend to be the most controversial, while questions about the design of the judicial and political system have increased in the last decade. Referendums are initiated by the government and all changes to the constitution (*Bunreacht na hÉireann*) require a referendum. Much has been written about the conduct of referendums in Ireland (Gallagher 1996, 2004; Sinnott 2001, 2002) but poor quality survey data largely accounts for the absence of substantive studies of campaign effects at referendums. Indeed, this paucity of data continues and constrains the analysis reported in this chapter.

There are some general points which should be made about referendums in Ireland. Ireland has a highly regulated campaign environment with an IDEA (2008) report concluding that Ireland has one of the most heavily regulated referendum campaign frameworks internationally. A Referendum Commission oversees the campaign and no public funding is provided to political parties or campaign groups participating in referendums. The government may campaign in favour of the proposed referendum but they are precluded from using public monies in the course of their campaign arising from a Supreme Court decision, known as the McKenna judgement. Only the Referendum Commission receives public funding (Reidy and Suiter 2015). As a result, the Referendum Commission is the dominant actor in advertising the referendum to the public and is responsible for providing information on the subject matter of the referendum, promoting awareness of the upcoming referendum and encouraging voters to turnout on referendum day. In carrying out these functions, the Commission runs a media campaign on television, radio and online and drops leaflets into all homes. However, it cannot give advice or arguments on either side of the discussion and is limited to increasing turnout following changes narrowing its remit in the Referendum Act of 2001. In fact, political advertising is banned in Ireland so there are no advertisements of any kind alerting voters to the arguments on either side of the debate. Campaign messages are relayed through television and radio debates on local and national stations as well as through the print media and the direct campaign activities of participants.

This chapter is focused on two referendums, which took place in October 2011 and May 2012. These are interesting cases for the study of campaign effects as returning to the LeDuc (2002) framework, the first one lies on the volatile end as it deals with political design. The second, an EU referendum, falls in the middle of the spectrum. There have been many EU referendums but the proposals do not draw from a particular cleavage in Irish politics. In both cases, it can be argued that the campaign matters.

In October 2011, the Referendum on Houses of the Oireachtas Inquiries (OI) was proposed as the thirtieth amendment to the constitution and arose from a Supreme Court decision, known as the Abbeylara judgement, which parliamentarians argued limited the type and scope of inquiries which parliament could conduct. While parliamentarians had grumbled about the consequences of the Abbeylara judgement for many years, the issue came into sharp focus in the aftermath of the financial crisis when public demands for an investigation into the causes of the banking and public finance crisis in Ireland became acute. Uncertainty surrounding the legal position of parliamentary inquiries was used as an argument to limit the role of parliamentarians in investigating and evaluating the causes of the financial crisis. High profile parliamentary investigations in other jurisdictions (the UK and the US) reinforced the weakness at the centre of parliamentary functions in Ireland. Consequently, in 2011 the newly elected coalition government decided to hold a referendum to change the constitution as it related to the powers of parliament. The core of the referendum proposal was empowering members of parliament to carry out investigations into matters of public import and significance. Studies of parliament in Ireland have tended to highlight its weakness. Executive dominance is seen as a particular problem and the parliament has been variously described by Dinan (1986) as 'a woefully inadequate institution' and by Chubb (1992) as a 'puny parliament'. These negative assessments have also been confirmed more recently by Gallagher (in Coakley and Gallagher 2012) and Martin (2013). While the financial crisis may have been the immediate precipitator of the OI referendum, it was also seen as a measure which would go some way to addressing the longstanding imbalance in parliament.

The OI referendum was held on the same day as a second referendum relating to the pay of judges as well as a presidential election. All three of the elections fall under the broad heading of second order contests but the referendums must also be classified as low information elections. Both were massively overshadowed by a tightly contested, melodramatic and personality focused presidential election (O'Malley 2012; Murphy and Reidy 2012). The referendum campaign was barely visible until the final week before voting. With a turnout of 55.4 per cent, the OI referendum was defeated by a margin of 111,167 votes or 52 per cent opposed to the proposal. As can be seen from Figure 18.1, there was a marked decrease in support for the proposal in the last week of the campaign (Suiter and Reidy 2013).

Low information alone cannot be used to explain the outcome as the referendum on reducing judge's remuneration was passed with a substantial 'yes' vote while the OI referendum was narrowly defeated. The OI campaign was influential and there was a sharp change in public opinion in the final stage of the campaign.

Figure 18.1: OI referendum – 'yes' support in opinion polls

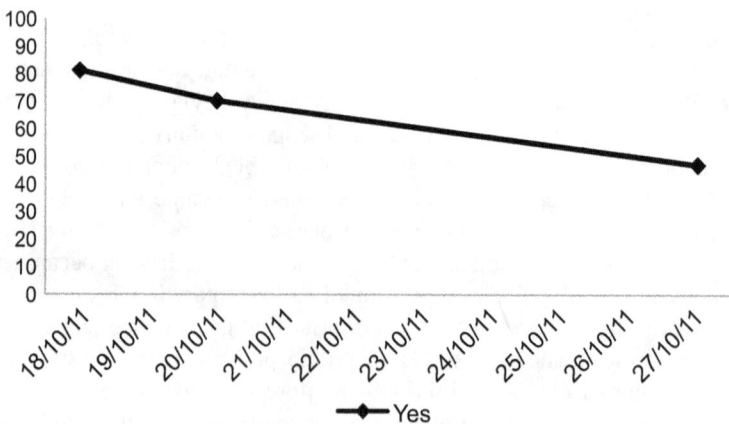

Source: Suiter and Reidy (2013)

The referendum on the Fiscal Treaty was held in May 2012. It was a stand-alone ballot, no other proposals were before the electorate on that day. EU treaties which involve the transfer of sovereignty must be passed by referendum in Ireland arising from the Crotty judgement of the Supreme Court in 1986. There was considerable trepidation among the pro-EU supporters in advance of the Fiscal Treaty vote, as Ireland had rejected the Nice and Lisbon treaties on their first appearance before the electorate, necessitating re-runs of both referendums. Ireland has what has been described by Hix (2005) as a pro-European cartel amongst its major parties and all three of the largest parties supported the Fiscal Treaty, as they have most major European Union (EU) treaties. Hayward (2002) speaks about Irish support for EU membership being based on comparatively low levels of knowledge about the EU. Much of the favourable view of the EU by Irish citizens is based on general impressions that membership has been good for Ireland (*see* also Sinnott *et al.* 2009). Hayward argues (specifically in relation to the Nice Treaty but it has wider applicability to other EU treaties) that EU referendum campaigns rely on rhetoric about Europe rather than the specific details of the Treaty on which the electorate are being asked to vote. This view can be applied to the Fiscal Treaty as much as to earlier campaigns (Costello 2014). The content of the Treaty was largely financial and related to changes in the budgetary requirements of EU member states. It could be said that the debate was more disciplined than usual with a lot of concentration on budgetary issues and the usual chestnuts of abortion, sovereignty, neutrality and the undemocratic nature of the EU making infrequent appearances. In contrast with the OI campaign, opinion polls were more stable for the Fiscal Stability Treaty as can be seen from Figure 18.2. The 'yes' side had an early lead, which they maintained into the final weeks. The last few points in the graph show the poll results from the weeks during the campaign but the major

Figure 18.2: Fiscal Treaty – change in support levels in opinions polls

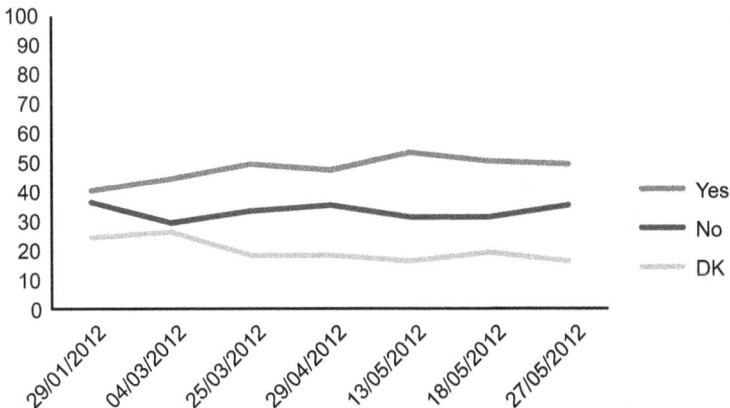

movements are largely accounted for by undecided voters making up their minds. With a turnout of just over 50 per cent, the Fiscal Treaty was passed by a margin of nearly 170,000 votes and 60 per cent of the poll.

Data and methods

A difficulty in studying campaign effects at referendums in Ireland is the lack of good data. The contests receive limited coverage in opinion polls, with intention to vote and political party preference usually being the only questions asked. There is no referendum study and the best opportunity for good data is when the government loses a referendum and needs to find out why. All in all, this means we have some very good information on the circumstances and reasons for the loss of certain propositions but we are considerably less informed on the reasons why propositions are passed.

Data for the OI referendum are drawn from a study commissioned by the Department of Public Expenditure and Reform, the lead government department sponsoring the referendum, some weeks after the vote. Polling firm Red C carried out 1,005 interviews with adults aged 18+ conducted between the 28 and 30 November 2011, utilising random digit dialling. Half of the sample was interviewed using an RDD landline sample, with the other half conducted using an RDD mobile phone sample. The interviews followed a fixed format, laid down in a detailed questionnaire. Questions were either closed or pre-coded and we must include the usual caveat that some voters when presented with a plausible reason to explain their voting may readily, but not necessarily accurately, select an option proffered by the interviewer. We use campaign message recall and reason for vote choice questions which we code as positive or negative to assess our first two hypotheses. We will then include demographic information and knowledge scales for the analysis relating to hypothesis three. Voter knowledge was measured using a ten-point Likert scale.

Data for the Fiscal Treaty referendum are drawn from an opinion poll taken by Millward Brown Lansdowne for the *Sunday Independent* in advance of the referendum. Interviews for the poll were conducted face-to-face, with a national sample and using demographic quotas. The questions were part of a multi-topic consumer research study (omnibus) and interviewing was conducted generally over a ten-day period. The company does not exclude respondents on the basis of their likelihood to vote and nor does it apply any post-data weights (apart from standard demographics). We use data from the questions which asked voters to give reasons for their voting intention. As with the OI data, questions are coded as positive or negative and as above, demographics and voter knowledge are included for hypothesis three. Voter knowledge was measured using a four-point Likert scale.

Results

Firstly, to provide context for the analysis, we briefly describe the key interventions during the campaigns for both referendums. Summary information including the political parties that were involved in the two referendum campaigns are included in Table 18.1.

First, we turn to the OI referendum. A striking feature of the referendum was the widespread consensus among all the political parties on the proposal. The campaign was one of low intensity, overshadowed by the presidential election but of the two referendums on that day, the OI proposal received more media interest and importantly in the last week of the campaign there were a number of high profile campaign interventions by civil society groups and actors on the 'no' side of the debate. The most prominent group was the Irish Council for Civil Liberties (ICCL) and they were active in a poster campaign, newspaper editorials and media debates in which they claimed that if passed, the proposal would undermine the democratic and legal rights of Irish citizens. Arguing the new powers would allow politicians to establish 'kangaroo courts' to adjudicate on the misdemeanours of citizens, they spread fear and uncertainty about the proposals (Suiter and Reidy 2013). Several media contributions involved the 'no' campaigners claiming that politicians would be able to search citizens' homes without search warrants and that existing legal provisions in relation to the 'good name' of a citizen would be reduced by the proposition.

A critical campaign intervention on the 'no' side occurred when eight former attorneys general (chief legal officer of the state) came out in opposition to the proposal just days before polling in a series of newspaper contributions, airing similar concerns to the ICCL. Their views were subsequently described as 'nonsense' by the Minister for Justice and the last few days of the campaign were passed in disagreement and recrimination (*see* O'Leary 2014 for more details). Despite the elite consensus among the parties, few resources were directed towards the referendum as most of them more closely focused on the outcome of the presidential election.

Table 18.1: Campaign summaries

Referendum	'Yes' – political parties and members of parliament	'No' parties	Campaign intensity	Campaign context
OI	Fine Gael, Labour, Fianna Fail, Sinn Fein, United Left Alliance, Non-Party	Non-Party	Low	Elite consensus
Fiscal Stability	Fine Gael, Labour, Fianna Fail, Sinn Fein, Non-Party	Sinn Fein, Socialist Party, People Before Profit, Non-Party	High	Pro-EU cartel but bi-directional messages

Figure 18.3 presents the arguments in favour of the proposal recalled by voters while Figure 18.4 presents the arguments against the proposal recalled by voters.

A notable point about both graphs is that a large number of voters included in the study are not listed as they were unable to recall arguments on either the 'yes' or the 'no' sides of the campaign. The survey was taken just three weeks after the referendum. Applying our definition of negative campaigning outlined in the introduction, in Table 18.2 we categorise the campaign messages.

Table 18.2 provides unambiguous data to address hypothesis one and hypothesis two. Negative campaign messages were clearly a feature at the OI referendum but more interestingly, there is a stark breakdown in the approach taken by campaigners on either side of the proposal with voters recalling the 'yes' side as having only positive campaign messages while voters recalled all negative messages from the 'no' side.

Turning to the Fiscal Treaty referendum, in the first instance there was a more diffuse information campaign with active engagement on both sides of the debate among political parties and civil society groups. The main opponents of the Treaty labelled it the Austerity Treaty and argued through the campaign that it would force more austerity and further budget cuts on the Irish population for decades to come.

Figure 18.3: 'Yes' arguments recalled by voters after the OI campaign

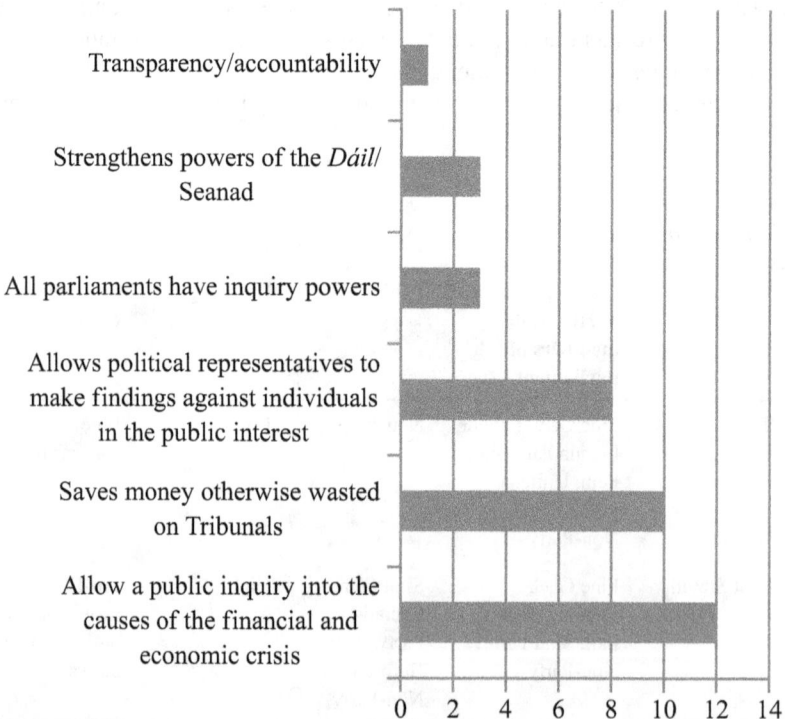

Figure 18.4: No arguments recalled by voters after the OI campaign

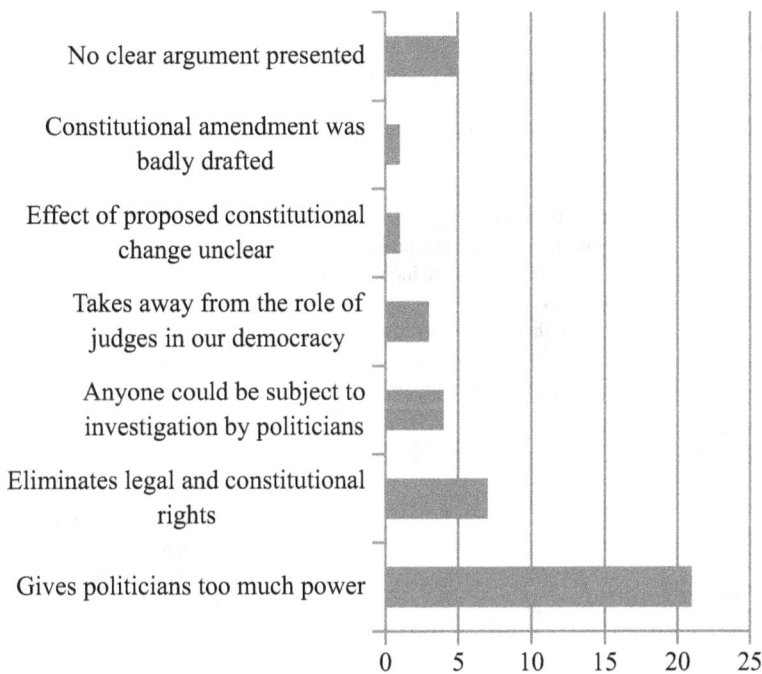

The 'yes' side focused on a more positive, if somewhat trite, message -'Vote Yes for Jobs'. The 'no' side used negative messages as the mainstay of their opposition to the proposal broadening the debate to include a range of topics which were unrelated to the Treaty, including the recently imposed property tax and water charges. Sinnott *et al.* (2009) have shown that where voters are unaware of the contents of an EU Treaty or believe things to be included which are not, they are among those most likely to vote 'no'.

On the 'yes' side there were occasional allegations that Ireland would go bankrupt if it did not ratify the Treaty as it would not have access to European Stability Mechanism funds in the event that a second bailout of the Irish state was required. The campaign was loud and enthusiastic with considerable effort from groups on both sides. The data we report were taken before the referendum and the question asked voters what arguments they could recall on both sides of the campaign as it was ongoing. Figure 18.5 reports the arguments cited by voters for voting 'yes' while Figure 18.6 reports the arguments cited by voters who were voting 'no'.

Table 18.3 paints a different picture to the OI campaign with negative messages a feature of both the 'yes' and 'no' campaigns. Again, voters cite only negative arguments for voting 'no' vote while voters intending to vote 'yes' cite both positive

Table 18.2: Campaign messages at the OI referendum

	Positive	**Negative**
'Yes' campaign	Allow a public inquiry into the causes of the financial and economic crisis Saves money otherwise wasted on tribunals Allows political representatives to make findings against individuals in the public interest All parliaments have inquiry powers Strengthens powers of the *Dáil/Seanad* Transparency/accountability	
'No' campaign		Gives politicians too much power Eliminates legal and constitutional rights Anyone could be subject to investigation by politicians Takes away from the role of judges in our democracy Effect of proposed constitutional change unclear Constitutional amendment was badly drafted No clear argument presented

and negative messages. Returning to our hypotheses, we find supporting evidence for both hypothesis one and hypothesis two at the Fiscal Treaty campaign. Negative campaign messages were used and they were used by both sides of the debate.

Returning to the OI referendum, from Table 18.2 we know that voters recalled only negative messages from the 'no' campaign and from Figure 18.4 we saw that the largest percentage of voters recalled that the proposal would give too much power to politicians. Also from Table 18.2 we remember that voters recalled only positive arguments from the 'yes' campaign with Figure 18.3 reminding us that the largest percentage of voters recalled that the proposal would allow for a public inquiry into the causes of the financial and economic crisis. We turn now to hypothesis three and examine differences among voters in the arguments that they recall from the 'yes' and 'no' campaigns. The analysis considers age, social class, gender and knowledge.

In the OI referendum, it is clear from Table 18.4 that across all age groups, a large majority were more likely to recall positive arguments (from the 'yes' campaign). The limited research on age effects and negative campaigning has

Figure 18.5: Arguments for voting 'yes' cited by voters during the Fiscal Treaty campaign

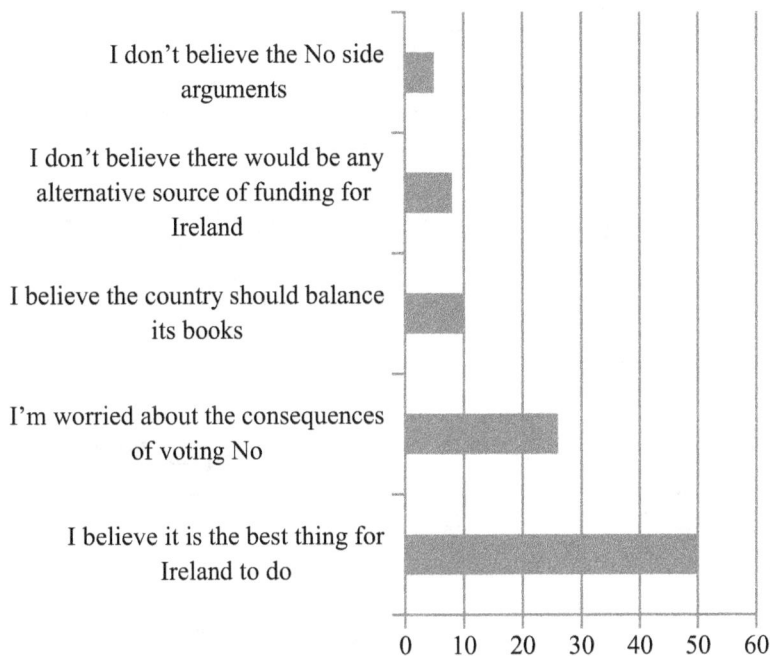

Figure 18.6: Arguments for voting 'no' cited by voters during the Fiscal Treaty campaign

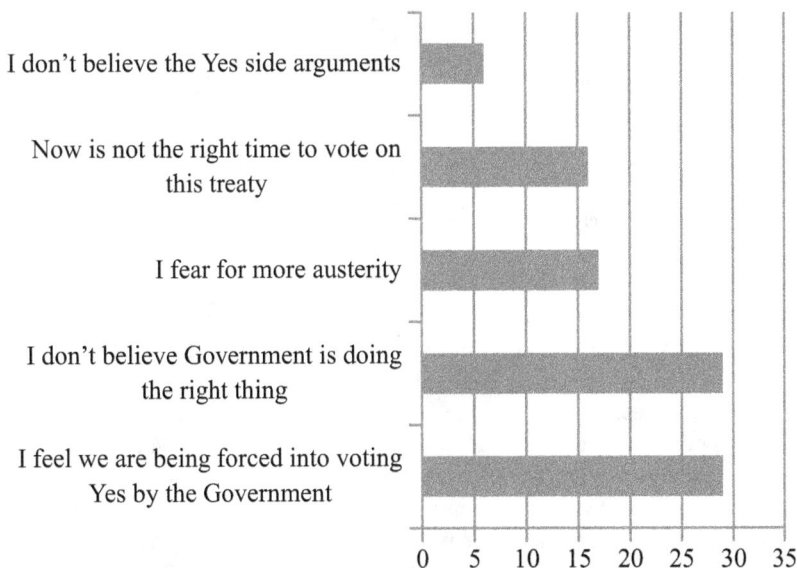

Table 18.3: Campaign messages at the Fiscal Treaty referendum

	Positive	**Negative**
'Yes' campaign	I believe it is the best thing for Ireland to do I believe the country should balance its books	I am worried about the consequences of voting No I do not believe there would be any alternative source of funding for Ireland I do not believe the No side arguments
'No' campaign		I feel we are being forced into voting Yes by the government I do not believe government is doing the right thing I fear for more austerity Now is not the right time to vote on this treaty I do not believe the Yes side arguments

Table 18.4: Reasons given for vote in OI referendum by age

	Negative	**Positive**
18–24	38	62
25–34	14	86
35–44	23	77
45–54	18	82
55–64	13	87
65+	18	82

Pearson chi2(10)=10.617 Pr=0.06 N=532
Figures reported row percentages.

focused on political cynicism in younger voters (*see* Elenbaas and de Vreese 2008) and consistent with the direction of that work we see that of all the age groups, those in the eighteen to twenty-four category were more likely to recall negative campaign messages.

Table 18.5 reports the findings for social class. Again all voters were more likely to recall positive arguments with C1 voters the most likely, followed closely by B and F voters. C2 voters were most likely to recall negative arguments.

From Table 18.6, we see that women were more likely to recall negative arguments from the campaign. Table 18.7 reports the details from the ten-point

Table 18.5: Reasons given for vote in OI referendum by class

	Negative	Positive
A (upper middle class)	21	79
B (middle class)	16	84
C1 (lower middle class)	15	85
C2 (skilled working class)	23	77
DE (working class + state income support)	19	81
F (farmer)	12	82

Pearson chi2(14)=3.2116 Pr=0.000 N=532
Figures reported row percentages.
A small number of arguments were excluded as they related to the second referendum.

Table 18.6: Reasons given for vote in OI referendum by gender

	Negative	Positive
Male	16	84
Female	22	78

N=532
Pearson chi2(2)=2.8286 Pr=0.093
Figures reported row percentages.
A small number of arguments were excluded as they related to the second referendum.

knowledge scale used in the OI study ('1' = not at all knowledgeable and '10' = extremely knowledgeable). Consistent with the information in the earlier tables, 'yes' arguments were more likely to be recalled by those across the knowledge scale with particularly high scores from those who felt very knowledgeable.

In Table 18.8 we report the results of a logistic regression for all the variables included in the descriptive discussion. All variables are significant. We can begin to develop a profile of voters and we find that older men, of higher social class and with more knowledge of the proposal are most likely to be able to recall campaign arguments on both sides of the campaign. This is largely consistent with the international voting and campaign literature.

The campaign arguments were more mixed at the Fiscal Treaty referendum with positive and negative reasons for vote choice recalled by voters from the 'yes' campaign. Table 18.3 also reported that voters provided only negative reasons for a 'no' vote. Turning to the demographic element, in Table 18.9 we report that

Table 18.7: Reasons given for vote in OI referendum by knowledge

	Negative	Positive
1 Not at all knowledgeable	23	77
2	17	83
3	33	67
4	30	70
5	18	82
6	16	84
7	15	85
8	8	92
9	8	92
10 Extremely knowledgeable	14	86

Pearson chi2(14)=21.7831 Pr=0.010 N=532
Figures reported row percentages.

Table 18.8: Logistic regression: Arguments recalled by voters from the OI referendum campaign

	Positive	Negative
Knowledge	0.22 (0.03)***	0.18 (0.03)***
Age	0.29 (0.05)***	0.32 (0.05) ***
Gender	−0.62 (0.14)***	−0.52 (0.14) ***
Class	−0.17 (0.34)***	−0.23 (0.04)***
Constant	−1.22 (0.34) ***	−1.06 (0.33)**
N	1005	1005
Log likelihood	−602.35	−610.05

*p<0.05, **p<0.01, ***p<0.001

Table 18.9: Reasons given for vote choice at Fiscal Treaty referendum by age

	Negative arguments ('no')	Negative arguments ('yes')	Positive arguments ('yes')
18–24	22	43	35
25–34	18	49	33
35–49	23	42	35
50–64	26	37	37
65+	31	21	48

Pearson chi2(8)=20.5693 Pr=0.004 N=711
Figures reported row percentages.

voters were more likely to recall arguments from the 'yes' side (positive and negative). Similar to the OI referendum, older voters were more likely to recall positive arguments although in the case of the Fiscal Treaty, those over sixty-five were most likely to recall positive arguments from the 'yes' side but they were also the most likely to recall negative reasons from the 'no' side.

In terms of class, Table 18.10 shows that again voters were more likely to recall the campaign messages from the 'yes' side. Farmers (F) and those in the upper middle and middle classes (AB) were most likely to recall positive reasons from the 'yes' campaign. In the Fiscal Treaty referendum, the greater propensity of farmers to recall positive arguments from the 'yes' side is not surprising as farmers have been among the most enthusiastic supporters and biggest financial beneficiaries of the EU since membership in 1973.

Table 18.11 reports the breakdown based on gender and we can see very little difference here. Knowledge is measured on a four-point scale in the Fiscal Treaty poll and the breakdown is presented in Table 18.12. Voters are more likely to recall the arguments for a 'yes' vote but there is a mixed picture with those at the top and the bottom of the knowledge scale being the least likely to recall negative reasons for their vote choice.

Table 18.13 reports the result of a logistic regression for the Fiscal Treaty vote. Voter knowledge is significant for voters intending to vote 'yes' whether they cite positive or negative reasons for their vote. There is no gender impact and as with the OI referendum, younger voters were more likely to provide negative reasons from the campaign.

Conclusion

Referendums, by their very construction require one side of the campaign to oppose. Opposition can take many forms and does not have to be explicitly negative but in many cases, the campaign actions of 'no' groups do conform

Table 18.10: Reasons given for vote choice at Fiscal Treaty referendum by class

	Negative arguments ('no')	Negative arguments ('yes')	Positive arguments ('yes')
	Negative	Negative for positive vote	Positive
AB (upper middle and middle class)	25	29	46
C1 (lower middle class)	31	31	38
C2 (skilled working class)	16	51	33
DE (working class plus state income support)	21	48	32
F (farmer)	33	23	44

Pearson chi2(8)=32.698 Pr=0.000 N=711
Figures reported row percentages.

Table 18.11: Reasons given for vote choice at Fiscal Treaty referendum by gender

	Negative arguments ('no')	Negative arguments ('yes')	Positive arguments ('yes')
Male	24	40	36
Female	25	38	38

Pearson chi2(2)=0.2879 Pr=0.866 N=711
Figures reported row percentages.

with what the negative campaign literature defines as negative campaigning. This chapter examined two referendum campaigns in Ireland. We have mixed quality data but we can see that negative campaign messages feature at both referendums with voters giving both positive and negative reasons for their vote intentions.

The dynamics are quite different at the referendums and negative and positive messages were used by the 'yes' side at the Fiscal Treaty while at the OI referendum, the arguments recalled for voting 'yes' were all positive. On the 'no' side, negative messages dominate with voters at both the Fiscal Treaty and OI referendums recalling only negative messages or giving only negative arguments to support their vote intention.

Table 18.12: Reasons given for vote choice at Fiscal Treaty referendum by understanding

	Negative arguments ('no')	Negative arguments ('yes')	Positive arguments ('yes')
I do not know what the issues are	13	53	33
I am only vaguely aware of the issues	29	41	29
I understand some of the issues	30	35	35
I have a good understanding	14	40	46

Pearson chi2(2)=26.96 Pr=0.0000 N=710
Figures reported row percentages.

Table 18.13: Logistic regression: Reasons given for vote choice at Fiscal Treaty referendum

	Negative arguments ('no')	Negative arguments ('yes')	Positive arguments ('yes')
	Negative vote	Negative for positive vote	Positive
Knowledge	0.12 (0.10)	0.47 (0.01)***	0.62 (0.09)***
Age	0.19 (0.07)*	−0.22 (0.06) ***	0.13 (0.06) *
Gender	−0.05 (0.17)	−0.07 (0.15)	0.07 (0.15)
Class	−0.13 (0.08)*	0.17 (0.07)***	−0.73 (0.07)
Constant	−2.12 (1.67)	−1.31 (1.41)	−3.96 (1.47)
N	1,025	1,025	1,025
Log likelihood	−457.203	−575.100	−550.19

*$p<0.05$, **$p<0.01$, ***$p<0.001$

The demographic picture is mixed and in the absence of better quality data, it is difficult to reach strong conclusions. Campaign messages resonate differently among groups of voters but, equally, there are differences across the two referendums. Knowledge is significant in the regression models for both referendums with a higher coefficient reported for positive arguments from the 'yes' side at both. At both referendums, older voters were more likely to recall positive arguments and, the higher social classes and farmers were more likely to recall positive messages. However, at the Fiscal Treaty referendum, older voters were also most likely to recall negative arguments from the 'no' side. This returns us to the truism of referendum research which states that in referendums, it is the question which matters most.

Chapter Nineteen

Where to Go From Here in the Study of Negative Campaigning: The Comparative Challenge Ahead

Annemarie S. Walter and Alessandro Nai

In this volume we have shown the wealth of research on negative campaigning. We have discussed the state of the art of this young field and presented several new studies alongside the three main questions asked by researchers, respectively what is negative campaigning and how can we measure it? What are the causes of going negative? What are the effects of negative campaigning? Instead of summarising the specific findings of the separate studies in this volume, we would like to reflect on the results of these studies in light of the goal set out in the introduction. In the introduction we stated that our hope is that this volume brings us closer to a general theory on negative campaigning. The development of such a general theory we believe to be impossible without broadening the scope of research beyond the United States (US) and 'true' comparative work that not only describes the level and features of negative campaigning across time and geographical contexts, but also examines its use and effectiveness (a feeling shared and expressed by Fridkin and Kenney 2014). This volume has definitely done the first by examining the features and use of negative campaigning in countries such as Austria, Switzerland, New Zealand, Turkey and Brazil (*see* Chapters Five, Seven, Eight, Nine, Ten, Eleven, Twelve, Thirteen, Sixteen and Seventeen). For the latter, this volume did include some cross-national examples (*see* Ridout and Walter, Chapter Sixteen) and single country cross-temporal studies (*see* for instance Toros, Chapter Twelve and Maier, Chapter Eight).

This edited volume helps pave the way for future large cross-national and cross-temporal work in the field of negative campaigning (note that a handful comparative studies already exists, *see* for instance Kaid and Holtz-Bacha 2006; Salmond 2011; Walter *et al.* 2014; Walter 2014b). The studies incorporated in this volume are diverse in nature (varying in theme, case studied, method *et cetera*), but also similar. What these studies share is that they point out 1) the need for comparative research; 2) the challenges that conducting comparative research poses; and 3) various suggestions to overcome these challenges.

The need for comparative research in the field of negative campaigning is mentioned explicitly by several scholars in this volume, but also becomes apparent implicitly when reading the chapters. In our overview chapter (Chapter Six) on the causes of negative campaigning we explain in detail why this part of the field in particular would benefit from comparative research. We argue that candidates and parties do not compete in a vacuum, but in the context of an election and a political system. As a result, the characteristics of the attacker and target are insufficient to explain fully why a candidate or party uses negative campaign tactics; the context that the candidate or party operates in should be taken into account as it affects the candidate/party's strategic behaviour. Cross-national research is a prerequisite to discover whether and in what way political system characteristics such as the electoral system, the party system, media system and institutional structure matter for the use of negative campaigning. In addition to cross-national research, cross-temporal research is needed to uncover the relationship between negative campaigning and campaign professionalisation, mediatisation, electoral volatility and party system polarisation. These four developments are argued to have increasingly stimulated the use of negative campaigning in election campaigns.

The chapters in the second part of the book on the causes of negative campaigning exemplify these arguments supporting our call for comparative research. First of all the chapters show the need for comparative research to cross-validate findings.[1] For instance, Bernard (Chapter Nine) finds that the 'no' campaign in eight Swiss direct-democratic campaigns is more attack-filled than the 'yes' campaign and Maier (Chapter Eight) shows that female candidates in forty-three German televised election debates do not differ from their male counterparts in attack behaviour. Notwithstanding the significance of these findings, the question remains whether these findings can be extrapolated to other geographical contexts. Are 'no' campaigns in direct-democratic campaigns in general more attack-filled than 'yes' campaigns? Do all female candidates in Europe behave similarly to male candidates when it comes to the use of negative campaigning? Second, the chapters show the need for comparative research to explain the differences in findings between studies on candidate/party behaviour conducted in different geographical contexts, in particular studies examining the US and non-US context. Maier's finding (Chapter Eight) that the gender of the candidate does not affect the use campaign tactics stands in stark contrast to many US studies (Benze and Declercq 1985; Kahn and Kenney 2004; Lau and Pomper 2004) that do find differences and refrains from pinpointing out what makes female candidates act differently in Germany than in the US. The same counts for Bol and Bohl (Chapter Seven) that attempt to explain why many European studies fail to find the strong relationship between competitiveness of the race and the use of campaign tactics that features prominently in US strategic studies. They argue that these studies fail to do so due to the need for coalition government formation and the existence of pre-electoral coalition agreements between parties in many

---

1. For this purpose the field needs comparative research, not just replication of research in different geographical settings, as we need to make sure that similar findings are found in different geographical and temporal contexts while controlling for all methodological variables. Currently in the field many single country studies exist that replicate US work, nevertheless they differ on (minor) methodological details, such as the unit of analysis, case selection, coding scheme etc. As a result, we cannot rule out that (minor) methodological differences affect the generalisability claim made by scholars.

European countries that have a proportional electoral system. Dolezal *et al.* (Chapter Ten) also point to the multiparty system and the need to form a coalition government after the elections for the deviating pattern in the use of negative campaigning and the choice of target in comparison to studies based on the US without cross-national research we are unable to find empirical support for the theoretical claim that systemic characteristics matter and we are unable to pinpoint which characteristics. Bol and Bohl (Chapter Seven) refer to the electoral system but Dolelzal *et al.* (Chapter Ten) refer to the party system, which are in general two highly intertwined systemic characteristics. Toros (Chapter Twelve) argues that the political culture of the political system might be the key to explaining the high levels of negative campaigning in the Turkish context. Borba (Chapter Eleven) shows that candidates make different strategic decisions in the different rounds of the Brazilian presidential election campaign, suggesting that the context of the rounds, the so-called situational determinants (*see* Chapter Thirteen) affect the behaviour of the candidates. To summarise, as argued extensively in Chapter Six the context in which political actors operate affects their strategic decision-making surrounding negative campaigning and if we wish to unravel which (systemic) factors and in what way they matter, comparative research is needed.

However, comparative research cannot only advance research on the causes of negative campaigning, but also research its effects. We do not expect that negative campaigning triggers different individual level psychological mechanisms across political systems; we believe that they will be the same. Thus, for instance we expect that independent of the political context negative campaigning has an impact on the information processing employed by voters as argued by Lau and Redlawsk (Chapter Fifteen) and on the evaluation of political candidates by voters as shown by De Nooy and Maier (Chapter Seventeen). Nevertheless, we claim that the setup of the political system can moderate how citizens respond to negative campaigning. It is important that this part of the field also starts to pay attention to the characteristics of the political system, as both candidates/parties and voters react to them.

Political system characteristics have implications for the strategic behaviour of voters and candidates/parties; the latter even make voters increasingly aware of these strategic considerations in their campaign messages during election campaigns (Van der Eijk and Franklin 2009). For instance, on the evening before election day in the 1998 Dutch parliamentary election campaign, Labour Party leader Wim Kok (PvdA) asked voters to vote for Democrats 66 (D66) if they wished continuation of the so-called 'Purple' government coalition. D66 was losing in the polls and both the Labour and Liberal party (VVD) only wished to continue the 'Purple' cabinet if D66 would remain part of it (Elzinga and Voerman 2002). Kok made voters increasingly aware of the different strategic considerations at play in the Dutch multiparty system and asked them not to consider solely their preferred party, but also their preferred coalition government when casting their vote. Although De Nooy and Kleinnijenhuis (Chapter Five) do not examine the influence of the systemic context on the use and effects of negative campaigning, they do reflect in their theory paragraph on voters' strategic considerations in a multiparty system. In a multiparty system a considerable number of voters vote 'strategically'. They try amongst others to use their vote to influence the coalition government using positive and negative campaigning as cues for potential coalition partners when pre-electoral coalition agreements are absent. Voters in a two-party system that have in general single party majoritarian governments do not have to take these considerations into account and do not see positive or negative campaign messages as signals of potential coalition partners.

In Chapter Six on the causes of negative campaigning in the second part of this edited volume, we argue how the party system moderates the effects of negative campaigning. Parties operating in a multiparty system have different strategic considerations than parties operating in a two-party system. A party's decision to refrain from negative campaigning in a multiparty system is not just based on the strategic consideration that a coalition government has to be built after the elections, and thus the risks of using negative campaign tactics are larger than in a two-party system. This decision is also based on how voters act in this environment, as party and voter behaviour are two phenomena that cannot be studied in isolation (Van der Eijk and Franklin 2009). In general, negative campaigning is thought to be less rewarding in a multiparty system than in a two-party system. Voters in a multiparty system do not respond the same way as voters in a two-party system when exposed to negative campaigning. As a result of exposure to negative campaigning voters in both party systems might have less positive feelings towards the attacked party and the expected utility for voting for the attacked party might decline. However, their actual behaviour in response to attack behaviour is likely to differ, as especially in multiparty systems, voters prefer or identify with more than one party, as it is likely that there are a number of fairly ideologically similar parties competing (Tillie 1995; Schmitt 2002; Van der Eijk and Niemöller 1983). The decline in voters' expected utility for voting for the attacked party may not result in an increase in the expected utility for the party doing the attacking. After the utility for the first preferred party is lowered, these voters are likely to vote for another party in their choice set. As voters in a two-party system are less likely to have a second preferred party and voting for the attacking party on the opposite side of the ideological spectrum is most likely a bridge too far, these voters are more likely to withdraw from the electoral process in contrast to voters in a multiparty system. As long as more voters vote for the attacking party than the opponent, negative campaigning is beneficial for a party operating in a two-party system, regardless whether the attacking party wins those voters or voters abstain from voting. For a party in a multiparty system, negative campaigning might not be rewarding, as voters can shift their support from one opponent to another. To summarise, the effectiveness of negative campaigning, i.e. the effect of negative campaigning on vote choice is likely moderated by the party system.[2]

---

2. *See* also the call for comparative research by Fridkin and Kenney (2012). They wonder whether the effectiveness of negative campaigning differs across institutional settings. However, they do not theorise in what way the institutional setting matters for the effectiveness of negative campaigning. The role of systemic factors in relation to negative campaigning has been neglected in literature, in particular by scholars who study effects of negative campaigning. Here we attempt to theorise in what way the party system would matter for the effectiveness of negative campaigning.

In addition, we refer in our overview chapter (Chapter Fourteen) to the effects of negative campaigning on other work (Dassoneville 2010) that seems to theorise that the political system moderates the effectiveness of negative campaigning. Dasonneville claims that the electoral system affects the importance of the size of groups of voters that are lost or gained as a result of exposure to negative campaigning. In the context of a backlash effect, i.e. the phenomenon that instead of winning, a party loses voters as they turn away in response to exposure to the party's attack behaviour, she argues that the size of a backlash effect matters less in a first-past-the-post electoral system than in a proportional representation electoral system. In a first-past-the-post electoral system a positive net gain suffices to win the elections, to gain office and policy influence. However, in PR elections each vote lost weakens the parties' power in parliament as well as in the government coalition after the election. This is another example of how the political system is likely to moderate the effects of negative campaigning. Regardless, the few studies that suggest that system characteristics matter comparative work testing whether this is the case and which characteristics moderate the effects of negative campaigning is still absent in the field.

Scholars that do take upon the endeavour of comparative research in the field of negative campaigning face various challenges. One of the challenges for comparative research is the definition used to measure negative campaigning. When studying negative campaigning in a comparative fashion one will by definition come across multiparty systems in which the formation of a coalition government after the elections is a general practice. As already suggested by several other scholars in the field (Walter 2014a; Hansen and Pedersen 2008; Elmelund-Præstekær 2010) the use of negative campaigning is more complicated in multiparty systems than two-party systems. Parties do not solely strive to win votes, but also strive to be part of the coalition government, which are often two conflicting goals in a multiparty setting (*see* also Chapter Six). De Nooy and Kleinnijenhuis (Chapter Five) point out in their chapter that to be able to understand the decision go negative in a multiparty system one should also take statements of support for other parties into account. Parties do not only make use of attack statements, but also support statements to strategically suggest potential coalitions to the electorate. Voters perceive attack statements as a signal that these parties fighting disagree with one another and are unlikely to govern together and they perceive support statements as a sign that these competing parties agree with another and regard each other as potential coalition partners. Voters have various motives to vote for a party, as already said previously we know that a part of the electorate in a multiparty system votes 'strategically' with the aim to influence the government coalition after the elections. The notion of support statements that voters use to derive information about potential coalitions currently falls outside the scope of positive campaigning, which is now defined as all self-praise and acclamation of a candidate and party. De Nooy and Kleinnijenhuis (Chapter Five) advocate the broadening of this definition to include these support statements, so that the concept is not tailored solely to the specifics of a two-party system.

Next to defining the concept of negative campaigning in such a way that it is applicable in all geographical contexts, scholars face the challenge of measuring negative campaigning. One issue that these scholars have to overcome is the choice of campaign materials. As pointed out in the introductory chapter the choice of campaign materials in general matters for measuring negative campaigning, as this can over or underestimate the level and specific content (in particular trait attacks) of negative campaigning. However, the choice of campaign materials becomes increasingly more difficult in the context of comparative research. As pointed out by Benoit (Chapter Two) and Gelineau and Blais (Chapter Four) campaign scholars do not have what party positions scholars have, namely a campaign mean that is available, is of similar importance and has a similar purpose across countries. Scholars who wish to measure party positions just simply turn to party manifestos. Political television advertisements in particular cannot be to campaign scholars what party manifestos are for party position scholars. Countries vary in media systems and electoral laws that affect the governing of political advertising. In some countries the purchase of airtime for political advertisements is not allowed and/or candidates and parties are limited in the time that they can air. Consequently, in these contexts televised political advertising is of no or lesser importance than for instance in the US. Benoit (Chapter Two) calls for awareness of these country differences, scholars should just not simply assume that (absence of) constraints in one country applies to others. Gelineau and Blais (Chapter Four) do not solely point out the difficulties, but also provide a suggestion to overcome these difficulties. They bring us the first methodological study on the use of expert judgements to measure negative campaigning. Although this method needs more testing, in particularly a test that applies this method across geographical contexts and elections, it is a research method that potentially can make conducting comparative research easier. It costs less time and effort to survey a range of experts on the tone of the campaign than to measure negative campaigning through systematic content analysis of one particular campaign mean. In addition, it would help to solve the challenge of what campaign materials to examine in a cross-national context and can even out distortions as it measures the tone of the campaign in general and not on the basis of one specific mean.

Related to the choice of materials is the choice of coding scheme, extensively discussed by Allen and Stevens in Chapter Three. The choice of coding scheme is, in general, of importance as it affects research findings in particular in effect research. Nevertheless, some coding schemes are more suitable than others for comparative research. Several coding schemes for measuring negative campaigning are developed on the basis of advertisements and have the advertisement as the unit of analysis. They are less suitable to measure negative campaigning on the basis of other campaign materials, as one can argue whether one can classify a two-hour debate or a ten-minute conference speech as positive, mixed or negative. In addition, one needs knowledge of the advertising restrictions in the countries as suggested by Benoit (Chapter Two) as it potentially provides information about which coding scheme might be more or less suitable for comparative research. To illustrate, Allen and Stevens (Chapter Three) find that Kahn and Kenney's method applied to the US context has the tendency to categorise more advertisements into the extreme negative category and shows that as a result different effects of negative campaigning are found in markets where few advertisements are aired. A finding that is likely to extrapolate to cross-national research, which would then imply different findings for countries with fewer advertisements aired, which might be a reason to be more reluctant to use Kahn and Kenney's method or to interpret the results yielded more conservatively. Allen and Stevens argue that the coding schemes of Jamieson and Geer (the latter is very similar to Benoit's method *see* Chapter Three, footnote two) are the ones that show most potential to measure across different campaign materials.

When one chooses to stick to the traditional method of content analysis for comparative research,[3] Allen and Stevens (Chapter Three) call for more awareness of the potential measurement problems that can arise and suggest when possible to measure negative campaigning on more than one type of campaign material.

In the wake of the findings in this volume and final thoughts expressed in this concluding chapter, how should the field of negative campaigning move forward? After finalising this project of a first edited volume with work from scholars that study both negative campaigning in the US, as well as in other parts of the world, we are still convinced that scholars in the field should commit themselves to producing work that contributes towards this goal of a general theory on negative campaigning – a theory that can explain the occurrence, use and effects of negative campaigning across temporal and geographical settings. As campaign scholars we are aware that there will always be idiosyncratic characteristics of a particular campaign that should be taken into account to explain the use and effects of negative campaigning in that campaign better, nevertheless there are many common patterns in the use and effects of negative campaigning moderated by (systemic) variables to be found. Therefore, we hope above all to welcome more truly comparative work in the field the upcoming years.

---

3.   The few cross-national studies that exist (*see* for instance Walter *et al.* 2014; Salmond 2011; Kaid and Holtz-Bacha 2006) rely on the traditional method of systematic content analysis of campaign materials to measure the level and use of negative campaigning.

Bibliography

Abbe, O. G., Herrnson, P. S., Magelby, D. B. and Patterson, K. D. (2001) 'Are professional campaigns more negative?', in Herrnson, P. S. (ed.) *Playing Hardball: Campaigning For The U.S. Congress*, Upper Saddle River: Prentice Hall, pp. 70–91.

Airne, D. and Benoit W. L. (2005a) '2004 Illinois U.S. Senate debates. Keyes vs. Obama', *American Behavioral Scientist*, 49(2): 343–352.

— (2005b) 'Political television advertising in Campaign 2000', *Communication Quarterly*, 53: 473–492.

Al-Rawi, A. K. and Gunter, B. (2013) 'Political candidates' coverage in the 2010 Iraqi general elections', *Journal of Middle East Media*, 9(1): 70.

Al-Yemeni, A. A. H. (2003) *The Dynamics of Democratisation: Political Parties in Yemen*, Bonn: Friedrich Ebert Stiftung.

Alinejad, M. (2009) *Between Defiance and Détente: Iran's 2009 Presidential Election and its Impact on Foreign Policy*, Sydney: Lowy Institute for International Policy.

Allen, B. and Stevens, D. (2013) 'Truth in advertising? Visuals, sound, and the factual accuracy of political advertising', paper presented at the Joint Session of Workshops of the European Consortium for Political Research, Mainz, 2013.

Allen, M. and Burrell, N. (2002) 'The negativity effect in political advertising: A meta-analysis' in Dillard, P. and Pfau, M. (eds) *The Persuasion Handbook: Developments in Theory and Practice*, Thousand Oaks, CA: Sage Publications, pp. 83–96.

Allport, G. W. (1954) *The Nature of Prejudice*, Cambridge: Addison-Wesley.

Alqaseer, J. (2013) *Political Advertising in Kuwait: A Functional Discourse Analysis*, Doctoral Dissertation, University of South Carolina.

Altmeyer, V. (2014) 'Intimidation versus inclusion: New strategies in Indonesian election campaigning', *ASEAS – Austrian Journal of South-East Asian Studies*, 7(1): 121–132.

Anderson, M. (2009) 'Beyond membership: A sense of community and political behavior', *Political Behavior*, 31(4): 603–627.

Andeweg, R. B. and Irwin, G. (2009) *Governance and Politics of The Netherlands*, Houndmills: Palgrave Macmillan.

Anduiza Perea, E. (2002) 'Individual characteristics, institutional incentives and electoral abstention in Western Europe', *European Journal of Political Research*, 41: 643–673.

Ansolabehere, S. and Iyengar, S. (1995) *Going Negative: How Attack Ads Shrink and Polarize the Electorate*, New York: Free Press.

Ansolabehere, S., Iyengar, S. and Simon, A. (1999) 'Replicating experiments using aggregate and survey data: The case of negative advertising and turnout', *American Political Science Review*, 93(4): 901–909.

Ansolabehere, S., Iyengar, S., Simon, A. and Valentino, N. (1994) 'Does attack advertising demobilize the electorate?', *The American Political Science Review*, 88(4): 829–838.

Arceneaux, K. (2006) 'Do campaigns help voters learn? A cross-national analysis', *British Journal of Political Science*, 36: 159–173.

Arceneaux, K. and Nickerson, D. W. (2005) 'Two field experiments testing negative campaign tactics', paper presented at the Annual Meeting of the American Political Science Association, Washington, 2005.

Åsard, E. (1989) 'Election campaigns in Sweden and the United States: Convergence or divergence', *American Studies in Scandinavia*, 21(2): 70–87.

Ashton, M. (2007) *Individual Differences and Personality*, Burlington: Elsevier Academic Press.

Aspinall, E., Dettman, S and Warburton, E. (2011) 'When religion trumps ethnicity: A regional election case study from Indonesia', *South East Asia Research*, 19(1): 27–58.

Attallah, P. and Burton, A. (2001) 'Television, the internet, and the Canadian federal election of 2000', in Pammett, J. H. and Dornan, C. (eds) *The Canadian General Election of 2000*, Toronto: The Dundurn Group, pp. 215–241.

Aziz, A. (2007) *Siyasal İletişim [Political Communication]*, İstanbul: Nobel.

Azpuru, D. (2010) 'The salience of ideology: Fifteen years of presidential elections in El Salvador', *Latin American Politics and Society*, 52(2): 103–138.

Baggaley, J. (1987) 'Continual response measurement: Design and validation', *Canadian Journal of Educational Communication*, 16(3): 217–38.

Bakari, M. and Makulilo, A. (2012) 'Beyond polarity in Zanzibar? The "silent" referendum and the government of national unity', *Journal of Contemporary African Studies*, 30(2): 195–218.

Bakker, R., De Vries, C., Edwards E., Hooghe, L., Jolly, S., Marks, G., Polk, J., Rovny, J., Steenbergen M. and Vachudova, M. A. (2015) 'Measuring party positions in Europe: The Chapel Hill expert survey trend file, 1999–2010', *Party Politics*, 21(1): 143–152.

Banducci, S. A., Gidengil, E. and Everitt, J. (2012) 'Women as political communicators: Candidates and campaigns', in Semetko, H. A. and Scammell, M. (eds) *The SAGE Handbook of Political Communication*, Los Angeles: Sage, pp. 164–172.

Barker, D. and Hansen, S. (2005) 'All things considered: Systematic cognitive processing and electoral decision-making', *The Journal of Politics*, 67(2): 319–344.

Barnes, W. A. (1998) 'Incomplete democracy in Central America: Polarization and voter turnout in Nicaragua and El Salvador', *Journal of Interamerican Studies and World Affairs*, 40(3): 63–101.

Bartels, L. M. (1988) *Presidential Primaries and the Dynamics of Public Choice*, Princeton: Princeton University Press.

— (2000) 'Campaign quality: Standards for evaluation, benchmarks for reform', in Bartels, L. M. and Vavreck, L. (eds) *Campaign Reform: Insights and Evidence*, Ann Arbor: University of Michigan Press, pp. 1–61.

Basil, M., Schooler, C. and Reeves, B. (1991) 'Positive and negative political advertising: Effectiveness of ads and perception of candidates', in Biocca, F. (ed.) *Television and Political Advertising,* Vol. 1, Hillsdale: Lawrence Erlbaum, pp. 245–262.

Baumeister, R., Bratslavsky, E., Finkenhauer, C. and Vohs, K. (2001) 'Bad is stronger than good', *Review of General Psychology*, 5(4): 323–370.

Bègue, L., Beauvois, J-L., Courbet, D., Oberle, D., Lepage, J. and Duke, A. (in press) 'Personality predicts obedience in a Milgram paradigm', *Journal of Personality* (DOI: 10.1111/jopy.12104).

Belch, G. E. (1981) 'An examination of comparative and noncomparative television commercials: The effects of claim variation and repetition on cognitive responses and message acceptance', *Journal of Marketing Research*, 18(3): 333–349.

Belley, S. (2003) 'L'élection municipale de 2001 à Québec: L'interventionnisme municipal de la ville-centre contre le populisme fiscal des banlieues', *Recherches Sociographiques*, 44(2): 217–238.

Beltran, U. (2007) 'The combined effect of advertising and news coverage in the Mexican presidential campaign of 2000', *Political Communication* 24(1): 37–63.

Bennett, L. W. (2005) *News: The Politics of Illusion*, 6th edition, White Plains: Longman.

Benoit, K. (2007) 'Electoral laws as political consequences: Explaining the origins and change of electoral institutions', *Annual Review of Political Science*, 10: 363–390.

Benoit, K. and Laver M. (2007) 'Estimating party policy positions: Comparing expert surveys and hand-coded content analysis', *Electoral Studies*, 26: 90–107.

Benoit, W. L. (1999) *Seeing Spots: A Functional Analysis of Presidential Television Advertisements from 1952–1996*, New York: Praeger.

— (2004) 'Election outcome and topic of political campaign attack', *Southern Communication Journal*, 69: 348–355.

— (2007) *Communication in Political Campaigns*, New York: Peter Lang.

— (2013) 'A functional analysis of the 2011 English language Canadian prime minister debate', *Contemporary Argumentation & Debate*, 32: 45–69.

— (2014a) *A Functional Analysis of Presidential Television Advertisements*, 2nd ed., Lanham: Lexington Books.

— (2014b) *Political Election Debates: Informing Voters about Policy and Character*, Lanham: Lexington Books.

Benoit, W. L. and Airne, D. (2009) 'A functional analysis of non-presidential TV spots in Campaign 2004', *Human Communication*, 12(1): 91–117.

Benoit, W. L. and Benoit-Bryan, J. M. (2013) 'Debates come to the United Kingdom: A functional analysis of the 2010 British prime minister election debates', *Communication Quarterly*, 61(4): 463–478.

— (2014) 'A functional analysis of UK debates in Northern Ireland, Scotland, and Wales', *Western Journal of Communication*, 78(5): 653–667.

Benoit, W. L. and Compton, J. (2012) 'A functional analysis of 2012 presidential primary TV spots', Orlando: National Communication Association Conference.

Benoit, W. L. and Glantz, M. (2012) 'A functional analysis of 2008 general election presidential TV spots', *Speaker & Gavel*, 49(1): 1–19.

Benoit, W. L. and Henson, J. R. (2007) 'A functional analysis of the 2006 Canadian and 2007 Australian election debates', *Argumentation & Advocacy*, 44: 36–48.

Benoit, W. L. and Klyukovski, A. A. (2006) 'A functional analysis of the 2004 Ukrainian debates', *Argumentation*, 20: 209–225.

Benoit, W. L. and Rill, L. A. (2012) 'A functional analysis of 2008 presidential primary TV spots', *Speaker and Gavel*, 49(1): 55–71.

Benoit, W. L. and Shaefer, T. (2006) 'Functional theory and political discourse: Televised debates in Israel and the United States', *Journalism and Mass Communication Quarterly*, 83(2): 281–297.

Benoit, W. L., Blaney, J. R. and Pier, P. M. (1998a) *Campaign '96: A Functional Analysis of Acclaiming, Attacking, and Defending*, Westport, CT: Greenwood Publishing Group.

Benoit, W. L., Compton, J. and Phillips, B. (2013a) 'Newspaper coverage of prime minister elections in Australia, Canada, and the United Kingdom', *Human Communication*, 16(4): 201–213.

Benoit, W. L., Delbert, J., Sudbrock, L. A. and Vogt, C. (2010a) 'Functional analysis of 2008 Senate and gubernatorial TV spots', *Human Communication*, 13(2): 103–125.

Benoit, W. L., Furgerson, J., Seifert, J. and Sargardia, S. (2013b) 'Newspaper coverage of Senate, gubernatorial and mayoral elections', *Human Communication*, 16(4): 215–229.

Benoit, W. L., Hansen, G. J. and Verser, R. M. (2003a) 'A meta-analysis of the effects of viewing U.S. presidential debates', *Communication Monographs*, 70(4): 335–50.

Benoit, W. L., Hemmer, K. and Stein, K. (2010b) 'New York Times' coverage of American presidential primary campaigns, 1952–2004', *Human Communication*, 13(4): 259–280.

Benoit, W. L., Leshner, G. M. and Chattopadhyay, S. (2007) 'A meta-analysis of political advertising', *Human Communication*, 10(4): 507–522.

Benoit, W. L., McHale, J. P., Hansen, G. J., Pier, P. M. and McGuire, J. (2003b) *Campaign 2000: A Functional Analysis of the Presidential Campaign at the Dawn of the New Millennium*, Lanhan: Rowman and Littlefield.

Benoit, W. L., Stein, K. A. and Hansen, G. J. (2005) '*New York Times*' coverage of presidential campaigns, 1952–2000', *Journalism and Mass Communication Quarterly*, 82: 356–376.

Benoit, W. L., Webber, D. J. and Berman, J. (1998b) 'Effects of presidential debate watching and ideology on attitudes and knowledge', *Argumentation and Advocacy*, 34: 163–172.

Benze, J. G. and Declercq, E. R. (1985) 'Content of television spot ads for female candidates', *Journalism Quarterly*, 62: 278–283.

Bernhard, L. (2012) *Campaign Strategy in Direct Democracy*, Basingstoke: Palgrave Macmillan.

Betz, H.-G. (1994) *Radical Right-Wing Populism in Western Europe*, Basingstoke: Macmillan.

Blais, A. (2010) 'Making electoral democracy work', *Electoral Studies*, 29(1): 169–170.

Blais, A. and Nadeau, R. (1996) 'Measuring strategic voting: A two-step procedure', *Electoral Studies*, 15(1): 39–52.

Blais, A. and St-Vincent, S. L. (2011) 'Personality traits, political attitudes and the propensity to vote', *European Journal of Political Research*, 50(3): 395–417.

Boas, T. C. (2005) 'Television and neopopulism in Latin America: Media effects in Brazil and Peru', *Latin American Research Review*, 40(2): 27–49.

— (2009) 'Going positive or going plausible? Campaign advertising effects in Chile's 1988 plebiscite', paper presented at the World Congress of the International Political Science Association, Santiago 2009.

Borba, F. (2012) 'Negative campaign and electoral law in presidential Brazilian elections', paper presented at the XXII World Conference of the International Political Science Association, Madrid 2012.

— (2013) 'Regras eleitorais e democracia em 11 países da América Latina' [Electoral rules and democracy in 11 Latin American countries], *Observador Online*, 8(11): 1–29.

Borghans, L., Heckman, J. J., Golsteyn, B. H. H. and Meijers, H. (2009) 'Gender differences in risk aversion and ambiguity aversion', *Journal of the European Economic Association*, 7(2–3): 649–658.

Bouandel, Y. (2004) 'Algeria's presidential election of April 2004: A backward step in the democratisation process or a forward step towards stability?', *Third World Quarterly*, 25(8): 1525–1540.

Bowler, S. and Donovan, T. (2000) *Demanding Choices, Opinion, Voting and Direct Democracy*, Ann Arbor: University of Michigan Press.

— (2002) 'Do voters have a cue? Television advertisements as a source of information in citizen initiated referendum campaigns', *European Journal of Political Research*, 41: 777–793.

Bowler, S. and Farrell, D. (1992) *Electoral Strategies and Political Marketing*, London: Macmillan.

Box-Seffensmeier, J. M., Darmofal, D. and Farrell, C. A. (2009) 'The aggregate dynamics of campaigns', *The Journal of Politics*, 71: 309–323.

Braden, M. (1996) *Women Politicians and the Media*, Lexington: University Press of Kentucky.

Brader, T. (2005) 'Striking a responsive chord: How political ads motivate and persuade voters by appealing to emotions', *American Journal of Political Science*, 49(2): 388–405.

— (2006) *Campaigning of Hearts and Minds: How Emotional Appeals in Political Ads Work*, Chicago: The University of Chicago Press.

Brader, T. and Corrigan, B. (2006) 'How the emotional tenor of ad campaigns affect political participation', paper presented at the Annual Meeting of the American Political Science Association, Philadelphia, 2006.

Brady, H. and Johnston, R. (eds) (2006) *Capturing Campaign Effects*, Ann Arbor: The University of Michigan Press.

Brandenburg, H. (2005) 'Political bias in the Irish media: A quantitative study of campaign coverage during the 2002 general election', *Irish Political Studies*, 20(3): 297–322.

Brants, K., Kok, W. and van Praag, P. (1982) *De strijd om de Kiezersgunst, Verkiezingscampagnes in Nederland*, Amsterdam: Kobra.

Brazeal, L. M. and Benoit, W. L. (2001) 'A functional analysis of congressional television spots, 1986–2000', *Communication Quarterly*, 49: 436–454.

— (2006) 'On the spot: A functional analysis of congressional television spots, 1980–2004', *Communication Studies*, 57: 401–420.

Brians, C. L. and Wattenberg, M. P. (1996) 'Campaign issue knowledge and salience: Comparing reception from TV commercials, TV news and newspapers', *American Journal of Political Science*, 40: 172–193.

Broder, D. (2002) 'Congress can't recognize vital issues', *Spokesman-Review*, 6 October 2002. Online. Available http://www.news.google.com/newsp apers?nid=1314&dat=20021006&id=5LszAAAAIBAJ&sjid=rPIDAAA AIBAJ&pg=2818,4320236&hl=fr (accessed 14 April 2012).

Brooks, D. J. (2006) 'The resilient voter: Moving toward closure in the debate over negative campaigning and turnout', *The Journal of Politics*, 68(3): 684–696.

— (2010) 'A negativity gap? Vote gender, attack politics and participation in American elections', *Politics and Gender*, 6: 319–41.

Brooks, D. J. and Geer, J. G. (2007) 'Beyond negativity: The effects of incivility on the electorate', *American Journal of Political Science*, 51(1): 1–16.

Brooks, D. J. and Murov, M. (2012) 'Assessing accountability in a post-Citizens United era: The effects of attack ad sponsorship by unknown independent groups', *American Political Research*, 40(3): 383–418.

Brooks, S. (1997) 'Negativity is in the eye of the beholder: Voter response to negative advertising', Paper prepared for delivery at the annual meeting of the American Political Science Association, Chicago, 1997.

Browne, W. J. (2004) *MCMC Estimation in MLwiN*, London: Centre for Multilevel Modelling.

Budesheim, T. L., Houston, D. A. and DePaola, S. G. (1996) 'Persuasiveness of in-group and out-group political messages: The case of negative campaigning', *Journal of Personality and Social Psychology*, 70: 523–34.

Budge, I. and Farlie, F. (1983) *Voting and Party Competition*, London: Wiley.

Budge, I., Ezrow L. and McDonald, M. D. (2010) 'Ideology, party factionalism and policy change: An integrated dynamic theory', *British Journal of Political Science*, 40: 781–804.

Buell, E. H. and Sigelman, L. (2008) *Attack Politics, Negativity in Presidential Campaigns Since 1960*, Lawrence: University Press of Kansas.

Bullock, J. G. (2011) 'Elite influence on public opinion in an informed electorate', *American Political Science Review*, 105: 496–529.

Bystrom, D. G. (2004) 'Women as political communication source and audiences', in Kaid, L. L. (ed.) *Handbook of Political Communication Research*, Mahwah: Erlbaum, pp. 435–459.

— (2006) 'Advertising, web sites and media coverage: Gender and communication along the campaign trail', in Caroll, S. J. and Fox, R. L. (eds) *Gender and Elections: Shaping the Future of American Politics*, Cambridge: Cambridge University Press, pp. 168–188.

Bystrom, D. G. and Kaid, L. L. (2002) 'Are women candidates transforming campaign communication? A comparison of advertising videostyles in the 1990s', in Simon Rosenthal, C. (ed.) *Women Transforming Congress*, Norman: University of Oklahoma Press, pp. 146–169.

Bystrom, D. G. and Miller, J. (1999) 'Gendered communication styles and strategies in Campaign 1996: The videostyle of women and men candidates', in Kaid, L. L. and Bystrom, D. G. (eds) *The Electronic Election: Perspectives on the 1996 Campaign Communication*, Mahwah: Erlbaum, pp. 81–95.

Cacioppo, J. T. and Bernston, G. G. (1994) 'Relationship between attitudes and evaluative spaces: A critical review with emphasis on the separability of positive and negative substrates', *Psychological Bulletin*, 115(3): 401–423.

Campbell, A., Converse, P., Miller, W. and Stokes, D. (1960) *The American Voter*, New York: Wiley.

Campbell, J. E. (2000) *The American Campaign: U.S. Presidential Campaigns and the National Vote*, College Station: Texas A and M Press.

Cappella, J. N. and Jamieson, K. H. (1997) *Spiral of Cynicism: The Press and the Public Good*, New York: Oxford University Press.

Caprara, G. V., Barbanelli, C. and Zimbardo, P. (2002) 'When parsimony subdues distinctiveness: Simplified public perceptions of politicians' personality', *Political Psychology*, 23(1): 77–95.

Caprara, G. V., Barbanelli, C., Fraley, C. and Vecchione, M. (2007) 'The simplicity of politicians' personalities across political context: An anomalous replication', *International Journal of Psychology*, 42(6): 393–405.

Cardona, E. (unpublished manuscript) 'Aproximación a los efectos de la negatividad político-mediática sobre la decisión electoral. El caso de la campaña presidencial uruguaya en 2009', Facultad de Ciencias Sociales-Universidad de la República (Uruguay).

Çarkoğlu, A. (2009) 'The March 2009 local elections in Turkey: A signal for takers or the inevitable beginning of the end for AKP?', *South European Society and Politics*, 14(3): 295–316.

Carlson, T. and Djupsund, G. (2001) 'Old wine in new bottles? The 1999 Finnish election campaign on the Internet', *The Harvard International Journal of Press/Politics*, 6(1): 68–87.

Carlson, T. and Strandberg, K. (2008) 'Riding the Web 2.0 wave: Candidates on YouTube in the 2007 Finnish national elections', *Journal of Information Technology & Politics*, 5(2): 159–174.

Carraro, L. and Castelli, L. (2010) 'The implicit and explicit effects of negative political campaigns: Is the source really blamed?' *Political Psychology*, 31: 617–645.

Carraro, L., Gawronski, B. and Castelli, L. (2010) 'Losing on all fronts: The effects of negative versus positive person-based campaigns on implicit and explicit evaluations of political candidates', *British Journal of Social Psychology*, 49: 453–470.

Carroll, J. S. and Johnson, E. J. (1990) *Decision Research: A Field Guide*, Beverly Hills: Sage.

Carsey, T. M., Jackson, R. A., Stewart, M. and Nelson, J. P. (2011) 'Strategic candidates, campaign dynamics, and campaign advertising in gubernatorial races', *State Politics & Policy Quarterly*, 11(3): 269–298.

Cartwright, D. and Harary, F. (1956) 'Structural balance: A generalisation of Heider's Theory', *Psychological Review*, 63: 277–293.

Carty, R. K. and Eagles, M. (1999) 'Do local campaigns matter? Campaign spending, the local canvass and party support in Canada', *Electoral Studies*, 18: 69–87.

Case, W. (2001) 'Malaysia's resilient pseudodemocracy', *Journal of Democracy*, 12(1): 43–57.

Center for Responsive Politics (2012) '2012 Presidential Race'. Online. Available http://www.opensecrets.org/pres12/index.php?ql3#out (accessed 12 November 2012).

Ceron, A. and D'Adda, G. (2013) 'Enlightening the voters: The effectiveness of alternative electoral strategies in the 2013 Italian election monitored through (sentiment) analysis of Twitter posts', paper presented at the General Conference of the European Consortium for Political Research, Bordeaux, 2013.

Chang, C. (2000) 'Political advertising in Taiwan and the U.S.: A cross-cultural comparison of the 1996 presidential election campaigns', *Asian Journal of Communication*, 10(1): 1–17.

Chang, C. and Hitchon, J. C. B. (2004) 'When does gender count? Further insights into gender schematic processing of female candidates' political advertisements', *Sex Roles*, 51(3/4): 197–208.

Cheibub, J. A. (2007) *Presidentialism, Parliamentarism, and Democracy*, Cambridge: Cambridge University Press.

Cho, S. and Benoit, W. L. (2006) '2004 presidential campaign messages: A functional analysis of press releases from President Bush and Senator Kerry', *Public Relations Review*, 32(1): 47–52.

Choi, Y. S. and Benoit, W. L. (2009) 'A functional analysis of French and South Korean debates', *Speaker and Gavel*, 46: 59–78.

— (2013) 'A functional analysis of the 2007 and 2012 French presidential debates', *Journal of Intercultural Communication Research*, 42(3): 215–227.

Cholova, B. (2013) 'Anti-establishment reform parties in Bulgaria: A decade of dominant populist rhetoric', paper presented at the General Conference of the European Consortium for Political Research, Bordeaux, 2013.

Chubb, B. (1992) *The Government and Politics of Ireland*, London: Longman.

Chung, K., Wallace, J., Kim, S.-Y., Kalyanasundaram, S., Andalman, A. S., Davidson, T. J., Mirzabekov, J. J., Zalocusky, K. A., Mattis, J., Denisin, A. K., Pak, S., Bernstein, H., Ramakrishnan, C., Grosenick, L., Gradinaru, V. and Deisseroth, K. (2013) 'Structural and molecular interrogation of intact biological systems', *Nature*, 497: 322–339.

Civettini, A. J. W. and Redlawsk, D. P. (2009) 'Voters, emotions, and memory', *Political Psychology*, 30(1): 125–151.

Çınar, M. (2011) 'Turkey's present ancient regime and the Justice and Development Party', in Caiser, M. and Jongerder, J. (eds) *Nationalisms and Politics in Turkey*, Oxon: Routledge, pp. 13–28.

Claassen, R. L. (2011) 'Political awareness and electoral campaigns: Maximum effects for minimum citizens?', *Political Behavior*, 33: 203–223.

Clarke, H., Sanders, D., Stewart, M. and Whiteley, P. F. (2003) *Content Analysis of Newspaper Coverage, British General Election, 2001*, Colchester: UK Data Archive.

Constante Fiscal, E. A. (2012) *Análisis de las estrategias de marketing político implementadas en la campaña electoral presidencial: Ecuador 2006*, Doctoral Dissertation, Universidad Politécnica Salesiana, Quito.

Cook, N. (2011) 'Cote d'Ivoire's post-election crisis', United States Congressional Research Service, 5 April 2011, RS21989. Online. Available http://www.refworld.org/docid/4db91c5e2.html (accessed 3 October 2014).

Costa, P. T. and McCrae, R. R. (1992) *NEO PI-R Professional Manual*, Odessa: Psychological Assessment Resources, Inc.

Costello, A. (2014) 'The Fiscal Stability Treaty referendum 2012', *Irish Political Studies*, 29(3): 457–470.

Coulter, K. (2008) 'The tri-mediation model of persuasion: a case for negative political advertising?', *International Journal of Advertising*, 27(5): 1–22.

Cox, G. W. and Shugart, M. S. (1996) 'Strategic voting under proportional representation', *Journal of Law, Economics, and Organization*, 12(2): 299–324.

Cox, G. W. and Thies, M. F. (2000) 'How much does money matter? 'Buying' votes in Japan, 1967–1990', *Comparative Political Studies*, 33(1): 37–57.

Craig, S. J. and Kane, J. G. (2000) 'Winning and losing, sour grapes, and negative ads: The impact of election campaigns on political support', paper presented at the annual meeting of the Midwest Political Science Association, Chicago, 2000.

Craig, S. J., Kane, J. G. and Gainous, J. (2005) 'Issue-related learning in a Gubernatorial campaign: A panel study', *Political Communication*, 22: 483–503.

Criegler, A., Just, M. and Belt, T. (2006) 'The three faces of negative campaigning: The democratic implications of attack ads, cynical news, and fear-arousing message', in Redlawsk, D. P. (ed.) *Feeling Politics: Emotion in Political Information Processing*, New York: Palgrave, pp. 135–163.

Curini, L. (2011) 'Negative campaigning in no-cabinet alternation systems: Ideological closeness and blames of corruption in Italy and Japan using party manifesto data', *Japanese Journal of Political Science*, 12(3): 399–420.

Curini, L. and Martelli, P. (2010) 'Ideological proximity and valence competition: Negative campaigning through allegation of corruption in the Italian legislative arena from 1946 to 1994', *Electoral Studies*, 29(4): 636–647.

Cyr, J. (2013) 'Que veinte años no es nada: Hugo Chávez, las elecciones de 2012 y el continuismo político venezolano', *Revista de Ciencia Política*, 33(1): 375–391.

D'Adamo, O. and Garcia-Beaudoux, V. (2004) 'Campañas electorales y efectos sobre la decisión de voto. Un análisis de la campaña para las elecciones presidenciales 2003 en Argentina', *América Latina Hoy*, 38: 163–179.

da Silveira, B. S. and de Mello, J. M. P. (2011) 'Campaign advertising and election outcomes: Quasi-natural experiment evidence from Gubernatorial elections in Brazil', *Review of Economic Studies*, 78: 590–612.

Dabelko, K. L. and Herrnson, P. S. (1997) 'Women's and men's campaigns for the U.S. House of Representatives', *Political Research Quarterly*, 50(1): 121–135.

Dachs, H. (1998) 'Wahlkampfkommunikation in der Zweiten Republik. Kontinuitäten und Brüche', in Panagl, O. (ed.) *Fahnenwörter der Politik. Kontinuitäten und Brüche*, Vienna: Böhlau Verlag, pp. 169–182.

Dalton, R. J. (2008) *Citizen Politics: Public Opinion and Political Parties in Advanced Industrial Democracies*, Washington, DC: CQ Press.

Damore, D. F. (2002) 'Candidate strategy and the decision to go negative', *Political Research Quarterly*, 55(3): 669–685.

Darcey, R. and Laver, M. (1990) 'Referendum dynamics and the Irish Divorce Amendment', *The Public Opinion Quarterly*, 54: 1–20.

Dassonneville, R. (2010) 'Negative campaigning effects: An analysis of the Belgian Election Survey for the Flemish Regional Election of June 2009', paper presented at the 9th Belgian-Dutch Political Science Conference, Leven, 27–28 May 2010.

Davis, M. L. and Ferrantino, M. (1996) 'Towards a positive theory of political rhetoric: Why do politicians lie?', *Public Choice*, 88(1/2): 1–13.

de Almeida, P. T. and Freire, A. (2005) 'Two overwhelming victories of the Portuguese left: The 2004 European election and the 2005 legislative election', *South European Society and Politics*, 10(3): 451–464.

de Nooy, W. (2011) 'Networks of action and events over time: A multilevel discrete-time event history model for longitudinal network data', *Social Networks*, 33(1): 31–40.

de Nooy, W. and Kleinnijenhuis, J. (2013) 'Polariziation in the media during an election campaign: A dynamic network model predicting support and attack among political actors', *Political Communication*, 30: 117–138.

de Vreese, C. H. and Semetko, H. A. (2004) *Political Campaigning in Referendums: Framing the Referendum Issue*, London: Routledge.

— (2002) 'Cynical and engaged: Strategic campaign coverage, public opinion, and mobilization in a referendum', *Communication Research*, 29(6): 615–641.

Dean, D. (2005) 'Fear, negative campaigning and loathing: The case of the UK election campaign', *Journal of Marketing Management*, 21(9–10): 1067–1078.

Deisseroth, K., Feng, G., Majewska, A. K., Miesenböck, G., Ting, A. and Schnitzer, M. J. (2006) 'Next-generation optical technologies for illuminating genetically targeted brain circuits', *The Journal of Neuroscience*, 26(41): 10380–10386.

Delli Carpini, M. and Keeter, S. (1996) *What Americans Know About Politics and Why it Matters*, New Haven: Yale University Press.

Denisov, Y. (1996) 'Pochemy Rossiyane ne priemlyut zolotoi serediy, ili ob umerennosti v politike [Why Russians don't accept the happy middle, or on moderation in politics]', *Polis*, 1: 177–180.

Denver, D. (2007) *Elections and Voters in Britain*, Houndmills: Palgrave Macmillan.

Deschouwer, K. (2004) 'Political parties and their reactions to the erosion of voter loyalty in Belgium: Caught in a trap', in Mair, P., Müller, W. C. and Plasser, F. (eds) *Political Parties and Electoral Change: Party Responses to Electoral Markets*, London: Sage, pp. 179–206.

Desposato, S. (2007) 'The impact of campaign messages in new democracies: Results from an experiment in Brazil', Manuscript, University of California, San Diego.

Deželan, T. and Maksuti, A. (2012) 'Slovenian election posters as a medium of political communication: An informative or persuasive campaign tool?', *Communication, Politics & Culture*, 45: 140–159.

Di Bonito, I. (2014) 'El uso de Facebook durante las campañas electorales. Reflexiones sobre las elecciones catalanas de 2010 y 2012', *Revista de la Asociación Española de Investigadores en Comunicación*, 1(1): 26–34.

Diamond, E. and Bates, S. (1992) *The Spot: The Rise of Political Advertising on Television*, Boston: MIT Press.

Dickenson, J. (2014) '"The politics of political advertising" in Australia and Britain, 1970–1989', *Australian Journal of Politics and History*, 60(2): 241–256.

Digman, J. (1990) 'Personality structure: Emergence of the Five-Factor Model', *Annual Review of Psychology*, 41: 417–440.

Dille, B. and Young, M. D. (2000) 'The conceptual complexity of presidents Carter and Clinton: An automated content analysis of temporal stability and source bias', *Political Psychology*, 21(3): 587–596.

Dinan, D. (1986) 'Constitution and Parliament', in Girvin, B. and Sturm, R. (eds) *Politics and Society in Contemporary Ireland*, Aldershot: Gower, pp. 141–168.

Ditonto, T. M., Hamilton, A. J. and Redlawsk, D. P. (2014) 'Gender stereotypes, information search, and voting behavior in political campaigns', *Political Behavior*, 36: 335–358.

Dolez, B. and Laurent, A. (2007) 'Une primaire à la française: La designation de Ségolène Royal par le parti socialiste', *Revue Française de Science Politique*, 57(2): 133–161.

Dolezal, M. and Zeglovits, E. (2014) 'Almost an earthquake: The Austrian parliamentary election of 2013', *West European Politics*, 37(3): 644–652.

Dolezal, M., Ennser-Jedenastik, L., Müller, W. C. and Winkler, A. K. (2014) 'How parties compete for votes: A test of saliency theory', *European Journal of Political Research*, 53(1): 57–76.

Dolezal, M., Haselmayer, M., Johann, D., Thomas, K. and Ennser-Jedenastik, L. (2014) 'Negative Campaigning' in Kritzinger, S., Müller, W. C. and Schönbach, K. (eds) *Die Nationalratswahl 2013: Wie Parteien, Medien und Wählerschaft zusammenwirken*, Wien: Böhlau, pp. 99–111.

Doron, G. and On, U. (1983) 'A rational choice model of campaign strategy', in Arian, A. (ed.) *The Elections in Israel, 1981*, Tel Aviv: Ramot Publishing, pp. 213–231.

Downs, A. (1957) *An Economic Theory of Democracy*, New York: Harper.

Druckman, J. and Kam, C. (2011) 'Students as experimental participants. A defense of the "narrow data base"', in Druckman, J., Green, D., Kuklinski, J. and Lupia, A. (eds) *Cambridge Handbook of Experimental Political Science*, New York: Cambridge University Press, pp. 41–57.

Druckman, J. N., Green, D., Kuklinski, J. and Lupia, A. (2011) 'Experiments: An introduction to core concepts', in Druckman, J. N., Green, D., Kuklinski, J. and Lupia, A. (eds) *Cambridge Handbook of Experimental Political Science*, Cambridge: Cambridge University Press, pp. 19–41.

Druckman, J. N., Kifer, M. J. and Parkin, M. (2010) 'Timeless strategy meets new medium: Going negative on congressional campaign web sites, 2002–2006', *Political Communication*, 27(1): 88–103.

Duch, R. M., May, J. and Armstrong, D. A. (2010) 'Coalition-directed voting in multiparty democracies', *American Political Science Review*, 104(4): 698–719.

Dunaway, J. (2008) 'Markets, ownership, and the quality of campaign news coverage', *The Journal of Politics*, 70(4): 1193–1202.

Dunn, S. W. (2009) 'Candidate and media agenda setting in the 2005 Virginia gubernatorial election', *Journal of Communication*, 59(3): 635–652.

Dyczok, M. (2005) 'Breaking through the information blockade: Election and revolution in Ukraine 2004', *Canadian Slavonic Papers/Revue Canadienne des Slavistes*, 47(3–4): 241–264.

Eagly, A. H. and Chaiken, S. (1993) *The Psychology of Attitudes*, Fort Worth: Harcourt Brace Jovanovich College Publishers.

Eagly, A. H and Johnson, B. T. (1990) 'Gender and leadership style: A meta-analysis', *Psychological Bulletin*, 108(2): 233–256.

Edegoh, L. O., Asemah, E. S. and Ezebuenyi, E. E. (2013) 'Television as a medium of political advertising during elections in Anambra State, Nigeria', *Asian Journal of Social Sciences and Humanities*, 2(3): 375–385.

Eemeren, F., Meuffels, B. and Verburg, M. (2000) 'The (un)reasonableness of ad hominem fallacies', *Journal of Language and Social Psychology*, 19(4): 416–435.

Elenbaas, M. and de Vreese, C. (2008) 'The effects of strategic news on political cynicism and vote choice', *Journal of Communication*, 58(3): 550–567.

Eligür, B. (2009) 'Turkey's March 2009 local elections', *Turkish Studies*, 10(3): 469–496.

Elmelund-Præstekær, C. (2008) 'Negative campaigning in a multiparty system', *Representation*, 44(1): 27–39.

— (2009) Kammertoner og unoder I dansk valgkamp, Partiernes positive og negative, person og politikfokuserede kampagner 1994–2007, Syddansk Universitet: Syddansk Universitetsforlag.

— (2010) 'Beyond American negativity: Toward a general understanding of the determinants of negative campaigning', *European Political Science Review*, 2(1): 137–156.

— (2011) 'Issue ownership as a determinant of negative campaigning', *International Political Science Review*, 32(2): 209–221.

Elmelund-Præstekær, C. and Svensson, H. M. (2014) 'Ebbs and flows of negative campaigning: A longitudinal study of contextual factors' influence on Danish campaign rhetoric', *European Journal of Communication*, 29(2): 230–239.

Elvestad, E. and Blekesaune, A. (2008) 'Newspaper readers in Europe: A multilevel study of individual and national differences', *European Journal of Communication*, 23(4): 425–447.

Elzinga, D. J. and G. Voerman (2002) *Om de stembus, Verkiezingsaffiches 1918–1998*. Den Haag: SDU.

Emruli, S., Zejneli, T. and Agai, F. (2011) 'YouTube and political communication – Macedonian case', *International Journal of Computer Science Issues*, 8(4): 460–466.

Erickson, L. (1997) 'Might more women make a difference? Gender, party, and ideology among Canada's parliamentary candidates', *Canadian Journal of Political Science*, 30(4): 663–688.

Evans, H. K., Cordova, V. and Sipole, S. (2014) 'Twitter style: An analysis of how House candidates used Twitter in their 2012 campaigns', *Political Science & Politics*, 47(2): 454–462.

Eysenck, H. (1976) *Sex and Personality*, Austin: University of Texas Press.

Faas, T. and Maier, J. (2004) 'Mobilisierung, verstärkung, konversion? Ergebnisse eines experiments zur wahrnehmung der fernsehduelle im vorfeld der bundestagswahl 2002', *Politische Vierteljahresschrift*, 45(1): 55–72.

Fact Check (2012a) 'Did Gingrich 'slash' federal spending?', 20 January 2012. Online. Available http://www.factcheck.org/2012/01/did-gingrich-slash-federal-spending/ (accessed 21 March 2012).

— (2012b) 'Florida ad war: Mitt pounds Newt', 26 January 2012. Online. Available http://www.factcheck.org/2012/01/florida-ad-war-mitt-pounds-newt/ (accessed 21 March 2012).

Fan, D. P. (1996) 'Predictions of the Bush-Clinton-Perot presidential race from the press', *Political Analysis*, 6(1): 67–105.

Farrell, D. M. (2005) 'Campaign modernization and the West European party', in Luther, K. R. and Müller, F. (eds) *Political Parties in the New Europe: Political and Analytical Challenges*, Oxford: Oxford University Press, pp. 63–83.

Farrell, D. M. and Schmitt-Beck, R. (eds) (2002) *Do Political Campaigns Matter? Campaign Effects in Elections and Referendums*, New York: Routledge.

— (2008) *Non-Party Actors in Electoral Politics: The Role of Interest Groups and Independent Citizens in Contemporary Election Campaigns*, Baden Baden: Nomos.

Fernandez-Albertos, J. and Martinez i Coma, F. (2014) 'Los efectos de la campaña electoral', in Anduiza, E., Bosch, A., Orriols, L. and Rico, G. (eds) *Elecciones Generales 2011*, Madrid: Centro de Investigaciones Sociologicas, pp. 103–125.

Fernández, O. (1994) 'Costa Rica. La reafirmación del bipartidismo', *Nueva Sociedad*, 131: 4–10.

Festinger, L. (1962 [1957]) *A Theory of Cognitive Dissonance*, London: Tavistock.

Finch, C. M. (2002) 'Mongolia in 2001: Political consolidation and continued economic reform', *Asian Survey*, 42(1): 39–45.

Finkel, S. E. and Geer, J. G. (1998) 'A spot check: Casting doubt on the demobilizing effect of attack advertising', *American Journal of Political Science*, 42(2): 573–595.

Finkel, S. E. and Schrott, P. R. (1995) 'Campaign effects on voter choice in the German election of 1990', *British Journal of Political Science*, 25(3): 349–377.

Flowers, J. F., Haynes, A. A. and Crespin, M. H. (2003) 'The media, the campaign, and the message', *American Journal of Political Science*, 47(2): 259–273.

Ford, K. J., Schmitt, N., Schechtman, S. L., Hults, B. M. and Doherty, M. L. (1989) 'Process tracing methods: Contributions, problems, and neglected research questions', *Organizational Behavior and Human Decision Processes*, 43: 75–117.

Fourie, L. (2011) 'The 2011 local elections campaigns in the Tlokwe municipality, North-West Province: Enhancing participatory governance?', *Communitas*, (16): 131–149.

Fourie, L. and du Plessis, N. (2011) 'The function of electoral communication in a developing democracy: The case of South Africa', *Journal of Public Affairs*, 11(4): 255–264.

Fowler, E. F. and Ridout, T. N. (2009) 'Local television and newspaper coverage of political advertising', *Political Communication*, 2(2): 119–136.

—   (2010) 'Advertising trends in 2010', *The Forum: A Journal of Applied Research in Contemporary Politics*, 8(4): 1–16.

—   (2012) 'Negative, angry and ubiquitous: Political advertising in 2012', *The Forum: A Journal of Applied Research in Contemporary Politics*, 10(4): 51–56.

Fowler, J. and Schreiber, D. (2008) 'Biology, politics and the emerging science of human nature', *Science*, 322(5903): 912–914.

Fraenkel, J. (2000) 'The triumph of the non-idealist intellectuals? An investigation of Fiji's 1999 election results', *Australian Journal of Politics & History*, 46(1): 86–109.

Francia, P. L. and Herrnson, P. S. (2007) 'Keeping it professional: The influence of political consultants on candidate attitudes toward negative campaigning', *Politics & Policy*, 35(2): 246–272.

Franklin, M., Marsh, M. and McLaren, L. (1994) 'Uncorking the bottle: Popular opposition to European unification in the wake of Maastricht', *Journal Of Common Market Studies*, 32: 455–72.

Franz, M. M., Freedman, P., Goldstein, K. and Ridout, T. N. (2008) *Campaign Advertising and American Democracy*, Philadelphia: Temple University Press.

Freedman, P. and Goldstein, K. (1999) 'Measuring media exposure and the effects of negative campaigning ads', *American Journal of Political Science* 43(4): 1189–1208.

—   (2002) 'Lessons learned: Campaign advertising in the 2000 elections', *Political Communication*, 19: 5–28.

Freiberger, O. (2009) 'Negative campaigning: Polemics against Brahmins in a Buddhist Sutta', *Religions of South Asia* 3(1): 61–67.

Freidenberg, F. (2007) 'Análisis de las elecciones en América Latina', Universidad de Salamanca.

—   (2010) 'Elecciones primarias en Panama: Claves para el diagnostico, buenas practices, y estrategias de reforma (1994–2009)', *Cuadernos de Desarrollo Humano*, 1: 73–138.

Fridkin, K. L. and Kenney, P. J. (2004) 'Do negative message work? The impact of negativity on citizens' evaluations of candidates', *American Politics Research*, 32: 570–605.

— (2008) 'The dimensions of negative messages', *American Politics Research*, 36(5): 694–723.

— (2009) 'The role of gender stereotypes in US senate campaigns, *Politics and Gender*, 5(3): 301–324.

— (2011a) 'Variability in citizens' reactions to different types of negative campaigns', *American Journal of Political Science*, 55(2): 307–325.

— (2011b) 'The role of candidate traits in campaigns', *The Journal of Politics*, 73(1): 61–73.

— (2012) 'The impact of negative campaigning on citizens' actions and attitudes', in Semetko, H. A. and Scammell, M. (eds) *The SAGE Handbook of Political Communication*, Los Angeles: Sage, pp. 173–185.

Fridkin, K. L., Kenney, P. J. and Woodall, G. S. (2009) 'Bad for men, better for women: The impact of stereotypes during negative campaigns', *Political Behavior*, 31(1): 53–77.

Fridkin Kahn, K. (1993) 'Gender differences in campaign messages: The political advertisement of men and women candidates for U.S. Senate', *Political Research Quarterly*, 46(3): 481–502.

Gallagher, M. (1996) 'Ireland: The referendum as a conservative device?' in Gallagher, M. and Uleri, P. V. (eds) *The Referendum Experience in Europe*, Basingstoke: Palgrave Macmillan, pp. 86–105.

— (2004) 'Referendum e campagne referendarie in Irlanda', *Quaderni dell'Osservatorio Elettorale*, 52(1): 61–82.

— (2012) 'The Oireachtas: President and parliament', in Coakley, J. and Gallagher, M. (eds) *Politics in the Republic of Ireland*, London: Routledge, pp. 198–229.

Gallagher, M. and Uleri, P. V. (1996) *The Referendum Experience in Europe*, Basingstoke: Palgrave Macmillan.

Gallagher, M., Laver, M. J. and Mair, P. (2005) *Representative Government in Modern Europe*, Boston: McGraw-Hill.

Gallucci, M. (2005) 'Argumentación y funciones estratégicas en el discurso político venezolano: El cierre de campaña del referéndum revocatorio presidencial', *Revista Latinoamericana de Estudios del Discurso*, 5(2): 49–75.

Galtung, J. and Ruge, M. H. (1965) 'The structure of foreign news', *Journal of Peace Research*, 2(1): 64–91.

Gamson, W. A. and Meyer, D. S. (1996) 'Framing political opportunity', in McAdam, D., McCarthy, J. D. and Zald, M. N. (eds) *Comparative Perspectives on Social Movements: Political Opportunities, Mobilizing Structures, and Cultural Framings*, Cambridge: Cambridge University Press, pp. 275–290.

García-Beaudoux, V. and D'Adamo, O. (2007) 'El anuncio político televisivo como herramienta de comunicación electoral. Análisis de caso: Los anuncios de la campaña para las elecciones legislativas de marzo de 2004 en España', *Revista de Psicología Social*, 22(1): 45–61.

Garramone, G. M. (1984) 'Voter response to negative political ads', *Journalism Quarterly*, 6: 250–59.

— (1985) 'Effects of negative political advertising: The roles of sponsor and rebuttal', *Journal of Broadcasting and Electronic Media*, 29: 147–59.

Garramone, G. M., Atkin, C. T., Pinkleton, B. E. and Cole, R. T. (1990) 'Effects of negative political advertising in the political process', *Journal of Broadcasting & Electronic Media*, 34: 299–311.

Geer, J. G. (2006) *In Defense of Negativity: Attack Ads in Presidential Campaigns*, Chicago: University of Chicago Press.

— (2009) *Fanning the Flames: The News Media's Role in the Rise of Negativity in Presidential Campaigns*, John F. Kennedy School of Government, Harvard University.

— (2012) 'The news media and the rise of negativity in presidential campaigns', *PS: Political Science & Politics*, 45(03): 422–427.

Gerber, A., Huber, G., Doherty, D. and Dowling, C. (2011) 'The Big Five personality traits in the political arena', *Annual Review of Political Science*, 14: 265–287.

Gidengil, E., Blais, A., Nevitte, N. and Nadeau, R. (2002) 'Priming and campaign context: Evidence from recent Canadian elections', in Farrell, D. M. and Schmitt-Beck, R. (eds) *Do Political Campaigns Matter? Campaign effects in elections and referendums*, New York: Routledge, pp. 76–91.

Glantz, M., Benoit, W. L. and Airne, D. (2013) 'A functional analysis of 2012 US presidential primary debates', *Argumentation and Advocacy*, 49: 275–285.

Globetti, S. and Heterington, M. J. (2000) 'The negative implications of anti-government campaign rhetoric', paper presented at the annual meeting of the Midwest Political Science Association, Chicago, 2000.

Glover, S. K. (2000) 'Namibia's recent elections: Something new or same old story?', *South African Journal of International Affairs*, 7(2): 141–149.

Golder, S. N. (2006) *The Logic of Pre-Electoral Coalition Formation*, Columbus: Ohio State University Press.

Goldstein, K. (1997) 'Political commercials in the 1996 election', paper presented at the annual meeting of the Midwest Political Science Association, Chicago, 1997.

Goldstein, K. and Freedman, P. (2000) 'New evidence for new arguments: Money and advertising in the 1996 Senate elections', *Journal of Politics*, 62: 1087–1108.

— (2002) 'Lessons learned: Campaign advertising in the 2000 elections', *Political Communication*, 19(1): 5–28.

Gordon, A., Shafie, D. M. and Crigler, A. N. (2003) 'Is negative advertising effective for female candidates? An experiment in voters' uses of gender stereotypes', *The International Journal of Press/Politics*, 8(3): 35–53.

Gosling, S., Rentfrow, P. and Swann, W. (2003) 'A very brief measure of the Big-Five personality domains', *Journal of Research in Personality*, 37(6): 504–528.

Grabe, M. E. and Kamhawi, R. (2006) 'Hard wired for negative news? Gender differences in processing broadcast news', *Communication Research*, 33(5): 346–369.

Grimmer, J. (2010) 'A Bayesian hierarchical topic model for political texts: Measuring expressed agendas in Senate press releases', *Political Analysis*, 18(1): 1–35.

Grimmer, J. and Stewart, B. M. (2013) 'Text as data: The promise and pitfalls of automatic content analysis methods for political texts', *Political Analysis* (DOI: 10.1093/pan/mps028).

Grossmann, M. (2009) 'What (or who) makes campaigns negative', paper presented at the Annual Meeting Midwest American Political Science Association, Chicago, 2009.

Gupta, M. P. (2000) 'Negative political advertising: Some effects from the 13th Indian general elections 1999', *Global Business Review*, 1(2): 249–277.

Gurian, Paul-Henri (1996) 'Eliminating Opponents in Presidential Nomination Campaigns', paper presented at the Annual Meeting of the Southern Political Science Association, Atlanta: Georgia, November 7–9.

Hai, L. H. and Ming, O. K. (2006) 'Electoral campaigning in Malaysia', in Schafferer, C. (ed.) *Election campaigning in East and Southeast Asia: Globalization of Political Marketing*, Aldershot: Ashgate, pp. 55–78.

Haigron, D. (2012) 'British party election broadcasts (2001, 2005 and 2010): Ideological framing, storytelling, individualisation', *InMedia*, 2.

Håkansson, N. (1999) *Valretorik: Om Politiskt Språk i Partipropagandan*, Göteborg: Statsvetenskapliga institutionen Göteborgs universitet.

— (2006) 'The same chatter wherever you go? Media logic and politicians' discourse in TV election debates', paper presented at the International Political Science Association World Congress, Fukuoka, 2006.

Hale, J. F., Fox, J. C. and Farmer, R. (1996) 'Negative advertisements in U.S. Senate campaigns: The influence of campaign context', *Social Science Quarterly*, 77(2): 329–343.

Hallin, D. C. and Mancini, P. (2004) *Comparing Media Systems: Three Models of Media and Politics*, Cambridge: Cambridge University Press.

Hänggli, R. (2010) 'Frame building and framing effects in direct-democratic campaigns', PhD thesis, University of Zurich.

Hänggli, R. and Kriesi, H. (2010) 'Political framing strategies and their impact on media framing in a Swiss direct-democratic campaign', *Political Communication*, 27(2): 141–157.

Hansen, K. M. and Pedersen, R. T. (2008) 'Negative campaigning in a multiparty system', *Scandinavian Political Studies*, 31(4): 408–427.

Haramija, P. and Poropat Darrer, J. (2014) 'Negative election campaigns – causes, effects and ethical dimension: Sample taken from the 2013 local self-management elections in the Republic of Croatia', *Obnovljeni život*, 69(1): 19–36.

Harmon-Jones, E., Gable, P. A. and Price, T. F. (2013) 'Does negative affect always narrow and positive affect always broaden the mind? Considering the influence of motivational intensity on cognitive scope', *Current Directions in Psychological Science*, 22(4): 301–7.

Harrington, J. and Hess, G. (1996). 'A spatial theory of positive and negative campaigning', *Games and Economic Behavior*, 17: 209–229.

Harris, D. (2003) 'Post-conflict elections or post-elections conflict: Sierra Leone 2002 and patterns of voting in Sub-Saharan Africa', *Cadernos de Estudos Africanos*, (5/6): 39–49.

Harris, P., Fury, D. and Lock, A. (2005) 'The evolution of a campaign: Tracking press coverage and party press releases through the 2001 UK general election', *Journal of Public Affairs*, 5 (1): 99–111.

—   (2006) 'Do political parties and the press influence the public agenda? A content analysis of press coverage of the 2001 UK general election', *Journal of Political Marketing*, 5(3): 1–28.

Hartlyn, J. (1990) 'The Dominican Republic's disputed elections', *Journal of Democracy*, 1(4): 92–103.

Hatemi, P. and McDermott, R. (eds) (2011) *Man is by Nature a Political Animal: Evolution, Biology, and Politics*, Chicago: The University of Chicago Press.

Hatfield, E., Cacioppo, J. T. and Rapson, R. L. (1994) *Emotional Contagion*, Cambridge: Cambridge University Press.

Hatfield, J. D. and Weider-Hatfield, D. (1978) 'The comparative utility of three types of behavioral units for interaction analysis', *Communication Monographs*, 45(1): 44–50.

Hayes, A. F. and Krippendorff, K. (2007) 'Answering the call for a standard reliability measure for coding data', *Communication Methods and Measures*, 1(1): 77–89.

Haynes, A. A. and Rhine, S. L. (1998) 'Attack politics in presidential nomination campaigns: An examination of the frequency and determinants of intermediated negative messages against opponents', *Political Research Quarterly*, 51(3): 691–721.

Haynes, A. A., Flowers, J. and Harman, J. (2006) 'Going negative: Press response to candidate attack messages', *Journal of Political Marketing*, 5(1–2): 105–125.

Haynes, A. A., Flowers, J. F. and Gurian, P. H. (2002) 'Getting the message out: Candidate communication strategy during the invisible primary', *Political Research Quarterly*, 55(3): 633–652.

Hayward, K. (2002) 'Not a nice surprise: An analysis of the debate surrounding the 2001 Referendum on the Treaty of Nice in the Republic of Ireland', *Irish Studies in International Affairs*, 13: 167–186.

Heider, F. (1946) 'Attitudes and cognitive organization', *Journal of Psychology*, 21: 107–12.

— (1958) *The Psychology of Interpersonal Relations*, New York: John Wiley and Sons.

Heinisch, R. (2003) 'Success in opposition – failure in government: Explaining the performance of right-wing populist parties in public office', *West European Politics*, 26(3): 91–130.

Helbling, M. and Tresch, A. (2011) 'Measuring party positions and issue salience from media coverage: Discussing and cross-validating new indicators', *Electoral Studies*, 30(1): 174–83.

Henson, J. R. and Benoit, W. L. (2010) '"Because I said so": A Functional Theory analysis of evidence in political TV spots', *Speaker and Gavel*, 47(1): 1–15.

Heper, M. and Sayarı, S. (2008) *Türkiye'de Liderler ve Demokrasi*, İstanbul: Kitap Yayınevi.

Heron, T. (2008) 'Political advertising and the portrayal of gender, colour and class in Jamaica's general elections 2007', *Gender and Governance*, 5: 59–104.

Herrnson, P. S. and Lucas, J. C. (2006) 'The fairer sex? Gender and negative campaigning in U.S. elections', *American Politics Research*, 34(1): 69–94.

Herstein, J. A. (1981) 'Keeping the voter's limits in mind: A cognitive process analysis of decision making in voting', *Journal of Personality and Social Psychology*, 40: 843–861.

Hibbing, J. R., Smith, K. B. and Alford, J. R. (2014) 'Differences in negativity bias underlie variations in political ideology', *Behavioral and Brain Sciences*, 37: 297–350.

Hinson, R. and Tweneboah-Koduah, E. Y. (2010) 'Political marketing strategies in Africa: Expert opinions of recent political elections in Ghana', *Journal of African Business*, 11(2): 201–218.

Hirschman, A. O. (1991) *The Rhetoric of Reaction*, Cambridge: Harvard University Press.

Hirsh, J. and Peterson, J. (2009) 'Extraversion, neuroticism, and the prisoner's dilemma', *Personality and Individual Differences*, 46: 254–256.

Hitchon, J. and Chang, C. (1995) 'Effects of gender schematic processing on the reception of political commercials for men and women candidates', *Communication Research*, 22: 430–458.

Hix, S. (2005) *The Political System of the European Union*, London: Palgrave Macmillan.

Hobolt, S. B., Spoon, J.-J. and Tilley, J. (2008) 'A vote against Europe? Explaining defection at the 1999 and 2004 European Parliament elections', *British Journal of Political Science*, 39: 93–115.

Hofer, T. (2007) 'Triumph des Negative Campaigning', in Hofer, T. and Tóth, B. (eds) *Wahl 2006. Kanzler, Kampagnen, Kapriolen. Analysen zur Nationalratswahl*, Vienna: Lit Verlag, pp. 5–31.

—   (2008) 'Die Kampagnen machten den Unterschied', in Hofer, T. and Tóth, B. (eds) *Wahl 2008: Strategien, Sieger, Sensationen*, Vienna: Molden, pp. 10–31.

Holbrook, T. M. (1996) *Do Campaigns Matter?*, Thousand Oaks: Sage.

Holtz-Bacha, C. (2001) 'Negative campaigning: In Deutschland negativ aufgenommen', *ZParl. Zeitschrift für Parlamentsfragen*, 32: 669–677.

Holtz-Bacha, C., Kaid, L. L. and Johnston, A. (1994) 'Political television advertising in Western democracies: A comparison of campaign broadcasts in the United States, Germany, and France', *Political Communication*, 11(1): 67–80.

Hölzl, N. (1974) *Propagandaschlachten. Die österreichischen Wahlkämpfe 1945 bis 1971*, Vienna: Verlag für Geschichte und Politik.

Hooghe, L., Bakker, R., Brigevich, A., De Vries, C., Edwards, E., Marks, G., Rovny, J., Steenbergen, M. and Vachudova, M. (2010) 'Reliability and validity of the 2002 and 2006 Chapel Hill expert surveys on party positioning', *European Journal of Political Research*, 49(5): 687–703.

Hooghe, M. and Vissers, S. (2008) 'Websites as a campaign tool for Belgian political parties. A comparison between the 2000 and 2006 local election campaigns', in Davis, R., Owen, D., Taras, D. and Ward, S. (eds) *Making a Difference: A Comparative View of the Role of the Internet in Election Politics*, Lanham: Lexington Press, pp. 171–196.

Hopkins, D. J. and King, G. (2010) 'A method of automated nonparametric content analysis for social science', *American Journal of Political Science*, 54(1): 229–247.

Hopmann, D. N., Elmelund-Præstekær, C., Albæk, E., Vliegenthart, R. and de Vreese, C. H. (2012) 'Party media agenda-setting: How parties influence election news coverage', *Party Politics*, 18(2): 173–191.

Horowitz, J. (2012) 'Campaigns and ethnic polarization in Kenya', PhD dissertation, University of California, San Diego.

Hoyle, T., Fejfar, M. and Miller, J. (2000) 'Personality and sexual risk taking: A quantitative review', *Journal of Personality*, 68: 1203–1231.

Hrbková, L. and Zagrapan, J. (2014) 'Slovak political debates: Functional Theory in a multi-party system', *European Journal of Communication* (DOI: 10.1177/0267323114544864).

Huang, L.-N. (2000) 'Examining candidate information search processes: The impact of processing goals and sophistication', *Journal of Communication*, 50: 93–114.

Huang, L.-N. and Price, V. (2001) 'Motivations, goals, information search, and memory about political candidates', *Political Psychology*, 22: 665–692.

Huddy, L. and Terkildsen, N. (1993) 'Stereotypes and the perception of male and female candidates', *American Journal of Political Science*, 37: 119–47.

Hughes, S. and Guerrero, M. A. (2009) 'Emotional attachment, social stratification, and mediated politics in Mexico's 2006 presidential election', *International Journal of Press/Politics*, 14(3): 353–375.

Hutcheson, D. (2001) 'Campaign in the Russian regions: The case of Ul'yanovsk', *Journal of Communist Studies and Transition Politics*, 17(2): 70–93.

IDEA (2008) *Direct Democracy: The International IDEA Handbook*, Stockholm: International Institute for Democracy and Electoral Assistance.

Ihonvbere, J. O. (1995) 'The "zero option" controversy in Zambia: Western double standards vis à vis safeguarding security?', *Africa Spectrum*, 30(1): 93–104.

İncioğlu, N. (2002) 'Local elections and political behaviour', in Sayarı, S. and Esmer, Y. (eds) *Politics, Parties and Elections in Turkey*, Boulder: Lynne Rienner Publishers, pp. 73–90.

Infante, D. and Wigley, C. (1986) 'Verbal aggressiveness: An interpersonal model and measure', *Communication Monographs*, 53(1): 61–69.

Inter-Parliamentary Union (2011) *Woman in Parliament in 2011: The Year in Perspective*, Geneva: Inter-Parliamentary Union.

— (2014) *Woman in Parliament: 50 Years of History at a Glance*, Geneva: Inter-Parliamentary Union.

Ito, T. A. and Cacioppo, J. T. (2005) 'Variations on a human universal: Individual differences in positivity offset and negativity bias', *Cognition and Emotion*, 19(1): 1–26.

Iyengar, S. (2011a) *Media politics: A Citizen's Guide*, 2nd edition, New York: WW Norton.

— (2011b) 'The media game: New moves, old strategies', *The Forum*, 9(1), Article 1.

Iyengar, S. and Kinder, D. (1987) *News That Matters: Television and American Opinion*, Chicago: The University of Chicago Press.

Iyengar, S. and Simon, A. F. (1993) 'News coverage of the Gulf crisis and public opinion: A study of agenda-setting, priming and framing', *Communication Research*, 20(3): 365–383.

— (2000) 'New perspectives and evidence on political communication and campaign effects', *Annual Review of Psychology*, 51(1): 149–169.

Iyengar, S., Norpoth, H. and Hahn, K. S. (2004) 'Consumer demand for election news: The horserace sells', *Journal of Politics*, 66(1): 157–175.

Iyengar, S., Sood, G. and Lelkes, Y. (2012) 'Affect, not ideology: A social identity perspective on polarization', *Public Opinion Quarterly*, 76 (3): 405–431.

Jackson, R. and Carsey, T. (2007) 'US Senate campaigns, negative advertising, and voter mobilization in the 1998 midterm election', *Electoral Studies*, 26(1): 180–195.

Jackson, R. A., Mondak, J. J. and Huckfeld, R. (2005) 'Campaign advertising and democratic citizenship: Evaluating the case against negative political ads', paper presented at the Annual Meeting of the American Political Science Association, Washington, 2005.

Jacobson, G. C. (1990) 'The effects of campaign spending in House elections: New evidence for old arguments', *American Journal of Political Science*, 34(2): 334–362.

Jacoby, J., Berning, C. K. and Speller, D. E. (1974a) 'Brand choice behavior as a function of information load', *Journal of Marketing Research*, 11: 63–69.

Jacoby, J., Speller, D. E. and Berning, C. K. (1974b) 'Brand choice behavior as a function of information load: Replication and extension', *Journal of Consumer Research*, 1: 33–40.

James, K. E. and Hensel, P. J. (1991) 'Negative advertising: The malicious strain of comparative advertising', *Journal of Advertising*, 20(2): 53–69.

Jamieson, K. H. (1992) *Dirty Politics: Deception, Distraction, and Democracy*, New York: Oxford University Press.

— (2000) *Everything You Think You Know About Politics ... and Why You're Wrong*, New York: Basic Books.

Jamieson, K. H. and Campbell, C. (1983) *The Interplay of Influence: Mass Media and their Publics in News, Advertising, Politics*, Belmont, CA: Wadsworth

Jamieson, K. H., Kensky, K. and Hardy, B. (2010) *The Obama Victory: How Media, Money, and Message Shaped the 2008 Election*, New York: Oxford University Press.

Jamieson, K. H., Waldman, P. and Sheer, S. (2000) 'Eliminate the negative? Categories of analysis for political advertisements', in Thurber, H. A., Nelson, C. J. and Dulio, D. A. (eds) *Crowded Airwaves: Campaign Advertising in Elections*, Washington: The Brookings Institution, pp. 44–64.

Jarman, J. W. (2005) 'Political affiliation and presidential debates: A real-time analysis of the effect of the arguments used in the presidential debates', *American Behavioral Scientist*, 49(2): 229–242.

Jensen-Campbell, L., Knack, J., Waldrip, A. and Campbell, S. (2007) 'Do Big Five personality traits associated with self-control influence the regulation of anger and aggression?', *Journal of Research in Personality*, 41: 403–424.

Jerit, J., Barabas, J. and Bolsen, T. (2006) 'Citizens, knowledge, and the information environment', *American Journal of Political Science*, 50(2): 266–82.

John, O. P., Donahue, E. M. and Kentle, R. L. (1991) 'The Big Five Inventory – versions 4a and 54', Berkeley: University of California, Berkeley, Institute of Personality and Social Research.

John, O. P., Naumann, L. P. and Soto, C. J. (2008) 'Paradigm shift to the integrative Big Five trait taxonomy: History, measurement, and conceptual issues', in John, O. P., Robins, R. W. and Pervin, L. A. (eds) *Handbook of Personality: Theory and Research*, New York, NY: Guilford Press, pp. 114–158.

Johnson-Cartee, K. S. and Copeland, G. A. (1989) 'Southern voters' reactions to negative political ads in 1986 election', *Journalism Quarterly*, 66(4): 888–893.

— (1991) *Negative Political Advertising: Coming of Age*, Hillsdale: Lawrence Erlbaum.

Johnston, A. and White, A. B. (1994) 'Communication styles and female candidates: A study of the political advertising during the 1986 Senate elections', *Journalism & Mass Communication Quarterly*, 71(2): 321–329.

Johnston, R., Michael, H. and Jamieson, K. H. (2004) *The 2000 Presidential Election and the Foundations of Party Politics*, Boston: Cambridge University Press.

Kagwanja, P. (2009) 'Courting genocide: Populism, ethno-nationalism and the informalisation of violence in Kenya's 2008 post-election crisis', *Journal of Contemporary African Studies*, 27(3): 365–387.

Kahn, K. F. (1993) 'Gender differences in campaign messages: The political advertisements of men and women candidates for U.S. Senate', *Political Research Quarterly*, 46(3): 481–502.

— (1996) *The Political Consequences of Being a Woman: How Stereotypes Influence the Conduct and Consequences of Political Campaigns*, New York: Columbia University Press.

Kahn, K. F. and Kenney, P. J. (1999a) 'Do negative campaigns mobilize or suppress turnout? Clarifying the relationship between negativity and participation', *American Political Science Review*, 93(4): 877–889.

— (1999b) *The Spectacle of U.S. Senate Campaigns*, Princeton: Princeton University Press.

— (2000) 'How negative campaigning enhances knowledge of Senate elections', in Thurber, J. A., Nelson, C. J. and Dulio, D. A. (eds) *Crowded Airwaves: Campaign Advertising in Elections*, Washington: The Brooking Institution, pp. 65–95.

— (2004) *No Holds Barred: Negativity in U.S. Senate Campaigns*, Upper Saddle River: Pearson Prentice Hall.

Kaid, L. L. (1997) 'Effects of television spots on images of Dole and Clinton', *American Behavioral Scientist*, 40: 1085–1094.

— (1999a) 'Comparing and contrasting the styles and effects of political advertising in European democracies', in Kaid, L. L. (ed.) *Television and Politics in Evolving European Democracies*, Commack: Nova Science Publications, pp. 219–236.

— (ed.) (1999b) *Television and Politics in Evolving European Democracies*, Commack: Nova Science Publications.

— (2004) *Handbook of Political Communication Research*, New Jersey: Lawrence Erlbaum Associate.

Kaid, L. L. and Gagnère, N. (2006) 'Election broadcasts in France', in Kaid, L. L. and Holtz-Bacha, C. (eds) *The Sage Handbook of Political Advertising*, London: Sage, pp. 83–96.

Kaid, L. L. and Holtz-Bacha, C. (1994) *Political Advertising in Western Democracies: Parties and Candidates on Television*, California: Sage.

— (1995) 'Political advertising across cultures', in Kaid, L. L. and Holtz-Bacha, C. (eds) *Political Advertising in Western Democracies*, Thousand Oaks: Sage, pp. 206–227.

—   (eds) (2006) *The Sage Handbook of Political Advertising*, Thousand Oaks: Sage.

Kaid, L. L. and Johnston, A. (1991) 'Negative versus positive television advertising in U.S. presidential campaigns, 1960–1988', *Journal of Communication*, 41: 53–64.

—   (2001) *Videostyle in Presidential Campaigns, Style and Content of Televised Political Advertising*, Westport: Praeger.

Kalaycıoğlu, E. (1989) 'Division of responsibility', in Heper, M. (ed.) *Local Government in Turkey: Governing Greater Istanbul*, London: Routledge, pp. 12–29.

Kangira, J. (2006) 'Negative advertising as a strategy of persuasion in the 2002 presidential election campaign in Zimbabwe', (unpublished manuscript).

Kaplan, N., Park, D. K. and Ridout, T. N. (2006) 'Dialogue in American political campaigns? An examination of issue convergence in candidate television advertising', *American Political Science Review*, 50(3): 724–736.

Karan, K., Gimeno, J. D. and Tandoc Jr, E. (2009) 'The Internet and mobile technologies in election campaigns: The GABRIELA Women's Party during the 2007 Philippine elections', *Journal of Information Technology & Politics*, 6(3–4): 326–339.

Kasmani, M. F. (2013) 'The BBC and Al Jazeera English: The similarities and differences in the discourse of the pre-election coverage of the 2009 Iranian election', *International Journal of Communication*, 7: 22.

Kavanagh, D. (1995) *Election Campaigning: The New Marketing of Politics*, Oxford: Blackwell.

Keman, H. (2007) 'Experts and manifestos: Different sources – same results for comparative research?', *Electoral Studies*, 26: 76–89.

Kennedy, J. R., Nadeau, C., and Roller, E. (1993) *Honduras 1993 Elections: Election Observation Mission Report*, Washington: Ifes.

Kennedy, R. (2006) 'A colorless election: The 2005 presidential election in Kazakhstan, and what it means for the future of the opposition', *Problems of Post-Communism*, 53(6): 46–58.

Kenny, D. (1987) *Statistics for the Social and Behavioral Sciences*, Boston: Little, Brown.

Kern, M. (1989) *Thirty Second Spots: Political Advertising in the Eighties*, New York: Praeger.

Kersting, N. (2009) 'Voting behaviour in the 2009 South African election', *Africa Spectrum*, 44(2): 125–133.

Khalifa, O. N. E. (2013) 'Discours présidentiels: Une analyse des prestations de trois candidats à la présidentielle sur le plateau d'un talk show', *Égypte/Monde arabe*, 10: 1–11.

Kibble, S. and Walls, M. (2012) 'Lessons from Somaliland's 2010 presidential elections: What democratic spaces, what opportunities?', in SORADI (ed.) *Reflections and Lessons of Somaliland's. Two Decades of Sustained Peace, Statebuilding and Democratzation*, Hargesia: Somaliland Development Series, pp. 23–43.

Kim, S. and Cho, K. (2004) 'Political cynicism, public interest blackballing and voter turnout: The case of South Korea's 2000 National Assembly elections', *Japanese Journal of Political Science*, 5: 91–111.

King, J. D. and McConnell, J. B. (2003) 'The effect of negative campaign advertising on vote choice: The mediating influence of gender', *Social Science Quarterly*, 84: 843–857.

Kleinnijenhuis, J. and Fan, D. P. (1999) 'Media coverage and the flow of voters in multiparty systems: The 1994 national elections in Holland and Germany', *International Journal of Public Opinion Research*, 11(3): 233–256.

Kleinnijenhuis, J. and Pennings, P. (2001) 'Measurement of party positions on the basis of party programmes, media coverage and voter perceptions', in Laver, M (ed.) *Estimating the Policy Positions of Political Actors*, London and New York: Routledge, pp. 162–182.

Kleinnijenhuis, J. and Takens, J. (2011) 'Het politieke nieuwsaanbod van dagbladen en televisie: Objectief en pluriform?, in Thomassen, J. and Andeweg, R. (eds) *Democratie Doorgelicht, Het Functioneren van de Nederlandse Democratie*, Leiden, Netherlands: Leiden University Press, pp. 407–424.

Kleinnijenhuis, J., Scholten, O., van Atteveldt, W., van Hoof, A. M. J., Krouwel, A., Oegema, D., de Ridder, J. A., Ruigrok, N. and Takens, J. (2007a) *Nederland Vijfstromenland*, Amsterdam: Bert Bakker.

Kleinnijenhuis, J., van Hoof, A. M. J., Oegema, D. and de Ridder, J. A. (2007b) 'A test of rivaling approaches to explain news effects: News on issue positions of parties, real-world developments, support and criticism, and success and failure', *Journal of Communication*, 57: 366–384.

Klotz, R. (1998) 'Virtual criticism: Negative advertising on the Internet in the 1996 Senate races', *Political Communication*, 15(3): 347–365.

Krasno, J. S. and Green, D. P. (2008) 'Do televised presidential ads increase voter turnout? Evidence from a natural experiment', *The Journal of Politics*, 70(1): 245–261.

Krebs, T. B. and Holian, D. B. (2007) 'Competitive positioning, deracialization, and attack speech: A study of negative campaigning in the 2001 Los Angeles Mayoral Election', *American Politics Research*, 35(1): 123–149.

Kriesi, H. (2005) *Direct Democratic Choice: The Swiss Experience*, Lanham: Lexington Books.

— (ed.) (2011) *Political Communication in Direct Democratic Campaigns: Manipulation or Deliberation?*, Basingstoke: Palgrave Macmillan.

Kriesi, H. and Trechsel, A. H. (2008) *The Politics of Switzerland: Continuity and Change in a Consensus Democracy*, Cambridge: Cambridge University Press.

Kriesi, H., Grande, E., Dolezal, M., Helbling, M., Höglinger, D., Hutter, S. and Wüest, B. (2012) *Political Conflict in Western Europe*, Cambridge: Cambridge University Press.

Kriesi, H., Grande, E., Lachat, R., Dolezal, M., Bornschier, S. and Frey, T. (2006) 'Globalization and the transformation of the national political space: Six European countries compared', *European Journal of Political Research*, 45(6): 921–956.

— (2008) *West European Politics in the Age of Globalization*, Cambridge: Cambridge University Press.

Krosnick, J. and Kinder, D. (1990) 'Altering the foundations of support for the president through priming', *The American Political Science Review*, 84(2): 497–512.

Krupnikov, Y. (2014) 'How negativity can increase and decrease voter turnout: The effect of timing', *Political Communication*, 31(3): 446–466.

Kumar, A. and Pathak, P. (2012) 'Political advertising in India: A perspective', *Management Insights*, 8(1): 15–29.

Kwon, H. and Lee, J. Y. (2004) 'NGO's political reform movement process via the Internet: Focusing on 'Election Defeat Movement' in Korea', *International Review of Public Administration*, 8(2): 49–57.

Lachat, R. and Sciarini, P. (2002) 'When do election campaigns matter, and to whom? Results from the 1999 Swiss election panel study', in Farrell, D. and Schmitt-Beck, R. (eds) *Do Political Campaigns Matter? Campaign Effects in Elections and Referendums*, New York: Routledge, pp. 41–57.

Ladd, J. M. (2012) 'When politicians attack: Party cohesion in the media', *Public Opinion Quarterly*, 76(1): 182–186.

Lal, B. V. (1988) 'Before the storm: An analysis of the Fiji general election of 1987', *Pacific Studies*, 12(1): 71–96.

Landers, R. and Lounsbury, J. (2006) 'An investigation of Big Five and narrow personality traits in relation to Internet usage', *Computers in Human Behavior*, 22(2): 283–293.

Lanoue, D. J. (1991) 'The "turning point": Viewers' reactions to the second 1988 presidential debate', *American Politics Research*, 19(1): 80–95.

— (1992) 'One that made a difference: Cognitive consistency, political knowledge, and the 1980 presidential debate', *The Public Opinion Quarterly*, 56(2): 168–184.

Lanz, S. and Nai, A. (2015) 'Vote as you think: Determinants of consistent decision making in direct democracy', *Swiss Political Science Review*, 21(1): 119–139.

Lappas, G., Chatzopoulos, S. and Yannas, P. (2008) 'Parliamentary candidates running on the Web for the 2004 Greek national elections', *Journal of Political Marketing*, 7(3): 256–277.

Lau, R. R. (1982) 'Negativity in political perception', *Political Behavior*, 4(4): 353–377.

— (1985) 'Two explanations for negativity effects in political behavior', *American Journal of Political Science*, 29: 119–138.

— (1995) 'Information search during an election campaign: Introducing a process-tracing methodology for political scientists', in Lodge, M. and

McGraw, K. M. (eds) *Political Judgment: Structure and Process,* Ann Arbor: University of Michigan Press, pp. 179–205.

— (2003) 'Models of decision making', in Sears, D. O., Huddy, L. and Jervis, R. (eds) *Oxford Handbook of Political Psychology,* New York: Oxford University Press, pp. 19–59.

Lau, R. R. and Pomper, G. M. (2000) 'Accentuate the negative? Effectiveness of negative campaigning in U.S. Senate elections', paper presented at the annual meeting of the American Political Science Association, Washington, DC, 2000.

— (2001a) 'Effects of negative campaigning on turnout in U.S. Senate elections, 1988–1998', *Journal of Politics,* 63: 804–819.

— (2001b) 'Negative campaigning by US Senate candidates', *Party Politics,* 7(1): 69–87.

— (2002) 'Effectiveness of negative campaigning in U.S. Senate elections', *American Journal of Political Science,* 46(1): 47–66.

— (2004) *Negative Campaigning: An Analysis of U.S. Senate Elections,* Oxford: Rowman and Littlefield.

Lau, R. R. and Redlawsk, D. P. (1997) 'Voting correctly', *American Political Science Review,* 91: 585–599.

— (2001) 'An experimental study of information search, memory, and decision making during a political campaign', in Kuklinski, J. (ed.), *Political Psychology and Public Opinion,* New York: Cambridge University Press, pp. 136–159.

— (2006) *How Voters Decide: Information Processing During Election Campaigns,* New York: Cambridge University Press.

Lau, R. R. and Rovner, I. B. (2009) 'Negative campaigning', *Annual Review of Political Science,* 12: 285–306.

Lau, R. R. and Sigelman, L. (2000) 'Effectiveness of negative political advertising in: J. A. Thurber, C. J. Nelsen and D. A. Dulio (eds) *Crowded Airwaves: Campaign Advertising in Elections,* Washington DC: Brookings Institute.

Lau, R. R., Siegelman, L., Heldman, C. and Babbit, P. (1999) 'The effects of negative advertisement: A meta-analytic assessment', *The American Political Science Review,* 93(4): 851–875.

Lau, R. R., Siegelman, L. and Rovner, I. B. (2007) 'The effects of negative political campaigns: A meta-analytic reassessment', *The Journal of Politics,* 69(4): 1176–1209.

Lavareda, A. (2009) *Emoções ocultas e estratégias eleitorais* [Hidden emotions and electoral strategies], Rio de Janeiro: Editora Objetiva.

Laver, M. J. (2005) 'Policy and the dynamics of political competition', *American Political Science Review,* 99(2): 263–281.

Laver, M. J., and Schofield, N. (1998) *Multiparty Government: The Politics of Coalition in Europe,* Oxford: Oxford University Press.

Lawrence, R. G. (2000) 'Game-framing the issues: Tracking the strategy frame in public policy news', *Political Communication,* 17(2): 93–114.

Lawton, L. D. and Freedman, P. (2001) 'Beyond negativity: Advertising effects in the 2000 Virginia Senate race', paper presented at the Annual Meeting of the Midwest Political Science Association, 2001.

Lazarsfeld, P. F., Berelson, B. R. and Gaudet, H. (1944) *The People's Choice: How the Voter Makes Up His Mind in a Presidential Campaign*, New York: Columbia University Press.

Leach, R., Coxall, B. and Robins, L. (2011) *British Politics*, Houndsmills: Palgrave Macmillan.

Lederer, A. (2010) 'Politische Werbung in der Wahlkampfarena: Analysen politischer Werberkommunikation', in Plasser, F. (ed.) *Politik in der Medienarena. Praxis politischer Kommunikation in Österreich*, Vienna: Facultas, pp. 241–272.

LeDuc, L. (2002) 'Opinion change and voting behaviour in referendums', *European Journal of Political Research*, 41: 711–732.

—— (2003) *The Politics of Direct Democracy: Referendums in Global Perspective*, New York: Broadview Press.

Lee, C. and Benoit, W. L. (2004) 'A functional analysis of presidential television spots: A comparison of Korean and American ads', *Communication Quarterly*, 52(1): 68–79.

Lees-Marshment, J. (2009) 'Political marketing and the 2008 New Zealand election: A comparative perspective', *Australian Journal of Political Science*, 44(3): 457–475.

Lemert, J., Wanta, W. and Lee, T.-T. (1999) 'Party identification and negative advertising in a U.S. Senate election', *Journal of Communications*, 49(2): 123–134.

Lengauer, G. (2012) 'PR-Input und Medien-Output: Kommunikationslogiken von Parteien und Massenmedien', in Plasser, F. (ed.) *Erfolgreich wahlkämpfen. Massenmedien und Wahlkampagnen in Österreich*, Vienna: Facultas, pp. 113–140.

Lengauer, G., Esser, F. and Berganza, R. (2012) 'Negativity in political news: A review of concepts, operationalizations and key findings', *Journalism*, 13(2): 179–202.

Lenz, G. S. (2009) 'Learning and opinion change, not priming: Reconsidering the priming hypothesis', *American Journal of Political Science*, 53(4): 821–837.

LePine, J. and van Dyne, L. (2001) 'Voice and cooperative behavior as contrasting forms of contextual performance: Evidence of differential relationships with Big Five personality characteristics and cognitive ability', *Journal of Applied Psychology*, 86(2): 326–336.

Li, C. (2008) 'From selection to election? Experiments in the recruitment of Chinese political elites', *China Leadership Monitor*, 26: 1–14.

Lijphart, A. (1997) 'Unequal participation: Democracy's unresolved dilemma. Presidential address of the American Political Science Association, 1996', *American Political Science Review*, 91: 1–14.

—   (1999) *Patterns of Democracy: Government Forms and Performance in Thirty-Six Countries*, New Haven: Yale University Press.

Lodge, M. and Taber, C. S. (2013) *The Rationalizing Voter*, Cambridge: Cambridge University Press.

Lodge, T. (2001) 'The South African local government elections of December 2000', *Politikon: South African Journal of Political Studies*, 28(1): 21–46.

Lord, C. G., Ross, L. and Lepper, M. R. (1979) 'Biased assimilation and attitude polarization: The effects of prior theories on subsequently considered evidence', *Journal of Personality and Social Psychology*, 37(11): 2098–2109.

Lovenduski, J. and Norris, P. (2001) 'Westminster women: The politics of presence', *Political Studies*, 51(1): 84–102.

Lowe, W., Benoit, K., Mikhaylov, S. and Laver, M. (2011) 'Scaling policy preferences from coded political texts', *Legislative Studies Quarterly*, 36(1): 123–155.

Lupia, A. and Philpot, T. S. (2005) 'Views from inside the Net: How websites affect young adults' political interest', *Journal of Politics*, 67(4): 1122–1142.

Luther, K. R. (2009) 'The revival of the radical right: The Austrian parliamentary election of 2008', *West European Politics*, 32(5): 1049–1061.

—   (2011) 'Of goals and own goals: A case study of right-wing populist party strategy for and during incumbency', *Party Politics*, 17(4): 453–470.

Magleby, D. B. (1984) *Direct Legislation: Voting on Ballot Propositions in the United States*, Baltimore: The John Hopkins University Press.

Maier, J. (2009) '"Frau Merkel wird doch noch kritik ertragen können...": Inhalt, struktur, wahrnehmung und wirkung des wirtschaftspolitischen teils der fernsehdebatte 2005', in Gabriel, O. W, Wessels, B. and Falter, J. W. (eds) *Wahlen und Wähler. Analysen aus Anlass der Bundestagswahl 2005*, Wiesbaden: Springer, pp. 177–201.

—   (2013) 'Measurement and effects of negativity in German televised debates', paper presented at the Joint Session of Workshops of the European Consortium of Political Research (ECPR), Mainz, 2013.

Maier, J. and Faas, T. (2003a) *Wortlaut und Wahrnehmung des ersten Fernsehduells im Bundestagswahlkampf 2002 – eine Dokumentation*, Bamberg: Universität Bamberg.

—   (2003b) *Wortlaut und Wahrnehmung des zweiten Fernsehduells im Bundestagswahlkampf 2002 – eine Dokumentation*, Bamberg: Universität Bamberg.

—   (2011) '"Miniature campaigns" in comparison. The German televised debates, 2002–09', *German Politics*, 20(1): 75–91.

Maier, J. and Jansen, C. (2013) 'Negativity in German televised debates, 1997–2012: A content analysis of candidate messages', paper presented at the Joint Session of Workshops of the European Consortium of Political Research (ECPR), Mainz, 2013.

Maier, J., Faas, T. and Maier, M. (2014) 'Aufgeholt, aber nicht aufgeschlossen. Wahrnehmungen und wirkungen von TV-duellen am beispiel von Angela Merkel und Peer Steinbrück 2013', *Zeitschrift für Parlamentsfragen*, 45(1): 38–54.

Maier, J., Maier, M., Reinemann, C. and Maurer, M. (2006) *Wortlaut der Fernsehdebatte im Bundestagswahlkampf 2005 und ihre Wahrnehmung im Ost-West-Vergleich*, Kaiserslautern: Technische Universität Kaiserslautern.

Mair, P. (1996) 'Party systems and structures of competition', in LeDuc, L., Niemi, R. G. and Norris, P. (eds) *Comparing Democracies: Elections and Voting in Global Perspective*, Thousand Oaks: Sage, pp. 83–106.

— (2006) 'Party system change', in Katz, R. S. and Crotty, W. (eds) *Handbook of Party Politics*, Thousand Oaks: Sage, pp. 63–74.

Mair, P., Müller, W. C. and Plasser, F. (2004) *Political Parties and Electoral Change: Party Responses to Electoral Markets*, London: Sage Publications.

Maisel, L. S. (2012) 'The negative consequences of uncivil political discourse', *PS: Political Science & Politics*, 45(03): 405–411.

Makamani, R. (2011) 'Contradictory HIV/AIDS rhetoric in Zimbabwe: An analysis of selected online media texts', *African Journal of Rhetoric: HIV/AIDS, Rhetoric and Associated Discourses-African Perspectives*, 3: 55–82.

Malhotra, N. and Kuo, A. G. (2009) 'Emotions as moderators of information cue use: Citizen attitudes toward hurricane Katrina', *American Politics Research*, 37: 301–326.

Mancuso, J. J., Kim, J., Lee, S., Tsuda, S., Chow, N. B. H. and Augustine, G. J. (2010) 'Optogenetic probing of functional brain circuitry', *Experimental Physiology*, 96(1): 26–33.

Marcus, G. E. (2002) *The Sentimental Citizen: Emotion in Democratic Politics*, University Park: The Pennsylvania State University.

— (2013) *Political Psychology: Neuroscience, Genetics, and Politics*, New York: Oxford University Press.

Marcus, G. E. and MacKuen, M. (1993) 'Anxiety, enthusiasm, and the vote: The emotional underpinnings of learning and involvement during presidential campaigns', *The American Political Science Review*, 87(3): 672–685.

Marcus, G. E., Neuman W. R. and MacKuen, M. (2000) *Affective Intelligence and Political Judgement*, Chicago: University of Chicago Press.

Mardin, S. (1973) 'Center-periphery relations: A key to Turkish politics?', *Deadalus* 102(1): 169–190.

Mark, D. (2006) *Going Dirty: The Art of Negative Campaigning*, Plymouth: Rowman and Littlefield.

Marks, G., Hooghe, L., Nelson, M. and Edwards, E. (2006) 'Party competition and European integration in the East and West: Different structure, same causality', *Comparative Political Studies*, 39(2): 155–75.

Marks, G., Hooghe, L., Steenbergen, M. R. and Bakker, R. (2007) 'Cross-validating data on party positions on European integration', *Electoral Studies*, 26: 23–38.

Marland, A. (2003) 'Political marketing in modern Canadian federal elections', paper presented at the annual meeting of the Canadian Political Science Association, Halifax, 2003.

Marquis, L. (2006) *La Formation de l'Opinion Publique en Démocratie Directe: Les Référendums sur la Politique Extérieure Suisse (1981–1995)*, Zurich: Seismo.

Marquis, L. and Bergman, M. M. (2009) 'Development and consequences of referendum campaigns in Switzerland, 1981–1999, *Swiss Political Science Review*, 15(1): 63–97.

Marsh, M. (2007) 'Referendum campaigns: Changing what people think or changing what they think about', in de Vreese, C. H. (ed.) *The Dynamics of Referendum Campaigns*, Basingstoke: Palgrave Macmillan, pp. 63–83.

Marsh, M., Suiter, J. and Reidy, T. (2012). *Report on Reasons Behind Voter Behaviour in the Oireachtas Inquiry Referendum 2011*, Dublin: Department of Public Expenditure and Reform.

Martin, P. (2004) 'Inside the black box of negative campaign effects: Three reasons why negative campaigns mobilize', *Political Psychology*, 25(4): 545–562.

Martin, S. (2013) 'Is all politics local? The role-orientation of Irish parliamentarians toward foreign policy', *Irish Political Studies*, 28(1): 114–129.

Martinez, M. D. and Delegal, T. (1990) 'The irrelevance of negative campaigns to political trust: Experimental and survey results', *Political Communication*, 7(1): 25–40.

Maru, M. T. (2012) 'Rethinking and reforming the African Union Commission elections', *African Security Review*, 21(4): 64–78.

Matchaya, C. G. (2010) 'The performance of the Malawi Congress Party in general elections: The role of sectionalism of a regional and ethnic nature', *African Journal of Political Science and International Relations*, 4(6): 221–230.

Mattes, K. (2007) 'Attack politics: Who goes negative and why?' *Caltech Social Science Working Paper*, 1256: 1–36.

— (2012) 'What happens when a candidate doesn't bark? "Cursed" voters and their impact on campaign discourse', *Journal of Politics*, 74(2): 369–382.

Mattes, K. and Redlawsk, D. P. (2015) *The Positive Case for Negative Campaigning*, Chicago: University of Chicago Press.

Mattes, K., Spezio, M., Kim, H., Todorov, A., Adolphs, R. and Alvarez, R. M. (2010) 'Predicting election outcomes from positive and negative trait assessments of candidate images', *Political Psychology*, 31(1): 41–58.

Maundeni, Z. (ed.) (2005) *40 Years of Democracy in Botswana, 1965–2005*, Gaborone: Mmegi Publishing House.

Maurer, M. and Reinemann, C. (2003) *Schröder gegen Stoiber. Nutzung, Wahrnehmung und Wirkung der TV-Duelle*, Wiesbaden: Westdeutscher Verlag.

— (2009) 'Schröder gegen Merkel. Eine analyse der zuschauereindrücke während des TV-duells', in Oberreuter, H. (ed.) *Unentschieden. Die erzwungene Koalition*, München: Olzog, pp. 119–140.

Mayer, W. G. (1996) 'In defense of negative campaigning', *Political Science Quarterly*, 111(3): 437–455.

Mazzoleni, G. and Schulz, W. (1999) '"Mediatisation"of politics: a challenge for democracy?', *Political Communication*, 16(8): 247–261.

McAllistar, I. (2007) 'The personalization of politics', in Dalton, R. J. and Klingemann, H.-D. (eds) *Oxford Handbook of Political Behaviour*, Oxford: Oxford University Press, pp. 571–588.

McClintock, C. (2006) 'An unlikely comeback in Peru', *Journal of Democracy*, 17(4): 95–109.

McCrae, R. R. and Costa, P. T. (2003) *Personality in Adulthood: A Five-Factor Theory Perspective*, New York: The Guilford Press.

McCrae, R. R., Costa, P. T., Martin, T., Oryol, V., Srnin, I. and O'Cleirigh, C. (2007) 'Personality correlates of HIV stigmatization in Russia and the United States', *Journal of Research in Personality*, 41: 190–196.

McCrae, R. R., Jang, K. L., Livesley, W. J., Riemann, R. and Angleitner, A. (2001) 'Sources of structure: Genetic, environmental, and artifactual influences on the covariation of personality traits', *Journal of Personality*, 69(4): 511–535.

McDonald, M. D., Mendes, S. V. and Kim, M. (2007) 'Cross-temporal and cross-national comparisons of party left-right positions', *Electoral Studies*, 26: 62–75.

McKelvey, R. D. and Ordeshook, P. C. (1972) 'A general theory of the calculus of voting', in Herdon, J. F. and Bemd, J. L. (eds) *Mathematical Applications in Political Science VI*, Charlottsville: The University of Virginia Press, pp. 32–78.

McKinney, M. S. and Carlin, D. B. (2004) 'Political campaign debates', in Kaid, L. L. (ed.) *Handbook of Political Communication Research*, Mahwah, NJ: Lawrence Erlbaum, pp. 203–234.

McKinney, M. S., Kaid, L. L. and Robertson, T. A. (2001) 'The front-runner, contenders, and also-rans: Effects of watching a 2000 Republican primary debate', *American Behavioral Scientist*, 44(12): 2232–51.

McKinnon, L. M. and Kaid, L. L. (1999) 'Exposing negative campaigning or enhancing advertising effects: An experimental study of adwatch effects on voter evaluations of candidates and their ads', *Journal of Applied Communication Research*, 27: 217–236.

McKinnon, L. M., Tedesco, J. C. and Kaid, L. L. (1993) 'The third 1992 presidential debate: Channel and commentary effects', *Argumentation & Advocacy*, 30(2): 106–118.

McNair, B. M. (2003) *An Introduction to Political Communication*, London: Routledge.

Meffert, M. F., and Gschwend, T. (2011) 'Polls, coalition signals and strategic voting: An experimental investigation of perceptions and effects', *European Journal of Political Research*, 50(5): 636–667.

Meffert, M. F., Chung, S., Joiner, A. J., Waks, L. and Garst, J. (2006) 'The effects of negativity and motivated information processing during a political campaign', *Journal of Communication*, 56(1): 27–51.

Melischek, G., Rußmann, U. and Seethaler, J. (2010) 'Agenda Building in österreichischen Nationalratswahlkämpfen, 1970–2008', in Plasser, F. (ed.) *Politik in der Medienarena. Praxis politischer Kommunikation in Österreich*, Vienna: Facultas, pp. 101–143.

Mény, Y. and Surel, Y. (eds) (2001) *Democracies and the Populist Challenge*, Basingstoke: Palgrave Macmillan.

Merritt, S. (1984) 'Negative political advertising: Some empirical findings', *Journal of Advertising*, 13(3): 27–38.

Merton, R. K. (1968) 'The Matthew Effect in Science', *Science*, 159(5): 56–63.

Mezquita, L., Stewart, S. and Ruiperez, A. (2010) 'Big-Five personality domains predict internal drinking motives in young adults', *Personality and Individual Differences*, 49: 240–245.

Midtbø, T. (2011) 'Explaining media attention for Norwegian MPs: A new modelling approach', *Scandinavian Political Studies*, 34(3): 226–249.

Min, Y. (2002) 'Intertwining of campaign news and advertising: The content and electoral effects of newspaper ad watches,' *Journalism and Mass Communication Quarterly*, 79(4): 927–944.

— (2004) 'News coverage of negative political campaigns: An experiment of negative campaigns effects on turnout and candidate preferences', *The International Journal of Press/Politics*, 9(4): 27–38.

Mintz, A., Geva, N., Redd, S. B. and Carnes, A. (1997) 'The effects of dynamic and static choice sets on decision strategy', *American Political Science Review*, 91: 553–566.

Miskin, S. and Grant, R. (2004) 'Political advertising in Australia', Briefing paper No. 5, Australian Parliamentary Library. Online. Available http://www.apo.org.au/node/504; (accessed 23 September 2014).

Mitchell, P. and Nyblade, B. (2008) 'Government formation and cabinet type', in Strøm, K., Müller, W. C. and Bergman, T. (eds) *Cabinets and Coalition Bargaining: The Democratic Life Cycle in Western Europe*, Oxford: Oxford University Press, pp. 201–235.

Molina, J. E. and Pérez Baralt, C. (1999) 'La democracia venezolana en una encrucijada: Las elecciones nacionales y regionales de 1998', *América Latina Hoy: Revista de Ciencias Sociales*, (21): 29–40.

Momoc, A. (2012) 'The presidential candidates on Twitter during the 2009 Romanian elections', *Romanian Journal of Communication and Public Relations*, 1: 21–37.

Mondak, J. (2010) *Personality and the Foundations of Political Behavior*, Cambridge: Cambridge University Press.

Mondak, J. and Halperin, K. (2008) 'A framework of the study of personality and political behaviour', *British Journal of Political Science*, 38(2): 335–362.

Mondak, J., Hibbing, M., Canache, D., Seligson, M. and Anderson, M. (2010) 'Personality and civic engagement: An integrative framework for the study of traits effects on political behavior', *American Political Science Review*, 104(1): 85–110.

Montigny, E. (2011) *Leadership et Militantisme au Parti Québécois*, Québec: Les Presses de l'Université Laval.

Moreno, A. (2004) 'The effects of negative campaigns on Mexican voters', in Domínguez, J. and Lawson, C. (eds) *Mexico's Pivotal Democratic Election: Candidates, Voters, and the Presidential Campaign of 2000*, Stanford: Stanford University Press, pp. 243–268.

Morris, P. (1998) 'The South Korean presidential election, 1998', *Electoral Studies*, 17(4): 581–583.

Mudde, C. (2007) *Populist Radical Right Parties in Europe*, Cambridge: Cambridge University Press.

— (2013) 'Three decades of populist radical right parties in Western Europe: So what?', *European Journal of Political Research*, 52(1): 1–19.

Mulgan, R. (2004) *Politics in New Zealand*, Auckland: Auckland University Press.

Müller, W. C. (1996) 'A vote for stability: The Austrian parliamentary elections of 1995', *Electoral Studies*, 15(3): 410–414.

— (2000) 'Austria: Tight coalitions and stable government', in Müller, W. C. and Strøm, K. (eds) *Coalition Governments in Western Europe*, Oxford: Oxford University Press, pp. 86–125.

— (2009) 'The snap election in Austria, September 2008', *Electoral Studies*, 28: 514–517.

Murphy, G. and Reidy, T. (2012) 'From partisan predictability to the end of loyalty, presidential elections in Ireland', *Irish Political Studies*, 27(4): 615–634.

Murray, D. (1996) 'The 1995 national elections in Thailand: A step backward for democracy?', *Asian Survey*, 36(4): 361–375.

Nagel, F. (2012) *Die Wirkung Verbaler und Nonverbaler Kommunikation in TV-Duellen. Eine Untersuchung am Beispiel von Gerhard Schröder und Angela Merkel*, Wiesbaden: Springer.

Nagel, F., Maurer, M. and Reinemann, C. (2012) 'Is there a visual dominance in political communication? How verbal, visual, and vocal communication shape viewers' impressions of political candidates', *Journal of Communication*, 62(5): 833–850.

Nai, A. (2013) 'What really matters is which camp goes dirty: Differential effects of negative campaigning on turnout during Swiss federal ballots', *European Journal of Political Research*, 52(1): 44–70.

—   (2014a) 'The Cadillac, the mother-in-law, and the ballot: individual and contextual roots of ambivalence in Swiss direct democracy', *Electoral Studies*, 33: 292–306.

—   (2014b) *Choisir avec l'esprit, voter avec le coeur. Causes et conséquences des processus cognitifs de formation de l'opinion en suisse lors des votations fédérales*, Zurich: Seismo.

—   (2014c) 'Does the electoral cycle matter for direct democracy? Evidence from citizens' attention to elites and negative campaigning effects on turnout in Switzerland', paper presented at the Annual Conference of the Australian Political Studies Association, Sydney, 2014.

—   (2015) 'The maze and the mirror: Voting correctly in direct democracy', *Social Science Quarterly*, 96(2): 465–486.

Nai, A. and Sciarini, P. (2015) 'Why 'going negative'? Strategic and situational determinants of personal attacks in Swiss direct democratic votes', Journal of Political Marketing, DOI: 10.1080/15377857.2015.1058310

Newhagen, J. and Reeves, B. (1991) 'Emotion and memory responses for negative political advertising', in Biocca, F. (ed.) *Television and Political Advertising: Psychological Processes*, Hillsdale: Routledge, pp. 197–220.

Newhagen, J., Lang, A. and Reeves, B. (1996) 'Negative video as structure: Emotion, attention, capacity, and memory', *Journal of Broadcasting & Electronic Media*, 40: 460–477.

Nicholson, N., Soane, E., Fenton-O'Creevy, M. and Willman, P. (2005) 'Personality and domain-specific risk taking', *Journal of Risk Research*, 8(2): 157–176.

Nikolayenko, O. (2012) 'Tactical interactions between youth movements and incumbent governments in postcommunist states', *Research in Social Movements, Conflicts and Change*, 34: 27–61.

Niven, D. (2006) 'A field experiment on the effects of negative campaign mail on voter turnout in a municipal election', *Political Research Quarterly*, 59(2): 203–210.

Norris, P. (1996) 'Women politicians: Transforming Westminster?', *Parliamentary Affairs*, 49(1): 89–102.

—   (2000) *A Virtuous Circle: Political Communications in Postindustrial Societies*, New York: Cambridge University Press.

Norris, P. and Lovenduski, J. (1989) 'Women candidates for parliament: Transforming the agenda?', *British Journal of Political Science*, 19(1): 106–115.

Norris, P. and Sanders, D. (2003) 'Message or medium? Campaign learning during the 2001 British general election', *Political Communication*, 20(3): 233–62.

Norris, P., Curtice, J., Sanders, D. and Scammell, M. (1999) *On Message: Communicating the Campaign*, London: Sage Publications.

Norris, P., Frank, R. W. and Martinez i Coma, F. (2013) 'Assessing the quality of elections', *Journal of Democracy*, 24(4): 124–135.

O'Keefe, D. J. and Jensen, J. D. (2008) 'Do loss-framed persuasive messages engender greater message processing than do gain-framed messages? A meta-analytic review', *Communication Studies*, 59(1): 51–67.

O'Leary, E. N. (2014) 'Oireachtas Inquiries referendum', *Irish Political Studies*, 29(2): 318–329.

O'Malley, E. N. (2012) 'Explaining the 2011 presidential election: Culture, valence, loyalty or punishment?', *Irish Political Studies*, 27(4): 635–655.

Ocampo Salgado, H. (2012) 'Performers y performensos: Performance y construcción de ciudadanía en las elecciones presidenciales del 2010 en Colombia', Master thesis, Universidad Nacional de Colombia.

Olatunji, R. W. and Adekunle Akinjogbin, S. (2011) 'Role of newspaper advertisements in the democratic process: The case of the 2007 presidential election in Nigeria', *Journal of Public Affairs*, 11(4): 265–278.

Olujide, J. O., Adeyemi, S. L. and Gbadeyan, R. A. (2011) 'Nigerian electorates' perception of political advertising and election campaign', *Research Journal of Social Sciences*, 1(5): 52–60.

Opeibi, T. (2005) 'Political marketing or political "macheting"? A study of negative campaigning in Nigerian political discourse' (unpublished manuscript).

Osgood, C. E., Saporta, S. and Nunnally, J. C. (1956) 'Evaluative assertion analysis', *Litera*, 3: 47–102.

Özkan, N. (2002) *Seçim Kazandıran Kampanyalar* [The Campaigns that Work], İstanbul: MediaCat.

Panagopoulos, C. (2004) 'Boy talk/girl talk: Gender differences in campaign communication strategies', *Women & Politics*, 26(3/4): 131–155.

Park, C. H. (1997) 'Electoral reform and the 1996 election', *Asia-Pacific Review*, 4(2): 143–168.

Pastor, R. A. (1990) 'The making of a free election', *Journal of Democracy*, 1(3): 13–25.

Patterson, T. E. and McClure, R. D. (1976) *The Unseeing Eye: The Myth of Television Power in National Politics*, New York: G. P. Putnam's Sons.

Pattie, C., Denver, D., Johns, R. and Mitchell, J. (2011) 'Raising the tone? The impact of "positive" and "negative" campaigning on voting in the 2007 Scottish Parliament election', *Electoral Studies*, 30(2): 333–343.

Payne, J. W., Bettman, J. R., and Johnson, E. J. (1993) *The Adaptive Decision Maker*, Cambridge: Cambridge University Press.

Pelletier, R. (ed.) (2012) *Les Partis Politiques Québécois dans la Tourmente*, Québec: Les Presses de l'Université Laval.

Perloff, R. M. and Kinsey, D. (1992) 'Political advertising as seen by consultants and journalists', *Journal of Advertising Research*, 32(3): 53–60.

Perron, L. (2009) 'Election campaigns in the Philippines', in Johnson, D. W. (ed.) *Routledge Handbook of Political Management*, New York: Routledge, pp. 360–369.

Peterson, D. A. and Djupe, P. A. (2005) 'When primary campaigns go negative: The determinants of campaign negativity', *Political Research Quarterly*, 58(1): 45–54.

Petrocik, J. R. (1996) 'Issue ownership in presidential elections, with a 1980 case study', *American Journal of Political Science*, 40(3): 825–50.

Petty, R. and Cacioppo, J. (1986) *Communication and Persuasion. Central and Peripheral Routes to Attitude Change*, New York: Springer-Verlag.

Pfau, M. and Burgoon, M. (1989) 'The efficacy of issue and character attack message strategies in political campaign communication', *Communication Reports*, 2(2): 53–61.

Pfau, M. and Kenski, H. (1990) *Attack Politics: Strategy and Defense*, New York: Praeger.

Pfau, M. and Louden, A. (1994) 'Effectiveness of adwatch formats in deflecting political attack ads', *Communication Research*, 21: 325–341.

Pinkleton, B. E. (1997) 'The effects of negative comparative political advertising on candidate evaluations and advertising evaluations: An exploration', *Journal of Advertising*, 26: 19–29.

Pinkleton, B. E. and Garramone, G. M. (1992) 'A survey response to negative political advertising: Voter cognition, affect, and behavior', Proceedings of the 1992 Conference of the American Academy of Advertising, 127–133.

Pinkleton, B. E., Um, N-H. and Weintraub Austin, E. (2002) 'An exploration of the effects of negative political advertising on political decision making', *Journal of Advertising*, 31(1): 13–25.

Pinkleton, B. E., Weintraub Austin, E. and Fortman, K. K. J. (1998) 'Relationship of media use and political disaffection to political efficacy and voting behavior', *Journal of Broadcasting & Electronic Media*, 42(1): 34–49.

Pitts, T. A. (2011) 'Politics as violence: A Girardian analysis of pre-genocide Rwandan politics', Masters dissertation, Virginia Polytechnic Institute and State University.

Piven, F. F. and Cloward, R. A. (1977) *Poor People's Movements: Why They Succeed, How They Fail*, New York: Vintage Books.

Plaisant, O., Courtois, R., Réveillère, C., Mendelsohn, G. A. and John, O. P. (2010) 'Validation par analyse factorielle du Big Five Inventory français (BFI-Fr). Analyse convergente avec le NEO-PI-R', *Annales Médico-Psychologiques*, 168: 97–106.

Plasser, F. (2000) 'American campaign techniques worldwide', *The Harvard International Journal of Press/Politics*, 5(4): 33–54.

Plasser, F. and Plasser, G. (2002) *Global Political Campaigning: A Worldwide Analysis of Campaign Professionals and their Practices*, London: Praeger.

— (2003) *Globalisierung der Wahlkämpfe: Praktiken der Campaign Professionals im weltweiten Vergleich*, Vienna: WUV.

Plasser, F., Scheucher, C. and Sommer, F. (1995) 'Massenmedien und Wahlkampf in Österreich: Personalisierung, Dethematisierung und Videopolitik', in Müller, W. C., Plasser, F. and Ulram, P. A. (eds) *Wählerverhalten und Parteienwettbewerb. Analysen zur Nationalratswahl 1994*, Vienna: Signum Verlag, pp. 227–264.

Plasser, F. and Ulram, P. A. (2007) 'Wählerbewegungen und Parteienkampagnen im Nationalratswahlkampf 2006', in Plasser, F. and Ulram, P. A. (eds) *Wechselwahlen. Analysen zur Nationalratswahl 2006*, Vienna: Facultas, pp. 19–37.

Plasser, F., Ulram, P. A. and Sommer, F. (2003) 'Kampagnedynamik, Mediahypes und Einfluss der TV-Konfrontationen 2002', in Plasser, F. and Ulram, P. A. (eds) *Wahlverhalten in Bewegung. Analysen zur Nationalratswahl 2002*, Vienna: WUV, pp. 19–53.

Polat, R. K. (2009) 'The 2007 parliamentary elections in Turkey: Between securitization and desecuritization', *Parliamentary Affairs*, 62(1): 129–148.

Polborn, M. and Yi, D. (2006) 'Informative positive and negative campaigning'. *Quarterly Journal of Political Science*, 1: 351–371.

Popkin, S. L. (1994) *The Reasoning Voter: Communication and Persuasion in Presidential Campaigns*, Chicago: University of Chicago Press.

Portillo, M. (2012) 'Campañas negativas y preferencias electorales: El caso de las elecciones presidenciales de México en 2006', *Razón y palabra*, (79): 33–18.

Premdas, R. R. and Steeves, J. S. (1981) 'The Solomon Islands: First elections after independence', *The Journal of Pacific History*, 16(4): 190–202.

Proctor D. E., Schenck-Hamlin, W. J. and Haase, K. A. (1994) 'Exploring the role of gender in the development of negative political advertisements', *Women & Politics*, 14(2): 1–22.

Rabinowitz, G. and Macdonald, S. (1989) 'A directional theory of issue voting', *American Political Science Review*, 83: 93–121.

Racine Group, The (2002) 'White paper on televised political campaign debates', *Argumentation & Advocacy*, 38(4): 199–218.

Rahn, W. M. and Hirshorn, R. M. (1999) 'Political advertising and public mood: A study of children's political orientations', *Political Communication*, 16: 387–407.

Rauschenbach, M. and Carey, S. C. (2013) 'Negative campaigning in Ghana's 2012 elections: A tool for mobilization or persuasion?', paper presented at the Joint Session of Workshops of the European Consortium for Political Research, Mainz, 2013.

Rawnsley, G. D. (1997) 'The 1996 presidential campaign in Taiwan: Packaging politics in a democratizing state', *The Harvard Journal of Press/Politics*, 2(2): 47–61.

Ray, L. (2007) 'Validity of measured party positions on European integration: Assumptions, approaches, and a comparison of alternative measures', *Electoral Studies*, 26: 11–22.

Redd, S. B. (2002) 'The influence of advisers on foreign policy decision making', *Journal of Conflict Resolution*, 46(3): 335–364.

Redlawsk, D. P. (2001) 'You must remember this: A test of the on-line model of voting', *Journal of Politics*, 63: 29–58.

—   (2002) 'Hot cognition or cool consideration: Testing the effects of motivated reasoning on political decision making', *Journal of Politics*, 64: 1021–1044.

—   (2004) 'What voters do', *Political Psychology*, 25: 595–609.

Redlawsk, D. P. and Lau, R. R. (2013) 'Behavioral decision making', in Huddy, L., Sears, D. O. and Levy, J. S. (eds) *Oxford Handbook of Political Psychology*, Second Edition, New York: Oxford University Press, pp. 130–164.

Redlawsk, D. P., Civettini, A. J. W. and Emmerson, K. M. (2010) 'The affective tipping point: Do motivated reasoners ever "get it"?', *Political Psychology*, 31: 563–594.

Reidy, T. and Suiter, J. (2015) 'Do rules matter? Categorizing the regulation of referendum campaigns', *Electoral Studies*, 38: 159–169.

Reif, K. (1985) 'Ten second-order elections', in Reif, K. (ed.) *Ten European Elections*, Aldershot: Gower, pp. 1–36.

Reinemann, C. and Maurer, M. (2005) 'Unifying or polarizing? Short-term effects and postdebate consequences of different rhetorical strategies in televised debates', *Journal of Communication*, 55(4): 775–794.

—   (2007) 'Populistisch und unkonkret. Die unmittelbare wahrnehmung des TV-duells', in Maurer, M., Reinemann, C., Maier, J. and Maier, M. (eds) *Schröder gegen Merkel. Wahrnehmung und Wirkung des TV-Duells 2005 im Ost-West-Vergleich*, Wiesbaden: VS Verlag für Sozialwissenschaften, pp. 53–89.

Restrepo Echavarría, N. J. (2012) 'La profesionalización de las campañas electorales: Las elecciones presidenciales de Colombia 2010', Universidad de Salamanca.

Reuster-Jahn, U. (2008) 'Bongo flava and the electoral campaign 2005 in Tanzania', *Stichproben, Wiener Zeitschrift für kritische Afrikastudien*, 14(8): 41–69.

Rhoads, E. (2012) 'Women's political participation in Indonesia: Decentralisation, money politics and collective memory in Bali', *Journal of Current Southeast Asian Affairs*, 31(2): 35–56.

Ridout, T. N. and Fowler, E. F. (2012) 'Explaining perceptions of advertising tone', *Political Research Quarterly*, 65(1): 62–75.

Ridout, T. N. and Franz, M. (2008) 'Evaluating measures of campaign tone', *Political Communication*, 25(2): 158–179.

—   (2011) *The Persuasive Power of Campaign Advertising*, Philadelphia: Temple University Press.

Ridout, T. N. and Holland, J. L. (2010) 'Candidate strategies in the presidential nomination campaign', *Presidential Studies Quarterly*, 40: 611–630.

Ridout, T. N. and Smith, G. R. (2008) 'Free advertising: How the media amplify campaign messages', *Political Research Quarterly*, 61: 598–608.

Ridout, T. N. and Walter, A. S. (2013) 'Party system change and negative campaigning in New Zealand', *Party Politics* (DOI: 10.1177/1354068813509522).

Riggle, E. D. B. and Johnson, M. M. S. (1995) 'Age differences in political decision-making: Strategies for evaluating political candidates', paper presented at the annual meeting of the Midwest Political Science Association, Chicago, 1995.

Riker, W. H. (1996) *The Strategy of Rhetoric: Campaigning for the American Constitution*, New Heaven: Yale University Press.

Roberts, B., Chernyshenko, O., Stark, S. and Goldberg, L. (2005) 'The structure of conscientiousness: An empirical investigation based on seven major personality questionnaires', *Personnel Psychology*, 58: 103–139.

Robertson, T., Froemling, K., Wells, S. and McCraw, S. (1999) 'Sex, lies, and videotape: An analysis of gender in campaign advertisements', *Communication Quarterly*, 47(3): 333–342.

Robinson, M. J. and Sheehan, M. A. (1983) *Over the Wire and on TV: CPS and UBI in Campaign '80*, New York: Russel Sage Foundation.

Roese, N. J. and Sande, G. N. (1993) 'Backlash effects in attack politics', *Journal of Applied Social Psychology*, 23: 632–653.

Rosema, M. (2007) 'Low turnout: Threat to democracy or blessing in disguise? Consequences of citizens' varying tendencies to vote', *Electoral Studies*, 26: 612–623.

Rosenthal, C. S. (ed.) (2002) *Women Transforming Congress*, Norman: University of Oklahoma Press.

Rozin, P. and Royzman, E. B. (2001) 'Negativity bias, negativity dominance and contagion', *Personality and Social Psychology Review*, 5(4): 296–320.

Rudd, C. and Hayward, J. (2005) 'Media takeover or media intrusion? Modernisation, the media and political communications in New Zealand', *Political Science*, 57(2): 7–16.

Rußmann, U. (2012) 'Themenmanagement der Parteien im Wahlkampf: Eine Analyse der Presseaussendungen', in Plasser, F. (ed.) *Erfolgreich wahlkämpfen. Massenmedien und Wahlkampagnen in Österreich*, Vienna: Facultas, pp. 141–162.

Sabatier, P. A. (1998) 'The advocacy coalition framework: Revisions and relevance for Europe', *Journal of European Public Policy*, 5(1): 98–130.

Salloukh, B. F. (2006) 'The limits of electoral engineering in divided societies: Elections in postwar Lebanon', *Canadian Journal of Political Science*, 39(03): 635–655.

Salmond, R. (2011) 'MeTube: Politicians, YouTube, and election campaigns in longstanding democracies', Paper presented at the annual meeting of the American Political Science Association, Seattle, 2011.

Samaras, A. N. and Papathanassopoulos, S. (2006) 'Polispots in Greece. Between partisanship and media logic', in Kaid, L. L. and Holtz-Bacha, C. (eds) *The Sage Handbook of Political Advertising*, London: Sage, pp. 211–225.

Sanders, D. and Norris, P. (2005) 'The impact of political advertising in the 2001 U.K. general election', *Political Research Quarterly*, 58: 525–536.

Sapiro, V., Cramer Walsh, K., Strach, P. and Hennings, V. (2011) 'Gender, context, and television advertising: A comprehensive analysis of 2000 and 2002 House races', *Political Research Quarterly*, 64(1): 107–119.

Savigny, H. (2005) 'Labour, political marketing and the 2005 election: A campaign of two halves', *Journal of Marketing Management*, 21(9–10): 925–941.

Sayarı, S. (2002) 'The changing party system', in Sayarı, S. and Esmer, Y. (eds) *Politics, Parties and Elections in Turkey*, Boulder: Lynne Rienner Publishers, pp. 9–32.

Scammell, M. and Langer, A. I. (2006) 'Political advertising in the United Kingdom', in Kaid, L. L. and Holtz-Bacha, C. (eds) *The SAGE Handbook of Political Advertising*, London: Sage, pp. 65–82.

Scammell, M. and Semetko, H. A. (2008) 'Election news coverage in the UK', in Strömbäck, J. and Kaid, L. L. (ed.) *The Handbook of Election News Coverage Around the World*, New York: Routledge, pp. 73–89.

Schafferer, C. (2006) 'Is there an Asian style of electoral campaigning?', in Schafferer, C. (ed.) *Election Campaigning in East and Southeast Asia: Globalization of Political Marketing*, Aldershot: Ashgate, pp. 103–140.

Scher, R. K. (1997) *The Modern Presidential Campaign: Mudslinging, Bombast, and the Vitality of American Politics*, New York: M. E. Sharpe.

Schiappa, E., Gregg, P. B. and Hewes, D. E. (2005) 'The parasocial contact hypothesis', *Communication Monographs*, 72(1): 92–115.

Schmidt, G. D. (2000) 'Delegative democracy in Peru? Fujimori's 1995 landslide and the prospects for 2000', *Journal of Interamerican Studies and World Affairs*, 42(1): 99–132.

Schmitt-Beck, R. and Farrell, D. (2002) 'Studying political campaigns and their effects', in Farrell, D. and Schmitt-Beck, R. (eds) *Do political campaign matter? Campaign effects in elections and referendums*, New York: Routledge, pp. 1–21.

Schmitt, H. (2002) 'Multiple party identifications', paper presented at the Conference of the Comparative Study of Electoral Systems (CSES) at the WZB in Berlin, 2002.

Schmitter, P. C. and Trechsel, A. H. (2004) *The Future of Democracy in Europe: Trends, Analysis and Reforms*, Strasbourg: Council of Europe.

Schrott, P. R. and Lanoue, D. J. (1992) 'How to win a televised debate. Candidate strategies and voter response in Germany, 1972–87', *British Journal of Political Science*, 22(4): 445–467.

Schultz, C. and Pancer, S. M. (1997) 'Character attacks and their effects on perceptions of male and female political candidates', *Political Psychology*, 18(1): 93–102.

Schumpeter, J. A. (1979) *Capitalism, Socialism and Democracy*, London: George Allen and Unwin.

Schuster, D. R. (2004) 'Elections on Guam, 1970–2002', *Pacific Studies*, 27(1/2): 22–67.

Schweitzer, E. J. (2008) 'Innovation or normalization in e-campaigning?', *European Journal of Communication*, 23(4): 449–470.

— (2009) 'Virtual mudslinging as a global challenge for democracy: Comparing the use of attacks on German and American campaign websites', paper presented at the Annual Conference of the Political Studies Association, Manchester, 2009.

— (2010) 'Global patterns of virtual mudslinging? The use of attacks on German party websites in state, national and European parliamentary elections', *German Politics*, 19(2): 200–221.

— (2011) 'Normalization 2.0: A longitudinal analysis of German online campaigns in the national elections 2002–9', *European Journal of Communication*, 26 (4): 310–327.

Seawright, J. and Gerring, J. (2008) 'Case selection techniques in case study research', *Political Research Quarterly*, 61(2): 294–308.

Seethaler, J. and Melischek, G. (2006) 'Die Pressekonzentration in Österreich im europäischen Vergleich', *Österreichische Zeitschrift für Politikwissenschaft*, 35(4): 337–360.

Semetko, H. A., Blumler, J. G., Gurevitch, M. and Weaver, D. H. (1991) *The Formation of Campaign Agendas: A Comparative Analysis of Party and Media Roles in Recent American and British Election Campaigns*, Hillsdale, NJ: Erlbau.

Sharan, T. and Heathershaw, J. (2011) 'Identity politics and statebuilding in post-Bonn Afghanistan: The 2009 presidential election', *Ethnopolitics*, 10(3–4): 297–319.

Sheckels, T. F. (1994) 'Mikulski vs. Chavez for the Senate from Maryland in 1986 and the "rules" for attack politics', *Communication Quarterly*, 42(3): 311–326.

Shih, C.-Y. (2001) 'Political culture of election in Taiwanese and Chinese minority areas', in Hua, S. (ed.) *Chinese Political Culture, 1898–2000*, New York: East Gate Book, pp. 276–297.

Sides, J., Grossmann, M., Trost, C. and Lipsitz, K. (2003) 'Candidate attacks and voter aversion: The uncertain link between negativity and campaign satisfaction', paper presented at the Annual Meeting of the American Political Science Association, Philadelphia, 2003.

Sides, J., Lipsitz, K. and Grossman, M. (2010) 'Do voters perceive negative campaigns as informative campaigns?', *American Politics Research*, 38(3): 502–530.

Sigelman, L. and Buell, E. (2003) 'You take the high road and I'll take the low road? The interplay of attack strategies and tactics in presidential campaigns', *Journal of Politics*, 65(2): 518–531.

— (2008) *Attack Politics, Negativity in Presidential Campaigns since 1960*, Lawrence: University Press of Kansas.

Sigelman, L. and Kugler, M. (2003) 'Why is research on the effects of negative campaigning so inconclusive? Understanding citizens' perception of negativity', *Journal of Politics*, 65(1): 142–160.

Sigelman, L. and Shiraev, E. (2002) 'The rational attacker in Russia? Negative campaigning in Russian presidential elections', *Journal of Politics*, 64(1): 45–62.

Simon, A. F. (2002) *The Winning Message: Candidate Behavior, Campaign Discourse, and Democracy*, Cambridge: Cambridge University Press.

Sinnott, R. (2001) *Attitudes and Behaviour of the Irish Electorate in the Referendum on the Treaty of Nice*, Dublin: Department of Foreign Affairs.

—   (2002) 'Cleavages, parties and referendums: Relationships between representative and direct democracy in the Republic of Ireland', *European Journal of Political Research*, 41: 811–826.

Sinnott, R. and Elkink, J. A. (2010) *Attitudes and Behaviour in the Referendum on the Second Treaty of Lisbon*, Dublin: Department of Foreign Affairs.

Sinnott, R., Elkink, J. A., O'Rourke, K. and McBride, J. (2009) *Attitudes and Behaviour in the Referendum on the Treaty of Lisbon*, Dublin: Department of Foreign Affairs.

Sjöblom, G. (1968) *Party Strategies in a Multiparty System*, Lund: Studentliteratur.

Skaperdas, S. and Grofman, B. (1995) 'Modeling negative campaigning', *American Political Science Review*, 89(1): 49–61.

Skarzynska, K. (2004) 'Politicians in television: 'The Big Five' in impression formation', *Journal of Political Marketing*, 3(2): 31–45.

Sniderman, P. (2000) 'Taking sides: A fixed choice theory of political reasoning', in Lupia, A., McCubbins, M. and Popkin, S. (eds) *Elements of Reason: Cognition, Choice and the Bounds of Rationality*, Cambridge: Cambridge University Press, pp. 67–84.

Sniderman, P., Brody, R. and Tetlock, P. (1991) *Reasoning and Choice. Explorations in Political Psychology*, Cambridge: Cambridge University Press.

Soroka, S. N. (2014) *Negativity in Democratic Politics*, Cambridge: Cambridge University Press.

Soroka, S. N. and McAdams, S. (2010) 'An experimental study of the differential effects of positive versus negative news content', paper presented at the Elections, Public Opinion and Parties Annual Conference, University of Essex, 2010.

Soroka, S. N., Maioni A. and Blake, A. (2006) *2006 Federal Election Newspaper Content Analysis* edited by Observatory on Media and Public Policy, Montreal: McGill University.

Southall, R. (1994) 'The 1993 Lesotho election', *Review of African Political Economy*, 21(59): 110–118.

Spieker, A. (2011) 'Licht ins dunkel der TV-duelle. Rhetorische strategien und ihre wirkungen im TV-Duell 2009. Eine empirische analyse mittels real-time-response measurement', in Haschke, J. F. and Moser, A. (eds) *Politik-Deutsch, Deutsch-Politik. Aktuelle Trends und Fachergebnisse*, Berlin: Frank & Timme, pp. 75–93.

Stanford, M., Houston, R., Mathias, C., Villemarette, N., Helfritz, L. and Conklin, S. (2003) 'Characterizing aggressive behavior', *Assessment*, 10(2): 183–190.

Steenbergen, M. and Ellis, C. (2006) 'Fear and loathing in American elections: Context, traits, and negative candidate affect', in Redlawks, D. P. (ed.), *Feeling Politics: Emotion in Political Information Processing*, New York: Palgrave, pp. 109–133.

Stevens, D. (2009) 'Elements of negativity: Volume and proportion in exposure to negative advertising', *Political Behavior*, 31(3): 429–454.

—— (2012) 'Tone versus information: Explaining the impact of negative political advertising', *Journal of Political Marketing*, 11(4): 322–352.

Stewart, C. J. (1975) 'Voter perception of mud-slinging in political communication', *Central States Speech Journal*, 26(4): 279–286.

Stewart, J. (2006) 'Political advertising in Australia and New Zealand', in Kaid, L. L. and Holtz-Bacha, C. (eds) *The Sage Handbook of Political Advertising*, London: Sage, pp. 269–284.

Strachan, J. C. and Wolf, M. R. (2012) 'Introduction to political civility', *PS: Political Science & Politics*, 45(03): 401–404.

Strandberg, K. (2007) 'It's the inside that counts? An explorative analysis of Finnish parties' opinions concerning the importance and use of their websites, and website contents, in relation to party characteristics', *Scandinavian Political Studies*, 30(4): 419–443.

Strøm, K. (1990) 'A behavioral theory of competitive political parties', *American Journal of Political Science*, 34(2): 565–598.

Strøm, K. and Müller, W. (1999) 'Political parties and hard choices', in Müller, W. and Strøm, K. (eds) *Policy, Office or Votes? How Political Parties in Western Europe Make Hard Decisions*, Cambridge: Cambridge University Press, pp. 1–35.

Strömbäck, J. (2007) 'Political marketing and professionalized campaigning: A conceptual analysis', *Journal of Political Marketing*, 6(2–3): 49–67.

Strömbäck, J. and Kaid, L. L. (2008) 'A framework in comparing election news coverage around the world', in Strömbäck, J. and Kaid, L. L. (eds) *The Handbook of Election News Coverage Around the World*, New York: Routledge, pp. 1–18.

Strömbäck, J. and Shehata, A. (2010) 'Media malaise or a virtuous cycle? Exploring the causal relationships between news media exposure, political news attention and political interest', *European Journal of Political Research*, 49: 575–597.

Suiter, J. and Reidy, T. (2013) 'It's the campaign learning stupid. An examination of a volatile Irish referendum', *Parliamentary Affairs* (DOI: 10.1093/pa/gst014).

Sullivan, J. (2008) 'Campaign advertising and democracy in Taiwan', *The China Quarterly*, 196: 900–911.

Sullivan, J. and Sapir, E. V. (2012a) 'Modeling negative campaign advertising: Evidence from Taiwan', *Asian Journal of Communication*, 22(3): 289–303.

—— (2012b) 'Nasty or nice? Explaining positive and negative campaign behavior in Taiwan', *China Journal*, 67: 149–168.

Sullivan, M. (2005) 'The parliamentary election in Cambodia, July 2003', *Electoral Studies*, 24(1): 129–136.

Surlin, S. H. and Gordon, T. E. (1977) 'How values affect attitudes toward direct reference political advertising', *Journalism Quarterly*, 77: 89–98.

Swanson, D. and Mancini, P. (eds) (1996) *Politics, Media, and Modern Democracy: An International Study of Innovations in Electoral Campaigning and their Consequences*, Westport: Praeger.

Swint, K. C. (1998) *Political Consultants and Negative Campaigning: The Secrets of the Pros*, Lanham: University Press of America.

Szczerbiak, A. (2001) 'Explaining Kwasniewski's landslide: The October 2000 Polish presidential election, *Journal of Communist Studies and Transition Politics*, 17(4): 78–107.

Taber, C. S. and Lodge, M. (2006) 'Motivated skepticism in the evaluation of political beliefs', *American Journal of Political Science*, 50(3): 755–769.

Taiwo, R. (2013) 'Emerging trends in English language in the news media: A case study of satire in Nigerian text messages', *Journal of the Nigerian English Studies Association*, 16(1): 58–73.

Tajfel, H. and Turner, J. C. (1979) 'An integrative theory of intergroup conflict', in Austin, W. G. and Worchel, S. (eds) *The Social Psychology of Intergroup Relations*, Monterey: Brooks/Cole, pp. 33–47.

Tak, J., Kaid, L. L. and Lee, S. (1997) 'A cross-cultural study of political advertising in the United States and Korea', *Communication Research*, 24(4): 423–430.

Tellis, G. J. (2004) *Effective Advertising: Understanding When, How, and Why Advertising Works*, Thousand Oaks: Sage.

Theilmann, J. and Wilhite, A. (1998) 'Campaign tactics and the decision to attack', *The Journal of Politics*, 60(4): 1050–1062.

Thomas, S. (1994) *How Women Legislate*, Oxford: Oxford University Press.

Thorson, E., Ogianova, E., Coyle, J. and Denton, F. (2000) 'Negative political ads and negative citizen orientations toward politics', *Journal of Current Issues and Research in Advertising*, 22(1): 13–40.

Tietaah, G. K. M. (2013) 'Negative political advertising and the imperative of broadcast regulation in Ghana', *Journal of African Media Studies*, 5(2): 203–217.

Tigasson, K-R. (2009) 'Strategic miscalculations: Election campaigns to the European Parliament in Estonia 2004', *Journal of Political Marketing*, 8: 46–58.

Tillie, J. (1995) *Party Utility and Voting Behavior*, Amsterdam: Het Spinhuis.

Timur, S. (2006) 'The 2005 presidential election in Zazakhstan: Problems and prospects for political liberalization', *Central Asia and the Caucasus*, 1(37): 44–54.

Tinkham, S. and Weaver-Lariscy, R. A. (1993) 'A diagnostic approach to assessing the impact of negative political television commercials', *Journal of Broadcasting & Electronic Media*, 37(4): 377–399.

Toros, E. (2012a) 'Forecasting Turkish local elections', *International Journal of Forecasting*, 28(4): 813–821.

— (2012b) 'The Kurdish problem, print media, and democratic consolidation in Turkey', *Asia Europe Journal*, 10(4): 317–333.

— (2013) 'Negative campaigning and voting behaviour in Turkish elections', paper presented at the Joint Session of Workshops of the European Consortium for Political Research, Mainz, 2013.

— (2015) 'Negative campaigning in Turkish elections', forthcoming at *Turkish Studies*.

Tremblay, P. and Ewart, L. (2005) 'The Buss and Perry Aggression Questionnaire and its relations to values, the Big Five, provoking hypothetical situations, alcohol consumption patterns, and alcohol expectancies', *Personality and Individual Differences*, 38: 337–346.

Trent, J. S. and Friedenberg, R. V. (2008) *Political Campaign Communication: Principles and Practices*, Lanham, MD: Rowman and Littlefield.

Trent, J. S. and Sabourin, T. (1993) 'Sex still counts. Women's use of televised advertising during the decade of the 80s', *Journal of Applied Communication*, 21(1): 21–40.

Turner, J. (2001) 'Trouble with Ken: New Labour's negative campaign in the selection and election process for London mayor', *Journal of Public Affairs*, 1(3): 239–253.

Urcuyo, C. (2010) 'Elecciones costarricenses: lucha por la continuidad', *Boletín Elcano*, 4: 1–8.

Valentino, N., Beckmann, M. and Buhr, T. (2001) 'A spiral of cynicism for some: The contingent effects of campaign news frames on participation and confidence in Government', *Political Communication*, 18(4): 347–367.

Valverde Loya, M. A. (2006) 'La publicidad negativa en la campaña presidencial mexicana de 2006', *Elecciones*, 5(6): 109–118.

van Atteveldt, W. (2008) *Semantic Network Analysis: Techniques for Extracting, Representing and Querying Media Content*, SIKS dissertation series, Charleston SC: BookSurge Publishing.

van Atteveldt, W., Kleinnijenhuis, J., Ruigrok, N. and Schlobach, S. (2008) 'Good news or bad news? Conducting sentiment analysis on Dutch text to distinguish between positive and negative relations', *Journal of Information Technology & Politics*, 5(1): 73–94.

van Cuilenburg, J. J., Kleinnijenhuis, J. and de Ridder, J. A. (1986) 'A theory of evaluative discourse: Towards a graph theory of journalistic texts', *European Journal of Communication*, 1(1): 65–96.

van der Eijk C. and Franklin, M. N. (2009) *Elections and Voters*, Houndmills: Palgrave Macmillan.

van der Eijk, C. and Niemöller, B. (1983) *Electoral Change in the Netherlands*, Amsterdam: CT Press.

van der Eijk, C., van der Brug, W., Kroh, M. and Franklin, M. (2006) 'Rethinking the dependent variable in voting behaviour, on the measurement and the analysis of electoral utilities', *Electoral Studies*, 25(3): 424–447.

van der Zee, K., Thijs, M. and Schakel, L. (2002) 'The relationship of emotional intelligence with academic intelligence and the Big Five', *European Journal of Personality*, 16: 103–125.

van Heerde-Hudson, J. (2011) 'The Americanization of British party advertising? Negativity in party election broadcasts, 1964–2005', *British Politics*, 6: 52–77.

van Kersbergen, K. and Krouwel, A. (2008) 'A double-edged sword! The Dutch centre-right and the "foreigners issue"', *Journal of European Public Policy*, 15(3): 398–414.

Vecchione, M. and Caprara, G. V. (2009) 'Personality determinants of political participation: The contribution of traits and self-efficacy beliefs', *Personality and Individual Differences*, 46: 487–492.

Vecchione, M., Schoen, H., Castro, J. L. G, Cieciuch, J., Pavlopoulos, V. and Caprara, G. V. (2011) 'Personality correlates of party preference: The Big Five in five big European countries', *Personality and Individual Differences*, 51: 737–742.

Venter, D. (2003) 'Democracy and multiparty politics in Africa: Recent elections in Zambia, Zimbabwe, and Lesotho', *Eastern Africa Social Science Research Review*, 19(1): 1–39.

Verba, S. and Nie, N. H. (1972) *Participation in America: Political Democracy and Social Equality*, New York: Harper and Row.

Vliegenthart, R. (2012) 'The professionalization of political communication? A longitudinal analysis of Dutch election campaign posters', *American Behavioral Scientist*, 56(2): 135–150.

Vliegenthart, R., Boomgarden, H. G. and Boumans, J. W. (2011) 'Changes in political news coverage: Personalization, conflict and negativity in British and Dutch newspapers', in Brants, K. and Voltmer, K. (eds) *Political Communication in Postmodern Democracy: Challenging the Primacy of Politics*, Houndmills: Palgrave Macmillan, pp. 92–110.

Volkens, A. (2007) 'Strengths and weaknesses of approaches to measuring policy positions of parties', *Electoral Studies*, 26: 108–120.

Volkens, A., Lacewell, O., Lehmann, P., Regel, S., Schultze, H. and Werner, A. (2012) *The Manifesto Data Collection: Manifesto Project (MRG/CMP/ MARPOR)*, Berlin: Wissenschaftszentrum Berlin für Sozialforschung (WZB).

Walter, A. S. (2009) 'Met Bos bent u de klos: Negatieve campagnevoering tijdens de Tweede Kamerverkiezingen van 2002, 2003 en 2006', in Voerman, G. (ed.) *Jaarboek Documentatiecentrum Nederlandse Politieke Partijen 2007*, Groningen: DNPP/Rijksuniversiteit Groningen, pp. 128–150.

— (2012) *Negative Campaigning in Western Europe: Beyond the Vote-Seeking Perspective*, Zutphen: Wöhrmann.

— (2013) 'Women on the political battleground: Does gender condition the use of negative campaigning', *Journal of Elections, Public Opinion and Parties*, 23(2): 154–176.

— (2014a) 'Choosing the enemy: Attack behavior in a multi-party system', *Party Politics*, 20(3): 311–323.

—   (2014b) 'Negative campaigning in Western Europe: Similar or different?', *Political Studies*, 62(1): 42–60.

Walter, A. S. and van der Brug, W. (2013) 'When the gloves come off: Inter-party variation in negative campaigning in Dutch elections, 1981–2010', *Acta Politica*, 48(4): 367–388.

Walter, A. S. and Vliegenthart, R. (2010) 'Negative campaigning across different communication channels: Different ballgames?', *The Harvard International Journal of Press/Politics*, 15(4): 441–461.

Walter, A. S., van der Brug, W. and van Praag, P. (2014) 'When the stakes are high: Party competition and negative campaigning', *Comparative Political Studies*, 47(4): 550–573.

Walters, T. N., Walters, L. M. and Gray, R. (1996) 'Agenda building in the 1992 presidential campaign', *Public Relations Review*, 22(1): 9–24.

Walton, D. (1998) *Ad Hominem Arguments*, Tuscaloosa: The University of Alabama Press.

Wanta, W., Lemert, J. B. and Lee, T. (1999) 'Consequences of Negative Political Advertising Exposure', in Johnson, T. J., Hays, C. E. and Hays, S. P. (eds), *Engaging the Public: How Government and the Media Can Reinvigorate American Democracy*, Colorado: Roman & Littlefield, pp. 97–109.

Wattenberg, M. P. and Brians, C. L. (1999) 'Negative campaign advertising: Demobilizer or mobilizer?', *American Political Science Review*, 93(4): 891–899.

Way, L. A. (2003) 'Weak states and pluralism: The case of Moldova', *East European Politics & Societies*, 17(3): 454–482.

Weible, C. M., Sabatier, P. A. and McQueen, K. (2009) 'Themes and variations: Taking stock of the Advocacy Coalition Framework', *Policy Studies Journal*, 37(1): 121–140.

Welch, S. (1985) 'Are women more liberal than men in the US congress?', *Legislative Studies Quarterly*, 10: 125–134.

Wen, W-C., Benoit, W. L. and Yu, T.-H. (2004) 'A functional analysis of the 2000 Taiwanese and US presidential spots', *Asian Journal of Communication*, 14(2): 140–155.

West, D. M. (2005) *Air Wars: Television Advertising in Election Campaigns, 1952–2004*, Washington: CQ Press.

West, D. M., Kern, M., Alger, D. and Goggin, J. (1995) 'Ad buys in presidential campaigns: The strategies of electoral appeal', *Political Communication*, 12: 275–290.

Whaley, B. B. and Holloway, R. L. (1997) 'Rebuttal analogy in political communication: Argument and attack in sound bite', *Political Communication*, 14(3): 293–305.

Whiteley, P. and Seyd, P. (2003) 'How to win a landslide by really trying: The effects of local campaigning on voting in the 1997 British general election', *Electoral Studies*, 22: 301–324.

Wicks, R. H. and Souley, B. (2003) 'Going negative: Candidate usage of internet web sites during the 2000 presidential campaign', *Journalism & Mass Communication Quarterly*, 80(1): 128–144.

Williams, K. (2003) 'Lustration as the securitization of democracy in Czechoslovakia and the Czech Republic', *Journal of Communist and Transition Politics*, 19(4): 1–24.

Williams, L. (1994) 'Political advertising in the "year of the woman": Did X mark the spot?', in Cook, E. A., Thomas, S. and Wilcox, C. (eds) *The Year of the Woman: Myths and Realities*, Boulder: Westview Press, pp. 197–215.

Willis, M. (2004) 'Morocco's Islamists and the legislative elections of 2002: The strange case of the party that did not want to win', *Mediterranean Politics*, 9(1): 53–81.

Wilson-Kratzer, J. M. and Benoit, W. L. (2010) 'A functional analysis of press releases from Senator Barack Obama and Senator John McCain during the 2008 primary presidential election', *Public Relations Review*, 36(2): 178–180.

Wilson, R. D. and Muderrisoglu, A. (1980) 'An analysis of cognitive responses to comparative advertising', in Olson, J. C. (ed.), *Advances in Consumer Research*, San Francisco: Association for Consumer Research, pp. 566–571.

Wilson, S. and Turnbull, N. (2001) 'Wedge politics and welfare reforms in Australia', *Australian Journal of Politics and History*, 47(3): 384–402.

Wisconsin Public Television (2001) *The 30 Second Candidate. Historical Timeline*. Online. Available http://www.pbs.org/30secondcandidate/timeline (accessed 8 March 2005).

Witt, L., Paget, K. M. and Matthews, G. (1994) *Running as a Woman: Gender and Power in American Politics*, New York: Free Press.

Witte, K. (1992) 'Putting the fear back into fear appeals: The extended parallel process model', *Communication Monographs*, 59: 329–349.

Yannas, P. and Lappas, G. (2005) 'Web campaign in the 2002 Greek municipal elections', *Journal of Political Marketing*, 4(1): 33–50.

Yanoshevsky, G. (2009) 'L'usage des vidéoblogs dans l'élection présidentielle de 2007. Vers une image plurigérée des candidats', *Mots. Les langages du politique*, 89: 57–68.

Yoon, K., Pinkleton, B. E. and Ko, W. (2005) 'Effects of negative political advertising on voting intention: An exploration of the roles of involvement and source credibility in the development of voter cynicism', *Journal of Marketing Communications*, 11(2): 95–112.

Young, L. and Soroka, S. (2012) 'Affective news: The automated coding of sentiment in political texts', *Political Communication*, 29(2): 205–231.

Zaller, J. R. (1992) *The Nature and Origins of Mass Opinion*, New York: Cambridge University Press.

— (1996) 'The myth of massive media impact revived: New support for a discredited idea', in Mutz, D. C., Sniderman, P. M. and Brody, R. A. (eds) *Political Persuasion and Attitude Change*, Ann Arbor: University of Michigan Press, pp. 17–78.

Zhang, Y. and Buda, R. (1999) 'Moderating effects of need for cognition on responses to positively versus negatively framed advertising messages', *Journal of Advertising*, 28(2): 1–15.

Index

Numbers in italics refer to Figures or Tables

www.ingramcontent.com/pod-product-compliance
Lightning Source LLC
Chambersburg PA
CBHW050559270326
41926CB00012B/2115